China's Challenges

CHINA'S CHALLENGES

Edited by

Jacques deLisle and Avery Goldstein

PENN

UNIVERSITY OF PENNSYLVANIA PRESS

PHILADELPHIA

Copyright © 2015 University of Pennsylvania Press

Published by
University of Pennsylvania Press
Philadelphia, Pennsylvania 19104-4112

Printed in the United States of America on acid-free paper
10 9 8 7 6 5 4 3 2 1

A Cataloging-in-Publication Record is available from the
Library of Congress
ISBN 978-0-8122-2312-5

CONTENTS

CHAPTER 1

China's Challenges: Reform Era Legacies and the Road Ahead

Jacques deLisle and Avery Goldstein

During 2012 and 2013, Xi Jinping, Li Keqiang, and other members of the "fifth-generation" cohort assumed the top political positions in China. They became leaders of a country that has achieved remarkable economic growth, political stability, and international influence over the past three decades and a regime that has, during those years, also weathered repeated crises and endured chronic problems. Under Xi, Li, and their colleagues, China now confronts a wide variety of challenges that are at least as daunting as—and perhaps more consequential for the future of the regime than—any it has faced since the reform era began at the end of the 1970s. This book examines some of the most important and some of the most urgent social, political, economic, legal, and international problems that China faces under the fifth-generation leadership.

Leadership in the Fifth Generation

The advent of new Chinese Communist Party (CCP) leadership seemed to confirm the stability of elite politics in China.[1] It was the second smooth transition in a row for a regime that in its first forty-five years had been rocked by sharp struggles over succession. Between 1949 and 1989, several putative successors and heirs apparent had fallen before a new paramount leader emerged.[2] When the founding leader of the reform era, Deng Xiaoping, selected Jiang Zemin as his successor after the June 1989 Tiananmen incident, it seemed initially to be yet another improvised and fragile succession plan. Indeed, many saw this as a continuation of the pattern set by Deng's personal endorsement of Zhao Ziyang in 1987 after he dismissed his previous choice, Hu Yaobang, in the wake of an earlier, smaller round of student protests.[3] But the selection of Jiang proved to be different. In 1992, the Fourteenth National Congress of the CCP formally ratified Jiang as its general secretary and, in 1993, the Eighth National People's Congress named him China's president, giving him the offices that—along with the chairmanship of the Central Military Commission (CMC)—clearly identified him as heading the regime's "third-generation" leadership.[4] Jiang went on to serve the two full five-year terms in each position permitted by party norms and the state constitution.

After Jiang, the head of the "fourth-generation" leadership, Hu Jintao, likewise served as general secretary and president—as well as (after a two-year delay) military commission chair—for the next decade. Like Hu, "fifth-generation" leader Xi Jinping was selected on schedule and in conformity with the formal rules of a process that seemed to have become remarkably predictable and institutionalized, if not entirely without political drama.[5] These three top leaders' time in office coincided with that of long-serving premiers Li Peng and Zhu Rongji under Jiang, Wen Jiabao under Hu and, if current expectations hold, Li Keqiang for a decade under Xi. A regime that long had been plagued by uncertainty and instability at the top, exacerbated by the concentration of power in the hands of charismatic leaders (first Mao, then Deng), had become a regime characterized by predictability and order, headed by long-rising organization men whose influence depended increasingly on their institutional roles and decreasingly on their personal qualities or ability to prevail in chronic factional infighting.[6]

On the other hand, the shift toward a more collective and stable leadership has coincided with new challenges. The ruthless struggles among a small circle of contenders within the CCP elite had reflected a comparatively simple logic of power politics. Today, conflicts are about how best to manage complex policy issues that defy simple solutions. Xi and his colleagues moved into the top posts at a time when many Chinese and foreign observers had become convinced that the country had arrived at a historic juncture, a crossroads for decision makers facing fateful choices with profound implications for the viability of CCP rule over the country it began to govern six decades earlier.[7] The recent changes in China's leadership and

China's problems may mean that the regime has less capacity to undertake the policy approaches needed to address the multifaceted and difficult challenges the country now faces. The cost of failure to address these challenges effectively could well be institutional and systemic.

The demanding tasks the new leaders face may be encouraging them not only to embrace a bolder reform agenda but also to strengthen Xi Jinping's power as first among equals. The policy innovations announced at the Third Plenum of the Eighteenth CCP Central Committee in November 2013 and detailed in subsequent meetings reflect a perceived need for decisive action to remedy numerous and varied shortcomings in China's model of development and, to a lesser extent, its model of governance. At the same time, China's media have made Xi Jinping an especially visible leader and cultivated his image as a man very much in charge of the party-state and in touch with the Chinese people's aspirations and concerns. Since late 2012, news reports and pictures have presented Xi invoking the legacy of Mao's mass line leadership style, dining with People's Liberation Army (PLA) servicemen, eating dumplings at a restaurant along with average Beijingers, and asserting his personal commitment to rooting out corruption and waste at all levels of officialdom in China. Although his high profile and apparent political savvy have led some to predict that Xi may emerge as the most dominant leader in China since Deng Xiaoping,[8] there has so far been little to indicate that, however much he might outshine and overshadow his immediate predecessors, Xi will circumvent the norms of collective leadership within the ranks of a Politburo Standing Committee (PSC) that includes members who represent powerful interests and institutions.

Economic Reform

China's economic challenges today have emerged against a backdrop of extraordinary economic growth and development over nearly three and a half decades.[9] A generation after the founding of the People's Republic in 1949, China remained a relatively poor country at the margins of the world economy. Under the leadership of Mao Zedong, repeated attempts to find a path to rapid economic development had produced violent policy swings and imposed staggering political, social, and economic costs.[10] These moves failed to deliver on the long-standing promise of all Chinese revolutionaries since the early twentieth century—building a prosperous China strong enough to protect its national interests in a dangerous world. When Deng Xiaoping and the second generation of CCP leaders consolidated their grip on power in the late 1970s, they inherited the troubled economic legacy of Mao's rule. Thirty years later, China had entered the ranks of middle-income countries. It is now home to the world's second largest economy and is among the top trading entities and recipients of foreign investment. China's economy has been transformed from a largely agrarian to a mostly industrial and service economy, with fast-growing higher value-added and knowledge-intensive sectors.

These dramatic achievements—and the path to them—were nearly unimaginable when reforms were launched a few years after Mao's death in 1976. The changes began during the 1980s, with a broad reform program for "enlivening the domestic economy and opening to the outside world" that liberated the productive energy of the Chinese people by relying on once-taboo material rewards. Decollectivization of agriculture, a shift toward markets, and greater autonomy for enterprises in the urban economy brought rapid growth. Policy changes also enabled China to benefit from international trade and investment, which had been shunned by the Mao-era regime that was committed to autarchy and revolutionary purity and that, in any event, faced economic isolation imposed first by the West and later by the Soviet bloc. The implementation of wide-ranging economic reforms in the early 1980s triggered a period of remarkable economic expansion and a sharp rise in standards of living.

By the end of the 1980s, however, the initially successful program faced difficulties. Within China, dissatisfaction was simmering. Some of this reflected unease with the consequences of the reforms that had been implemented, especially the increased job insecurity and price inflation that accompanied the shift from state socialism toward market economics.[11] Doubts about political stability faded after the regime survived the massive demonstrations during spring 1989 that culminated in a bloody confrontation in Tiananmen Square—the tragic end to nationwide pro-democracy protests that had also given students and workers an opportunity to vent economic grievances. Yet, concerns remained about the prospects for pursuing an agenda of sustained economic reform. In the 1990s, looming challenges included the need to address remaining distortions in an economy where reforms were incomplete and in which inefficient state enterprises continued to play an outsized role, supported by nonperforming loans made by state-owned banks on the basis of policy mandates rather than commercial risk. Under the third-generation leadership of Jiang Zemin and Zhu

Rongji, new policies addressed these problems. In an increasingly market-based environment, township and village enterprises mushroomed in the first part of the 1990s, while private, foreign-invested, and hybrid enterprises grew rapidly throughout the decade, effectively shrinking the share of the traditional state-owned sector in the economy.

China's integration with the global economy intensified as Beijing moved to make China's currency freely convertible for trade (although not for capital flows), adopted ever more flexible foreign investment policies, and liberalized policies and laws governing trade. These measures, combined with China's immense, inexpensive, and compliant labor force, and a generally pro-growth and foreign-investment-friendly regulatory environment, attracted large inflows of investment, especially to export-oriented industries in coastal regions. As foreign trade and investment grew, and eastern urban areas boomed, many tens of millions of rural residents migrated in search of better-paying jobs in the factories that were making China the new workshop of the world.

China's economic achievements during the 1990s and into the early years of the new century were in many respects impressive, with double-digit growth rates in most years. Such accomplishments, when contrasted with the troubles besetting the former Soviet states, seemed to vindicate the Chinese leadership's decision to give priority to economic change and to postpone political reform. In addition, China's ability to emerge from the Asian Financial Crisis of 1997–1998 relatively unscathed enhanced confidence in the implicit Chinese model, particularly in comparison to the suddenly battered East Asian model. Just after the end of this period, China's overall economic success was reflected in and supported by China's accession to the World Trade Organization (WTO) in 2001, a decade and a half after China first sought to join the global trade regime.

Still, in the 1990s, progress in economic development continued to be accompanied by recurrent bouts of inflation, rising job insecurity among the vast numbers of workers employed in state-owned enterprises plagued by inefficiency and facing new pressures from market competition, and resistance to market-oriented reforms from some sectors and institutions. Increasingly, the benefits of rapid growth became unevenly distributed. Per capita income surged, but inequality spiked, with one common measure (the Gini coefficient) climbing to levels not seen before in the PRC or in most of industrial East Asia. Fueled in part by foreign investment and trade, the economies of coastal cities raced ahead of those in inland and rural areas. While newly prosperous entrepreneurs and leaders of huge state-linked enterprises accumulated great wealth, the social safety net that rural collectives and urban work units had once provided for the less fortunate frayed, further exacerbating inequality.

When the fourth generation leaders took office in 2002–2003, they faced the twin challenges of trying to sustain and extend their predecessors' record of economic progress at home and economic integration abroad while also dealing with the Chinese development strategy's shortcomings and adverse effects. Although the leadership headed by Hu Jintao sought to sustain high growth rates, it pledged to ameliorate some of the inter-regional and social class inequalities that had emerged when the regime had focused overwhelmingly on rapid national economic development during the preceding decade. It proffered "scientific" or all-around "human" development to replace a one-sided emphasis on increasing the country's GDP. More concretely, it also adopted new policies that reduced burdensome taxes on farmers and moved toward building state-funded social insurance programs.

The success in sustaining China's swift modernization was impressive. During the Hu years, the country maintained double-digit or near-double-digit growth rates. China's GDP surpassed that of all other countries but the United States, and per capita incomes rose sufficiently for China to become an upper-middle-income country, as classified by the World Bank.[12] China greatly expanded its international economic presence, with trade and investment relationships—including rapidly growing outbound investment—reaching well beyond Asia and the developed market economies. Although the Global Financial Crisis in 2008 and the deep worldwide recession that followed created headwinds for China's still export-dependent economy, China recovered remarkably quickly. Increasingly self-confident Chinese leaders claimed a major role in the new G-20 group of leading economies and held forth on the flaws of U.S.-style capitalism that they alleged had produced an international crisis.

Efforts by Hu and his colleagues to address China's intensifying inequality, however, failed to fundamentally alter the prior pattern of rapid but uneven growth. Moreover, despite the maintenance of impressive economic expansion, near the end of the Hu years, skeptics were expressing doubts that China's long run of success would continue. Attention shifted from the extraordinary record of achievement to vexing problems that China's leaders seemed unable or unwilling to tackle. Although China initially withstood the great recession better than most major economies, the policies that helped make this possible (especially a stimulus package ramping up investment, renewed emphasis on financial support for the state-linked sector, and promotion of exports) remained in place after the crisis faded, and they were in tension with the resumption of reforms that many saw as necessary to ensure the sustainability of China's economic success.[13]

Several concerns contributed to fears that China might slide into protracted stagnation of the sort that had plagued Japan's once soaring economy after the late 1980s, and that China would suffer this fate at a time when it had not yet achieved Japan's level of broad-based prosperity. The emphasis on investment spending was deepening local government indebtedness and potentially generating or worsening a real estate bubble fueled by expectations that appreciating property values would bring higher returns than the low state-set interest rates for savings accounts into which citizens with few alternatives deposited much of their wealth.[14] More broadly, the later Hu years had been marked by *guojin mintui* ("the state sector advances and the private sector retreats")—a pattern that favored the entrenched economic interests of large state-owned firms, disadvantaged previously dynamic sectors, and threatened to impede further reform. Flagging demand for China's products in recession-plagued Europe and America had accelerated the decline of what had been a major driver of China's economic growth over the preceding decades. With so large an economy and with trading partners increasingly challenging what they charged were China's unfair trade and exchange rate policies, China could no longer so heavily rely on exports for growth. At the same time, efforts to sustain the country's impressive record of economic expansion faced formidable challenges that reflected the consequences of reform era policies: an aging society (produced by strict birth control regulations in place since the 1970s), corruption (born of the opportunities that a rapidly growing but incompletely reformed economy presented), and environmental pollution (worsened by lax regulation and policies that prioritized growth).

Social Issues

The prospect of a long-lasting economic slowdown is especially troubling for China's leaders, and for China and the wider world, because China's social stability in the decades since Mao's death has depended so much on ever-rising prosperity. Especially against the background of the social upheavals

of the People's Republic's first thirty years, more than three decades of reform have transformed society in ways that most Chinese have welcomed.[15]
Hundreds of millions have escaped poverty. Relaxation of the *hukou* system
of household registration and the shift to economic markets have freed Chinese citizens from serflike bondage to their rural locales and urban employers.
The waning of formerly pervasive demands for ideological conformity has
made room for diverse and critical views—increasingly expressed through
new media—and enabled individuals to pursue their own privately defined
goals in life.

Despite these significant advances, however, new and serious social
challenges have arisen. The first waves of market-oriented reforms increased
unemployment and insecurity among state-owned enterprise workers, dis-
rupted once-stable communities as many tens of millions moved in search
of work and opportunity, and eroded the formerly comprehensive, if rudi-
mentary, system of social security that collectives and work units had previously provided. A predictable effect of the regime's successful implementation
of a so-called "one child" policy to limit the country's population growth has
been a rapidly aging populace whose social welfare and health care needs will
have to be funded by a shrinking workforce. A vast cohort of rural-to-urban
migrants have lived a precarious existence as a "floating population," often
consigned to the least desirable jobs and at times vulnerable to "repatriation"
to their home areas because they have not had legal status as city residents.
Discontent about inequality, disappointment over economic conditions (especially among internal migrants and laid-off workers), and complaints about
wealth that too often comes from personal connections and corruption rather
than from hard work, talent, or luck have been increasingly serious problems
since the 1990s. Violent crime, organized crime, and other social ills have
spread as well. And, as a growing number of Chinese have joined unauthorized
groups—including underground "house churches" and the Falun Gong—a
wary and threatened regime has responded with harsh repression.

These and other changes have led to the alarming rise of an array of
social conflicts: about compensation for land that developers have expropri-
ated with the collaboration of local officials; about the environmental and
public health impact of economic development; about working conditions
and wages in China's myriad factories; about the safety of consumer products and foodstuffs marketed by poorly regulated enterprises; about pervasive corruption among officials who have leveraged their control of economic
assets for personal gain; about the unaccountability of imperious officials and

their families, who have accumulated vast wealth and abused their power and privilege, often with impunity; and about the shortcomings of a legal system that—despite striking if uneven progress—has not been robust enough either to enforce existing rules that might forestall many conflicts or to provide an effective venue for redressing many grievances. In response to such growing social strains, the Hu-era leadership promised to foster a "harmonious society" (*hexie shehui*), in part through addressing the needs and wants of those left behind during China's long economic boom. But where "disharmony" persisted and conflict loomed, the regime made clear that it would prioritize maintaining "social stability" (*weiwen*) over protecting "individual rights" (*weiquan*), even if the latter were enshrined in the regime's own laws and policies.[16]

Political Order

In China's political system, the reform era had begun with a repudiation of the toxic combination of tyranny and chaos that had characterized the Cultural Revolution decade (1966–1976).[17] Victims of purges during Mao's final years were rehabilitated and returned to positions of power and pledged support for socialist democracy and political liberalization. From Democracy Wall at the end of the 1970s to the democracy salons and think tanks proposing systemic reforms in the middle 1980s, from the demonstrations on college campuses in late 1986 to the popular Tiananmen Democracy Movement of 1989, the first decade of the post-Mao period was punctuated by recurrent calls, and hopes, for fundamental political change. Victories by independent candidates in a few local legislative elections and in some elections for village leadership during the 1980s also suggested the possibility of further steps toward democratic reform. Yet, such developments instead encountered repeated frustration or blunt repression. Broadly similar efforts in more recent times—such as the Charter 08 proposal for a liberal, democratic, constitutional order based on the rule of law; campaigns by a new wave of anti-establishment candidates for local people's congresses; the rise of "rights protection lawyers" who combine litigation and political activism on behalf of victims of misuses of state power; and the widely publicized demands by the villagers of Wukan in 2011–2012 seeking the implementation of laws protecting property rights and promising democratic elections—have been relatively few and have not fared better than their predecessors during the 1980s.

The fate of various democratic reform proposals and of many advocates of political change reflects the determination of the CCP to retain its monopoly of power. The regime, overall, has shown greater tolerance of heterodox and critical views among intellectuals and the broader public, supported moves toward more extensive, partially institutionalized consultation between the party-state and those affected by its policies, allowed (and at times encouraged) citizens to seek redress for local authorities' lawless or undisciplined behavior through administrative lawsuits, petitions to higher-level authorities (most prominently through *xinfang* or "letters and visits"), and even accommodated public protests and some of the demands they have put forth. Significant as such changes have been, however, they do not imply abandonment of the "four cardinal principles" (*si xiang jiben yuanze*) articulated by Deng Xiaoping in 1979 and written into the Chinese constitution in 1982: upholding the socialist path, the people's democratic dictatorship, the leadership of the party, and Marxism-Leninism-Mao Zedong thought.

The durability of China's version of Communist authoritarianism in the reform era has surprised many. Although moves toward democracy in East Asia and Soviet leader Mikhail Gorbachev's innovative ideas about political reform in Communist systems provided a catalyst for the massive protests in China in the spring of 1989, the third wave of democratization and the collapse of the Soviet Union did not lead to similarly sweeping change in China. When the Chinese leadership responded to the 1989 demonstrations with a forceful crackdown that did nothing to address the root causes of discontent, it cast doubt on the future of the entire reform agenda and triggered an angry international reaction and the prospect of China's ostracism. A widespread view at the time among outside observers was that the CCP regime was an anachronism likely to share the fate of similar authoritarian regimes, especially those in the Soviet bloc.[18] Such expectations proved to be incorrect. After Deng Xiaoping and his cadre of senior leaders concluded that their coercive response had consolidated the regime's hold on power, they moved to reinvigorate the reform program and to ensure that leadership passed to successors who would carry forward their agenda for change guided by the ruling Communist Party.[19]

With rapid economic growth, international engagement, and political stability restored, a new conventional wisdom took hold during the 1990s— that China had found a viable formula, whether labeled "market Leninism" or "resilient authoritarianism" or something else.[20] The prevalent view among analysts was that the CCP regime was "here to stay." In the first decade of the new century, however, new doubts began to arise.[21] Skeptics could point to: rising social unrest, with "mass incidents" surpassing 100,000 per year and larger-scale ethnic and religious uprisings erupting in Tibet and Xinjiang; slowing growth, which could imperil the economic performance that has been the principal basis for the regime's legitimacy for more than a genera-tion; expanding access to information and ideas among an increasingly well-educated, well-traveled, Internet-surfing and social media-using society; and seemingly mounting public disillusionment with the regime, coupled with possibly rising public demands for accountability and input in politics and policy. Nevertheless, at the end of the Hu years, such concerns still did not clearly pose an existential crisis for what had proved to be a remarkably adaptable authoritarian regime.

Foreign Relations

In engaging the world as well, China's reform era leaders have accomplished much, although not without encountering serious challenges.[22] China's broad opening to the outside made dramatic progress during the 1980s. Al-though the international opprobrium that followed the violent suppression of the protests at Tiananmen in 1989 seemed to jeopardize the country's ties to the international community, its effects proved to be shallow and short lived. The 1990s and early 2000s brought new, if less dramatic, setbacks for China's foreign relations. Recurrent frictions with the United States over trade, human rights, and security issues at times strained the relationship. Tension spiked during 1995–1996 in a confrontation over Chinese missile tests that sought to influence voters in Taiwan's first fully democratic presi-dential election and prompted President Clinton to dispatch U.S. naval forces near the Taiwan Strait. In early 2003, the international community again reacted with alarm and outrage to Beijing's secrecy and mishandling of the outbreak of Severe Acute Respiratory Syndrome (SARS) and the re-sulting threat of a global public health crisis. Despite such difficulties, how-ever, the predominant trend in China's foreign relations during the period was one of increasing acceptance, integration, and stature in the interna-tional system. By the early twenty-first century, China had joined every major international organization, had recovered the former British and Portuguese colonies of Hong Kong and Macao, and had sharply reduced the prospect that Taiwan would press for formal independence.

By the middle of the 2000s, the perception outside China, and to some extent in China, was that China's steeply upward economic trajectory—as well as a military modernization program and ambitious diplomatic initiatives that Beijing's new wealth underwrote—marked the dawn of an era that would be defined by "China's rise." Peaking around the time of the 2008 Olympics in Beijing, the new conventional wisdom held that, after two centuries of decline and failed attempts at revival, China's return to international prominence was at hand. As the advanced industrial economies struggled with the effects of the Great Recession, the perception that the downturn was enabling China to accelerate its gains relative to others deepened. The implications of this incipient shift in global power became a focus of analyses by scholars, pundits, and policymakers.[23]

At the end of the decade, however, as domestic troubles were mounting, China also faced new and growing challenges in its foreign relations. Disputes over conflicting territorial claims strained China's relations with Japan, the Philippines, and Vietnam. China's muscular and uncompromising response to increased tensions in the South and East China Seas dramatically undercut what had been Beijing's successful, decade-long effort to convince others that it sought "peaceful development" and a "peaceful rise."[24] Neighbors who recently had been reassured by China's generally responsible international behavior and "charm offensive" became alarmed by what many labeled "China's new assertiveness"—all the more so given deepening doubts about the U.S. commitment to the region and its ability to sustain its traditional postwar role as guarantor of regional stability and security.[25] Although China soon attempted to assuage its neighbors' concerns and to convince them of its benign intentions, Beijing's words were not matched by clear and consistent changes in behavior. Consequently, relations with key countries from Northeast through Southeast Asia remained unstable.

Moreover, China's increasingly fraught relations with states in its region coincided with a downturn in its most important bilateral relationship, that with the United States. From early in the George W. Bush administration and through the opening year of the Barack Obama administration, U.S.-Chinese ties were generally in good shape.[26] Beginning in 2010, however, frictions rose amid a series of disagreements about: U.S. arms sales to Taiwan; how to respond to North Korea's provocative behavior; the best approach to managing sovereignty disputes in the South and East China Seas; long-festering economic issues such as trade policy, exchange rates, and intellectual property protection; and a revival of U.S. criticisms of China's human rights record. In 2011, the Obama administration announced that it would shift more of America's strategic focus from the Middle East and Central Asia to the Asia Pacific, a region expected to be of continued and increasing importance for U.S. interests. Despite emphasizing that this "strategic rebalancing" was neither aimed at China nor simply about military deployments, the Obama administration was unable to alter the Chinese view that this new American initiative reflected a strategy designed to contain China's rise. Beijing insisted that the new emphasis in U.S. policy was aggravating tensions in the region, especially between China and neighboring countries. According to Beijing, those states had both encouraged and enthusiastically welcomed the American "pivot," and, as it unfolded, were emboldened by the perceived boost in U.S. support for them to press their disputes with China.

Troubled relations with states in its region and with the world's sole superpower meant that the stable and peaceful external environment, which China had long insisted it needed to complete the unfinished task of economic modernization, was looking more fragile than at any time since the early 1990s. As Hu's fourth-generation leadership prepared to hand over power to its successors, China faced the prospect of a more hostile atmosphere abroad and, as a result, a heavier burden of military expenditures at a time when it also faced large demands on national resources to address formidable domestic challenges.

Challenges Ahead

When they came to power in 2012–2013, the PRC's fifth-generation leaders appeared to recognize that China's domestic circumstances and international situation presented them with tough policy problems that, if not addressed adequately, could bring dire consequences. One of their first challenges was the need to manage the criminal case against Bo Xilai, who had been expelled from the CCP and arrested during the last months of the Hu era. Prior to his downfall in March 2012, Bo had been an aspiring member of the uppermost elite. His rule as party leader in Chongqing had won support in some circles for its populism and Maoist nostalgia, but elicited alarm in other quarters for its brutality, corruption, and revival of the state's role in the economy. But perhaps most troubling at the moment of impending transition among the top leadership, his unusually public bid for power had threatened to disrupt the norms of orderly succession. After completing the prosecution of those charged in connection with Bo's activities (most notably, his wife Gu Kailai and his police chief Wang Lijun), the CCP's new leaders tried Bo and sought to put the sensational case behind them in late summer 2013. An anticorruption drive launched by the Xi leadership, however, has brought trouble for other recent members of the top elite, including a reported investigation of Zhou Yongkang, the Politburo Standing Committee member and head of the CCP's Political Legal Committee under Hu Jintao.

With respect to the broader policy challenges, President and General Secretary Xi Jinping and Premier Li Keqiang began publicly asserting the imperative to do more than better implement the economic and social policies of their predecessors. Xi touted a "China dream" that included greater prosperity and national rejuvenation. In their early months in power, the new leadership floated proposals for a new round of economic reforms for rebalancing the economy away from relying on investment-driven growth fueled by easy credit and export-dependent growth supported by low production costs and a favorable exchange rate.[27] They frankly acknowledged the inadequacy of excessively focusing on high rates of economic growth without paying sufficient attention to the quality of growth, including its impact on the environment that was becoming a major focus of popular discontent.[28]

In November 2013, the CCP's Eighteenth Central Committee convened its Third Plenum—a point in the Chinese policy cycle that during the reform era has often produced significant agendas for economic reform. The ensuing "Sixty-Point Decision" statement of the plenum's reform plans included several potentially significant, if limited and general, initiatives including: allowing market forces to play the "decisive role" in allocating economic resources, altering the nature and role of state-owned enterprises, moving to more liberal and market-oriented policies for the financial sector, providing a more level playing field for private enterprises, opening more sectors to foreign investment, reforming long-troubled local government finance, expanding land-use rights for farmers, unifying urban and rural markets for construction land (to address problems of land expropriation that have fueled peasant anger), strengthening the social safety net, and assigning greater weight to environmental and quality of life concerns in evaluating cadres' performance.[29] The document also endorsed further urbanization, portending an extension of trends that have transformed China from a majority agrarian to a majority city-dwelling society. And it pledged, and formal steps soon followed, to implement a much-anticipated reform to relax the three-decade-old "one child" policy and permit couples to have a second child if one of the parents is an only child.

Xi and Li pledged a reinvigorated struggle against official corruption and extravagance, including a campaign to clean house and attack both "tigers and flies" (both high- and low-ranking targets) that might be described as Maoist party rectification with Internet age characteristics. This campaign seeks a more effective approach to dealing with this insidious and growing threat to the regime's legitimacy. The Third Plenum's blueprint for reform included a broad pledge to "contain power within the cage of law."

As the fifth-generation leadership came to power, advocates of political and legal reform eagerly anticipated new openings for progress. Implementing a pledge from the Third Plenum, the National People's Congress Standing Committee approved, in December 2013, the end of the system of "reeducation through labor" (*laojiao*) that imprisoned hundreds of thousands without the minimal protections afforded by the process of criminal prosecution and conviction in China's courts, and that had long been a target of reform advocates and human rights critics. Passages in the post–Third Plenum Sixty-Point Decision concerning law and legal issues (including promises to address structural underpinnings of "local protectionism" and political interference in judicial decision making), the selection and early official acts of Zhou Qiang as president of the Supreme People's Court, and remarks by Xi Jinping at a central political and legal work conference in January 2014 all suggested, at least to hopeful pro-reform observers and advocates, that prospects were improving for a turn back to rule-of-law—or at least stronger rule-by-law—agendas, renewed reliance on formal laws and legal institutions, and progress for long-percolating reforms in administrative law mechanisms to increase the accountability of state actors.[30]

To tackle China's recently more difficult circumstances in foreign affairs, Xi made a successful push for an early, informal summit meeting with President Obama aimed at reversing the slide into mistrust, mutual recrimination, and growing suspicion that marred U.S.-China relations during the final years of the Hu era. Because Beijing seemed to believe that much of the reason for renewed tensions with its neighbors was an American policy that encouraged them to challenge China, reducing these frictions, along with improving ties with Washington, was among the evident goals of the new leadership's attempt to recast U.S.-China ties as a "new type of great power relationship" (*xinxing daguo guanxi*). The announcement of a pilot "free trade zone" in Shanghai and pledges of greater access to the Chinese market for foreign firms and investors appeared to be early signals from the Xi administration of progress in some aspects of continuing to deepen China's international economic engagement.

However urgent the many tasks at hand, Xi and his colleagues also seemed to recognize that a push for bold new reforms would confront predictable obstacles and could lead to unpredictable effects. Their caution and determination were both on display at the trial of Bo Xilai, which proved to be an ambivalent affair. The regime's desire to convey an impression of due process clashed with concerns about the trial's broader implications when Bo's defense turned out to be pugnacious and irreverent. By focusing on long-past corruption and the cover-up of a tawdry murder, the trial sought to sidestep the more delicate and potentially explosive task of addressing a wider pattern of behavior that would resonate with those leveling fundamental criticisms against the regime, but it also risked inviting questions about why Bo had not been stopped sooner. Amid the fifth-generation leadership's much-trumpeted drive against corruption, foreign news media encountered blocked Web sites and threats of visa denials to their journalists, reportedly because of their exposés of corruption among family members of Xi, Wen, and other top leaders. In addition, foreign investment banks were forced to forgo deals with China, reportedly because of investigations into their hiring of close relatives of top Chinese officials.

Concerning larger questions of new economic, social, or political reforms, the new leadership could foresee criticisms from both flanks. One side might object to policy innovations as ill-advised steps that would jeopardize the substantial achievements of the reform era as well as their personal and institutional stakes in the status quo. The other side might object to these innovations as insufficient to address the major and mounting problems China now faces. Perhaps anticipating resistance from a diverse coalition of skeptics, as the new leaders began to roll out their agenda in 2013, they gave no indication that they planned to include major reforms of the political system—or more than gradual reforms to the legal system—that matched the relative boldness of their vision in other areas, primarily economic policy and perhaps foreign policy.

On the contrary, there were signs that they intended to resist, rather than accommodate, pressures for major political reform, possibly because such changes could weaken the grip on power they saw as necessary for pushing through changes in other areas. Outspoken advocates of political and legal reforms came under new pressure as the regime targeted and detained prominent critics (including Xu Zhiyong, a leader of the Open Constitution Initiative—*gongmeng*—and the New Citizen Movement—*xinmin yundong*), issued an ominous "Document No. 9" that reportedly declared several "Western" legal and political ideas (including judicial independence, universal values, and some forms of constitutionalism) off-limits for open discussion, and opened the door to a stream of similarly minded commentaries in official media. The regime has generally tightened control over public debate. New restrictions have especially targeted popular social media which now face the chilling effect of detentions, prohibitions and sanctions, including those aimed at so-called "Big V" bloggers (who have large numbers of followers) and more ordinary Internet users whose posted "rumors" have been reposted more than 500 times or seen by more than 5,000 viewers.[31] It remains to be seen whether the steps to rein in heterodox views in 2013 were the beginning of a long-term trend toward a less tolerant political climate in China under Xi Jinping or simply a reprise of what has become a familiar ebb and flow.

The fifth-generation's early moves in foreign policy combined efforts that sought to ease tensions and deepen integration while also responding to significant domestic criticism of Hu and his leadership group for being insufficiently insistent on China's stature and interests in the world. Xi's "new type of great power relationship" and his China Dream—which included national rejuvenation and military strength—seemed to address these critiques and to signal a vigorous stance. Beijing's November 2013 proclamation of an Air Defense Identification Zone (ADIZ) over the East China Sea reflected the new leadership's attempts to manage the tensions inherent in its new foreign policy direction. Having caught the international community off-guard and having initially cast China's policy in terms that seemed unusually strict and possibly provocative, the ADIZ announcement was quickly softened in official explanations that pledged enforcement consistent with international norms, in response to alarmed reactions from China's neighbors and the United States.

Overall, the new leaders were generally continuing an approach typical of their reform era predecessors: assign top priority to agendas in economic and foreign policy while insisting that success in these areas depends on maintaining social stability at home; the need for social stability, in turn, counsels postponing difficult political and related reforms that might constrain or threaten the regime's power to manage China's development and protect China's interests in the world. This approach undoubtedly seems prudent from the perspective of China's leaders in light of the regime's track record over the last few decades. But for a regime otherwise avowedly dedicated to reinvigorating the reformist agenda, this kind of cautiousness also carries risks. Decisively tackling some of the problems to which official policies attach high priority (including corruption, worker and product safety, and environmental degradation) may well depend on deepening political and legal reforms.

The November 2013 Third Plenum of the Eighteenth Central Committee and its early aftermath reflected ambivalence and uncertainty about an agenda for ambitious reform in China in the early years of the fifth-generation leadership. In the months-long run-up to the plenum, there were heady discussions of potential change across a wide range of policy areas. At the plenum's conclusion, initial reports elicited disappointment from those who had thought that discussion over the preceding months had foreshadowed a more sweeping push for major reforms suited to the scale of China's deepening challenges. The more detailed Sixty-Point Decision, setting forth the scope of the new leaders' reform ambitions, revived optimism.

Like the plenum's wide-ranging but still sparse and as-yet-largely-unimplemented policy initiatives, the plenum's announcement of two new leadership groups might, or might not, signal significant policy change. One of these groups, a vaguely described State (sometimes translated as "National") Security Council, is to focus on coordinating the tasks of ensuring international and domestic security. The other, a Leading Small Group for Comprehensively Deepening Reform, is to be a select body chaired by Xi Jinping that will take charge of guiding a renewed push for sweeping reforms—in the economy, politics, society, culture, the environment, and party building. If successfully implemented, and if it enables China's leaders to grapple effectively with the challenges the country faces in the new millennium's second decade, the reform package—and the organizational changes to support it—will herald a dramatic new vision for China, and the Third Plenum of the Eighteenth CCP Central Committee will have been a watershed moment, a historic turning point second in significance only to the

Third Plenum of the Eleventh CCP Central Committee in December 1978 that launched the post-Mao reforms. If, however, the regime's actions fail to match the bold rhetoric and meet the expectations raised by the ambitious agenda China's new leaders announced, then the November 2013 meeting is more likely to be seen as simply a tactical adjustment by a leadership unable or unwilling to take innovative and risky measures to tackle the country's difficult challenges inherited from their predecessors.

The following chapters examine some, though certainly not all, of the major issues that face China under the fifth-generation leadership, and consider the prospects for the country's leaders to address them successfully. The contributors examine key areas that pose pivotal challenges, focusing on illustrative, or especially difficult, or particularly important questions within the broader fields of social, economic, political-legal, and foreign policy.

Jane Duckett and Guohui Wang, Yong Cai, and Zai Liang consider various aspects of inequality and its relationship to China's changing demography. Duckett and Wang assess the coexistence of a significant drop in absolute poverty with a sharp rise in income inequality during the reform era, attributing the latter in part to the commodification of access to education, health care, housing, and jobs, and the broader logic of China's growth model. Looking forward, they discern an apparently serious and self-interested commitment by the leadership to address relative poverty. But they warn of the dangers that high and rising inequality create for social stability, and the difficulty of taking needed policy measures as growth slows and as redistributionist measures threaten the interests of the reform era's "winners."

Liang addresses inequality associated with the *hukou* system of household registration, which, during the reform era, eroded as a rigid barrier to mobility but emerged as a basis for inequality within fast-growing urban regions between local *hukou* holders and roughly two hundred million internal migrants. This created a two-tier system in terms of access to employment, housing, education, social services, and political influence. Liang discerns a significant commitment among the new leadership to address these issues and the perils they pose for the regime's agenda and for maintaining social stability. But he cautions that the scale of the challenge (particularly of addressing the educational needs of children "left behind" in the countryside and children who have migrated with their parents to the cities), resistance to radical *hukou* reform from city governments (which face vastly increased costs or dilution of benefits if migrants receive equal access), and the growing impatience and activism of migrants seeking educational opportunities for their children all complicate the effort to implement major changes in the *hukou* system.

Cai focuses on another, fundamentally demographic inequality: the gender imbalance that has arisen from the combination of reform era anti-natalist population policies, long-standing social norms, and rational economic calculations in China's marketized economy—which lead families to favor boys—and the availability of sex-selective abortions. Ahead, Cai points to significant ongoing risks to social stability from a large cohort of economically disadvantaged, unmarried young men concentrated in a few geographic areas. But he foresees positive longer-term trends toward redressing sex ratios with increasing urbanization, the growing power in the marriage market of the relatively small cohort of young women, women's improved education levels and economic opportunities, and the regime's relaxation of the single-child family policy.

Yasheng Huang and Barry Naughton each address economic challenges that have emerged from China's remarkably sustained rapid economic growth during the reform era. Huang continues the preceding chapters' focus on inequality, tracing the shift from declining inequality in the 1980s to rising inequality in the 1990s and early 2000s. This trend has yielded a level of inequality (as measured by the Gini coefficient) that has soared past that of Brazil, India, and China's more developed East Asian neighbors, notwithstanding some amelioration of inegalitarian trends in China recently. Huang argues that these trends are not the inevitable accompaniments of economic development but reflect policy choices, including pro-rural and pro-market policies in the 1980s, a shift to pro-urban policies and partial reversal of rural reforms in the 1990s, and a reduction in antirural bias amid partial erosion of pro-market approaches to urban policy in the later 2000s. Huang finds somewhat hopeful signs in some policies of the Hu-Wen era upon which the Xi-Li leadership may build, but he concludes that difficult, fundamental reforms to statist economic and political institutions are needed to address inequality effectively.

Naughton turns to economic imbalance of another sort, engaging the debate over China's need to "rebalance" its economy from exports toward domestic demand, from investment toward consumption, and from hyper-growth to more moderate growth. He finds that the increase in imbalance toward exports was short-lived and declined quickly after the Global Financial Crisis, but that dependence on investment-heavy growth has been a major, durable feature of reform era Chinese policy, further reinforced by stimulus measures undertaken in the wake of the 2008 downturn. Naughton concludes that a fundamental imperative to rebalance stems from the unsustainability of investment-driven growth as China exhausts the "demographic dividend" of a large ratio of working-age population to dependent population, moves beyond the "followership" stage when building infrastructure and industry contributes to high growth, and exits a phase when market-oriented reforms and government-led construction are mutually reinforcing. As China confronts the long-term transition to a middle-income society with markedly slower growth, its leaders face near-term policy challenges to recalibrate the roles of—or to move away from—state-directed industrial policy and state control of large portions of the economy.

Melanie Manion, Daniela Stockmann, and Benjamin L. Liebman analyze domestic political challenges facing China today, focusing on three aspects of concerns about stability and the regime's responses to them. Manion examines corruption, which China's leaders and public opinion polls identify as a major problem that generally—and in Manion's view rightly—is seen as having become more large scale and more threatening to economic performance and political legitimacy over the last two decades. Rooted in 1990s reforms that increased the value of economic opportunities controlled by state agents while preserving the discretion of officials to grant access to such opportunities, new types of corruption became especially serious. These include sale of official positions, judicial corruption, real estate profiteering, and financial corruption (especially misappropriation of public funds). Manion argues that the shifting emphasis in anticorruption efforts from routine or intensive campaign-based enforcement toward prevention is a relatively promising change. Although cautiously optimistic about the new leadership's initiatives to have officials disclose their assets and, especially, to reduce the scope of activities requiring government approvals, she cautions that altering the problematic incentive structures that foster corruption and, in turn, imperil the regime's stability is a difficult, long-term project.

Stockmann examines China's changing media and its implications for political stability. She finds that reforms creating a more market-based traditional media sector and the rise of new media have created novel threats to the regime's stability by giving rise to autonomous sources of information and arenas for critical public discourse. But, at least for now, Stockmann finds that a long-standing and adaptable infrastructure of party and state institutions for controlling the media, and for supporting the dissemination of regime-favored news and views, remains in place and is being supplemented by new mechanisms such as defamation suits and norms of journalistic "social responsibility." With these mechanisms, the regime has been able to maintain a balance between liberalization and control that has helped sustain its grip on power. The question ahead is whether it will be possible to continue a "responsive authoritarian" approach to media—one that allows society to communicate information that the state needs to hear in order to govern effectively yet retains the state's capacity to guide public opinion.

Assessing a "law and stability paradox," Liebman asks why a regime that invested in building a legal system in the 1980s and 1990s seemed to turn, in the 2000s, away from courts (and toward stability maintenance organizations) and away from formal legality within the courts (and toward more ad hoc responses to discontent). Liebman points to several interrelated developments. The perception of rising social instability during the Hu-Wen years shifted the always fraught balance between reform and stability toward the latter and reinvigorated traditions of populism that are at odds with legal professionalism. The leadership's view that law was not adequate to maintain order dovetailed with popular perceptions that the legal system favored the rich and powerful or produced outcomes inconsistent with popular preferences and demands. This encouraged citizens to seek, and courts and officials to be overly responsive in granting, relief where none was legally warranted. Liebman concludes that the Xi-Li leadership has signaled a possible reversal of these trends and that a more rule-governed system might serve the regime's interests. But he also finds that the new leadership's messages have been mixed and notes that the law's potential contributions to stability in a time of rapid transition for China are debatable.

M. Taylor Fravel, Andrew S. Erickson, and Robert Sutter analyze the growing difficulties that China faces in its international relationships. They address overlapping aspects of China's troubled security relations. Erickson argues that China's reform era drive for military modernization has been limited in its effectiveness because wary neighbors (many of them embroiled in territorial and jurisdictional disputes with China) perceive China's growing capability as a threat and are reacting accordingly, and because China's increasingly global aims and interests demand a profound increase in China's military capacity if it is to be able to defend those aims and interests unilaterally. In Erickson's view, China has an opportunity to secure its most important, realistic aims with a comparatively modest improvement in capabilities and the pursuit of diplomatic cooperation with the United States and others. But the prospects for such cooperation are limited. China's quest for regional influence (and territorial gains) conflicts with the interests of the militarily still-dominant United States. American interests include sustaining a postwar status quo that the United States sees as having served its own interests and those of the region to which it has recently recommitted itself, with its "rebalancing" to Asia.

Fravel focuses on China's maritime disputes with its neighbors, which, especially since 2008, have unraveled the policies of good neighborliness and "win-win" approaches to regional relations that Beijing had pursued throughout much of the reform era. Fravel attributes the change to China's growing economic and, in turn, military power and its use of that power to resist what it sees as other states' encroachments on China's important interests in the South and East China Seas. A security dilemma has emerged between China and China's neighbors (which increasingly have sought and received U.S. support), with each side seeing its own actions as justified and defensive and the other side's as assertive and status quo-challenging. China has attempted to contain the damage to its foreign policy interests with intermittent tactical moderation in its approach to maritime territorial claims, efforts to insulate other aspects of relations with disputant states from the conflicts over sovereignty, and attempts to improve relations with the United States. But Fravel concludes that these measures may be too little and too late, and that China's poor relationships with its neighbors are likely to cause lingering and significant harm to its security interests.

Sutter examines China's—and the world's—most important bilateral relationship. With Xi and the fifth-generation leadership in power, Sutter foresees a continuation of the pattern in recent years of volatility in U.S.-China relations and a decline of the pragmatic engagement that had long characterized bilateral ties. Although numerous, regular, high-level meetings, warming relations across the Taiwan Strait, and cooperation on specific issues reflect continuing engagement, China's assertive and nationalist stance on maritime territorial disputes and the related, broader rise in competition between the United States and China for influence in Asia indicate a troubled relationship. Sutter attributes this partly to a legacy of mistrust with roots in decades of sporadic conflicts over many issues, but he argues that domestic politics are a major source of the problem. While domestic politics in the United States have at times pressed leaders in Washington to pursue harder-line China policies that have ill-served U.S. interests, today elite and mass political opinion in China also pushes leaders in Beijing toward unwise approaches to foreign policy. Returning this volume to its opening focus on China's domestic issues, Sutter links this foreign policy nationalism to a legitimacy-challenged regime's propagation of a narrative asserting that China was a victim of nineteenth-century imperialist depredations and is a singularly benign, righteous, and rightful great power today.

Although the high politics of security affairs are only one dimension of the multifaceted foreign policy challenges facing contemporary China, these issues are among the most fundamental and the most urgent. Trade and investment disputes, climate change and cross-border pollution, energy security, and nontraditional security threats ranging from terrorism to infectious diseases to natural disasters are important as well. But many of these are longer-term concerns that are unlikely to elicit major responses from a Chinese party-state facing numerous, more pressing problems. And progress in addressing many of these other international issues depends on China's ability to avoid military conflict or even severe crises in its security affairs.

How—and how well—China under the fifth-generation leadership copes with the social, economic, political, and international challenges discussed in this volume (and other challenges as well) will do much to define China's trajectory for years to come. Given the magnitude of these challenges and China's significance for the region and the world, its success or failure will matter far beyond its borders.

CHAPTER 2

Poverty and Inequality

Jane Duckett and Guohui Wang

China has made impressive progress in reducing poverty over the last three decades. According to the most recent World Bank data, the percentage of the Chinese population living on less than $1.25 a day had fallen from 60 percent in 1990 to 13 percent in 2008, and China accounted for 510 million out of the 600 million people lifted out of poverty across the world over that eighteen-year period. This impressive record, however, still leaves over 170 million Chinese people in severe poverty, and a total of nearly 400 million (30 percent) living on less than $2 a day. Altogether almost one billion Chinese people (72 percent) are living on less than $5 a day, the World Bank's measure of less severe poverty.[1]

At the same time, China has experienced substantial increases in inequality—in incomes and assets, and in access to housing, education, and health care. Of these, it is the increases in income inequality that have garnered the most attention, as stark rises in China's Gini index (from a low 32 in 1990 to at least 49 by 2008) apparently transformed it from one of the most equal to one of the most unequal societies in the world in less than twenty years.[2] But income inequalities in turn exacerbated inequalities in other dimensions because they occurred at the same time as housing markets appeared and school, university, and medical fees increased. Stark differentials across all these dimensions exist not only between individuals but also between rural and urban areas, and between regions.

A significant challenge, then, for China's new leaders is to sustain the decline in poverty while at the same time reducing high levels of inequality. If Xi Jinping, Li Keqiang, and their allies at the top of the party-state do not meet this dual challenge they may face both economic slowdown and political opposition. High levels of poverty and inequality can be obstacles to economic growth.[3] The poor, moreover, may mobilize in unequal societies, and inequality is associated with political instability—whether bottom-up democratic transitions, top-down political coups, or widespread social unrest.[4]

Indeed the domestic pressure on the government to act has grown in China. There has been a steady rise in public protest, with the number of "mass incidents" increasing to 180,000 per year. And while these incidents are often catalyzed by specific, localized problems such as unpaid pensions or wages, poor working conditions, land seizures, and pollution incidents, some believe them to be underpinned by a simmering resentment over rising inequality.[5] Although opinion surveys do not all support this view—one study of attitudes in the early twenty-first century argued that there was little anger with income inequality[6]—a recent poll showed dissatisfaction to have risen.[7] Just as importantly, China's leaders believe that high levels of poverty and inequality are a political problem—contributing to "social instability" and reducing the Chinese Communist Party's (CCP's) political legitimacy.[8] As a result, over the last decade leaders have increasingly prioritized social policies that address inequality and (to a lesser extent) poverty.

But reducing deprivation and inequality will not be easy. Much of China's remaining serious poverty is the most entrenched, for example in remote and mountainous regions. In any case, as overall living standards rise, so will expectations of minimally acceptable livelihoods and poverty thresholds. Poverty is a moving target, and policies to help the poorest raise their incomes and living standards will need to evolve. Effective policies for reducing inequality meanwhile require targeting investment at the poor to provide social services, income support, unemployment benefits, state pensions, and assistance with access to education, health care, and housing. The difficulty here is to change incentives for local governments—the main source of social spending—which currently invest much more in infrastructure (especially roads, rail, and buildings) to support economic growth than in what they see as "unproductive" social goods.

Other policies to reduce inequality, such as introducing progressive taxation and land reform, also face obstacles. First, they are undermined by a weak tax administration and corruption. Second, because they are redistributive, they are likely to meet opposition in the form of preemptive resistance or overt political challenge from beneficiaries of the status quo. Political coups tend to follow periods of steep *decline* in inequality under populist regimes in the developing world. This suggests that when governments successfully reduce inequality they may be challenged by elites who are unhappy with their redistributive policies.[9] Indeed elite opposition to redistribution in China may explain why—despite progress over the last twenty years—pro-poor policies have been underfunded while new old age and health insurance programs have disproportionately benefited the urban middle classes.

The next section of this chapter sets out the historical context to the challenge today of reducing poverty and inequality in China. It looks at how the policies of the 1949–1978 "Mao era" tackled them on some dimensions but also entrenched inequalities between urban and rural areas. It then discusses how China's post-Mao economic strategy much more successfully reduced poverty but allowed individual and household income inequalities to rise.[10] The subsequent sections then examine in more detail the main dimensions of poverty and inequality in contemporary China, recent policies to tackle them, and the obstacles that they have faced. In the concluding section we look at the prospects for China's current leaders to meet the challenge.

Historical Context: Reconfiguring Poverty and Inequality, 1949 to the Twenty-First Century

The Mao Era: A Focus on Reducing Inequality

When the Chinese Communist Party (CCP) came to power in 1949 after more than a decade of war, the vast majority of the population lived in extreme destitution amid small pockets of wealth. Over the next three decades the new regime—led by Mao Zedong—set about tackling many of these problems. Its approach was egalitarian: addressing class-based inequalities by redistributing land and other property, and setting up governing institutions across countryside and cities that provided basic safety nets for the poorest.[11] This approach raised living standards for many, and reduced inequalities, in part by extending basic education, sanitation, and health care facilities across rural areas.

The new CCP regime's egalitarian approach was founded on radical land reform. It seized the property of rural landlords and reallocated it on a per capita basis—doing much to reduce rural inequalities and equalize living standards. The regime then collectivized land and farm tools, and by the end of the decade set up communes to organize production as well as extend basic education and health services nationwide. The communes also provided meager safety nets to the very poorest rural households (the so-called "five guarantee households," *wubaohu*). Beyond this, poverty reduction for the main part involved providing financial subsidies to poor rural areas to help those in poverty maintain a very basic standard of living and production. There was a particular focus on relief for areas impoverished by natural disasters and famine.[12]

Despite the CCP's pro-rural inclinations, the new regime was in the 1950s strongly influenced by the Soviet Union's model of state-led industrialization and set up a state planning system that financed heavy industry by squeezing agriculture and keeping rural incomes low. It effectively underpaid farmers for their produce so as to provide cheap food in the cities where the CCP felt it needed to build and maintain support. At the same time, a household registration system, introduced in 1958, prevented farmers from migrating to the cities. So while it kept incomes and living standards relatively equal within localities, it allowed inequalities *between* them—and especially between rural and urban areas—to grow. By the 1970s, average urban incomes were three times higher than those in the countryside.[13]

In the cities, redistribution in the 1950s and 1960s involved nationalizing businesses and redeploying most of the population to public sector work. In conjunction with state planning, this gave the party-state the power to redistribute wealth, primarily by limiting the acquisition of private property and virtually equalizing wages.[14] Urban dwellers benefited from higher living standards than their rural counterparts, in part because the state guaranteed jobs and provided much urban housing, as well as subsidizing food and financing relatively high standards of education and health care, given China's low level of economic development. Poverty was seen as a rural rather than an urban problem and social relief in the cities provided for the tiny proportion of the population with no work, no family, and no other means of support (the so-called *san wu* or "three nos").[15]

The Early Post-Mao Period: Reducing Poverty
and Raising Living Standards

All this changed starting in the late 1970s. After Mao Zedong's death in 1976, and Deng Xiaoping's accession to power in late 1978, the CCP adopted a radically different development strategy—one that prioritized not egalitarianism but rapid economic growth. In the early post-Mao period, the Chinese government's goal was to reduce poverty and raise living standards by stimulating agricultural and light industrial development—and economic policies drove much of China's poverty reduction. There was at this early stage little concern with wealth distribution, though Deng Xiaoping clearly encouraged the emergence of some inequality when he argued that it was acceptable "to let some people get rich first."

In line with its growth-led antipoverty strategy, the government—while maintaining its very minimal individual social relief programs—also began to invest in developing rural economies in deprived localities.[16] The main program identified "poor counties" on the basis of whether local average per capita incomes fell below a poverty line. These counties (as well some townships and villages not in official "poor counties") were targeted with poverty reduction loans (micro-credit), food-for-work programs and Ministry of Finance grant funds. Aimed at tackling the worst deprivation, this focus on poor localities meant the neglect of many poor people in better off areas.

Although in the 1990s CCP leader Jiang Zemin was apparently unconcerned with rising inequalities,[17] the party-state did introduce social policies to deal with poverty, especially the urban deprivation created by massive layoffs during state enterprise reform. It extended eligibility for material social relief in principle (though not fully in practice) to all the urban poor through a new income support program known as the "minimum livelihood guarantee."[18] This program was mandated in all cities from 1999 and became an important—though only very basic—safety net that was expanded to growing numbers of poor people as unemployment from state enterprises surged.[19] It provided means-tested benefits using a locally determined minimum cost of living based on a basket of essential food, clothing, shelter, and other necessities. It helped reduce opposition to the politically sensitive state enterprise reforms that raised unemployment just as the state also deregulated grain prices and commodified housing, health care, and education.[20] But it was underfunded because city governments saw benefits as fostering dependency and they had stronger incentives to invest directly in economic growth.

The Chinese government also introduced unemployment insurance and reemployment service centers to limit political opposition to state enterprise reform.[21] At the same time, it announced new policies to deliver old age and health insurance to the urban employed.[22] Jiang and his premier, Zhu

Rongji, also targeted support at the poorest rural areas, usually in the interior or "West" of the country and especially in remote mountainous regions.[23] Then, in 2000, they announced a major new project aimed at rebalancing unequal regional development and reducing poverty through "major development of the Western regions" (*xibu da kaifa*). Over the first six years the government targeted more than a trillion yuan, or 125 billion U.S. dollars, for infrastructure (railways and highways, hydropower, and pipelines), education, and ecological protection.[24] Finally, toward the end of the Jiang and Zhu leadership in 2002, the government also announced policies to try and reduce the rural-urban divide by introducing "New Cooperative Medical Schemes" (NCMS) and cutting the tax burden on farmers.[25]

All these efforts to reduce poverty and inequality were undermined, however, by policies—such as privatizing provision or permitting providers to charge fees for education and health treatment—that commodified goods previously provided by the state. Starting in the 1980s private education and health service providers appeared, while in the 1990s schools and universities began to charge fees—if not for tuition then for equipment and other "extras."[26] Although the education and health infrastructure benefited from the extra income, rural dwellers and the poor were disadvantaged by rising costs.[27] Their problems accessing health care were further compounded by the nationwide collapse of rural cooperative medical schemes in the early 1980s and the erosion of urban health insurance in the 1990s.[28] Also in the 1990s, urban housing, previously available at very low rental prices, was commercialized.[29] Again, although housing quality improved for those who were better off, housing markets pushed up prices, contributing to urban poverty and exacerbating inequalities.

Policies were also limited by political opposition. Wealthy local governments opposed efforts to change the fiscal system and give the center more redistributional capacity. Although tax reforms in the 1990s did increase the center's fiscal revenues and are credited with increased central spending on poverty reduction, they did not fundamentally change the decentralized tax system that left revenue generation and social spending decisions in the hands of local governments. Similarly, better-off localities opposed efforts to introduce provincial- or national-level risk pooling in social insurance because it would have entailed them subsidizing poorer areas and reducing benefits to their own residents.[30] Middle-class representatives to local people's congresses meanwhile sometimes opposed efforts to cut their social insurance entitlements, while medical professionals resisted health reforms that threatened lucrative sources of income.[31]

Into the Twenty-First Century:
Time to Tackle Inequality Again?

Into the first decade of the twenty-first century, China's deprivation-related social problems became increasingly evident, and provided impetus for new policies to tackle poverty and inequality. The CCP's top leader from 2002, Hu Jintao, and his premier, Wen Jiabao, were driven by fears of political instability, but they were also influenced by advisers aware of changing conceptions of poverty and inequality internationally. Their government began first with policies aimed at reducing poverty in the countryside and tackling rural-urban inequalities in access to education and health care. These policies were soon packaged as "Building a New Socialist Countryside,"[32] and included measures to abolish agricultural taxes in a move significantly more radical than the prior Jiang and Zhu-era proposals to lighten the tax burden on farmers.

Next, the government expanded NCMS, investing more in subsidies and, at the same time, setting concrete targets for local governments to enroll (voluntarily) the vast majority of villagers.[33] Then, in 2006, it announced that all children would receive nine years of free education and began implementation in western and central rural districts, extending it nationwide by September 2008.[34] Beginning in 2007 the government formally announced that the means-tested "minimum livelihood guarantee" program operating in the cities since the 1990s would be introduced across all rural areas.[35] In 2009 it established a national framework for rural pensions, the Rural Pension Pilot Program, and has since extended its coverage. By 2013, 790 million Chinese were said to be included in national pension endowment schemes.[36]

Under Hu and Wen the government also plugged holes in the previous government's urban social policies. In 2007 it introduced an Urban Residents' Health Insurance for the nonworking population—to tackle criticisms that its social health insurance for urban employees (introduced in the late 1990s) had left too many without protection.[37] And, in April 2009, the government announced a major overhaul of the health system, committing itself to achieving universal access to basic health care for all by 2020.[38] In 2011 it then began to push the extension of rural pensions and announced national pilot Urban Residents Pension Scheme.[39] Finally, with late 1990s promises to deliver low-cost housing in the cities unmet, the Hu and Wen leadership renewed this goal, as house price inflation became one of the greatest sources of popular disquiet. Along with these social welfare reforms, there was also some improvement—though locally very variable—in the rights of rural migrant workers.[40]

Finally, in March 2011, the Hu and Wen government published the Twelfth Five-Year Plan (2011–2015; hereafter, the Plan): its blueprint for economic and social development into the Xi Jinping and Li Keqiang leadership term. This long document committed the government to continuing the social reforms of the previous eight years—reducing rural poverty, increasing social assistance payments for the poor, raising the minimum wage, extending participation in social insurance schemes, and decreasing not only unequal income distribution between individuals and households (through pro-poor growth and progressive tax reforms), but also regional gaps and rural-urban inequalities in access to public services such as education and health.[41] The Plan bridged the change of leadership, providing continuity and direction for the next "generation" of leaders as well as indicating the challenges as perceived at the end of the Hu and Wen period (2012–2013).

Rising to the Challenge Today: The Obstacles

Sustaining Poverty Reduction

Thus, tackling poverty remained on the leadership agenda into the second decade of the twenty-first century despite China's impressive poverty reduction since the late 1970s—especially when compared with other countries internationally.[42] Using the World Bank's poverty threshold of $1.25 dollars a day, China's fall from 60 to 13 percent of the population living in poverty between 1990 and 2008 was slightly greater than Vietnam's, where the proportion living in poverty fell from 56 percent to 14 percent over the same period. And China performed significantly better than India, which reduced its poverty ratio from 49 percent in 1995 to 33 percent in 2010, and also better than South Africa, whose poverty ratio fell from 24 percent in 1993 to 14 percent in 2010. China's gains are proportionally bigger than these other nations, but also, because its population is so large, China has contributed significantly to achieving the United Nations' Millennium Development Goal of halving world poverty (at $1.25 a day) between 1990 and 2015.

By 2008, the global number in poverty had fallen from 2 billion (1990) to 1.4 billion, with China contributing 510 million of the 600 million reduction.[43]

The challenge for new leaders Xi Jinping and Li Keqiang, then, is to sustain this trend. But there are many obstacles. China's severest poverty may be the most entrenched, and perceptions of poverty change as average living standards rise and expectations grow—both domestically and internationally—and benchmarks change. Indeed the Chinese government has already raised its benchmarks for measuring poverty using a daily or yearly individual consumption level expressed in its domestic currency, *renminbi*. The most recent rise, in November 2011, took the threshold to 2,300 yuan in income per year, meaning that by official calculations, China in 2011 had 128 million poor people—100 million more than estimated using the previous poverty line of 1,274 yuan.[44] Because the new threshold is based on the cost of living in eleven cities, it overstates rural poverty, but it still is considered low in comparison with international poverty lines.[45] The World Bank 2008 threshold of $1.25 a day,[46] for example, added almost 50 million to the Chinese government's 2011 number for people living in poverty, and its $2-a-day threshold added over 200 million.

Even these international thresholds are likely to be questioned, however, as living standards rise. They are established by measuring income and consumption and concentrating on the household revenue necessary to achieve some basic level of sustenance and nutrition. They are useful for establishing levels of "absolute" poverty,[47] and for comparing poverty levels between nations. But they fail to show where the poorest sit in relation to the rest of society. For this reason, many (wealthier) countries prefer to measure relative poverty, usually defined as the proportion of the population living on less than 60 percent of the median income.[48] China has not yet adopted this approach, but if average incomes continue to rise, its government will likely come under domestic pressure not just to eliminate the worst deprivation, but also to tackle relative poverty.

Income-based measures also of course miss nonincome features of poverty such as housing deprivation or lack of access to education and health care, all of which may contribute to entrenching poverty in families and communities.[49] To incorporate wider dimensions of poverty, the United Nations Development Programme (UNDP) has encouraged a focus on "human poverty," defined as "the denial of opportunities and choices most basic to human development: to lead a long and healthy life and to enjoy a decent standard of living, freedom, dignity, self-esteem and the respect of others."[50] The International Labour Organization (ILO) similarly encourages a relative deprivation approach that takes into account the resources needed for living standards and activities that are the norm in a society.[51]

As international approaches to defining and measuring poverty have moved beyond income, consumption, and "basic human needs" over the last two to three decades, to focus on "human poverty" and relative deprivation, international organizations have made specific recommendations to the Chinese government. These include not only raising the poverty line and basing it on relative rather than absolute poverty, but also providing basic public services such as health and education directly to the poor. In relation specifically to urban poverty, the UNDP and ILO have recommended taking into account nonmonetary income (because of indications that some residents receive almost a third of their income in in-kind benefits) and access to welfare and social services. They were aided in this by an international collaboration on the China Household Income Project (CHIP), which sought to assess the distribution of personal income through surveys in both rural and urban areas in 1988, 1995, and 2002 that defined income to include cash payments and a range of additional components such as payments in kind, agricultural output produced for self-consumption, ration coupons and other direct subsidies, and the imputed value of housing.[52]

International organizations have also encouraged China to develop new monitoring systems to establish better measures of urban poverty, to allow rural migrants access to services in urban areas, and to directly subsidize the health care costs of the poor.[53] In addition, income support for the poor needs to be higher, better targeted, and more flexible, while more low-cost urban housing needs to be built. Here, as with improving access to education, more investment is important. But this will require either greater central government funding, or incentivizing local governments to invest in these areas. While central policies have begun to encourage spending on social housing, health insurance (or other health subsidies), and education, there is still a need to change the dominant view among local decision makers that equity and efficiency are incompatible.

Reducing Inequality

Although spending on the poor is crucial for reducing inequality, redistributive policies, too, are important. But the obstacles to reducing inequality may be even greater than those to cutting severe poverty. This may be why, despite the ameliorating social policies of Hu Jintao and Wen Jiabao and the continued decline in severe deprivation, inequality continued to rise for most of the first decade of the twenty-first century.

In the late Mao era—the 1970s—income inequality had been very low. Using the most common measure of inequality, the Gini index, China at that time—alongside other state socialist countries—was one of the most equal societies in the world. As market-oriented reforms began to bite, however, inequality rose—particularly in the 1990s. According to World Bank data, in 1990 China's inequality measured 32 on the Gini index, still low on international comparisons, but it had risen to 39 by 1999 and to 43 by 2005.[54] When the Chinese government released its own Gini calculation in January 2013—the first time it had done so since 2000—it was at 47, though reportedly down slightly from 49 in 2008.[55] Another recent study, however, found the Gini index to be 60, suggesting that even the high official figures may substantially understate the problem.[56] They nevertheless put inequality in China at higher than relatively unequal industrialized nations such as the United States (38 in 2010) and the United Kingdom (34, in 2010),[57] higher than India at 33 (in 2009) and Vietnam at 36 (in 2007), and in (or close to) the same bracket as highly unequal societies such as Brazil (55, 2009) and South Africa (63, 2009).[58]

The Gini index indicates China's high income (and asset) inequality between individuals and households and as well as (on average) between people living in urban versus rural areas and between those living in eastern versus western provinces. But it does not tell us a great deal beyond that about the distribution of inequality and how people experience it. In addition to high income inequalities, however, there are inequalities in access to education, health care, and housing between rich and poor as well as between urban and rural residents. For the most deprived, poor access to these goods threatens to entrench poverty by reducing the next generation's opportunities. The unequal treatment of rural migrants to China's cities—especially in their access to urban jobs and public services—is another widely reported dimension of the problem.[59] Due to the birth registration system set up in 1958, an estimated 206 million of China's 666 million urban dwellers are thought to be formally registered as "agricultural" and so often unable to educate their children in city public schools and ineligible for urban health insurance as well as some housing and jobs.[60] Finally, discrimination and unequal opportunities for women, for example in employment and pay, are further—and still deeply entrenched—facets of inequality.

Inequalities can be tackled through progressive growth—for example, by adjusting the taxation structure to raise the threshold for paying tax on the one hand and to increase the tax contributions of the richest on the other.[61] In fact the Chinese government committed to doing this in the Twelfth Five-Year Plan. However, corruption and a weak administrative and legal capacity to enforce tax obligations (common in developing countries) are likely to undermine achievement of this objective. Indeed, it was in part because of poor administrative capacity that the government abolished agricultural taxes early in the first decade of the twenty-first century. This radical move however reduced local government funding and in some localities hit spending on education, health, and social services. It thus prevented the tax cuts being supplemented by important investment in human capital to help the poorest—often those in the agricultural sector—to move into higher productivity work.[62] Although the Plan also set out a parallel goal of improving government tax administration, it will take time to achieve nationwide.

Other problems are equally difficult to solve. For example, to deliver health care more equitably, China needs to restrain cost inflation, better manage health service providers, improve primary care, and develop doctor training, each an enormous task in itself. Similarly, with China's elderly population set to rise to over 200 million for the first time in 2013, and with a recent Chinese Academy of Social Sciences survey reporting that only 17 percent of elderly people thought their pensions were minimally sufficient, establishing an adequate and sustainable pension system may be one of the Chinese government's greatest challenges.[63]

Reducing the inequities experienced by rural migrants to the cities is also fraught with difficulty. Although the central government has announced experiments with reform of the household registration system, there has been no major nationwide reform. Most recently, in 2012, it announced that it would become easier for migrants to transfer their registration to county and prefecture-level cities, and it planned to reduce the welfare restrictions associated with "agricultural" registration. But, this does not solve the problems of the majority of migrants in the largest cities. A major obstacle is decentralized fiscal arrangements that mean local governments would be shouldered with paying for the provision of services to people from other localities. The same fiscal arrangements have blocked efforts to create national, or even provincial, social insurance schemes. And they have produced an overreliance by the central government on transfers.[64] But changes to the fiscal system are likely to be blocked by richer localities that do not want to subsidize poorer ones. With no independent labor unions, workers are unable to counter either these regional interests or opposition to policy changes from employers, managers, and the middle classes more generally.[65]

Recent and Current Attempts to Tackle Poverty and Inequality

Toward the end of the Hu Jintao and Wen Jiabao leadership era in June 2012, elite commentators argued that the fight against poverty remained important, but was moving to a "new stage" as part of efforts to reduce inequality and its political consequences:

> Food is no longer the biggest challenge. What China's poor people need most is equal access to improve their livelihoods and participate in China's development. . . . Fighting against poverty in China, which used to be a special task, should be integrated into the larger project of China's economic and social development. To some extent, poverty alleviation provides a good opportunity for China to construct a fair and harmonious society, which cannot be realized with a widening income gap.[66]

This indicates not only that the understanding of poverty and inequality is changing, but also that tackling them is now seen by China's elite as integral to the national development project. Indeed, both issues remained high on the agenda in Xi Jinping and Li Keqiang's accession speeches, where they signaled that inequality in particular will be the priority.[67] Both Xi and Li are likely to remain committed to the goals and targets of the Twelfth Five-Year Plan, which they will have played a role in formulating. In November 2012, moreover, just a few months before he became premier, Li Keqiang (then a vice-premier), set out in a speech to the Eighteenth Party Congress the challenges that China faced. Among these was the challenge arising from what he referred to as the "middle income trap" of the "gap between rich and poor," and he acknowledged the "gap in income distribution between residents" in

China. Li also stressed the importance of reducing regional (East-West) as well as rural-urban gaps, providing social safety nets and social housing, equalizing compulsory education provision, promoting urban and rural pensions, and ensuring basic health care for all.[68]

Since 2013 Li Keqiang has also taken health care system and public hospital reform as one of his work priorities, aiming to tackle the most serious gaps—between cities and countryside and between regions—so that ordinary people, especially those in central, western, and rural areas, really benefit.[69] In his first press conference after the first session of the Twelfth National People's Congress, he stressed that maintaining economic growth, improving people's livelihoods, and safeguarding social justice were the three top tasks of the newly installed government. On improving people's livelihoods, Li said "it means to continuously improve people's livelihoods by raising the income of urban and rural residents, in particular that of the poverty-stricken people, and expand the size of the middle-income class."[70] He emphasized the significance of creating a strong social safety net to safeguard basic welfare for all Chinese people including compulsory education, medical care, social insurance, and housing. A subsistence system and medical assistance must be in place for the poor to fall back on when in difficulty: "If those people fall into plight, the moral and psychological basic line of the society will be at stake. The government shall make the utmost efforts to mobilize all possible resources to safeguard the subsistence and dignity of the needy." Calling social fairness "a source of creativity" and "a yardstick" by which to measure public satisfaction with the government, Li said his government would strive to ensure all Chinese enjoy equal opportunities and receive due rewards for their hard work, whatever social or family backgrounds they have. To this end, the government has begun to set new targets. For example, in recommitting to increasing the supply of housing for people on lower incomes, it set a target of 4.7 million units of subsidized urban housing units to be built in 2013.[71] And crucially, the new leadership has announced new investment to back up some of its poverty-reduction goals.[72]

In November 2013, a year after Xi and Li assumed power, the Third Plenum of the Eighteenth CCP Central Committee passed a major Decision setting out the new leadership's policy orientation.[73] On inequality and poverty, the Decision stated a commitment to "better securing and improving the people's livelihood," "further promoting social equity and justice," creating a fairer income distribution system, promoting "common prosperity," and "equalizing basic public services." It specified that public services and the social welfare system, including education, pensions, and health care, should be extended and improved to make them fairer and more equal. Rural-urban development should be rebalanced to accelerate the development of rural areas and integrate rural dwellers and migrant workers into urban development so that they can "equally participate in the process of modernization and jointly share the benefits of modernization." Finally, the Decision revealed a concern to provide for the elderly in China's rapidly ageing population.

The Third Plenum also agreed to reforms in other policy areas because of concerns about inequality. Its Decision reiterated the central government's greater fiscal responsibility toward poor areas and vowed to reform the current tax system to make it fairer. It set fiscal reform as a priority for the coming years, in part to help "equalize basic public services."[74] The Decision also emphasized the new central leaders' determination to tackle corruption—seen as an important part of improving social fairness and tackling social inequality. This built on Xi and Li's anticorruption measures from the end of 2012: between November 2012 and December 2013, eighteen ministerial/provincial-level officials were dismissed, investigated, and punished.[75] And, according to the latest figures published by the CCP's Central Commission for Discipline Inspection (CCDI) and the Ministry of Supervision, in the year 2013, they formally investigated 172,000 cases and punished 182,000 officials.[76]

Conclusion

The CCP since 1949 has in different periods adopted very different approaches to dealing with poverty and inequality. While in the Mao era it focused on class-based inequalities and the "contradictions" they created, it left many millions in severe poverty. But its post-Mao growth-led poverty reduction—in the absence of mitigating policies and inattention to the problems that came with commodifying the provision of housing, education, and health services in the 1980s and 1990s—contributed to high levels of inequality. Into the twenty-first century, however, political expediency refocused the CCP's attention on poverty, inequality, and encouraging economic development that benefits the wider population. Apparently driven by fears of destabilizing social unrest, it preferred however to emphasize its efforts at promoting social harmony rather than to discuss reemerging contradictions.

Can China's new leaders rise to this challenge? Based on their early performance and the policy orientation that emerged from the 2013 Third Plenum, it looks likely that improving people's livelihood and tackling inequality will remain on the agenda. But whether leaders' aspirations will be translated into workable policies and backed with adequate resources remains to be seen. In addition to the problems China faces because of changing understandings of poverty and inequality, rising expectations, poor state capacity (for example, in tax administration) and corruption, it is likely to be operating in a very different economic environment. High growth rates have made the greatest contribution to reducing absolute poverty. The question now is how poverty reduction can be sustained when—as seems likely—economic growth moderates. There will be pressure on policymakers to make difficult judgments about where to invest state funds for pro-poor growth while at the same time sustaining overall growth levels.

Slowing growth may help reduce income inequalities, which tend to rise during the early stages of industrialization and economic development. But there is still scope for government policies to prevent the worst inequities, especially the very unequal access to health, education, and housing.[77] In the early twenty-first century, social policies were having only a very slight equalizing effect.[78] The Hu and Wen government has since then extended provisions to provide income-based safety nets for the poorest and introduced a range of new social policies. But these schemes have provided only the most meager support or cut taxes, rather than tackling the roots of deprivation. Although they may have contributed to the slight fall in income inequality announced in 2012, they need to be sustained and deepened if those gains are to be consolidated.

The indications are that Xi and Li would like to increase the opportunities for the poorest to make better lives for themselves by reversing some of the inequities in access to health, education, and housing. But reducing these structural sources of deprivation may involve taking resources away from current reform winners and the CCP's key support bases: urban elites, the middle classes, and wealthy local governments. Political science tells us that threats to authoritarian rulers may come not only from restive and dissatisfied economic development losers, but also from among elites opposed to redistribution. Whether or not people actually press for political change because of perceived distributional injustices depends on many factors, including how powerful they are and whether their interests are sufficiently concentrated to enable collective action. But perhaps the greatest challenge for Xi and Li is to identify and navigate a route between the distinct and divergent interests in China today.

CHAPTER 3

Migration, *Hukou,* and the Prospects of an Integrated Chinese Society

Zai Liang

It is often said that "demography is destiny." For the past three decades in China, the migrant population (also known as the "floating" population), has supplied much needed inexpensive labor for China's economic growth.[1] The migrant population has also been capturing recent mass media head-lines. From the heart-breaking reports of serial suicides in Foxconn facto-ries to unpaid wages for migrant workers, from the shortage of migrant labor to the massive return migration during the Global Financial Crisis and the Chinese New Year, migration stories are everywhere.[2] Some of these migration stories have triggered violence, as manifested in riots during 2009, first in Guangdong, and then Urumqi, where conflicts between Han Chinese and the Uyghur minority erupted.[3]

The extensive and broad media coverage of migration is certainly con-sistent with the rise and spatial diversification of the floating population in China.[4] Recent data from China's 2010 census confirm that the floating population had reached 221 million. In 2011, for the first time in Chinese history, China reached a milestone: over half of the population was found to reside in urban places. The floating population has overwhelmingly contributed to China's rising level of urbanization and urban growth. These migrant workers have also contributed enormously to China's eco-nomic miracle in the past three decades as they have built China's sky-scrapers and labored in China's world factories that supply goods across the globe.

Although associated with China's urbanization process for the past three decades, China's floating population is far from fully integrated in urban society. They are in the city, but not part of the city. The next decade or more will test if China can accept this floating population as full members of the urban society. This challenge is clearly on the agenda for the Chinese government. On March 17, 2013, after the close of the Twelfth National People's Congress (NPC) in Beijing, the new premier, Li Keqiang, held a press conference in the Great Hall of the People. Responding to a question on urbanization in China, Premier Li highlighted several features of China's plans for a new type of urbanization. The fundamental idea of this new type of urbanization is a people-centered approach (*yi ren wei ben*). Premier Li stressed that urbanization is a long-term and complex process that needs the support of employment as well as social security. He also mentioned that there were more than five hundred proposals about China's urbanization submitted during the National People's Congress. His remarks on urbanization as well as the vetting of such a large number of proposals during the NPC underscored the importance of migration and urbanization for China's next stage of development.[5]

China's migrant population is an extremely important issue. One reason is its ever-increasing size. At 221 million people, the floating population is larger than all but four of the world's countries. This tremendous size means that its impact is not only domestic but also international. In addition, the migrant population has also contributed to China's spectacular economic growth, and the availability of this supply of labor could help sustain continued growth in years to come. But at the same time, by virtue of not having urban household registration (*hukou*), China's migrant population has been treated as second-class citizens, not eligible to enjoy the same rights all urban citizens take for granted. As the second largest economy in the world with growing international influence, China now faces an imperative to address the disadvantages facing migrants, even if this means other interest groups could suffer. Doing so will reduce currently dangerous levels of inequality, enhance stability, and create a more just society that motivates its members to achieve their highest potential.

In this chapter, I review literature on the current state of knowledge about internal migration in China and highlight critical issues related to migrants in China. I first discuss the brief history of *hukou* and its impact from the founding of the People's Republic to the dawn of China's reform program. I then focus on how migration and the role of *hukou* have changed over the last three decades. Finally, I discuss challenges for reform of China's *hukou* system in the years to come. The key issue I discuss in depth is the education of migrant children—of those left behind in rural areas and especially of migrant children in the cities. Education issues include compulsory education and the recent debate about the location of college entrance exams for migrant children.

Migration and *Hukou* Legacy in China

On September 25, 1954, nearly five years after the founding of the People's Republic of China, the National People's Congress (China's national legislature) approved a Constitution.[6] Article 90 of the Constitution stated that "citizens of China have the rights of residence and the freedom to move." However, citizens would only have four years to exercise this right. In 1958, the NPC passed the *hukou* regulations (*hukou dengji tiaoli*).[7] Among the twenty-four articles in these regulations, three have had the most important lasting impact. First, every citizen of China needs to be registered either in an urban or rural place. Second, prior to migration, permissions must be obtained both from the place of origin and the place of destination. The *hukou* regulations stipulate that "individuals who migrate from rural to urban places must hold a certificate of a job offer, a school acceptance letter, or proof of urban *hukou* migration." Third, temporary migrants in cities for more than three days need to obtain a temporary residence card from urban local authorities. The specific reference to migration of rural residents to urban places is not an accident—it reflects the central concern behind the 1958 *hukou* regulations, namely, to control rural to urban migration.

The 1958 *hukou* regulations clearly achieved their intended results as far as restricting rural to urban migration. In practice, however, *hukou* has done more than just control geographic mobility. Because *hukou* has been linked with entitlements and benefits for individuals in China, it has helped define China's stratification system and contributed to urban-rural inequality.[8] For a long time, an urban *hukou* ensured the privilege of employment, food ration coupons (*liang piao*), health insurance, housing, and schooling for children. The idea of food ration coupons may sound odd nowadays given China's current level of prosperity, but it was an important part of daily life in China for the three decades prior to the economic reforms implemented after 1978. In fact, this mechanism for the allocation of food by urban *hukou* status was important, because it meant that without an urban *hukou* it was difficult for anyone to survive in the cities, let alone find a job. As a result, the *hukou* system of control produced a unique pattern of migration from 1950 to 1978.

Unlike migration patterns in other countries that reflect regional economic development, internal migration in China during the period of 1950 to 1978 was largely determined by political factors and campaigns.[9] The movement of population to the frontier areas of Xinjiang and Heilongjiang, for example, reflected the central government's plan to control border regions and to counter the potential threat from the former Soviet Union.[10] Likewise the migration of millions of urban youth to rural China mainly reflected the political ideology of Mao Zedong rather than opportunities attracting urban youth to the Chinese countryside.[11] Thus migration theories developed in the context of Western societies are not particularly useful for explaining Chinese migration patterns during these early decades of the PRC. The fundamental assumption of most Western migration theories is the existence of a market economy, and these theories give short shrift to the political and institutional factors that prevailed in China.[12] Understanding migration in China requires accounting for the country's unique context, especially the central significance of the *hukou*.

Market Transition, the Rise of Migration, and *Hukou* Reforms

Since the late 1970s, two driving forces have provided the impetus for reform of the *hukou* system. The fundamental driving force is the development of a market-oriented economy in China, first in Special Economic Zones and then gradually throughout the rest of the economy. As an experiment in the early 1980s, China began to designate several southern Chinese cities as "Special Economic Zones" to attract international investment.[13] Three out of the four cities—Shenzhen, Shantou, and Zhuhai—designated as Special Economic Zones were located in Guangdong Province (the fourth city, Xiamen, was in Fujian Province). As a consequence, early in China's reform era migration often meant moving to Guangdong, the most desirable destination until around 2005.[14] In addition, the implementation of the household production responsibility system in agriculture in 1982 increased the efficiency of farming and generated a huge surplus of rural labor. As foreign investment poured into China's coastal Special Economic Zones, and a factory boom took root there, redundant rural labor migrated to the cities in large numbers seeking jobs in the new industries.

While peasant workers began to be on the move in the early 1980s, the central government's changes in migration policy were slow in coming. Bai and Song give a thorough review and assessment of migration-related policies during the period 1979–2002.[15] Several critical policy changes occurred during this period. Between 1979 and 1983, the policy mainly aimed to control the flow of migrants. One of the first significant changes was in 1984. People who had jobs or conducted businesses in market towns (*jizhen*), had a stable place of residence, and could supply their own grain would be permitted to obtain local *hukou* in these market towns. The new policy also called for the local government to facilitate migrants' need for building, purchasing, or renting houses. The significance of this 1984 policy is that it was the first sign of a loosening of the strict 1958 *hukou* regulations. The connection between migration and poverty alleviation was also manifested in a policy from the Ministry of Labor (*laodong bu*) in 1988 that called for making effective use of labor from high-poverty regions, essentially embracing labor migration as a strategy for poverty alleviation.[16]

There was another step forward in 1997 when the State Council allowed migrants who met certain conditions in small towns to receive local *hukou*. Thus, the door was open wider for rural residents to get an urban *hukou*, from allowing them to get a *hukou* in market towns in 1984 to getting a *hukou* in small towns in 1997. This was a period when the strategy for developing small towns was favored by policymakers as township and village enterprises (TVE) were growing fast.[17] Even though small towns were generating ample employment opportunities for migrants, a significant number of migrant workers preferred to travel long distances to other provinces, especially to the coastal regions—a preference reflected in the popular saying "if you want to make money, go to Guangdong" (*dong xi nan bei zhong, fa cai dao Guangdong*). Indeed, by 2000 Guangdong accounted for a quarter of China's interprovincial floating population. This clearly indicated that *hukou* reform restricted to small towns would not be sufficient.

Perhaps the most important change was in 2001 during meetings of the National People's Congress. For the first time, the idea of *hukou* reform was written into the tenth five-year plan for China's economic and social development.[18] The document calls for breaking down the rural-urban divide and reforming the *hukou* system. Though the language is vague, leaves a lot of room for interpretation, and the proposal was more symbolic than substantive at that point, the essential message of the document—that it is high time to reform the *hukou* system—is unmistakable. In fact, several cities had been implementing what is called a "blue-shield *hukou*" (*lanyin hukou*) since the early 1990s. Shenzhen, one of the cities with the highest proportion of floating population, began implementing this blue shield system in 1994. Its two most important requirements were investment of over one million yuan for a business operation and having paid taxes of over 100,000 yuan for the preceding three years. Wang labels this the "urban *hukou* for sale," since only rich people can meet its requirements.[19] A major advantage of this blue-shield *hukou*, however, is that migrants can enjoy the same benefits as local residents. In most cases, after seven years in blue-shield *hukou* status, migrants are eligible to receive a regular, official local *hukou*. Other major destinations for China's migrants, such as Guangzhou and Shanghai, have implemented similar policies. As expected, due to its demanding criteria, only a small number of migrants (the rich and well educated) are able to follow this path to obtaining an urban *hukou*.

In recent years, *hukou* reform has taken place in other cities, such as Shijiazhuang, Wuhan, and, more recently, Chongqing, with a population of twenty-seven million, China's largest city. Chongqing took the biggest step in 2010.[20] The Chongqing government has the goal of transferring ten million peasants currently registered in the Chongqing metropolitan area with a rural *hukou* into urban residents in ten years. The policy has three main layers that address the issue of getting urban *hukou* in three kinds of locations—central city, thirty-one remote counties, and other towns and townships—with declining levels of restrictions. But the most important and common qualifications are: (1) duration of residence in an urban location; (2) purchase of commodity housing; and, (3) investment. For example, to apply for an urban *hukou* in central city Chongqing, one needs to meet one of the following three conditions: having resided in the central city for more than five years, having purchased commodity housing, or having invested in a business with three years of cumulative tax revenue totaling 100,000 yuan or a single-year tax revenue of 50,000 yuan. The big advantage of becoming urban *hukou* in Chongqing is to enjoy all the benefits for urban residents such as eligibility for public housing or low-income housing, medical insurance, access to local public schools for children, and no-cost training for technical skills and business formation. In return for an urban *hukou*, peasants must give up their farmland as well as the land on which their residence sits, though they receive some compensation.

The Chongqing *hukou* reform is quite a big step. But it differs from most other reforms in one key aspect: the goal in Chongqing *hukou* reform is to transfer Chongqing's own registered peasants into urban *hukou* status, excluding interprovincial migrants from other places. This may not be a big issue for Chongqing because it is not a major destination for interprovincial migrants. The Chongqing story does, however, highlight some key principles that are often seen as the basis for *hukou* reform in other locations. First is the idea of long-term residence (in Chongqing's case for central city *hukou*, it is five years). This criterion suggests that *hukou* reform caters to people who have already stayed in the city for a long period of time and are likely to have a stable job. The second criterion, purchasing local commodity housing, suggests the reform is designed for individuals who have invested in the local housing market, reinforcing the commitment to long-term residence. The final criterion indicates that reforms aim at individuals who are already contributing to the local economy by paying taxes. One element missing in the case of Chongqing *hukou* reform, but often a key element in *hukou* reforms in other locations, is the requirement of education credentials. In this respect, the door to rural migrants in Chongqing is open much wider than in other cities.

The Difficult Road Ahead

It has been said that China's economic reform program has now entered the deepest waters of the river. Likewise, China's *hukou* reform also has entered a critical stage. Progress has clearly been made and there is a broad base of unified support for reform among the mainstream media. Perhaps even more importantly there is strong endorsement for fundamental *hukou* reform from the two most important political institutions in China: the CCP and the NPC, as reflected in documents issued during annual meetings in recent years. However, rhetoric is no longer sufficient; concrete and perhaps bold steps are urgently needed. Overall, it is going to be an uphill battle. In the current climate of fiscal decentralization, the central government has been taking a hands-off approach, letting provincial/city-level governments make these decisions. City-level policies are often proposed and approved by city People's Congresses. Unfortunately, in these settings migrant workers do not have a strong political base to make their voices heard. In the People's Congress of Guangdong Province, for example, with a total of 787 elected delegates, there are only 10 delegates who represent a migrant population of over 20 million. At this stage, I view the following three areas as the critical battlegrounds for the struggle of China's migrants to gain full citizenship: (1) minimum support (*dibao*) for low-income households, (2) low-income housing (*baozhang fang*), and (3) education of migrant children.

In this section, I focus on the issue of the well-being of children of migrants, especially on educational opportunity, because education is the engine of modern economic growth and, in an increasingly market-oriented economy like China's, education is certain to remain important for career success in the years ahead. In this regard, a good education is essential for the intergenerational mobility of migrant children. We need to examine the educational challenges for two groups of children. One is the education of so-called "left behind children" whose parents moved to work in Chinese cities. The second is the education of the children of migrants who actually live in Chinese cities. In a paper published several years ago, Yiu Por Chen and I refer to the children of migrants as "the forgotten story of China's urbanization."[21] Today they are no longer forgotten, but much more careful research is needed to examine the conditions facing both groups of migrant children, as their fate will have major implications for the future of both rural and urban China.

The Story of Left Behind Children in Rural China

The massive flow of China's migrant population has led to a very large contingent of left behind children. Recent estimates place the size of this group at about fifty-eight million.[22] Admittedly, this is a global phenomenon also occurring in other developing countries undergoing rapid urbanization in Africa, Asia, and Latin America.[23] However, China stands out in this regard not only because of the enormous size of this population, but also because of other characteristics of the Chinese case. For example, the lack of urban *hukou* continues to be a major barrier for migrant children to be enrolled in local public schools. Another major concern is the long duration of the separation of China's left behind children from their parents. Ye Jingzhong, one of the leading experts on this topic, has shown that nearly 50 percent of his sample of China's left behind children have fathers with seven years of migration experience, and 44 percent of his sample have mothers with seven years of migration experience.[24] Seven years is a very significant period of time in any child's life. This long-term separation of migrant parents and children is in part due to the soaring price of urban housing, which makes it much harder for migrant households to settle in Chinese cities.

The left behind children have drawn major media attention in recent years. Reports by newspapers often provide a negative portrait of their situation, as manifest in rates of school drop-out, smoking, drinking, Internet addiction, delinquency, and in some cases suicides.[25] In 2008, two popular books written by Chinese writers underscored the plight of left behind children.[26] The recent report of the death of five left behind children (resulting from carbon monoxide poisoning while sleeping in a dumpster) has again drawn high-profile, dramatic attention to the situation.[27]

Among researchers, Ye Jingzhong and his research team have conducted the most systematic study on the situation of left behind children.[28] Their research conducted in western China identified major problems facing left behind children: lack of supervision for school work, lack of communication with parents, lack of emotional support from parents, an increased burden for household chores, and, in some cases, the burden for farm work. The most important finding from Ye's research is evidence about the psychological development of these children. They are less likely to talk to others or to have a curiosity for life, more likely to feel lonely, and more likely to give up when facing difficult circumstances.[29] Research by Wen and Lin echoes the findings of Ye and his coauthors.[30] When I interviewed some left behind children in a middle school in Jintang County near Chengdu (fifty miles away), I was very surprised to learn that some of these children's parents, working in Chengdu, only came home once or twice a year, and that the children only talk to their parents once or twice a month.[31]

A recent paper by Lu using school enrollment measures from rural China suggests that although the migration of siblings can benefit children who remain behind, younger left behind children are especially likely to suffer negative consequences.[32] Ye and Pan also found that although there is no significant difference in student academic performance between left behind children and other children, the grades of left behind students dropped after parental migration.[33]

Results from studies in Western societies provide overwhelming evidence that family disruption leads to negative consequences for children and that, in some cases, the consequences can be long term. McLanahan and Sanderfur find that children whose parents live apart are twice as likely to drop out of high school as those in two-parent families, are one-and-a-half times more likely to be idle in young adulthood, and twice as likely to become single parents themselves.[34] China's migrant parents usually do send remittances to their children left behind. But money, while helpful, cannot substitute for other types of support, especially the healthy emotional bonds between children and migrant parents.

The issue of China's left behind children presents several major challenges. First, it underscores the impact of China's migration on families in rural areas. The large size of this population (fifty-eight million), the longtime separation of these children from their parents, the lack of healthy psychological development, and the increased household burden raise alarms for policymakers about the urgency of the problem. The difficulty for migrant parents to obtain an urban *hukou* is at least partly to blame. In addition, the strain on the emotional bonds between parents and left behind children raises doubts about the future of intergenerational relationships and the prospects for children providing old age support for their parents, a long-standing traditional norm among rural Chinese households.

Migrant Children in Urban China

The second aspect of the educational issue for children of migrants is the fate of those who reside with their parents in the cities where they have moved. For much of the past two decades, scholars have studied the education of migrant children with a focus on school-enrollment issues. Where do migrant children go to school? Local urban public schools, or somewhere else? The education of migrant children has become a major issue in part because city education bureau officials claim that their education budgets are based only on the registered population. Thus, any additional, unregistered children enrolled in local public schools increase a city's fiscal burden. As migrants have settled for longer duration in cities, increasing numbers of migrants have been bringing their children with them, increasing the demand on the cities' educational resources. In earlier years, many local public schools would charge "education endorsement fees" (*jiaoyu zanzhu fei*). Given the high cost of school enrollment in local public schools, especially for the majority of the migrant workers who earn meager salaries, these workers search for alternative schools for their children. As a result, many migrant-sponsored schools (*dagong zidi xuexiao*) have appeared in China's cities. By some accounts, there were over two hundred migrant-sponsored schools in Beijing during the 1990s.[35]

These migrant-sponsored schools have lower tuition and flexible payment plans and they attract lots of migrant children. However, migrant-sponsored schools are far from ideal, as they often struggle with teacher qualifications, teacher retention, less than adequate equipment and classrooms, and safety and sanitation concerns. On my visits to migrant-sponsored schools in Fuzhou, Xiamen, Shanghai, and Beijing, conditions reminded me of elementary schools in the Chinese countryside.[36] Moreover, most migrant-sponsored schools are not registered with the City Education Bureau and cannot, therefore, issue graduation certificates. Overall, there is good reason to believe that the education of migrant children is severely compromised by enrolling in migrant-sponsored schools, with the exception of the few such schools licensed by city education bureaus.

The central government policy on education of migrant children in the cities has undergone significant changes. Prior to 1998, the policy can be summarized as either absent or very vague. In 1998, the Ministry of Education issued the Document "Temporary Plan for Education of Migrant Children," which placed the issue on policymakers' agenda.[37] Subsequent policies have been issued as well over the years. These policies exemplify major government efforts to improve educational opportunities for migrant children. Although they are based on the idea that governments of both migrant-sending and migrant-receiving communities should work together to resolve the issue of migrant children's education, they fall short of assigning the responsibilities of educating migrant children to schools in destination cities. In addition, they are not well implemented because they depend on decisions by local governments regarding the allocation of financial resources. Consequently, most migrant children still face steep educational challenges in the cities where their parents are working.

In 2006, the State Council issued an unambiguous document calling for procedures to solve the problem of migrant children education. The document requires schools in cities that are the destination for migrants to bear the major responsibility for ensuring that children of migrants are enrolled in local public schools without any extra fees.[38] In addition, the document explicitly stated that fiscal planning by the destination cities' governments must take into account the education of migrant children. In other words, the destination areas should treat these children of migrants as equal to the children from families with a local urban *hukou*. At least on paper, this reform indicates the greatest progress so far in providing education for migrant children. Of course, the reality is often more complex, since schools are still able to devise alternative fees for migrant enrollees.

Although the above-mentioned policy change clearly benefits migrant children, it applies only to the nine years of compulsory education. It does not apply to high school or college education. In the past three years the most contentious battle has been about migrant children's right to take the college entrance examination in their parents' place of destination (*yidi gaokao*). This battle is fundamentally different from the matter of providing nine-year compulsory education for migrant children in local public schools in migrant destinations because it challenges the current system in two ways. First, it challenges the existing *hukou*-based education system that requires students take college entrance examinations at their place of household registration. For most migrant children, this means rural areas, but for others it could mean another urban area in a different province. Second, it challenges the current unequal system of allocating education resources that favors large cities (such as Beijing, Shanghai, and Guangzhou (often referred to as *bei shang guang*, using the first Chinese character of each city). Much discussion about educational inequality has focused on rural-urban educational inequality, understandably given China's large rural population.[39] However, there are substantial interregional inequalities in education as well. A child with either urban *hukou* or rural *hukou* in Hebei Province (or any other province) faces a different educational opportunity compared to a child with Beijing *hukou*. This is reflected clearly in recent evidence about where migrant children can take college entrance examinations. Big cities such as Beijing or Shanghai have many of the top-rated universities in China, and their universities often allocate a large quota of enrollment for students with a local *hukou*. For this reason, the minimum test score to go to Peking University for Beijing *hukou* students is lower than students with *hukou* from another province. Table 3.1 presents the required minimum scores for Beijing *hukou* holders and nearby Hebei *hukou* holders to attend Peking University in natural science fields. In 2011, Beijing *hukou* students needed to get a minimum of 630 points in testing scores to be eligible for Peking University, as compared to 681 points for students with *hukou* from nearby Hebei Province.[40] Furthermore, in 2011, the quota set

Table 3.1. *Hukou* and Unequal Access to Elite Universities in China, Natural Science Fields, 2011

Hukou Status	Beijing	Hebei	Hukou Status	Guangdong	Hunan
Minimum score for PKU	630	681	Minimum score for SYSU	590	620
Quota	144	8	Quota	938	156
Population size in 2010 (in millions)	12.55	71.91	Population size in 2010 (in millions)	85.02	70.78

Note: PKU refers to Peking University in Beijing and SYSU refers to Sun Yat-sen University in Guangzhou.

for the number of Beijing *hukou* residents to attend Peking University in the natural sciences was 144, but only 8 for Hebei *hukou* students. Since Hebei has nearly six times the population of Beijing, the probability of a Hebei student being accepted by Peking University is much lower than for a student with a Beijing *hukou*. A similar story can be told about Guangdong *hukou* holders and Hunan *hukou* holders (again see Table 3.1).[41] This system has been in place ever since the national college entrance examination was adopted and is yet further evidence about how significantly a *hukou* can affect a young person's life chances.[42] If migrant children were allowed to take the college entrance examination in Beijing, it would improve their life chances but would also be very likely to reduce the greater opportunities to attend universities that Beijing *hukou* students currently enjoy.

The demographic foundation of this issue is clear: after thirty years of migration in China, a large number of migrant children have joined their parents in cities. Data from the 2010 Chinese census show that there are fourteen million migrant children in the 15–19 age group who are potential candidates to go to college in the next few years.[43] For some ambitious migrant children who want to pursue a college education, the only choice they have had for a long time has been to return to their hometowns (often in rural areas) to take the national college entrance examination. This poses enormous problems for migrant children who have lived in cities for a long time; indeed, some have been born in cities.

In early 2010, a group of parents in Beijing whose children were in line to take the college entrance exam started a grassroots-level campaign aiming to change the country's education policy. They named their effort "Citizens' United Action for Equal Rights of Education" (*jiaoyu pingdeng gongmin lianhe xingdong*). Soon the movement spread into other cities and they gathered signatures and drafted a proposal calling for a change in policy.[44] They received support from lawyers and, by October 2011, had issued a draft of a reform proposal to the public that clearly accelerated the momentum of this campaign. Under such pressure from a public campaign, the government decided to allow each province to draft a plan. In August 2012, the Ministry of Education issued a document that required every province (and Shanghai and Beijing) to release their plans on middle school and college entrance examinations (*zhongkao he gaokao*) for migrant children by December 31, 2012.

Among the supporters of the migrant education proposal is Professor Zhang Qianfan of Peking University. Zhang received a Ph.D. in physics from Carnegie-Mellon University and has become a public intellectual of sorts in recent years. In October 2012, Professor Zhang, along with thirty other scholars, offered a draft proposal that was subsequently submitted to the State Council and the Ministry of Education, as well as the education bureaus in three locations: Beijing, Shanghai, and Guangdong. When the December 2012 deadline for release of provincial policies arrived, most provinces issued policies regarding education of migrant children that stipulated certain conditions. In Heilongjiang Province, for example, as long as migrant children have been attending high school for three years and have a stable residence in the city, they are allowed to take the college examination in Heilongjiang Province (including cities in that province).

Not surprisingly, Beijing, Shanghai, and Guangdong, the most desirable migrant destinations, have much stricter policies. In fact, Beijing's policies allow migrant children to take the exam for technical high schools or three-year colleges in Beijing, but not four-year colleges and universities. Shanghai has a similar policy.[45] Guangdong adopted a two-step process. For now, migrant children who meet certain conditions can take the exams for technical high schools or three-year colleges. By 2016, the province will allow migrant children with no local *hukou* but who meet certain conditions (three-year high-school record, three-year stable place of residence, and three years of participation in the social security program by migrant children's parents) to take college entrance exams in Guangdong. Guangdong also set one more condition—the parents of these children must have had residence cards in Guangdong (easier to get than local *hukou*) for three years.[46] Many parents of migrant children have been disappointed with these conditions, which reserve certain privileges for parents of children with local urban *hukou*.

Conclusion

In this chapter, I examined some of China's internal migration and policy changes since the founding of the People's Republic, focusing on the decades after the late 1970s when China initiated its economic reform program. I reviewed the social and economic consequences of *hukou* for migrant workers. It is clear that policy changes in the *hukou* system have greatly facilitated the migration of record numbers of people in China. Compared to the prereform era, there is no doubt that the role of *hukou* has been significantly weakened. However, even in the twenty-first century, and after three decades of economic reform, the *hukou* continues to be a major hurdle that prevents many migrants and their children from reaching their highest potential.[47]

Since 1958, the *hukou* has divided Chinese society and especially affected the life chances of millions of individuals with rural origins. It generated a strong sense of inequality among China's citizens.[48] Even today, the *hukou* system has the potential to exert negative consequences for at least 221 million Chinese who comprise the country's "floating population." Its negative consequences for migrant workers are manifest in the many challenges they face trying to secure occupational opportunities, living wages, housing, welfare support, and the education of their children. As far as education is concerned, not having an urban *hukou* has probably cut down the ambition and dreams of many migrant children. Instead of pursuing higher education, they may instead opt for a job immediately after completing their compulsory education.[49] Other migrant children are forced to stay away from their parents for a substantial period of time to attend high school and take college entrance exams in their hometowns. The long-term separation from their parents is likely to have long-term psychological consequences. It is by now a consensus among policymakers at the highest level in China as well as among scholars that the *hukou* should be removed or fundamentally changed to ensure a more equal and open Chinese society. Some have argued that removal of *hukou* will broaden opportunities for migrant workers, raise their salaries, and help stimulate the greater consumer demand that the Chinese economy badly needs.[50]

Hukou reform will not be easy. It would break down a two-tier social system that has prevailed in China since 1958. The steps taken thus far in *hukou* reform have been relatively easy. Allowing migrant workers to obtain *hukou* in small towns went well because there are not many benefits associated with small town *hukou* in the first place. Likewise, allowing migrant workers to work in cities like Beijing, Shanghai, or Guangzhou faced little resistance because migrant workers supply the needed labor for factories and construction sites and provide a variety of services that urban households now depend on. Highways are congested and subways are crowded in the big cities, but people have learned to tolerate it or get used to it.

Allowing migrant children to take the college entrance exam in Beijing, however, is a very different story. It is likely to face strong resistance from people who have benefited from the existing system for many years. This is another matter in which there is constant negotiation between state and civil society.[51] In the case of Beijing, while parents of migrant children gather signatures supporting a new college exam proposal, local Beijing *hukou* holders express their strong resistance to changes that would reduce the benefits their own children now enjoy. Both sides have taken advantage of the Internet and Microblogs (*weibo*) to spread their ideas and get more support and leverage. Parents who hold the Beijing *hukou* argue that allowing migrant children to take the college exam in Beijing will only attract more migrants and their children to the city, severely reducing the educational opportunities that Beijing's local *hukou* children now have as a birthright. To be fair, the potential reallocation of opportunities is significant. In 2012 there were 421,000 migrant children with no Beijing *hukou* enrolled either in elementary school or middle school. This is about 41 percent of the total Beijing student population who could take the college entrance exam in Beijing if policy allowed them to do so.[52] So far, the central government has been watching from the sidelines and leaving much of the decision making to the local governments.

Successfully reforming the college entrance exam policy for migrant children would set a good precedent for major reforms of other aspects of the *hukou* system. As mentioned briefly above, two other issues are on the policy agenda for every city government: low-income housing and minimum income support for poor urban households. Will local governments make these available to migrant households? In general, despite strong resistance from some parents of local *hukou* students, it is still relatively easier to get public support on the issue of expanding college exam opportunities for migrant children than on covering migrant households for low-income housing and minimum income support. The latter two would involve a much larger population and have much greater fiscal implications. The good news is that this is also in the blueprint laid out in the Sixty-Point Decision following the Third Plenum of the Eighteenth CCP Central Committee in November 2013. This document explicitly states that the central government encourages a people-centered approach (*yiren weiben*) toward migrants and that migrants in cities should be integrated into the urban housing and social security system.[53] Furthermore, during December 12–13, 2013, the CCP Central Committee held another meeting centered on urbanization. The importance of the meeting can be seen from the fact that both President Xi Jinping and Premier Li Keqiang delivered major speeches and that the five other members of the Standing Committee of the Politburo were all in attendance. One of the six key tasks outlined in this meeting was to make urbanization a major part of strategic plans for the next stage of China's economic growth. In particular, the meeting highlighted the importance of urbanization in generating domestic consumption demand and upgrading China's industry structure.[54]

Judging from the document following the Third Plenum of the Eighteenth CCP Central Committee, initial policies on taking college entrance exams for migrant children, and other recent *hukou* reform experiences in China, the path for future *hukou* reform seems to be taking shape. First, the CCP Central Committee does not want a one-size-fits-all approach to urbanization (and *hukou* reform). Specifically, the document reiterates China's urbanization policy of allowing the flexibility of getting urban *hukou* for small, medium, and even large cities, but strictly controlling the population size of mega cities (e.g., Beijing, Shanghai, and Guangzhou). Thus, just as the Chinese city system has a strict hierarchy, getting urban *hukou* follows another system of hierarchy, from easy, to difficult, to perhaps nearly impossible.

Second, obtaining urban *hukou* seems likely to be considered for migrants with the following characteristics: relatively long duration of residence in the cities, purchase of commodity housing, payment of taxes for a certain time period, and a record of continuous high school attendance in cities (for migrant children to take college entrance exams). These are criteria that reflect a compromise likely to achieve acceptance among both local *hukou* holders and migrants. However, one big decision is whether to include education credentials as a criterion for obtaining urban *hukou*. The

2010 census shows that only 10 percent of China's migrant population has a college education. If college education is used as a criterion for urban *hukou* applications, 90 percent of the migrant population would be excluded. Given the association between education and income/housing quality, limiting urban *hukou* to migrants with higher education would reduce the fiscal burden on cities for providing low-income housing and minimum income support.[55] But this begs a tough question: Will China choose to exclude its truly disadvantaged members from becoming urban citizens?

Given the extremely large number of migrants in China and the potentially huge fiscal implications of granting them urban *hukou*, dramatic change is not likely to happen overnight. Nor is it likely that the whole system will quickly be dismantled. The more likely sequence will be a piece-by-piece approach: remove one *hukou*-related privilege at a time.[56] The process may often be more akin to a zero-sum game than a win-win situation for both migrants and local *hukou* holders. The fact that this difficult debate has been kept alive and that some progress has been made suggests that China is determined to move toward giving equal rights to migrants and migrant children. The recent experience with the reform of educational opportunities for migrant children has demonstrated the growing significance of a civil society in China where citizens have greater scope to voice their opinions. This suggests that such pressure may provide the initial impetus for fundamental policy changes to other aspects of the *hukou* system in the not-so-distant future. China's leaders have often invoked the popular metaphor of "crossing the river while feeling the stones" (*mozhe shitou guohe*) to describe the path they have followed in economic reform. Reforming the *hukou* system demands that China's leaders similarly figure out how to meet the challenges posed by another deep river that must be crossed.

CHAPTER 4

China's Demographic Challenges:
Gender Imbalance

Yong Cai

Gender imbalance in China's population has been a major concern for the past three decades. Under normal circumstances, the sex ratio at birth (SRB) is determined mostly by biological factors, and is generally bounded in a small range of 103 to 106 boys for every 100 girls.[1] SRB in China has been rising steadily over the last thirty years. According to China's most recent census, the ratio reached 118.1 in 2010. This high SRB, in combination with unfavorable mortality rates for female infants and children, has created an enormous gender imbalance in China, on the order of 20 to 30 million.[2] The gender imbalance in China, with its large scale and long duration, has changed China's demographic landscape, and will continue to affect China's demography and society for generations to come.

There is general agreement on the causes of this imbalance—as for demographic context: a strong son preference embedded in Chinese culture and low fertility, and as for its main mechanism: sex-selective abortion—but there is still considerable uncertainty about the severity of the imbalance and in turn about its social and demographic consequences. Even more uncertain is how long this gender imbalance will continue. Three decades after the initial jump in SRB, and despite numerous government and social programs to control the problem, there has yet to be a clear sign of a reversal.

In this chapter, I begin with a review of China's gender imbalance in historical and global context. I update the estimate of "missing girls" in China using newly released 2010 census data. I then turn to the future. Using data from the 2000 and 2010 censuses, I predict that there is hope on the horizon: China's SRB is likely to begin a gradual decline soon. A return of SRB to a biologically normal level is likely decades away because a population's overall SRB can be skewed by the behavior of a relatively small proportion of families, and because the preference for sons has such deep roots in China. I conclude with a discussion of the social and policy implications of gender imbalance.

China's Gender Imbalance in Historical and Global Context

Gender imbalance is neither a new nor a uniquely Chinese phenomenon. The rising gender imbalance in China over the past three decades must be considered in a broader social context. From a historical perspective, China has a long history of discrimination in favor of sons: sex-biased neglect and infanticide go back centuries.[3] From a global perspective, gender imbalance exists in many countries.[4] According to a recent United Nations Population Fund (UNFPA) report, a total of 117 million women were "missing" worldwide in 2010: "The trend has shifted geographically over time, beginning in a number of Asian countries (China, India, and the Republic of Korea) in the 1980s, followed by some countries of the Caucasus (Azerbaijan, Armenia, and Georgia) in the 1990s, and has more recently been followed by Montenegro, Albania, and Vietnam."[5] Despite the enormous socioeconomic and cultural diversity across the world, three main features are shared by those countries with escalating sex imbalances: strong son preference, rapid decline of fertility, and increased availability of sex-selection technology.

Gender imbalance is a result of parental choice, reflecting a strong son preference that is deeply rooted in some societies.[6] Son preference comes from the normative roles and values associated with sons that are embedded in particular types of family systems, especially the patrilineal family system, which is characterized by patrilineally organized kinship groups, patrilocal marital residence, and inheritance practices favoring sons. As Skinner argues, "Patrilineal joint family systems, which obtain in one variant or another in a continuous belt of agrarian societies stretching from China across South Asia and the Middle East into Eastern Europe and North Africa, present the extreme examples of consistent, thoroughgoing male bias."[7] Despite major socioeconomic changes and influence from the outside over the past several decades, these societies, including China, have maintained strong patrilineal traditions. Under a patrilineal joint family system, as in China and India, having sons is one of the most critical measures of a family's success, or even a condition for its survival. As Confucius said: "among three major offenses against filial piety, having no male descendent is the gravest." In such a social context, sex selection is a natural component of demographic control, just like birth control. When families see the need to achieve fertility control, compelled or voluntary, sex selection becomes not only a desirable, but a necessary strategy.[8]

Most sex-biased selective behaviors, although affecting family composition, do not necessarily change gender balance at the population level. Common sex-selective behaviors include giving away daughters for adoption or stopping having children after reaching some ideal family size and/ or composition. Those acts are balanced by families that adopt in daughters and by the fact that stopping having children itself has minimal effect on the sex of the next child.[9] Only the bluntest versions of sex-biased selection, such as neglect and infanticide, would change a population's sex composition.[10]

The conflict between the need for a small family and the desire for sons is intensified when fertility drops down to a low level. Like fertility control more generally, the sex of a child could be part of the rational calculus of family reproduction when son preference provides both material motivations and ideational justifications for gender discrimination.[11] Pressure for low fertility, whether an internal drive to control individual or family life, economic factors such as the high costs of raising children, or state compulsion like China's draconian One-child policy, pushes families to shift their fertility strategies from "quantity" to "quality."[12]

Modern prenatal sex determination and selection technologies, especially the use of ultrasound machines, provide a relatively easy and less painful solution for families to satisfy both the demand for low fertility and son preference. Ultrasound machines became widely available in China and India in the 1980s, when the initial signs of the current round of high SRB were observed. In China, some even proposed that the government should use sex-detection technology to help families achieve both ideal family compositions (one son and one daughter) and the government's fertility control goals. In India, billboards were put up to advertise the use of ultrasound machines for selective detection.[13] Similar correlations are also observed in other countries like Albania, Korea, and Vietnam.[14]

Effective sex-selective abortion makes the numerator (male births) and denominator (female births) move in opposite directions, resulting in a greatly exacerbated gender imbalance in a population, even when only a relatively small proportion of families undertake sex selection. The high effectiveness of sex-detection technologies ensures that most aborted female fetuses are replaced by a male birth, thus greatly reducing the "wastage" in fertility. Figure 4.1 illustrates the effect of sex-selective abortion on SRB, assuming a normal SRB of 106 (boys per 100 girls) and 100 percent success rate of selection and replacement. The effect of sex-selective abortion on SRB is exponential, as shown in the first panel. For example, the SRB would be over 1,000 if 40 percent of births were selected through abortion; at a 20 percent practice rate, SRB would still be over 250; a 10 percent practice rate produces an SRB of 159.4. The middle panel shows that the currently high SRB (about 120) observed in China requires only that 3.1 percent of births are affected by sex-selective abortion. A sex ratio of 110 suggests a practice rate of only 0.9 percent. Even if only 0.5 percent of births were the product of sex selection, it would still push the SRB to over 108 (panel 3). The distorting effect of the actions of a small proportion of families in a large social context of son preference makes gender imbalance an extremely difficult problem to eradicate.

A combination of cultural, social, economic, and political factors makes China especially susceptible to sex selection. First and foremost is the strong son preference in China. According to Chinese tradition, continuation of family lineage is the foremost responsibility. Because family name and lineage

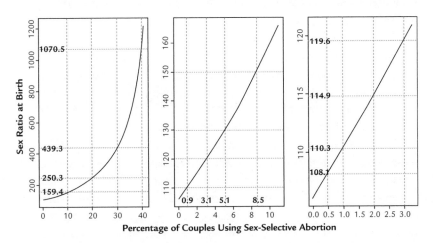

Figure 4.1. Effects of sex-selective abortion on sex ratio at birth.

can only be passed down through sons, having sons is both a basic necessity for a family's survival and for its prosperity. The end of a family lineage threatens not only the livelihood of the living members of the family, but also the status of the dead—it is the utmost failure of life to leave ancestors as "lonely ghosts."

The second factor is what Greenhalgh has insightfully called "fertility as mobility."[15] In a society characterized by extreme economic rationality and weak intermediate or moderating social institutions, families make their fertility decisions according to narrow cost-benefit calculations. The economic reforms launched in the late 1970s re-created a pernicious environment for gender equality as some protective measures installed under socialism receded and market forces put more pressure on families. It is no surprise that the gender imbalance worsened rapidly in China once economic liberalization threw most Chinese families into relentless market competition with little social protection. The rising cost of living, especially the cost of educating children, and drastic increases in economic inequality further increased the economic pressures favoring low fertility. China's low fertility today is as much a matter of family preferences for few children as of government-enforced limits on family size.[16]

The third factor is the social and cultural acceptance of abortion as a method of fertility control. This acceptance might be linked to the traditional view of when a life starts, which was built on the assumption of high infant and child mortality. In the past, many Chinese families would not formally name their newborn until the child survived to his or her first birthday. When induced abortion was discussed as a birth control method in the 1950s, most opposition focused on its potential harm to the mother's health, not the rights or protections of the fetus.[17] From 1964, induced abortion became widely used as a birth control method.[18] According to the *Health Statistics Yearbook of China*, between 1971 and 2011, 336 million abortions were performed. Even if only a small proportion of these were sex selective, they would still have resulted in millions of missing girls.[19]

The last factor, but not the least, is China's One-child policy. The One-child policy has accelerated and magnified the escalation of gender imbalance.[20] The policy treats births merely as numbers to be managed and thus justifies any measure for achieving its goals.[21] The draconian policy not only left families no options in achieving a desired number of sons, but also fostered the use of sex-detective technology. One early use of ultrasound machines in China was for checking IUDs. It did not take long for people to realize that the same technology could be used for sex detection. Moreover, the sex-biased policy in rural areas, that if the first child is a girl, couples are allowed a second child (the so-called 1.5 child policy), acknowledges and perpetuates strong son preferences.[22] The most egregious gender imbalances in China are found in areas with the so-called 1.5 child policy.[23]

All these factors together create an environment for extreme rationality around fertility control in China. The Chinese government has long promoted fertility control with arguments that a small family is a rational choice, both for individual and familial economic welfare, and for the country's or the world's collective future. Social and economic rationality pushes families to leave nothing to chance: if a son is so strongly desired, any measure and cost are justified. Government pressures leave families with still less flexibility.

Coale and Banister have charted the course of sex ratio changes in China over the five decades before 1990.[24] Their analysis reveals that sex imbalance in China in the prerevolutionary period was even higher than the current level: the proportion of missing females for cohorts born in 1936–1940 was over 15 percent.[25] Their analysis further suggests that sex imbalance prior to 1950 was largely attributable to excess female mortality, probably due to infanticide, but has declined precipitously, to 5 percent in early 1950, and to 2 percent by the late 1960s, with a disruption by the Great Leap Forward famine of 1959–1961. The reduction was partly because of a strong government that promoted gender equality with policies that attempted to dismantle traditional practices that it deemed backward and harmful, such as infanticide and child marriage, and partly because some of the collective economy mitigated the economic incentives and burdens associated with having "extra" female children. Traditional son preference continued to exert its influence, however, as the proportion of missing never declined to zero.

As soon as the Chinese government started its birth planning programs (in the 1960s in urban areas, and the early 1970s nationwide), pressure from policies demanding low fertility pushed families to make more conscious choices, now within a more clearly defined "quantity" limit. In this period, sex-selective behavior, in the form of fertility control through stopping having children, again emerged as a common family strategy: couples tend to stop after having at least one son (or two sons).

The One-child policy, officially announced in 1980, imposed a stringent restriction on families in China to have only one child; it thus created a sharp conflict between the traditions of strong son preference and demand for low fertility—the once soft boundaries of family size had become an official red line that families were not to cross.[26] The One-child policy marked the reemergence of rising gender imbalance in China, as predicted by the policy's critics and acknowledged by the policy's designers.[27] Achieving the goal of having at least one son while complying with government restrictions was made much easier by modern fetal sex-detection technologies, particularly the ultrasound B machines that became widely available across China in the 1980s. The reported SRB jumped from 108.5 in 1982 to 110.9 in 1990, and reached 118.1 in 2010.

There is some confusion and controversy over these statistics. Three hypotheses are proposed to explain to the rapid rise in gender imbalance: sex-selective abortion (with help from modern technology such as ultrasound B machines), sex differentials in mortality among infants (by neglect or infanticide of females), and underenumeration of female infants and children (by not recording or reporting female births).[28] Among these three, only sex-selective abortion would affect the true SRB. Sex-differential mortality affects sex ratio *after* birth, not *at* birth. Underenumeration, due to adoption or hiding, should not affect actual sex ratios.[29] All three causes have undoubtedly contributed to the rise of the "missing females," yet there is no consensus on their proportional contributions.[30]

The use of modern sex-selective technologies both guarantees a satisfactory result and also lessens the moral and psychological discomfort associated with traditional sex-selection practices, such as adoption or infanticide. Evidence for the use of sex-selection techniques can be found in the low sex ratio (few males, many females) of aborted fetuses and the high sex ratios of hospital births, where underreporting of new births or infanticides is low.[31] Fearing the misuse of newly available technologies, the Ministry of Health and the State Family Planning Commission (SFPC) issued a decree prohibiting sex screening during pregnancy as early as 1986. More regulations restricting the use of sex-detection technologies followed. Nevertheless, in a country where abortion is both legally sanctioned and widely available as a birth control method, despite heavy government regulation, sex-selective abortion is still widely available in China.[32]

Direct and systematic evidence of infanticide is hard to come by, but higher female infant and child mortality rates suggest that it must exist and is significant. In normal circumstances, female infants and children tend to have lower mortality rates than their male counterparts. This was true in China until the 1980s, although to a lesser degree than in other populations.

Figure 4.2 compares the sex ratios of infant mortality in China over the past few decades with corresponding (matching female life expectancy) values from Coale and Demeny's Model West life tables.[33] The 1990 census first reported a female infant mortality rate that was higher than the male infant mortality rate. By the 2000 census, the female infant mortality rate exceeded the male rate by 40 percent.[34] The data from the 2005 mini-census and the 2010 census suggest a possible reversal of this trend, but the accuracy of this reported trend is uncertain due to possible data problems: the infant mortality rates from the two sources are suspiciously low, with the infant mortality rates reported in the 2010 census being among the lowest in the world.

The hypothesis that missing girls are merely hidden from census enumerators has very different demographic and social implications than do the hypotheses of differential mortality and abortion rates, which assume the missing girls are truly absent from the population. Stories from the field and examination of data suggest that the problem of underreporting is rampant

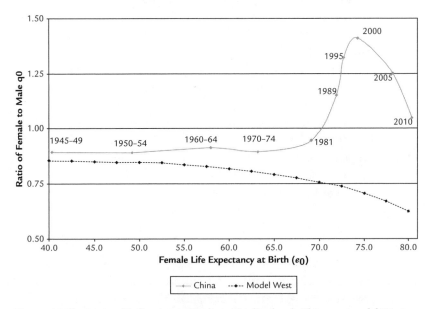

Figure 4.2. Sex ratio of infant mortality by mortality level: China vs. model West.
Sources: Coale and Demeny, *Regional Model Life Tables and Stable Population*; Huang, Rongqing and Liu Yan (eds). 1995. *Mortality Data of China Population*. Data User Service Series No. 4. CPIRC/UNFPA. Beijing: China Population Publishing House; National Bureau of Statistics of China (NBS), *China Population Statistical Yearbook*, 1996, 2002, 2006, 2012.

and widespread.[35] The One-child policy gives families and local governments strong incentives to hide births, especially for births that are not within a "quota." An increasingly mobile society provides opportunities for such hiding. Cai and Lavely estimate, using the 2000 census data, that over one-quarter of the number of missing girls between 1980 and 2000 might be attributed to underreporting.[36]

Hidden or Gone? Estimating Missing Girls in China between 1980 and 2010

The release of the 2010 census offers a new opportunity for assessing the extent of underreporting and updating our understanding of the scale and trend of gender imbalance in China. Examination of the data suggests that the 2010 census is of reasonable quality, but that underreporting exists on a substantial scale, especially for infants, and possibly for young males who are in the prime age range for internal migration.[37]

Two factors primarily contribute to population underreporting in China: the One-child policy and a rise in population mobility. The One-child policy affects population registration for several reasons: 1) the government uses the denial of registration as a punishment for policy violators or as a mechanism for enforcement, including by conditioning registration on payment of fines for unauthorized births; 2) local governments manipulate statistics for administrative/political purposes; and 3) families hide children in order to avoid penalties or to seek opportunities for having more children. It is expected that One-child policy-related underreporting is more likely to affect infants and children. Given the critical importance of having a household registration (*hukou*) in China for schooling and for accessing social benefits, as a child ages, he or she is more and more likely to be picked up by the system.

Increasing population mobility also affects population enumeration in China. As in many other countries, it is much more difficult to get an accurate count of people on the move. The problem is exacerbated by two institutional elements in China. First, with more and more people working and living in places other than where they are registered, the *hukou* system, which was designed to administer an immobile population, has created confusion about where people should be counted—at their place of formal registration or actual residence. Second, government officials are evaluated partly on the basis of statistics tied to population-related measures such as their jurisdiction's conformity to the One-child policy and the GDP per capita. These metrics give local officials strong incentives not to count certain "undesirable" groups such as migrants.[38] The migration-related underreporting is more likely to affect those in the age ranges where mobility is highest.

These two kinds of underreporting have very different effects on the reported sex ratio. For child underreporting, given the strong son preference in China, it is expected that more female children would go underreported, especially in cases of so-called "out-of-plan" births, and in cases of families seeking opportunities to have another child. This type of underreporting would push up the reported sex ratio higher relative to the actual ratio. That is, many missing girls are not truly missing from the population, but merely are unreported and hidden in the population. For migrant underreporting, because males are more mobile, it is expected that more males would be missed by the reporting system. Thus, this type of underreporting would push down the reported sex ratio, making gender imbalance appear to be less severe in certain age groups than it is in reality.

Figure 4.3 compares the SRB cohort reported in the three recent Chinese censuses (1990, 2000, and 2010), along with data from sixteen recent annual population-change sampling surveys within the same twenty-year period. These surveys are conducted by the National Bureau of Statistics (NBS) of China to monitor population change, usually with a sample rate of around one per thousand, but augmenting to 1 percent in years ending in "5."[39] For the 1990 census and surveys of 1991–1993, the standard time for sampling is July 1. Starting from 1994, the standard time has been moved to November 1. The military population is included in the censuses, but not in the sampling surveys. Figure 4.3 simply lines up data by cohorts as they were counted in each survey or census; no adjustment is made for the difference in date of measurement or for the effect of including military personnel in the censuses but not the surveys, or for the effect of sex-differential mortality. Data from the three censuses are represented by bold lines, and data from surveys are in thin lines.

The three censuses show remarkable consistency for cohorts born before 1970. The change in sex ratio fits well with general mortality patterns: adult survival favors females, the sex ratio declines with age—in this case, in later enumerations. Even the small swings observed from year to year are consistent across those three enumerations. Such consistency attests to the accuracy of Chinese age counting and the general quality of Chinese census data.

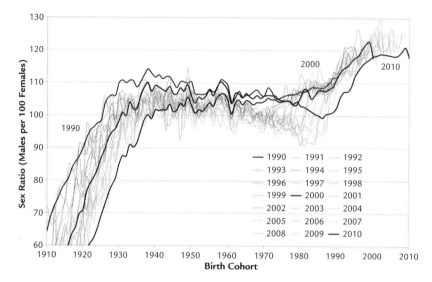

Figure 4.3. Sex ratio by birth cohort reported in the Chinese censuses and surveys. Sources: NBS, *China Population Statistical Yearbook*, 1989–2012.

The patterns are significantly different for cohorts born after the 1970s. While the lower sex ratios in more recent censuses seem to support the "hidden girls" hypothesis on the surface, the sex ratios of the 1980s cohorts reported in the 2010 census are just too low to be true. The ratios even dropped to below 100 at one point. If those sex ratios were accurate, they would imply "missing boys" instead of "missing girls" for those cohorts. Cross-checking the 2010 census with other data sources (*hukou* data and education enrollment data) suggests that the 2010 census data underreported males in migration-prone ages.[40] Apparently, the two kinds of sex-selective underreporting discussed above are both occurring, and having opposite effects, making it difficult to determine the magnitude or trend in either type of underreporting. The question is how much confidence we can have in the 2010 census data if they badly miscount the 1980s cohorts.

Adding the sampling survey data to the picture provides some clues for understanding the problem. It is no surprise that sex ratios from the sampling surveys are more volatile, because the calculation of sex ratios is highly sensitive to sampling errors. Nevertheless, three interesting patterns emerge. First, for cohorts born in the 1950s, there is reasonable consistency across censuses and surveys. Second, for cohorts born between 1950 and 1990, the sampling surveys tend to report lower sex ratios than the censuses, especially for cohorts born between 1960 and 1990. This can be explained by the fact that the sampling surveys are more likely than censuses to miss people who are on the move because the sampling surveys are less rigorously organized and implemented than the censuses, and because military personnel, mostly males, are not included in the sampling surveys. Third, for cohorts born after 1990, the sampling surveys are generally in line with the 2000 census, making the 2010 census an outlier. This raises the question of whether there was something different about the 2010 census that explains its unusual results.

Indeed, the 2010 census introduced a new method of enumeration.[41] Unlike previous censuses and surveys that only counted "residents," the 2010 census counted both *de jure* registered residents and *de facto* populations. A computer algorithm was then applied to the data to determine whether a person should be counted as a resident. This new method was designed to minimize underenumeration of migrants who live in places different from their official household registration—a major problem encountered in the previous censuses, especially in the 2000 census.[42] The lower sex ratios in the 2010 census suggest that the 2010 census picked up more "hidden girls." Because sex ratio is a relative measure, it is still necessary to examine the detailed counts of population by sex.

Figure 4.4 presents the tracking of cohort sizes and sex ratios across enumerations and over time. To reduce the volatility associated with single-age data, as shown in Figure 4.3, five-year age groups are used. Six birth cohorts are traced sequentially from the earliest enumeration to the latest. For example, the birth cohort of 1980–1984 has twenty-four data points, each representing one enumeration from 1987 to 2011 (no data from 1988). The most recent cohort, born in 2005–2009, only has three data points, from the 2009 survey, the 2010 census, and the 2011 survey. Despite considerable variation within each cohort across different enumerations, two unambiguous trends emerge: the sex ratio rose from the earliest to the latest cohorts, and cohort size declined from 1985–1989 to 2005–2009, reflecting the decline of fertility. A cohort-by-cohort analysis helps to identify features unique to each cohort and patterns shared across cohorts.

The 1980–1984 Cohort

Tracing this cohort across the twenty-four enumerations confirms the existence of both kinds of underreporting: underreporting of infants and children

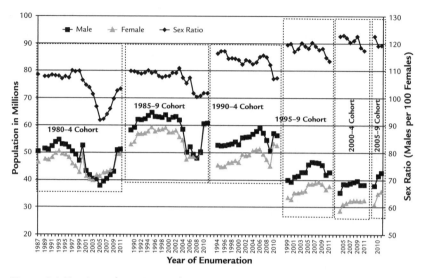

Figure 4.4. Tracing cohort sizes and sex ratios across years.
Sources: NBS, *China Population Statistical Yearbook*, 1989–2012.

and underreporting of migrants. When the 1980–1984 cohort was first counted in the 1987 1 percent sampling survey, the cohort sizes were 50.5 million for males, and 46.5 million for females, and the sex ratio was 108.5. In the next five enumerations, each round picked more "hidden" boys and girls. The cohort sizes reached 54.7 million for males, and 50.6 million for females in the 1993 survey, when the cohort was aged between 9 and 13 years— around primary school age. This suggests that the underreporting was substantial, but with relatively limited sex bias. The sex ratio of the 1993 counting was 108.1, slightly lower than the 1987 counting, before taking into account sex-differential mortality. In other words, from those five enumerations, for the 1980–1984 cohort, "missing girls" is a real phenomenon, not a statistical artifact. From the 1994 survey on, the enumerations of the 1980–1984 cohorts became more and more contaminated by underreporting, because this cohort was in a migration-prone age. Each enumeration of the cohort became smaller, for both males and females, with the sole exception of the 2000 census. The decline did not stop until reaching nadirs in 2003 for females and in 2005 for males. The underreporting is substantial: the count of males in 2005 is just shy of 70 percent of the 1993 tally; the count of females in 2003 is just shy of 80 percent of the number in 1993. The cohort sizes then recovered gradually before jumping to close to their 1993 level in the 2010 census, probably as a result of the new enumeration method. The sex ratio also inched back up from 2005, with a big jump in 2010. As the migration-driven under-reporting hypothesis posits, the underreporting in the high migration age range is highly sex selective, more severe for males than females. By 2011, the reported female cohort size is 98 percent of the maximum size as counted in 1993; the male cohort size is only 94 percent of the 1993 count. This suggests that there was still a large group of males missed by enumerators in 2011.

The 1985–1989 Cohort

This cohort has twenty-three observations. They share some patterns with the 1980–1984 cohort: child-age underreporting declined gradually until the co-hort reached primary school age (around 1996). The underreporting of chil-dren in the cohort's first enumeration was about 10 percent, and with a small sex bias. Underreporting rose again as the cohort entered the migration-prone ages, but was largely gone by the 2010 census. Migration-related underreport-ing was highly sex selective. The number of females for this cohort in the 2010 census—when the cohort was in the age range associated with high rates of migration—is close to its early peak level, but not the number of males.

The 1990–1994 Cohort

The underreporting of children in this cohort's early years gradually de-clined until 2006, when the cohort size was about 12 percent larger than its initial counting. This was followed by a steep, and sex-imbalanced, decline in the next three enumerations. For females, the 2010 census seems to have been the most complete ever. Because this cohort was in the most migration-prone age during the 2010 census, the counting of males is likely to suffer from underreporting.

The 1995–1999 Cohort

As with the 1990–1994 cohort, the underreporting of this cohort when it was in the child-age range gradually abated until 2010, when the cohort size had a sudden drop, more for males than for females. In light of the underreporting patterns observed in the preceding three cohorts, the drop was most likely due to migration. Notwithstanding the new enumeration method introduced in the 2010 census, cohort sizes dropped in the 2010 census, although not by very much. The drop was more for males than for females. Prior to that, there was no obvious pattern of sex bias in underreporting patterns.

The 2000–2004 and 2005–2009 Cohorts

The data cover these cohorts only through childhood age. The members of these cohorts have yet to enter their prime migration years by the 2011 survey. The steady reduction of underreporting among these child-age cohorts is the most obvious trend. For the 2000–2004 cohort, there was a sudden sex-skewed drop in the 2010 and 2011 data. For the 2005–2009 cohort, the data series is too short to make any conclusive observation besides the decline in undercounting each year.

To sum up, some commonalities emerge from careful examination of Figure 4.4, and are useful for understanding gender imbalance in the Chinese demographic data over the past two decades. First, child-age underreporting exists, at around 10–15 percent, but there is not a strong and consistent sex bias. Underreporting occurs for both boys and girls, at a roughly comparable scale. Second, migration-age underreporting is a much more severe problem, both in scale and in its strong sex bias. Third, the enumeration of the female population in the 2010 census shows reasonable consistency with previous censuses and surveys. Fourth, because of data problems in the 2010 census data, especially the severe underreporting of males in the high-migration-age range, the sex ratios from the 2010 census should not be directly used to estimate the number of missing girls.

Based on the data and assessments above, it is possible to provide an estimate of the number of missing girls in China. Given the limited quality of the data, the estimate can provide only a ballpark understanding. Two assumptions are made in formulating this estimate: first, the count of the female population in the 2010 census is close to accurate; and second, the sex ratio report for a cohort before it reaches migration age is a good approximation of the real sex ratio.

Table 4.1 presents an estimate of missing girls for the thirty-one cohorts born between 1980 and 2010. The first two columns are enumerations taken directly from the 2010 census. The third through fifth columns are the sex ratios of each cohort, as enumerated in the 2010 census, as expected from Coale and Demeny's model West life tables and as adjusted using the survey and census data.[43] The expected sex ratio is based on assuming a sex ratio at birth of 106, adjusted for mortality rate between the time of birth and the 2010 census. The adjusted sex ratios are derived as follows: for the first four cohorts, sex ratios of the cohort at ages 10–14 are assumed; for the last two cohorts, sex ratios from the 2010 census are used. The "nominal" missing girls number is calculated as the difference between the expected sex ratio and the enumerated sex ratio (i.e., $[6] = [2] * ([3]/[4] − 1)$). The "actual" missing girls number is calculated as the difference between the expected sex ratio and the adjusted sex ratio (i.e., $[7] = [2] * ([5]/[4] − 1)$).

The total number of "missing girls" between 1980 and 2010 is estimated at twenty-two million. The "nominal" number of missing girls observed in the 2010 census is substantially smaller than the "actual" missing, because of underreporting of males for the 1980s birth cohort in the 2010 census. Since 1990, on average, close to one million "missing girls" are removed from the Chinese population each year. The estimate offered here is somewhat lower than UNFPA's estimated 23.7 million "missing girls" for the ages 0–19 cohort in the 2010 census,[44] and also lower than the "40 million extra boys" estimated by Poston, Conde, and DeSalvo.[45]

It should be emphasized that the estimates in Table 4.1 are only ballpark estimates. There are some uncertainties in the more recent cohorts because

Table 4.1. Estimates of Missing Girls, China 1980–2010

Birth Cohort	2000 Census (Millions)		Sex Ratio (Boys per 100 Girls)			Missing Girls (Millions)	
	Male (1)	Female (2)	Census (3)	Model West (4)	Adjusted (5)	Nominal (6)	Actual (7)
1980–1984	50.9	49.6	102.7	103.6	107.1	−0.4	1.7
1985–1989	60.6	59.6	101.8	104.1	108.0	−1.3	2.2
1990–1994	57.1	53.3	107.1	104.5	112.4	1.3	4.0
1995–1999	42.0	36.5	114.9	104.9	118.3	3.5	4.7
2000–2004	38.3	32.3	118.6	105.2	118.6	4.1	4.1
2005–2010	49.1	41.2	119.0	105.4	119.0	5.3	5.3
Total	297.9	272.5	109.3	104.5	108.1	12.5	22.0

Sources: Author's calculation based on the 2010 census, and Coale and Demeny, *Regional Model Life Tables and Stable Population* (Model West).

the data series is not long enough. The implementation of the new method of counting both *de jure* and *de facto* populations could have led to some over-enumeration in certain cohorts in the 2010 census. Nevertheless, the data from multiple enumerations and the assessment of that data undertaken here do provide reasons for confidence in the estimates.

Demography Is Destiny: Where Is the End?

Having long recognized the dire consequences of serious gender imbalance, China has fought a long battle against son preference and sex-selective abortion. Some optimism has been expressed recently, with suggestions that there has been an incipient decline of sex imbalance.[46] For example, Ma Jiantang, the head of China's National Bureau of Statistics, offered a bit of "good news" at the news conference releasing the 2010 census data: "The sex ratio at birth is 118.06 (for every 100 girls), up by 1.2 percentage points over the 116.86 in 2000. But there is a drop of 0.53 percentage points if compared with the 118.59 from the sample survey in 2005, and a decline of 1.39 percentage points over the 119.45 from the sample survey in 2009." He suggests that "measures taken extensively by relevant government agencies are successful, such as the Care for Girls Campaign."[47]

While it clearly is premature to declare victory and to attribute success to the government's efforts, the 2010 census does provide some support for the argument that gender imbalance in China is peaking. Figure 4.5 compares SRB by region (thirty-one provincial-level units) between 2000 and 2010. Because subnational-level birth parity data are from the census long form, the sex ratios at birth are somewhat different from those calculated from the short forms, used for the data cited above.[48] Using the long-form data, the sex ratio at birth is slightly higher, at 119.9 in 2000, and 121.2 in 2010 at the national level. At the subnational level, among thirty-one provincial-level units, eighteen had an increase and thirteen had a decrease. The change in SRB at provincial levels between 2000 and 2010 showed two high correlations: a high positive correlation (r = .79) between regions with high SRB in 2000 and high SRB in 2010, and a high negative correlation (r = -.64) between SRB in 2000 and change over the following ten years (i.e., regions with high SRB in 2000 were more likely to observe a decline between the two censuses).

The increase in SRB is concentrated in a few regions: the most drastic increases were in Shangdong and Guizhou. Shangdong's SRB increased

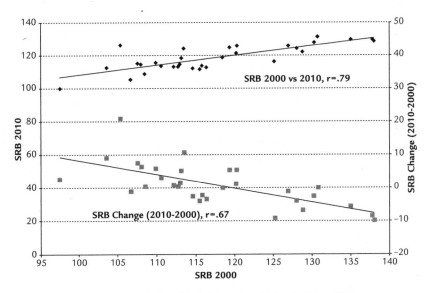

Figure 4.5. Changes in sex ratio at birth by region, China 2000 vs. 2010.
Sources: NBS, *China Population Statistical Yearbook*, 2002, 2012.

from 113.5 in 2000 to 124.3 in 2010, an almost 11-point increase in ten years; Guizhou's SRB increased from 105.4 in 2000 to 126.2 in 2010, a 21-point increase in ten years. If those two provinces were excluded from the analysis, the sex ratio at birth in 2010 would be lower than that in 2000. Meanwhile, there were also dramatic decreases in some regions, such as Jiangxi, Guangdong, and Shaanxi. Overall, SRB has converged at the subnational level: high gender imbalance has spread to more regions; at the same time, the regions with the highest imbalance in 2000 saw a decline. Between 2000 and 2010, while the average of SRB increased about 1 point, the variability across the regions (measured by standard deviation) decreased by 2.7 points—a strong signal of converging and peaking.

The regional convergence and peaking are easier to comprehend in Figure 4.6, which depicts the regional differences of gender imbalance by birth parity with maps. For births of all parities, the comparison of 2000 and 2010 maps shows an unmistakable trend: gender imbalance has spread to all of China, with the exception of Tibet and Xinjiang. At the same time, the pattern of large contiguous regions with especially high gender imbalances seems to be disintegrating.

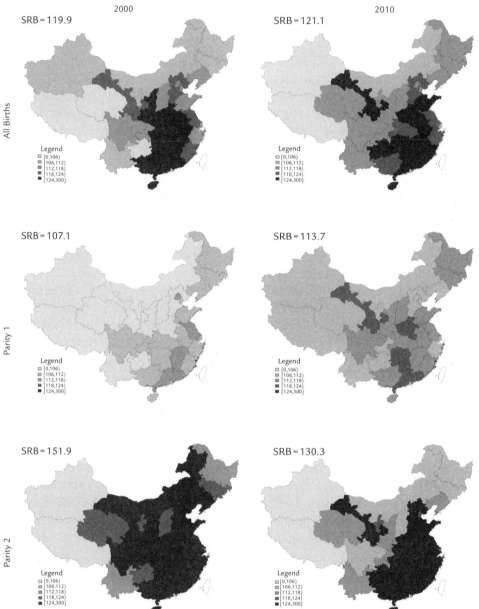

Figure 4.6. Sex ratio at birth by region and parity, China 2000 vs. 2010.
Sources: NBS, *China Population Statistical Yearbook*, 2002, 2012.

The picture looks less promising if the focus is on parity 1. Unlike in 2000, when SRB for parity 1 was "normal" for most of provincial level units, in 2010, no region in China had a SRB below the normal 106 (boys per 100 girls) threshold. A jump from a SRB of 107.1 to 113.7 suggests that sex selection, which used to occur at high parities, is now being practiced at parity 1. This seems to contradict the assessment that sex imbalance in China is peaking, as it is a nationwide increase. However, as illustrated in Figure 4.1, increasing SRB from 107.1 to 113.7 is equivalent to increasing the proportion of sex selection from .26 percent to 1.75 percent. This is not an unexpected result, given the very low fertility in China. Especially under the "one child" norm, a few more families opt for just one son.

Evidence for optimism about reducing gender imbalance in China comes from the changes at parity 2. Between 2000 and 2010, the SRB of parity 2 declined more than 20 points, from 151.9 to 130.3. If the drop was mostly due to reduction in sex-selective abortion, it would mean reducing the proportion of parity 2 births with sex selection from 8.8 percent to 5.1 percent. More importantly, the decline was broad based, with the exceptions only of Beijing, Jiangxi, Shandong, and Ningxia. Provinces with the highest SRB saw the ratio fall between the two censuses. Both the overall drop and the reversion to norms suggest peaking, if not yet the beginning of major decline, in gender imbalance.

The overall increase in SRB in China from 2000 to 2010 can be partially attributed to population structure: the vast majority of births in China were at parity 1, and the most populous provinces, such as Guangdong and Henan, still had highest sex ratios. Parities 1 and 2 together account for over 90 percent of all births in China, with parity 1 births twice as numerous as parity 2 births. Thus, even a dramatic decline in SRB at parity 2 is outweighed by a moderate increase at parity 1. There was also a small decline at parities higher than 3 (not shown). With most populous regions continuing to have high gender imbalances, the return of SRB to normalcy at the national level is likely to be a slow process.

There are other encouraging signs in the comparison of 2000 and 2010 census data. Table 4.2 compares SRB by women's education level across the two censuses. Two trends are clearly represented in the data: an almost linear association between education level and fertility, and a nonlinear relationship between education and sex ratio. The highest SRB is found among women with primary school education. By 2010, sex selection existed across all education groups, and was higher in earlier periods (especially parity 1). Peaking and convergence can be seen across education levels.

Table 4.2. Sex Ratio at Birth by Parity and Women's Education Level, China 2000 vs. 2010

Year	Education	Women 15–49	Births				Sex Ratio		
			Total	% of Parity 1	% of Parity 2	TFR	Total	Parity 1	Parity 2
2010	Total[i]	35,788,094	1,190,060	62.2	31.3	1.18	121.2	113.7	130.3
	No Education	633,141	14,910	30.9	39.2	1.53	123.5	111.5	129.6
	Primary School	6,156,409	162,771	39.9	44.5	1.60	126.8	115.4	128.0
	Middle School	17,646,606	693,064	58.9	35.0	1.35	125.0	113.4	137.1
	High School	6,476,047	147,549	76.8	21.2	0.91	119.0	112.3	141.4
	College	2,797,412	81,250	88.9	10.5	0.83	114.1	111.3	138.0
	University	2,078,479	57,726	93.8	5.9	0.81	110.0	108.4	136.6
2000	Total	32,853,082	1,181,803	68.1	26.1	1.22	119.9	107.1	151.9
	No Education	2,019,324	62,508	39.0	37.4	1.93	109.8	90.5[iii]	124.2
	Primary School	14,411,173	348,895	53.2	37.3	1.48	123.6	104.6	147.3
	Middle School	15,132,669	578,931	72.5	24.1	1.25	121.2	108.0	162.4
	High School	5,125,437	136,782	89.2	9.8	0.95	114.8	111.1	150.0
	College	1,174,548	42,460	96.1	3.7	0.88	109.9	108.8	139.4
	University	456,453	12,227	96.8	3.1	0.74	107.3	106.8	130.0

Sources: NBS, *China Population Statistical Yearbook*, 2002, 2012.
[i] There is a discrepancy in the released 2010 census tabulation data. The total number of birth by parity (1,190,060) in Table 6-1 (Birth by Region, Sex, and Parity) and 6-3 (Fertility by Women's Age and Parity) is different from that (1,157,270) in Table 6-2 (Childbearing Women by Age, Education, and Birth Parity). The discrepancy could be due to how childbearing mothers were counted in case of multiples or because of a missing education variable, but NBS provides no explanation to address these issues.
[iii] One possible explanation for the unusually low SRB in this group is sex-selective abortion to ensure a girl as first birth, which leads to an opportunity of having a second child in areas with a "1.5 child" policy.

Table 4.2 also shows that women's education levels are changing rapidly. In 2000, women with middle school or lower education were the predominant groups, accounting for 96 percent of women of reproductive age. By 2010, their share had declined to 68 percent, and more women had high school education and above than primary school or lower. Projecting ten years beyond 2010, most women in prime reproductive age at that time will have at least a middle school education, and a quarter to a third are expected to have a college education. Research has shown again and again that women's education level is one of the most important factors affecting fertility change, and higher education levels are associated with reduced son preference.[49] If the pattern of educational effect on sex ratio holds for the future in China, SRB should begin to decline soon.

The decline of China's SRB is likely to be slow. Son preference remains strong in rural China;[50] the 2010 census actually shows that son preference has spread to a wider population: among urbanites, among people with higher education, and at first birth parity. Son preference is so deep and entrenched that changing it will require fundamental change in the social institution of the patrilineal joint family. Moreover, because a small proportion of families can drive up SRB, as shown in the discussion of Figure 4.1, even in a "best-case scenario" projection, cultural gender bias and the problem of sex selection will continue to affect sex ratios in China.

Conclusion

Gender imbalance in China is a result of families complying with a strong social desire for sons under conditions of constrained fertility. From 1980 to 2010, China accumulated about twenty-two million "missing girls." Trends in demographic and social change do offer hope for amelioration, but this imbalance is likely to continue for some time.

As much other research has argued or suggested, the shortage of girls in the marriage market generates risks of serious tension or disorder in Chinese society.[51] Nothing can change this demographic fact in the short term: for a generation, as many as 20 percent of the males in some birth cohorts will not be able to find suitable marriage partners. In a society that highly values marriage, marriage is once again becoming a social privilege, a reflection of social and economic success.[52] Traditions of age and social status hypergamy (women "marrying up" in age and status) further exacerbate the problem of a shortage of brides: men not marrying women of higher status pushes highly educated women out of the marriage market, and men marrying younger women combines with shrinking cohort sizes to create an even larger imbalance between marriageable males and females in the rising cohorts.

Rising economic inequality and some aspects of migration patterns mean that bachelors with poor economic prospects will concentrate in certain population sectors and geographic regions.[53] As Greenhalgh artfully puts it, China is creating a social class of bachelors who are "socially marginalized," "economically at risk," "politically excluded," and "reproductively extinguished."[54] This class is also likely to be socially stigmatized and psychologically stressed.

There are ample reasons to be concerned about the social ills possibly associated with this group of bachelors as a product of gender imbalance: crime, violence, STDs, even global instability.[55] Most of these are still speculative dangers, or at most perceived threats, and not real problems yet. But China will live under these perils for generations to come, and there is no easy solution.

On the positive side, China may be at a turning point on gender imbalance, as new social trends seem likely to lead to a diminution in the traditional son preference. First, rapid urbanization dismantles patrilineal communities and family structures, and, in turn, erodes cultural bases of son preference. Second, because they are relatively fewer in number, women could enjoy greater power in the marriage market, giving them more choices and opportunities, and thus potentially changing parents' rational calculations about the relative value of sons and daughters. Third, the increase in women's education is likely to provide a stimulus for change in culture. For the first time in history, China is sending more women than men to college. Such a structural shift will affect women's status and value.

Another major positive development in China's combat against gender imbalance is the newly announced relaxation of the One-child policy. The ambitious agenda presented by the Third Plenum of the Eighteenth CCP Central Committee includes a major reform of the One-child policy: families in which at least one parent was an only child are now allowed to have a second child themselves. Demographically, it is a relatively small step, as the new exemption applies mostly to urban families. Nonetheless, such a policy alleviates some state-imposed constraints that have limited many families' fertility choices. Such a policy change also has important political and psychological effects: it raises the hope for the eventual return of reproductive freedom to the Chinese people.

CHAPTER 5

Policy Model and Inequality:
Some Potential Connections

Yasheng Huang

According to a report in *Caijing*, the all-China Gini coefficient was 0.474 for 2012.[1] This was based on the estimates provided by the National Bureau of Statistics (NBS). For four years in a row, according to NBS, the all-China Gini declined from a peak of 0.491 in 2008. In the accompanying report, the NBS attributed this decline of the Gini to the effectiveness of the government's social and income support programs.

That China has a high level of income inequality is an established fact. The debates are about three issues. First, just how high is China's income inequality? Independent academics have provided different estimates on the Chinese Gini from the ones provided by NBS. Gan Li, director of the China Household Finance Survey at the Southwestern University of Finance and Economics in Chengdu, estimates that the all-China Gini in 2010 was 0.61. By contrast, the NBS estimate is only 0.481 for 2010. Another independent academic, Li Wei, a sociologist at the Chinese Academy of Social Sciences, estimated the Gini to be 0.54 in 2008, compared with the 0.491 figure provided by NBS.[2]

The most likely reason for the difference between these alternative estimates and the estimates by NBS results from the differences in the sampling frames. As Gan Li pointed out, NBS's surveys undersample both households at the low-income spectrum and households at the high-income spectrum, which leads to biased estimates. While it is not the job of this chapter to resolve this methodological dispute, it should be noted that NBS has never made available its survey data and that it has not disclosed refusal rates by the respondents, a standard disclosure in any survey research. By contrast, the disclosure by Professor Gan Li is far more substantial and detailed. All else being equal, Professor Li's findings should be given more credence than those provided by NBS.[3]

The second debate is about the consequences of China's high income inequality. Some observers cite the close correlation between the rising incidence of what are known as "mass riots" and income inequality to argue that income inequality has contributed to social instability. This is debatable. It is possible that the rising incidence of mass riots and growing income inequality are jointly caused by omitted variables (such as forcible evictions of farmers). Survey research by a Harvard sociologist, Martin Whyte, shows that Chinese people are not unduly concerned about rising inequality.[4] He argues that it is a myth that inequality has created "a social volcano" in China. This finding by Whyte is based on large-scale and systematic survey research. On methodological grounds, it is a strong finding.

It should be noted that the finding by Professor Whyte was generated when the Chinese economy was growing robustly. The political and economic consequences of inequality can be argued to be "contingent." They are contingent on a host of other factors that are well beyond the purview of Professor Whyte's survey project. For example, it is entirely possible that the consequences of inequality can be benign when growth is fast but can turn malicious when growth slows down. As China faces a near certain prospect of an economic slowdown (relative to its historical norm), one would advise Chinese leaders against taking the findings by Whyte too much at face value.

This perspective is partially informed by an argument proposed by Benjamin Friedman in his book *The Moral Consequences of Economic Growth*.[5] Friedman argues, mostly referring to the United States, that economic growth is a vital source of elements of a good society (such as political tolerance and openness). Growth stagnation, on the other hand, contributes to a deterioration of these qualities of a society. If this is true for a country at a high income level and with a relatively developed social safety net, the social and political effects of growth are probably a magnitude larger in a country such as China. Think of the contrast between Indonesia and South Korea. Both countries were hit by an external financial crisis in 1998, but in the case of Indonesia, a country with a high level of extant income inequality, the financial crisis led to the crumbling of the Suharto regime and political chaos. South Korea, on the other hand, not only survived the financial crisis intact, but also implemented pro-active political and economic reforms with minimal political and social instability.

The third debate revolves around why and how income inequality has gotten so high in China. This is the main focus of this chapter. On this issue, there are two contrasting views. One holds that the rising income inequality is a natural product of China's stages of development.[6] The rationale commonly invoked to support this view is the so-called Kuznets curve. The idea of the Kuznets curve is that inequality has an inverted-U shape, that is, inequality first rises as development occurs (driven by market forces and urbanization), and then inequality falls as the economy reaches a higher level of economic development. The problem is that the Kuznets curve does not hold up either against general economic evidence or against China-specific empirics. Acemoglu and Robinson, for example, found no empirical evidence in support of the Kuznets curve, and the political economy implications they drew from their study of the Kuznets curve are almost diametrically opposed to the conclusions of those who invoke it to show that rising inequality in China is benign.[7] They show that development induces both improving and deteriorating equality, with no clear patterns, and that those economies with rising inequality are more likely to experience political instability (and also demands for political transition). Later in this chapter I present evidence that within China there is no correlation between growth and patterns of income inequality.

The alternative view in this debate is that policies matter, both given a certain level of development as well as relative to the effect of development stage. This is my view in this chapter. Specifically, I group economic policies into two broad categories: those policies that are pro-rural and those policies that are pro-urban. This categorization of economic policies is often confused with an economically regressive stance against urbanization when in reality it is fundamentally orthogonal to the whole discussion on urbanization. Some habitually view pro-rural policies as automatically anti-urbanization when in fact a pro-rural policy is more about conditions under which urbanization proceeds, not about forces for or against urbanization per se. The best contrast is between urbanization in East Asia (South Korea and Taiwan) and urbanization in Latin America. Both regions experienced substantial urbanization, but in East Asia urbanization occurred with relative rural-urban income parity, whereas in Latin America urbanization proceeded with substantial rural deprivation.

The overall argument of this chapter is that China's reform era can be broadly—or even crudely—decomposed into a pro-rural policy period and a pro-urban policy period. The pro-rural policy period roughly corresponds to the first half of the reform era (from 1978 to roughly 1993); the rural bias period roughly goes from the mid-1990s to 2002. Since 2002, there has been some moderation of this rural bias, but the fundamental direction of the policy has remained one of substantial pro-urban biases. I show that the patterns in the empirics on inequality in China are broadly consistent with this demarcation of the policy episodes.

The vast majority of studies on income inequality in China are efforts to estimate its level and to demonstrate its developments over time. The purpose of this chapter is to relate the well-documented facts on Chinese income inequality with policy models and episodes. Before I proceed, let me note a number of caveats. One has to do with how inequality is measured. Economists and sociologists often measure equality/inequality by metrics in addition to income. For example, asset or consumption inequality is also estimated. In this chapter, the primary metric is the income equality. This is a measure most frequently used in research, and the data on income are more consistent in availability and in quality, therefore making the estimates based on these data more reliable. It is possible, although unlikely, that consumption and asset inequality shows an entirely different pattern from the one established by income inequality.

The second caveat is that we observe the connections between the posited policy episodes and patterns of income inequality at a high level of aggregation. This chapter offers no statistical evidence that the two are connected. For these and other reasons, this chapter is mainly speculative. I will offer a view of what China policy models consist of and then provide some tentative ideas about how particular aspects of the China policy model may—or may not—matter for income inequality. I will do my best to offer some support for these ideas by attributing not just income inequality per se, but some of its specific manifestations to one feature of the China model—its pro- or anti-rural bias. In other words, this is a think piece, and the motivation is to provide grounds for discussion and maybe some ideas for further research.

The third caveat is that I did not generate the empirical findings on income inequality. All the estimates are cited from research done by economists who have studied this issue in great detail. This paper makes no *original* contributions to this growing and important empirical literature on income inequality. (The tables and figures are all reprinted from the cited papers.) My task here is to take these research findings more or less as given and then throw on top of them some ideas of how certain features of the China model may have contributed to them (or at least appear to be consistent with them). I take as a starting premise that features of the China model contributed to inequality, but it is possible that others would argue for a reverse causality— that somehow inequality played a role in shaping the design of the China model. The latter hypothesis is possible, but not probable. Some empirical papers do show the effect of a number of policies on income inequality. The potentially contentious issue is whether these policies are unique features of the China model. I will touch on—but largely sidestep—that debate here.

The first section of this chapter summarizes a number of empirical studies on inequality in China. The second section focuses on one aspect of this inequality—the rural-urban income gap, which is the biggest component of China's overall income inequality and links this component of inequality with the anti- or pro-rural biases of the China model. The third section provides a conclusion.

Some Stylized Facts

The Overall Trends

The most consistent finding on inequality in China is that it has increased substantially during the reform era. In "A Comparative Perspective on Poverty Reduction in Brazil, China and India," Martin Ravallion of the World Bank estimated that China's Gini coefficient has been rising at the trend rate of 7 percent per decade. He posited that if it continued at that rate, it would reach the level of Brazil in 2025. (It should be noted that China most likely already reached the level of Brazil as of 2014.)

Table 5.1 is reproduced from Ravallion's paper. It shows that China started out in 1981 with the lowest Gini of the three countries in the table: Brazil, China, and India. By 1993, China surpassed India, and, by 2005, its Gini was substantially greater than that of India. A recent estimate by Gan Li, director of the School of Economics at the Southwestern University of

Table 5.1. From Martin Ravallion's Paper

Table 1: Summary statistics

	Brazil			China			India		
	1981	1993	2005	1981	1993	2005	1981	1993	2005
Average income or consumption									
GDP per capita ($PPP per year)	7072.8	7241.0	8471.0	543.5	1505.5	4076.3	901.4	1274.1	2233.9
PCE per capita ($PPP per year)	3727.3	3711.1	4408.6	248.9	635.4	1336.6	642.5	790.3	1208.8
Survey mean ($PPP per year)	2367.5	3091.4	3344.2	300.2	571.8	1294.8	494.5	560.3	642.2
Mixed mean ($PPP per year)	2323.7	2473.0	3030.0	382.3	597.5	1219.6	613.9	699.3	841.0
Inequality and human development									
Gini index (%)	57.5	59.7	57.6	29.1	35.5	41.5	35.1	30.8	33.4
Infant mortality rate (deaths per 1000 births)	72.2	49.2	21.8	45.8	36.3	21.4	113	80	57.7
Life expectancy at birth (years)	62.8	66.6	71.81	65.5	68.3	72.6	55.7	59.7	64.0
Primary enrollment rate (Female/male, %)*	136.7	141.0	136.9	111.7 (86.9)	127.5 (93.3)	111.2 (99.5)	81.6 (67.6)	93.6 (76.7)	114.6 (97.6)

Secondary enrollment rate (Female/male, %)*	47.2	54.2	105.5	43.2	37.7	75.5	33.1	41.3	54.0
				(73.2)	(75.1)	(100.8)	(49.3)	(59.7)	(82.3)
Literacy (% of people age 15+) (Female/male, %)*	74.6	86.4	89.6	65.5	77.8	93.3	40.8	48.2	66.0
				(64.6)	(78.2)	(93.3)	(48.7)	(54.7)	(70.9)
Poverty									
Headcount index ($1.25; %)	17.1	13.0	7.8	84.0	53.7	16.3	59.8	49.4	41.6
Headcount index using mixed method ($1.25; %)	17.6	18.1	9.7	73.0	45.0	12.1	42.3	30.4	20.3
Headcount index ($2.00; %)	31.1	24.7	18.3	97.8	78.6	36.9	86.6	81.7	75.6
Headcount index using mixed method ($2.00; %)	31.7	31.5	21.1	95.4	78.4	33.9	77.0	68.4	57.0

Notes: GDP, per capita consumption expenditure (PCE) and the survey mean are all at PPP for 2005 and 2005 constant prices and annual. Survey means relate to household income per person for Brazil and China and household consumption expenditure per person for India. Adult literacy rate for Brazil is 2006 and 2007 for China and India. Enrollment rates are 1980 and 2006 for China. *: Enrollment and literacy rates have been approximately equal for Brazil since the 1970s, and so are omitted.

Sources: Poverty and inequality measures are from *PovcalNet*. All other data are from the World Bank's Development Data Platform.

Reproduced from Martin Ravallion, "A Comparative Perspective on Poverty Reduction in Brazil, China and India," The World Bank Policy Research Working Paper 5080, 2009. Used with permission from World Bank.

Finance and Economics, shows that China's income Gini as of 2010 is around 0.60, substantially more than 0.576 for Brazil as of 2005.[8] (Since 2005, Brazil's Gini has declined.) China is possibly among the most unequal countries in the world in terms of income inequality.

This finding on the rise of inequality is not sensitive to the particular measures used. Based on different measures of income inequality, including the Gini coefficient, the mean logarithm deviation of income (MLD), and comparisons of quintile ranges, Wu and Perloff find that both within-rural and within-urban income inequalities have increased in 1985–2001, with urban income inequality rising relatively faster.[9] Income inequality in rural areas has been greater than urban areas throughout the period. The details of their findings are reported in Table 5.2.

Measures of income inequality are somewhat sensitive to spatial differences in price data. Demurger, Fournier, and Li restudied urban income inequality in China by applying spatial price deflators to CHIP data from 1988, 1995, and 2002.[10] Their results show that when spatial price differentials are

Table 5.2. National Income Inequality Measures

| Year | Gini | MLD | | |
		Total	Within	Between
1985	0.310	0.164	0.111	0.053
1986	0.311	0.169	0.121	0.048
1987	0.317	0.175	0.117	0.058
1988	0.337	0.201	0.135	0.066
1989	0.342	0.208	0.138	0.070
1990	0.327	0.186	0.124	0.062
1991	0.345	0.215	0.144	0.070
1992	0.361	0.231	0.147	0.084
1993	0.380	0.255	0.150	0.105
1994	0.381	0.252	0.136	0.116
1995	0.382	0.266	0.169	0.096
1996	0.349	0.215	0.131	0.084
1997	0.375	0.258	0.143	0.116
1998	0.378	0.257	0.154	0.103
1999	0.389	0.272	0.157	0.115
2000	0.407	0.305	0.174	0.131
2001	0.415	0.317	0.178	0.139

Source: Wu and Perloff, "China's Income Distribution, 1985–2001."

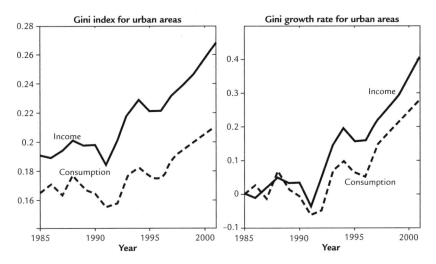

Figure 5.1. Gini index and growth rate for urban areas, 1985–2001.
Source: Wu and Perloff, "China's Income Distribution, 1985–2001."

taken into account, both urban inequality and the contribution of regions (coastal, central, and western) decrease substantially, though interprovincial inequality is still a very important contributor to urban inequality. In addition they show that within-urban income inequality decreased after 1995.

Consumption inequality displays a similar rising trend to income inequality, which suggests that the rise of inequality is not due to how inequality is measured. The two graphs shown in Figure 5.1 were generated by Wu and Perloff. The solid line represents income inequality and the dotted line represents consumption inequality. As seen in the graphs, there is significant comovement between the two measures. The data are for the urban areas only.

Within-Group Inequality

There are also studies that estimate rural and urban income inequality separately. The within-group inequality is important because it implicitly controls for the group-fixed effects, such as the *hukou* status. Also many of the Chinese household surveys (such as NBS' household surveys and CHIP) have different sampling frames for rural and urban residents, making it difficult to undertake direct comparisons. Estimating rural and urban income inequality separately should help achieve some precision in the estimation. However, it is interesting to note that results on within-group inequality are quite unstable. Sources of data and how the reform era is periodized all seem to have nontrivial effects on the findings. The instability of the within-group findings makes it difficult to generate broad policy and research implications.

Cai, Chen, and Zhou compute consumption inequality in urban China for the years 1992–2003. Household consumption in their study includes expenditures on nondurable goods (food, clothes, utilities, communication, etc.) as well as durable goods (electronic appliances, cars, etc.).[11] There is also a significant co-movement between income inequality and consumption inequality. However, what is unusual in this study is that their estimates on consumption inequality are consistently higher than their estimates on income inequality throughout the entire period. The pattern generated by Wu and Perloff is more conventional and more consistent with traditional consumption theory.[12] That consumption inequality is greater than income inequality is quite unusual and warrants further research.

Rural consumption inequality also increased, as shown in Benjamin, Brandt, and Giles.[13] Consumption is calculated as the sum of expenditures on food and nondurable goods purchased during the year, the value of home-produced goods consumed, the value of the flow of services from the household's stock of durable goods and housing, and the value of services (education, health care, and other) purchased by the household during the period. Consumption inequality in rural China increased in the period and, similar to Wu and Perloff, the Gini coefficient of consumption is lower than income Gini. The trend and overall time pattern are almost the same.[14]

Against this overall rising trend of inequality there are also findings on the periodized variances in the inequality estimates, although the estimates are not consistent across different studies. For example, Ravallion reports that inequality declined in the early 1980s, in the mid-1990s, and in 2004. Using CHIP data from 1995 and 2002, Khan and Riskin find that within-rural and within-urban income inequality both decreased from 1995 to 2002.[15] In their study, the aggregate income inequality during this period did not decline, but remained more or less constant, suggesting that rural-urban income inequality increased, but within-group inequality did not increase.

The findings on the stability of within-group inequality are not replicated in other studies. Contrary to Khan and Riskin, within-urban income inequality increased substantially after 1995 in Cai, Chen, and Zhou.[16] Benjamin, Brandt, and Giles also show an increase in rural income inequality in China from 1986 to 1999.[17] Income inequality increased from 1987 to 1999, mostly from increases in the years 1995 to 1999, contradicting Khan and Riskin. In other words, there is considerable consistency in the estimates of inequality level and dynamics over the entire reform era, but there are some disagreements about whether specific subperiods within those thirty years are associated with increase or decrease in income equality, or whether or not within-group inequality was stable relative to between-group inequality. Results in Benjamin, Brandt, and Giles also differ from Gustafsson and Li on changes in within-rural income inequality before 1995.[18] Gustafsson and Li find that income inequality in rural China increased significantly from 1988 to 1995.[19] The MLD-index in their estimations increased from 0.178 to 0.288, or by 62 percent, while the Theil-index increased from 0.181 to 0.339, or by 87 percent. However, increases in income inequality before 1995 were small in Benjamin, Brandt, and Giles.[20]

Cai, Chen, and Zhou use data compiled from the Urban Household Income and Expenditure Survey (UHIES), which covers all provincial units in China in 1992–2003 (but migrants are excluded).[21] Household income in Cai, Chen, and Zhou refers to household disposable income, which includes wage earnings, business income, asset income, and transfer income.[22] Their findings contradict those reported by Khan and Riskin in that within-urban income inequality increased substantially after 1995.[23]

Regional Inequality

Despite different measures and data sources, studies on the 1980s and 1990s have yielded rather consistent observations about interprovincial and interregional inequalities: namely, interprovincial inequality declined during the 1980s and showed signs of increase in the 1990s, while inequality between the eastern coastal region and the rest of China was on an upward trajectory since the 1980s.[24]

Using rural and urban per capita consumption data at the provincial level for 1952–2000, Kanbur and Zhang construct and analyze a long-run time series for regional inequality in China from the Communist Revolution to the present.[25] As indicated by the graphs in Figure 5.2, there have been three peaks of inequality in the last fifty years, coinciding with the Great Famine of the late 1950s, the Cultural Revolution of the late 1960s and 1970s, and finally the period of openness and global integration in the late 1990s.

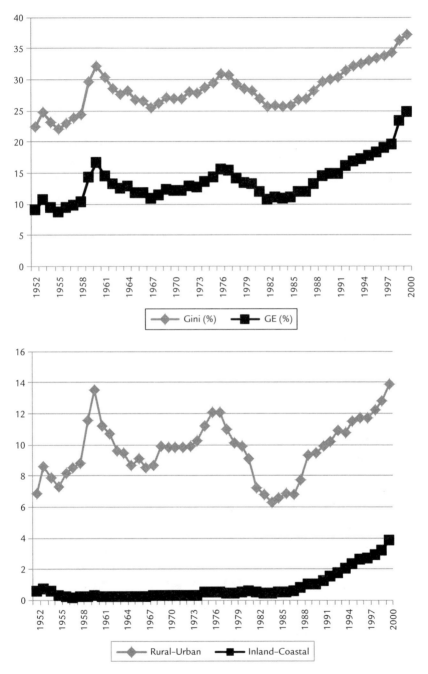

Figure 5.2. Trends of regional inequality.
Source: Kanbur and Zhang, "Fifty Years of Regional Inequality in China."

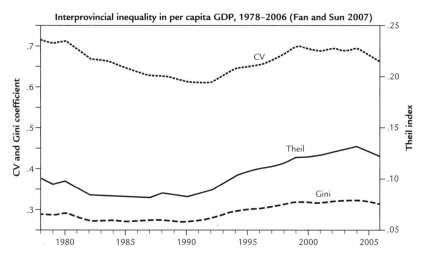

Figure 5.3. Interprovincial inequality in per capita GDP, 1978–2006.
Source: Fan and Sun, "Regional Inequality in China, 1978–2006."

As shown in Figure 5.3, using the most recent per capita GDP data, Fan and Sun demonstrate that interprovincial inequality declined during the 1980s, increased in the 1990s, was relatively stable from the late 1990s to 2004, and has declined thereafter.[26] They show how the trend in interprovincial inequality up to 2004 was shaped by countervailing patterns in (declining) intraregional inequality and (increasing) interregional inequality. Since 2004, however, the study reveals that both interregional and intraregional inequalities have declined, reflecting convergence in growth rates among provinces and among regions.

Inequality and the China Model

It is important to distinguish between the effect of the China model and the effect of economic growth on inequality. Some observers and scholars argue that the high growth of China is somewhat responsible for rising inequality. Within China and among some of the Western academics, the Kuznets curve is often invoked to explain China's rising income inequality. It is often forgotten that the region often associated with Kuznets tradeoffs between growth and equity turned out to be most disappointing in terms of economic growth—Latin America. By contrast, the economies that performed

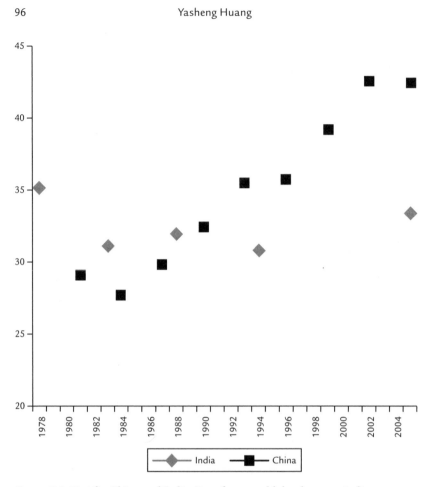

Figure 5.4. Gini for China and India: Data from world development indicators. Source: World Bank, available at http://data.worldbank.org/data-catalog/world -development-indicators.

the best—those in East Asia—exhibit no Kuznets tradeoffs at all. As demonstrated in Figure 5.4, recent economic performers, such as India, also did not experience a sharp acceleration of the Gini index in the way China has. India in 2004 had a lower level of inequality relative both to China in 2004 and to itself in 1981.

The Kuznets curve is not borne out by Chinese data. Ravallion shows that increasing inequality is not the price of growth and poverty reduction. Specifically, he reports the following findings:

The period of most rapid growth was accompanied by decreased inequalities (1981–85 and 1995–98).

The sub-periods of highest growth in the primary sector (1983–84, 1987–88 and 1994–96) did not typically come with lower growth in other sectors.

The provinces with more rapid rural income growth did not experience a steeper increase in inequality; if anything it was the opposite.[27]

A second important point to note is that the most consistent findings on income inequality are about the increases in overall trends over time. One way to summarize the findings is that inequality initially declined in the 1980s but began to rise in the 1990s and experienced some moderations after 2004. Yes, there are findings that show declining or stable inequality in the mid-1990s, but as the summary above shows, those findings are less consistent across different papers and across data sources. In particular, the supposed stability of Gini between 1995 and 2002 (i.e., between the two waves of CHIP) seems to be principally driven by the stability of within-group Gini, but findings on the within-group Gini seems to be the least robust and credible.

A third important point is that rural income and urban income behave very differently in terms of their contributions to overall inequality. Rural income tends to have an equalizing effect, whereas urban income tends to have a disequalizing effect. Taking these three points together suggests a way to speculate about the effect of the China model on income inequality. First, the China model here is assumed to have an effect on income equality. Second, if the China model is assumed to have an effect, then the variances of that model must be consistent with the variances in the overall trends of income equality documented above. Third, how rural income performs under different phases of the China model is a central component in the effect of the China model on overall income inequality.

Let me put forward the following simple—even simplistic—hypothesis: The anti-rural biases of the China model tend to worsen China's overall income equality; pro-rural biases of the China model tend to improve it. Here is one way to conceptualize the evolution of the China model: 1) in the 1980s, the China model was trending toward pro-rural biases, mainly through liberalization; 2) in the 1990s, the China model was turning sharply away from the pro-rural biases; and 3) since 2003, the Hu-Wen leadership modified some of the worst anti-rural biases of the 1990s. They began to invest in public goods in the rural areas, such as health and education, and they also increased the provisions of finance in the rural areas.

But there are some critical differences with the 1980s, the most important of which is that the Hu-Wen leadership modified the anti-rural biases of the China model mainly through massive state-led investments and state-directed provisions in the rural areas. There was almost no liberalization of policies and institutions (such as land or *hukou* reforms).[28] The other problem with the Hu-Wen era, as is well known, is that they were either unwilling or ineffective in dealing with what can be viewed as the root institutional causes of inequality—such as corruption, financial repression, and so forth. It is possible that while rural-urban inequality—which is the biggest component of China's overall inequality—may have moderated, within-group inequality may have increased during this period.

I will now present evidence—produced by other scholars—on the close link between rural income and overall income inequality and will then present more details on the reform periodization along the evolution of the China model described above.

Rural Income and Inequality

That an increase in rural income tends to improve overall equality is well documented in the literature. The important role of rising rural income in decreasing national income inequality is confirmed in Kahn and Riskin.[29] By comparing the urban Gini and rural Gini with the national Gini index, Kahn and Riskin conclude that rural income has a strong equalizing influence on the distribution of overall income, while the role of urban income is mainly disequalizing. According to their calculations, every 1 percentage point shift in the share of income from urban to rural population would reduce the overall national Gini by 0.007, or 1.5 percent.

There are also decomposition studies for rural and urban income groups. Sources of rural income inequality are analyzed in Benjamin, Brandt, and Giles.[30] By comparing decomposition results in 1987 and 1999, they explain the rising rural income inequality during this period by identifying the decline of the source of income that is most equalizing—farm income. Relative to this equalization effect of farm income is the rise of the disequalizing income from nonfarm family businesses and wage income. For the subperiod of 1988 to 1995, decomposition results in Gustafsson and Li show that increases in income inequality in rural China were more than fully due to money income (wages, salaries, net cash income from family enterprises and property income), while increases in income inequality in urban China were mainly due to imputed rents of private housing, which is the dominant part of subsistence income.[31]

Reforms and Rural Policy Biases

Many of the sources quoted above conduct accounting—rather than explanatory—exercises, and they are very useful in identifying the direction in which we can search for the underlying causes behind China's overall level and trend of inequality. Two aspects are important for our discussion. The first is the evidence on the equalizing effect of rural income developments; the second is identifying those policies and reforms that have the biggest effects on rural income developments.

The second point above leads to a discussion of how we should think about reforms in the past thirty years. There is a long, respected, and well-established perspective among China scholars of many disciplines, for example, economics, political science, and sociology, that Chinese reforms have been gradual and have been gradually progressive (in the sense of denoting motions of actions, not in the sense of denoting progressivity of policies, as in the "Progressive Era" in the United States). My own research rejects this view. My view is that the evidence is stronger in supporting the opposite view—that China initially started with some substantial and indeed even radical reforms (almost all of them in rural China), but the Chinese leadership reversed almost all of them in the early 1990s. (However, the leadership in the 1990s did undertake urban reforms, such as SOE privatization and WTO accession.) In the 2000s, under the Hu-Wen leadership, two things happened: 1) reversals of rural reforms were not stopped, but the anti-rural biases associated with the reform reversals were reduced and modified, and, 2) since 2008, there may have been some reversals of *urban* reforms. This is the idea behind the so-called *guojin mintui* (or "advancing state, retreating private economy").

Grafting this way of interpreting Chinese reforms in the last thirty years onto the various findings on income inequality produces the following postulation:

- The rural reforms in the 1980s improved rural income substantially and contributed to *some* leveling of the biggest component of China's overall income inequality—the rural-urban income gap;
- The reversals of rural reforms in the 1990s and the simultaneous acceleration of urban reforms contributed to the rising gap between rural and urban incomes by slowing down the equalizing effect of rural income on the one hand and accelerating the disequalizing effect of urban income on the other;
- It is harder to generalize about the Hu-Wen era in part because the research on both their policies and on income inequality during this era is partial, but their mixed policies could have led to some moderation of the rural-urban income gap and to rising within-group income inequality (especially since 2008).

That the leadership in the 1990s reversed rural reforms is not a consensus view among China scholars, and the issue is sufficiently complex that forming a consensus view on this issue is difficult. There are at least two sources of interpretative complication. One is whether or not the evidence on policy reform reversals is strong enough. The other issue is more of a "So what?" question. One can argue that even if reversals of rural reforms happened, they should not have had the kind or magnitude of effect as postulated here. After all, in the 1990s, the Chinese leadership undertook urban reforms, which could have completely offset or more than compensated for the negative effects of reform reversals in the rural area. One specific mechanism linking urban reforms with rural welfare is labor migration, which increased sharply beginning in the early 1990s.

The evidence on the policy reversals comes from voluminous policy documents going back to the late 1970s that I have examined carefully and presented in a number of publications.[32] (Together with another scholar, I have also conducted statistical research documenting the policy reversal. We found substantial evidence in support of the reversal hypothesis.[33]) Let me give an example. China scholars widely believe that informal finance played a critical role in funding the growth of China's private sector. However, the view is that this critical role of informal finance was limited geographically, to places such as Wenzhou, where the private sector flourished despite tight controls of finance by the government. Another, although more implied than stated, view is that informal finance is more of a phenomenon of the 1990s. This perspective is not stated explicitly, but it is true that the work on informal finance was mostly done in the late 1990s.[34]

In reality, documentary research shows that informal finance probably reached its peak in the late 1980s and was geographically distributed. It was active in Wenzhou, for sure, but also in Guizhou, Guangxi, and Jilin provinces. In fact, in the 1980s, informal finance, which is basically financial intermediation by private entrepreneurs, was not that informal. Let me quote two statements from that period below:

1) Chen Muhua: "In addition to the capital provided by the state banks and rural credit cooperatives, there are now various kinds of businesses with deposit-taking and lending operations. Non-governmental capital mobilization and non-governmental rural cooperatives have emerged. The various methods of financial mobilization have made a positive contribution to local economic development."[35]

2) Han Lei: "Rural areas need state-owned banks and credit cooperatives for finance but at the same time, under bank supervision, we need to allow the existence of private free lending and borrowing."[36]

These are not two liberal academic economists advocating reforms. Chen Muhua and Han Lei were, respectively, the governor of the People's Bank of China, China's central bank, and the chairman of Agricultural Bank of China, arguably the most important state-owned bank in China in the 1980s, given the pioneering rural reforms. Several bank documents from that era justified informal finance on competitive grounds—that they competed with and therefore helped improve the state-owned banks.

In the 1990s this encouraging stance on informal finance was reversed. In fact, informal finance was criminalized. (The restrictive stance on informal finance still persists to this day, although the enforcement has been varied.) What is interesting about Wenzhou is that the authorities in Wenzhou chose not to crack down on informal finance as hard as the rest of the country did. The so-called Wenzhou model is in fact nothing more or less than continuing with the model from the 1980s. We do not know enough about the political economy of Wenzhou at the time to explain why this region seemed to be able to continue with the reforms of the 1980s into the 1990s with apparent impunity, but the claim that informal finance is unique to Wenzhou is not supported by the data.

The "So what?" question is more complicated to address, and to some extent there is a judgment call that one has to make because we do not have the kind of data to answer the question definitively. The judgment call rests on two factors. One is the degree to which initial conditions—social, economic, and even cognitive—are complementary with policy reforms in rural vis-à-vis urban China. The other is the base effect—which China, rural or urban, has a bigger base along the relevant dimensions for which welfare and institutional change matter.

The base effect is straightforward and straightforwardly in favor of the view that rural China mattered more than urban China. In the 1980s and the 1990s, rural China had a bigger population share, and this is one reason why rural income growth was intrinsically equalizing. Thus, reversing reforms that affect negatively the welfare of more people in theory cannot be automatically offset by advancing reforms that affect a smaller number of people.

The initial conditions also matter. All things being equal, initial conditions in rural China were more conducive to the development of capitalism than those in urban China. Let me reproduce this formulation here:

A key insight here rests on some fundamental differences between rural China and urban China. Chinese capitalism is rural in origin and rural capitalism is highly entrepreneurial in a Schumpeterian sense. Urban China, by contrast, is far more state-controlled. The urban reforms since the early 1990s have led to the rise of a politically-connected, rent-seeking private sector (the most prominent example of which is the real estate private firms) whereas the reversals of rural reforms have been at the expense of a more arm's-length, entrepreneurial type of private sector. The effects of rural policy reversals go beyond rural China; they may have slowed down the overall pace of market transition.[37]

Conclusion

This chapter discusses some possible connections between two different policy episodes during the reform era and the patterns of income inequality.

In this aspect it is interesting to note the recent decline of Gini measures as estimated by NBS, from the peak level in 2008 at 0.491 to 0.474 in 2012. We should distinguish between the factors affecting the level estimates and the factors affecting the trend estimates of Gini. As pointed out before, the level estimates are heavily influenced by the sampling frame of the NBS household surveys, which is potentially problematic. However, given the same problematic sampling frame, the trend estimates can still be reliable (or at least they can be more reliable than the level estimates). Thus a legitimate question is why China has begun to experience some improvement in Gini in recent years, and whether the pro- or anti-rural policy framework proposed here can accommodate this development.

The answer is yes. One of the underreported achievements of the Hu-Wen era is that they did succeed in reversing some of the worst anti-rural policy biases from the 1990s. They began the process of rebuilding rural health community insurance schemes and reduced educational surcharges in rural schools. They also reversed the decline of a critical rural financial institution—rural credit cooperatives—and increased the supply of rural credits. Beginning in 2006 and 2007, the Hu-Wen leadership substantially reduced rural income taxes and then waived them altogether. Collectively these policy measures improved the growth rates of rural household income. Thus, the recent reported improvement in Gini is entirely consistent with these policy developments and with the framework proposed in this paper.

It is unlikely that the Hu-Wen policies completely erased or reversed China's antirural policy biases. One problem is that their policy adjustments are completely administrative in nature, unlike the 1980s, when the unleashing of the market forces contributed to a substantial moderation of urban policy biases. These policy adjustments are likely to produce one-time effects of relatively short duration. In the long run, to really solve the problem of high inequality requires not just policy adjustments but also institutional changes. Institutions such as rural *hukou*, state ownership of land, and restrictions on private entry into financial intermediation are likely to be a bigger contributing factor to inequality than the income distribution policies favored by the Chinese policymakers.

This is China's next big challenge, and it will—or will not—occur under the watch of Xi Jinping and Li Keqiang: how to move China away from its fundamentally statist economic and political institutions. So far, the evidence is that the Xi-Li leadership seems to believe that they can implement economic reforms while tightening the political grip of the Party. It is not at all clear that this combination of economic liberalism and political illiberalism is the right path toward institutional reforms. The most likely direction under the Xi-Li leadership is that income inequality will be treated as a social issue requiring redistribution of income and wealth rather than as an institutional issue, as argued in this chapter.

CHAPTER 6

Economic Rebalancing

Barry Naughton

There is broad agreement that China's economy is unbalanced, and many worry that these imbalances may mean that China's growth is unsustainable. It follows that "rebalancing" is desirable, and maybe even essential. But what exactly is "rebalancing"? The truth is that since there is no commonly accepted definition of a "balanced economy," there is also no precise definition of "rebalancing." Moreover, "unbalanced growth" is not necessarily a bad thing: any dynamic economy will experience periods of unbalanced development as it pushes to a higher level. In this chapter, I argue that the basic idea of rebalancing can be clarified, but that in order to understand the challenges facing the Chinese economy, the concept of rebalancing must also be expanded. In this broader sense, rebalancing includes the need for the Chinese economy to make an effective transition to the end of the hypergrowth era and to reduce the imbalances that concentrate power and resources in government-run sectors of the economy. The revitalization of market-oriented economic reform launched at the Third Plenum in November 2013 shows that policymakers are willing to take the first steps in this direction. However, the path is long and arduous, and if rebalancing is not successfully undertaken, the Chinese economy may face a rough transition.

A Narrow Definition of Rebalancing

When economists use the term *rebalancing*, they typically use it in a relatively narrow sense, to refer to two changes in the way in which output is used. As laid out in the "expenditure side" of the national accounts, gross domestic product (GDP) has only three uses: consumption, investment, and net exports. China's economy has been considered unbalanced because net exports, investment, or both, are unusually high, and therefore consumption is an unusually small share of total output. The U.S. economy is also sometimes considered to be unbalanced, for exactly the opposite reason: net exports are a large negative number (reflecting a large trade deficit), and investment is low, so that consumption is an unusually large share of total output (over 65 percent). These concepts are perfectly straightforward, but the problem is that there are no absolute yardsticks for these judgments. Who is to say that Americans consume too much? Who is to say that Chinese invest too much?

Only with respect to net exports (or external surplus) is there even a rough benchmark. The external surpluses of all the countries in the world, added together, must equal zero, so there has been a long history of discussion and practical policy disputes among countries and economists about what constitutes a large surplus or deficit. A basic rule of thumb that has emerged is that an external surplus substantially over 3 percent of GDP is considered "big," and there are periodically attempts to pressure countries to adjust once their surpluses reach 4 percent of GDP. There is no similar benchmark for the investment rate: there is no immediate logical constraint on how high an investment rate can be, and one country's investment rate doesn't constrain any other country. The normal constraint on investment is simply that people want to consume: living a better life means consuming more. As an empirical matter, very few countries in history have ever had investment ratios over 40 percent. The East Asian miracle economies have high investment rates (relative to historical precedent and other developing countries), but for Japan, Korea, and Taiwan this meant investment rates that peaked out in the 35–39 percent range. Thailand, Malaysia, and Singapore all experienced investment rates over 40 percent for two or three years at a time, but this was a short-lived phenomenon in the wake of large inflows of foreign investment. We can adopt 40 percent as a rule of thumb for high investment, in the same general sense that 3 percent is a benchmark for a large trade surplus, but with less clear normative value.

With these benchmarks in mind, we can turn to China's recent history of balance and imbalance, shown in Figure 6.1.[1] The story is particularly straightforward with respect to external imbalance. China's external surplus, traditionally of modest size, began to grow after 2004, and became very large, peaking at nearly 9 percent of GDP in 2007. This huge external surplus was not, of course, solely the fault of Chinese economic policy: this was the period when loose U.S. macroeconomic and regulatory policy was creating a massive housing bubble, and indirectly causing huge U.S. trade deficits, comparable in scale to the Chinese surplus. In any case, the Chinese surplus has come down substantially since 2007, and in 2012 was only 2.7 percent of GDP (according to Chinese national accounts). While China's bilateral surplus vis-à-vis the United States is still large, China's global surplus no longer exceeds the rule-of-thumb standard for a "big" surplus. So long as China can stabilize—or perhaps slightly reduce—this global surplus, the problem is not large.

The story on the investment side is quite different. China has long been a high-investment economy: indeed, during the Maoist period, it is no exaggeration to say that economic growth depended almost entirely on maintaining a high investment effort. The economic reform era at first led to lower investment rates: the fact that growth was maintained and even accelerated

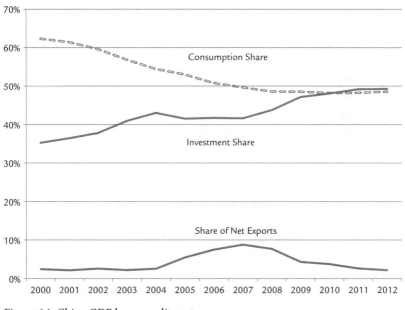

Figure 6.1. China GDP by expenditure type.
Source: NBS, *Zhongguo Tongji Zhaiyao 2013*.

during this period showed that reform brought enormous productivity benefits to the Chinese economy. From the late 1990s, China's investment rate started to climb again. By 2004, the investment rate had been pushed up to 43 percent, putting it unambiguously into the range of unusually high (and historically rare) investment rates. Over the next few years, as China's trade surplus widened and the investment rate remained high, the share of consumption in China's GDP steadily eroded, dropping below 50 percent in 2007. Concerns about unbalanced growth began to be articulated both in China and abroad.

Still, it is what happened *after* 2007 that is most remarkable. It turned out that the first round of imbalance had indeed been unsustainable, but the problem was with the U.S. economy. As the U.S. financial system foundered at the end of 2008 and world trade plunged, China responded with a dramatic stimulus program that pumped billions of dollars into the economy, both through direct government investment and loose credit policy that channeled billions to local governments and state-owned enterprises. The additional investment kept growth high and fully compensated for the decline in net exports, which otherwise would have reduced growth. As Figure 6.1 shows, the consumption share did not increase. Instead, the reduction in the external surplus was 100 percent offset by an increase in investment. The already high investment rate now climbed to new levels, unprecedented in world economic history: from 2009 through 2013, investment has averaged 48 percent over a five-year period, with no apparent tendency to decline. External imbalance became internal imbalance. Given that the external surplus is no longer "large," rebalancing today must mean tackling the extraordinarily high investment rate, and shifting to a growth strategy that gives higher priority to consumption growth.

China's High Investment Rate and Rebalancing

The extraordinary dependence of the Chinese economy on investment is evident in two respects. First, the share of output going to investment—consistently now over the past five years—far surpasses that of any other large economy in world history. The closest competition was provided by tiny, highly open Singapore, which rode massive foreign investment inflows to a total investment share averaging 42 percent over fifteen years from 1971 to

1985. By contrast, China's investment is virtually all generated and financed domestically. This aspect of China's economic experience is completely unprecedented. Second, for the past five years, China has depended on investment to sustain rapid growth. While growth has inched downward from just over 10 percent per year to just under 8 percent per year (between late 2009 and the end of 2013), this growth decline would have been much more rapid without the strong increases in investment. Thus, both as its steady state and as its growth engine, China displays an unprecedented dependence on investment.

Even a casual visitor to China can see the evidence of this economic structure. Shiny new airports mark even middle-sized cities, high-speed rail lines connect major urban nodes, and vast new housing estates continue to spring up everywhere. Industrial capacity has quadrupled and quintupled in many industries over the past decade. Often, these new facilities seem underutilized: airports with three concourses use only one, high-speed trains leave the station with many empty seats, and empty and sometimes half-finished housing blocks are a common sight.

By definition, the high investment share means that household consumption is a small share of total output. Household consumption was a little over 50 percent of GDP in the 1980s and 45 percent of GDP through most of the 1990s, but since 2008 has been only 35 percent of GDP. (Government consumption has ranged between 13 and 16 percent of GDP, recently near the bottom of that range.) Like the investment ratio, this household consumption ratio is unprecedented: there is no large economy that has ever consumed such a small portion of its total output. In this sense, China's economy is very unbalanced indeed.

However, it is important to clarify what this means. While consumption is "low" as a proportion of total output, consumption is *not* low relative to consumption in the past. Indeed, over the past two decades, China's consumption has grown faster—much faster—than that of virtually any other country in the world. Rapid economic growth has enabled rapid consumption growth, even as consumption as a share of GDP has inched downward. In other words, over the past few decades, it is not only China's investment rate that has been high, China's growth rate has also been extraordinarily high. From the beginning of economic reforms in 1978 until 2003, China's GDP grew at an average annual rate of 9.6 percent. Then, after 2003, as economic imbalances worsened and the Global Financial Crisis hit, China's

GDP growth rate . . . accelerated. From 2003 through 2012, growth inched upward, hitting an average annual rate of 10.4 percent. With this super-heated overall growth, consumption growth remained strong, running at 9.2 percent per year between 2003 and 2012.

The relationship between these numbers is more than just an arithmetical curiosity. The truth is that China's growth rate has been high *because* it has made a massive investment effort. It is not simply that China today has an unbalanced economy, it is that China has consistently followed an unbalanced growth strategy for the past two decades. From the mid-1990s onward, China has intentionally stimulated investment, built out its infrastructure ahead of demand, and driven the economy forward through the processes of industrialization and urbanization. In this sense, China's extreme imbalances after 2007 have simply been the logical extension of China's growth strategy up until 2007. While increases in investment were used to drive growth in the earlier period, an extra dose of investment was used counter-cyclically during the Global Financial Crisis (GFC) to sustain these extraordinarily high growth rates in the face of adverse external conditions. China is thus undeniably an unbalanced economy, but most people would say that the unbalanced growth strategy has worked rather well for China.

We must keep these relationships in mind as we consider the question of rebalancing. Given that China's external account is roughly in balance, a more "balanced" Chinese economy means only that the external surplus does not again begin to grow, which means that expansion of net exports will be a small contributor to China's overall growth rate in the coming years. The bulk of rebalancing would then mean a reduction of the rate of investment from "extremely high" to simply "high." This would imply a reduction in the total investment rate of perhaps 10 percentage points of GDP, from 48 percent in 2012 to 38 percent, which is at the high end of "normal" high-investment economies. Assuming that the external surplus stabilizes at 2 percent of GDP, China's total consumption would be 60 percent of GDP, and if government consumption remains stable at 13 percent of GDP, household consumption would reach 47 percent of GDP. In comparative terms, China's consumption share would still be at the low end of the spectrum, and would simply have returned to the level of the late 1990s. Nevertheless, such rebalancing would imply a massive shift of resources. About a trillion U.S. dollars—six trillion RMB—would be shifted to household consumption, increasing overall consumption by about 30 percent.

This is implicitly what many people have in mind when they discuss the need to "rebalance" the Chinese economy. Why would you want to do this? The benefits of a trillion dollars of increased consumption would be considerable: many people in China are poor or lower-middle income. Increases in their consumption would contribute enormously to human welfare. Moreover, consumption would use much less energy and generate much less pollution than an equivalent amount of investment. And after all, there is no purpose to economic growth beyond consumption, so rebalancing in this sense means enjoying the benefits of growth sooner, rather than later. The change is good in itself.

And yet, there are doubts. In the first place, if the current trajectory is sustainable, it doesn't make sense to disrupt it. If high investment could sustain GDP and consumption growth at 8 to 10 percent per year, it would only take a few years to reach the same absolute level of consumption anyway. If past relationships were to prevail, an extra ten percentage points of GDP in investment would lead to an extra 2.5 percentage points of growth: it would only take four years to make up for the foregone consumption.[2] More broadly, a few economists point out that the current, rather casual way of referring to rebalancing implicitly treats investment as a waste: when people say that China "invests too much," they essentially treat the "excess" portion of investment as wasted output. In fact, however, investment is a key component of growth, not just in China, but in every economy. When we discuss policies that would lower investment, we need to exercise the utmost caution.[3] Moreover, while the basic arithmetic relationships among output, investment, and growth can tell us a lot, they can't tell the whole story. We need to look more broadly at the history of the economy and the structural factors that drive specific phases of growth.

A Golden Age of High Investment and Rapid Growth

The command economy, in the Maoist era, was an economy of imbalance. It relied on investment almost entirely to drive growth, and sacrificed productivity growth in the process. One of the great achievements of the early reform period (in the late 1970s and early 1980s) was to reduce imbalances as the reform process began. Investment rates came down, but productivity growth more than compensated for slower investment. Fewer new assets were created, but the existing assets were used more efficiently. As a result, the economy was able to produce more consumption goods without sacrificing growth. During the subsequent decades, investment rates gradually began to increase, but crucially, the ability of the economy to generate steady gains in efficiency also remained strong. As market reforms were generally successful, and as Chinese imported cutting-edge practices and technologies from abroad, productivity gains continued to support rapid growth. China achieved the best of both worlds: an economy driven both by high investment and by rapid productivity growth. It is not surprising, then, that China's growth has been miraculous: China has grown faster, longer than any economy in history.

In retrospect, three major structural factors supported this growth. First, in common with previous Asian "miracle economies," China grew fast in an environment of abundant labor. With falling mortality, China enjoyed the "demographic dividend," of having an unusually large share of the population at working age, and a low dependency burden. Under these circumstances, the amount of new capital provided by investment was the key driver of growth: as the machines and structures were put in place, there were plenty of farmers ready to move to factory jobs, and as they did so, productivity and total output grew. Investment was the key facilitator of this process of structural change. As rural-to-urban migration became large, China's economy shifted into overdrive.

Second, in China's "follower" economy, there were myriad opportunities for transplanting business models, technologies, and infrastructure patterns from developed countries. Businesses were rewarded for moving fast, and planners could adapt infrastructure solutions from developed countries. China built out grids of highways and electric power, and later airports and high-speed rail. The basic pattern and scale of these infrastructure solutions were copied wholesale from developed countries. Chinese policymakers argued that it was more important to build these networks quickly than it was to have each node in the network appropriately adapted to local demand. They were right: China built out infrastructure ahead of demand and drove the growth process. Moreover, during the course of the 1990s, the institutional set-up was adapted, in myriad ways, to support the high investment imperative. The system delivered investment, and investment delivered growth.

Third, and finally, a whole series of new sources of demand developed during the 2000s, well beyond what most economists had anticipated. China developed a much "heavier" industrial structure during the 2000s because of two dramatic changes in the structure of demand: the housing boom and the restructuring of China's export economy. Both of these changes in the structure of demand should be recognized as imperfectly foreseen outcomes of the reform process China undertook in the 1990s. The housing boom developed after the privatization of urban housing at the end of the 1990s. Housing construction is itself investment, and it also created new demand for capital-intensive steel, cement, and aluminum industries which expanded enormously, generating a further round of heavy industry investment. The housing boom affected both saving behavior and investment. Chinese households increasingly began saving in order to afford housing, investment in construction soared, and derivative investment in supporting heavy industries increased as well.

China's foreign trade changed dramatically after membership in the World Trade Organization (WTO) began to phase in after 2001. WTO membership brought a wholesale reorganization of China's traded goods sectors. Liberalization did not so much produce a flood of imports as it did a flood of new ways to produce industrial goods cheaply and efficiently. With imported parts and components, China's industry cut costs dramatically. Export growth accelerated to 30 percent per year after 2003, and this was only part of the story. The other part of the story was rapid import substitution, concentrated in the machinery industry. China imported fewer foreign machines, and greatly expanded its domestic machinery industry. Construction machinery firms such as Sany and Zoomlion developed thriving businesses, listed on overseas stock markets, and made overseas acquisitions. It is, of course, normal for an economy to develop new, more sophisticated heavy industrial sectors as it begins to move into middle-income status, as China did in the 2000s. This industrial maturation is often accompanied by higher investment levels. This was seen clearly in Japan (in the late 1960s and early 1970s) and Korea (in the 1990s after, arguably, a false start in the late 1970s). However, since China had such a strong heavy industry legacy coming out of the Maoist period, it was not clear in advance whether or not a similar shift to a "heavier" industrial structure would take place in China during the 2000s. In fact, it did.

These elements of the story of China's "unbalanced growth strategy" provide us additional insight into China's current challenges. In the first place—and most broadly—when we look at something as general as the rate of investment, we are looking at a broad, synthetic indicator of multiple changes in an economy. The economy's investment rate is not an *instrument* that is under the direct control of policymakers. Rather, it is an *outcome*, the comprehensive reflection of a whole series of macroeconomic, budgetary, and regulatory policies. Investment levels are the result of decisions made by households and foreign and domestic businesses, as well as by government. The investment level reflects the incentives of businesses to invest in specific projects, and also their profitability in recent operations. It reflects the incentives of households to consume today, or to invest in housing, and to spread that consumption over a prolonged period.

When we look back at the Chinese experience since the mid-1990s, we see that the increase in the investment rate has not been *primarily* the result of top-down government policies. Rather, the spread of market forces has opened up new areas in the dynamic Chinese economy that have elicited new investment. The unbalanced growth strategy has primarily been an unanticipated consequence of successful market-oriented reforms.[4] To be sure, Chinese governments both at the central and local levels also stepped up their investment in infrastructure. Thus, government actors also deserve some credit for the dynamic growth strategy. But overall, the increase of investment was the result of increasingly market-oriented actors responding to real incentives. As a result, the Chinese economy was able to sustain the best of both worlds: rising real investment accompanied by sustained high productivity growth. This "explains" why Chinese economic growth has been so rapid. Clearly, high investment has been a positive contributor to the Chinese growth miracle thus far.

Is It Sustainable?

In this author's view, none of the three structural factors that sustained the combination of high investment and rapid productivity growth are likely to be continued over the next decade. First, as I discuss below, demographic and labor force characteristics are changing rapidly, spelling the end of China's "demographic dividend," and signaling an inevitable reduction in the growth rate. Second, China is moving partially out of the "followership" position, particularly when it comes to building infrastructure and developing industries. Third, China is no longer in the "sweet spot" of combining spreading marketization with government infrastructure construction. Put together, these changes mean that China will almost certainly have to transition to a slower growth path, and one with a lower steady-state investment rate. In short, China will be forced to rebalance. If this process is undertaken successfully, China will continue to be one of the most dynamic economies in the world, growing at a sustained 5–6 percent per year. But the transition is difficult and fraught with uncertainties: indeed, it might turn out to be driven by economic crisis. However, policymakers have an opportunity to get out in front of this change, if they are able to adopt policies that lead to further economic reforms and accommodate a graceful shift to a lower investment rate and growth rate.

The Inevitable End of the Hypergrowth Phase

Asia since World War II has seen repeated "growth miracles," in which GDP has grown at over 8 percent per year for more than twenty years. Japan was the first of these; China is the most recent. Although China's growth has been exceptional—even faster and longer than previous growth miracles—it has also shared many features of previous episodes of hypergrowth. Hypergrowth occurs while economies are reaping their "demographic dividend"— that is, when the working-age population is growing more rapidly than the population overall, and dependency rates are declining. Under these conditions, economies can move into hypergrowth if they can facilitate rapid structural change, that is, labor moving out of agriculture and into more productive industrial and urban service jobs. To support this transformation, two things are needed: a large accommodative market that can absorb rapid increases in output; and an investment rate that is high enough to equip new workers with the machines, factories, roads, and housing that they need. All the East Asian miracle economies, including China, brought these growth components together, typically through an export-oriented development strategy. Once in place, these components can sustain extremely rapid growth for more than two decades. Then, as these positive structural conditions fade, growth miracles also come to an end. The changes that ultimately bring the end of the hypergrowth phase are gradual. However, in all of the previous cases, the end of the hypergrowth phase has been rather abrupt, and caught many people by surprise. A growth slowdown was triggered by some external event, which seemed unique and transient, but after the passing of the event, the economy never resumed the hypergrowth dynamic. Figure 6.2 shows the basic contours of the hypergrowth era for Japan, Korea, and Taiwan.[5] Japan's growth miracle ended abruptly in 1973;

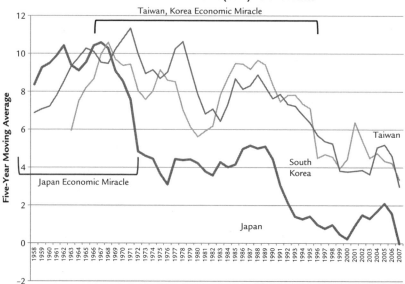

Figure 6.2. East Asian GDP growth rates.
Source: World Bank, World Development Indicators. Online Database. Access at
http://databank.worldbank.org/data/ or http://data.worldbank.org/data-catalog
/world-development-indicators.

Korea and Taiwan not quite as abruptly, but just as decisively, in the mid-
1990s.

This process is most obvious—and also most relevant to China—with
respect to changing conditions in the labor market. Up through the first
years of the twenty-first century, China experienced rapid growth in the
population at working age, augmented with extremely rapid rural-to-urban
migration. Labor supply was therefore inexhaustible. But after around 2004,
the demand for unskilled labor began to increase more rapidly than supply,
with the result that the wages of unskilled, and especially migrant, workers
began to increase rapidly. Feng Lu of Peking University has compiled available studies into a consolidated series for migrant worker wages: he finds that
between 2003 and 2012, real migrant wages (corrected for inflation) increased
at an average annual rate of 10.8 percent, so that 2012 wages were almost
exactly two and one-half times what they had been in 2003.[6] To some extent,
this rapid increase reflects the earlier "imbalance" discussed above: the ex-

traordinary rise of Chinese exports in the mid-2000s began to push up migrant wages after a decade of very slow growth. The increase in wages was
thus a natural part of the rebalancing process that took place at mid-decade.
However, this increase in wages has been sustained in subsequent years,
notwithstanding much slower growth of Chinese exports.

This pattern suggests to many Chinese economists that China has passed
through a so-called "Lewis turning point." The Lewis turning point refers to
a point in the development process when abundant supplies of "surplus"
labor are exhausted, and wage increases are necessary to draw workers out of
the agricultural sector (that is, the supply of labor becomes less than perfectly
elastic).[7] According to the original Lewis model, these changes primarily
reflect changing conditions in the rural economy: as agriculture becomes
more productive, and most of the young workers have already left the countryside, there is no longer a pool of "surplus labor" willing to move to the
cities or export zones. Changes of this sort occur in all successful developing
economies. Clearly they have occurred in China: in many accessible rural
areas, all the young people have left, nonagricultural jobs are available nearby,
and older people are not willing to leave the farm. These labor force changes
force broader structural changes in the economy.

However, these changes will be especially dramatic in China because
they correspond with an additional set of demographic changes. The age
structure of China's population (shown in Figure 6.3) is unusual, primarily
because of China's draconian birth control policies. Figure 6.3 shows the size
of each population cohort in the year 2010, starting from the bottom, with
children less than a year old, and proceeding upward to those one hundred
years old.[8] To simplify the story considerably, the figure shows a very large
proportion of the population at working age, and particularly large birth
cohorts between the ages of twenty and fifty (in 2010). This pattern exists
because China began a massive baby boom in the early 1960s, and then, after
1990, the absolute number of births dropped substantially. Looking backward, China got an extra growth impetus—a demographic dividend—as this
huge group went to work between 1980 and 2010. This period of rapid labor
force growth is now over. From now on, nearly as many workers will retire
every year as enter the labor force. By 2020, at the very latest, China's labor
force will be declining significantly.

Exactly when the labor force begins to decline depends on when older
workers retire. The legal retirement age in China is sixty for men and fifty-

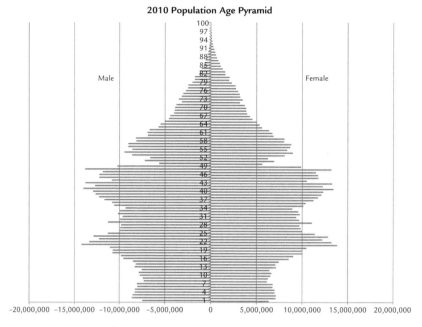

Figure 6.3. 2010 Population age pyramid.
Source: China 2010 Census, Summary Volume, Table 3-1, "Population by Age and Gender."

five for women, but in practice people retire much earlier. In 2002, the average age of retirement from formal sector jobs was fifty-three for both sexes combined. Although there have been discussions on raising the retirement age, the idea is extremely unpopular, and government officials have repeatedly declared they are not contemplating this step.[9] According to the National Bureau of Statistics, the population at working age (fifteen to fifty-nine years) has already begun to shrink, declining 3.45 million in 2012.[10] This small reduction (less than 0.4 percent) may or may not signal the beginning of a declining labor force. But what is absolutely clear is that the era of rapid labor force growth has ended, and China is now in a transition phase that will, within a few years, lead to a consistently declining labor force. The demographic dividend is over, and as China's population begins aging, policymakers will have to cope with a demographic deficit.

While the "Lewis turning point" and the end of the demographic dividend are related, they are not at all the same thing. The first predominantly reflects the relationship between the rural economy and the rural labor supply, while the second reflects the growth of different age cohorts and the relationship among those cohorts. The two things do not necessarily coincide in time. The declining size of the labor force has generally come *after* the slowdown from the hypergrowth era, which is commonly associated with the Lewis turning point. This was the case in Japan, where the slowdown from the high growth period occurred in 1973, but the labor force continued to grow until 1998 (twenty-five years later). In Korea, the slowdown from the high growth period occurred in 1997, but the labor force continued to grow until 2012 (fifteen years later). China, however, is facing the Lewis turning point and beginning to exit the high growth era, but is already facing a declining labor force. These two labor force shifts are occurring at the same time.

These structural changes will have an especially profound effect on the supply of nonskilled labor, because they correspond with changes in the education system that are drawing more young people into university education. In 2013, and for each of the next five years, about seven million middle-school students will go to university or technical schools, and about the same number of students, seven million, will graduate from these tertiary institutions. This is a very large proportion of the fifteen to sixteen million total young people in each of those annual age cohorts. Labor force entrants with less than a college education will be eight to nine million per year, already much less than the number of less-educated workers in their fifties who are retiring. In other words, China's less-skilled labor force is already shrinking in absolute terms, and at a fairly rapid pace. With supply reduced, wages for unskilled workers have been increasing robustly over the past few years, even as overall growth slows, and exports (which rely heavily on unskilled labor) struggle. Conversely, the economy is under pressure to provide jobs for the rapidly growing supply of college-educated workers.

How does this affect the challenge of rebalancing? As argued above, during the period of rapid labor force growth, maximizing investment was a successful policy because it equipped the largest possible number of workers to shift into new occupations. Today, however, the challenge is completely different. It is no longer particularly important to provide new factory jobs for unskilled workers, and, in fact, those jobs are now starting to decrease. However, a new challenge is to provide high-skilled jobs to China's rapidly growing group of college graduates. Of course, it takes investment to create jobs for these people as well, but the challenge is in discovering which new sectors will expand, defining the new types of jobs that will be created, and responding to new sources of demand. The quantity of investment is less important, and the ability to match specific sources and supplies of investment is becoming much more important. Alternatively stated, it is no longer possible to copy export industries already familiar from earlier developing economies. Instead, China's demographic changes are leading to the end of a phase of hypergrowth. As that phase ends, China will also cease to be a "follower economy" to the extent that it was in the past, and will be forced to upgrade the quality of its jobs and the quality of its investment. Jobs in high-tech sectors and sophisticated services do not necessarily require the same value of investment as factory jobs: however, they are far more demanding in terms of the sophisticated business models needed to survive in a highly competitive global environment. Adjusting to a different, less-unbalanced growth strategy will be essential.

Looking at the same issue from a slightly different perspective, we see that in forerunner miracle economies the end of hypergrowth is accompanied by a reduction in investment rates from their highest levels at the peak of the hypergrowth period. Some of this no doubt reflects the life cycle changes associated with the demographic structure changes we have just been discussing: young, high-saving households mature into older, dissaving households. But more broadly, saving and investment rates reflect complex adjustments to the whole range of economic institutions and structural opportunities. That means that *if* the investment rate was appropriate for the high growth phase—as it seems to have been—then a lower overall investment rate is almost certainly more appropriate now. China's shift into a middle-income economy brings new challenges and new demands for rebalancing.

End of the "Sweet Spot": Searching for a New Government-Market Accommodation

Considering the long sweep of Chinese economic development in the 1990s and 2000s, I argued above that the spread of markets, combined with Chinese government investment policy, led to the best of both worlds: market-based efficiencies were reaped, while the government built out infrastructure ahead of demand. This happy combination solidified China's hypergrowth phase because it allowed growth from more inputs (capital) as well as higher efficiency. However, this happy confluence of policies has now disappeared.

In the first place, the emergence of an unbalanced economy after 2004—most obvious in the rapidly expanding external surplus—was accompanied by a shift in China's macropolicy orientation. As Lardy has argued,[11] the emergence of imbalances after 2004 was associated with the rise of financial repression. Policymakers contained inflationary pressures to a certain extent, but at the cost of capping nominal interest rates below the rate of inflation, penalizing savers and forcing banks to allocate loans to favored borrowers. The financial system was in a less favorable position to efficiently allocate credit to investment projects. These emerging problems were greatly intensified after the government launched its massive stimulus program in 2009. To counteract the effects of the Global Financial Crisis, credit was pumped into numerous projects, particularly local government projects. During 2009, overall credit expanded by ten trillion yuan, over a third of GDP. Inevitably, credit was pumped into projects of relatively poor quality.

A massive stimulus program like this has both benefits and costs. As noted above, the stimulus program allowed China to escape the worst impact of the Global Financial Crisis, and the Chinese growth rate remained high. The cost, however, was the creation of a large number of unfunded investment projects. Local governments set up local government financing vehicles (LGFV) to borrow from state-owned banks and rapidly launch new investment projects. These LGFVs quickly ran up large debts: by one official account they owed 7.38 trillion RMB at the end of 2009 (almost exactly half of that year's GDP), and other estimates are even higher. The debt total has continued to grow, albeit more slowly in the years since.[12] But this is not a sustainable funding model: according to an extensive survey of these LGFVs, only about 10 percent of local funding platforms are able to repay loans from revenues raised directly from their investment projects; the large majority expect to repay loans from the increased value of land sold in the wake of those investment projects.[13] China's overall government debt is only moderate, so the government has the ability to restructure these flimsy investment vehicles, but doing so will require time, resources, and careful attention from policymakers.

How does this affect the challenge of rebalancing? The answer is that in the 1990s and early 2000s, government support for investment was consistent with spreading marketization. In the recent five-year period—the period when growth has been driven by investment to an unprecedented degree—government investment promotion has begun to interfere with marketization of the economy. Thus, while increasing investment coincided with increasing productivity in the earlier period, this is much less likely to be true now. Indeed, the opposite is more likely: high investment was used to prop up short-term growth, and also corresponded with an increase in direct government intervention in market forces. As a result, a reversal—or at least a slowing—of productivity gains will likely depress growth rates. These problems are then likely to spill over into financial markets. The presence of these large and fragile investment vehicles will inevitably draw from future resources. While misallocated investments mainly represent wasted resources (a sunk cost), restructuring failed investments requires resources, and these deferred costs will eventually have to be paid. Similar effects are evident in many other sectors of the economy: increased government intervention will have limited the impact of spreading marketization, inhibiting robust efficiency gains. No longer will Chinese policymakers have the best of both worlds: instead, they have overdue bills that need to be paid.

Conclusion

The challenges of development change as a country enters middle-income status, but they do not necessarily become easier. Examining the experience of earlier developing East Asian economies provides some clear lessons for China. The hypergrowth phases of these earlier developers came to an end. Their slowdowns occurred following long-run structure changes and in the wake of gradually changing conditions, but the actual slowdown occurred rather abruptly in each economy, and in response to apparently unrelated external shocks. Moreover, in the face of their growth slowdowns, the earlier developing East Asian economies have typically responded by adopting policies that are less top down, more open, more market oriented, and more democratic than those they adopted during the hypergrowth period. Industrial policies are still adopted, but with a "lighter" touch. As these countries close in on the technological frontier, they seed their high-tech sectors, rather than trying to steer the entire economy. So far, such a movement has not been evident in China: indeed, if anything, China has moved in the opposite direction over the past decade.

Rebalancing, then, presents both a long-term and a short-term challenge. In the long term, rebalancing will ultimately be part of China's evolution into a middle-income society. It is difficult to see how China can assume technological leadership, support a more prosperous and diverse society, and develop a healthy and sustainable environment without a substantial economic rebalancing. In the short term, there are two immediate worries. First, if China *doesn't* take steps to rebalance the economy—that is, if China tries too hard to keep the growth rate high—it risks the creation and continuous re-creation of numerous asset bubbles, flimsy financial structures, and investment projects of declining quality. Such policies increase the risk of a significant financial crisis in the economy and increase the size of the shock when the inevitable day of reckoning comes. Second, in recent years, China's technology and income policies have moved in the direction of increased direct government steerage. For example, the government has moved aggressively to support the development of "strategic emerging industries," thus stepping up government intervention in the most dynamic sectors of the economy. Will the emphasis on a top-down, state-directed program of innovation, combined with state control of large swathes of the economy, actually end up retarding China's essential graduation toward an innovative, diverse, and resilient economy? If so, this will again retard the adjustment to a more balanced economy and create more difficult-to-manage shocks when larger adjustments are ultimately required.

Xi Jinping and Li Keqiang, China's top leaders since 2012, used the occasion of the November 2013 Third Plenum of the 18th Central Committee to relaunch programs of market-oriented reform. Particularly striking was the creation of a special Leadership Small Group (chaired by Xi Jinping) to design, coordinate, and supervise the implementation of reforms. This clearly shows that the leadership has the desire to address the long-run structural and institutional problems that cause the problems of economic imbalance, and have committed substantial political capital to the effort. As Premier Li Keqiang has repeatedly emphasized, successful reforms will create a "reform dividend," which is the only way to replace the disappearing demographic dividend. More broadly, a reform dividend would provide new sources of growth that could sustain development during the difficult transition when traditional drivers of growth are winding down. Thus, economic reform could be the best way to carry out a program of economic rebalancing, stabilizing growth at a lower, but more sustainable, level, and creating a new dynamic that would substitute for the current overreliance on investment.

At the same time, the actual reform program has barely begun, and success can hardly be assumed. In the short run, the imperatives of reform could actually work against prompt rebalancing of the economy. Reformers need to bring new groups of "winners" on board, decentralize some control of decision making, and open up sectors of the economy that have been closed off to domestic and foreign private businesses. All of these changes might increase investment in the short run, while households might "wait and see" before increasing their consumption. In the short run, then, reform is not equivalent to rebalancing, and China's leaders, at least initially, have emphasized reform far more than rebalancing. If successful, though, market-oriented reforms will ultimately lead to a longer-run rebalancing of the economy. This is because successful reforms would reduce the concentration of economic resources in selected, often state-run, sectors of the economy, and create a more "level playing field." In such an outcome, a smaller total volume of investment resources would likely be distributed more efficiently (and in smaller quantities) among newer, more dynamic sectors of the economy. This would enable China to transition to a slower, but more sustainable, balanced growth process. Without this, it is difficult to envision China's economy moving up beyond middle-income status and into the top tier of global economies.

CHAPTER 7

The Challenge of Corruption

Melanie Manion

Scholars who study corruption in China generally agree that it is now far more extensive than in the Maoist era, that its characteristics have evolved over the past three decades of reform, and that it is a serious problem both politically and economically, notwithstanding China's spectacular growth record. Chinese scholars and top Chinese leaders also broadly air these views. There is no consensus, however, as to whether corruption in China is intensifying or whether the regime's anticorruption reform effort has been at all successful (or even sincere). Similarly, there is no consensus as to whether corruption in China can be significantly reduced without fundamental regime change. For sure, we lack good measures of corruption (and, therefore, good data). On some of these issues, our assessments may largely reflect fundamentally held perspectives on Chinese politics and the Chinese political economy. As to whether the frequency, scope, and seriousness of corrupt acts have increased in recent years, officially and informally revealed corruption does suggest to me an increase along all dimensions. At the same time, my best guess is that the regime is sincere in its anticorruption effort, even as the effort seems highly flawed. In this chapter, I focus mainly on issues around which consensus exists. In particular, I focus on changes in forms of corruption in the post-Mao (and especially the post-Deng) era. I also weigh in on the issue of anticorruption reform.

From a comparative perspective, looking at Transparency International scores, for example, China ranks as a fairly (but not spectacularly) corrupt country; in most years it is in the bottom third of all countries ranked. On a scale from 0 to 100, with higher scores signifying less-perceived corruption, experts now give China a score of 39, roughly the same as India (at 36) but significantly better than Russia (at 28) and Ukraine (at 26).[1] Looking specifically at corruption vulnerability in defense agencies, experts give China a grade of D-.[2] Post-Mao leaders in Beijing publicly acknowledged corruption as a serious (indeed, existential) threat to Communist Party rule as early as 1982 and as recently as 2013. Corruption's harm is reflected in the diversion of state revenues to private pockets, although the magnitude of losses is impossible to estimate accurately. Estimates range from 2–3 percent to a staggering 15 percent of GDP for the late 1990s,[3] for example, but the high estimates include categories that are not strictly unlawful uses of official power. More to the point, the crux of the corruption challenge is more political than economic. Stories of venal (or just stupendously licentious) officials spread like wildfire on the Chinese social media, prompting the Chinese blog *Danwei* to pronounce 2012 the year of "trial by *weibo*" (the Chinese hybrid of Twitter and Facebook) for officials.

The chapter begins with a summary of relevant conclusions from an empirical comparative literature on corruption and a survey of the ways scholars measure Chinese corruption. Next I briefly contextualize contemporary Chinese corruption historically. Then I turn to the core of the chapter: the current challenge of corruption. I associate current forms of corruption with new reforms and then select for more pointed discussion four types of corruption that seem to pose especially serious challenges: sale of official positions, judicial corruption, real estate profiteering, and financial corruption. In the next section I assess the regime's anticorruption efforts. I conclude by speculating about prospects for successfully meeting the challenge of corruption, especially in light of what we know about correlates of corruption generally. First, however, I offer a straightforward definition for an elusive concept: following others, corruption here is the use of public power for private gain.[4]

Correlates and Measurement

As Treisman concludes in his survey of empirical cross-national research on the problem of corruption,[5] not only are the methodological issues difficult to solve, but also (and more importantly): "There is no widely accepted theory on which to base an empirical model. What theory there is relates to the micro level—an exchange is imagined between an individual citizen and an official—and the terms of this exchange are traced by sometimes tortuous logic to characteristics of countries on which data are available."[6] In this characterization, Treisman ignores forms of corruption, common in China as elsewhere, that are abuses of public power to prey on public resources and do not involve exchanges at all; that would not fundamentally change the conclusion, however. Treisman's strategy is to eschew theory altogether and focus on what we know about corruption's correlates. This seems a sensible analytical lever to adopt as a point of departure here too, situating the problem of corruption in contemporary China in the context of relevant knowledge about its correlates in other countries. I postpone consideration of theory until later on. Since 1995, most of the cross-national empirical research on corruption uses scores derived from subjective perceptions (usually by surveys of risk analysts) of corruption, but some headway has been made to survey ordinary citizens and firm managers on experiences of corruption. Data of the first sort are available for a larger number of countries for a greater number of years (and so are more widely used), but it is worth noting that conclusions from the two sorts of data can differ.[7] With this caveat, what relevant knowledge from cross-national empirical research can we bring to bear on the issue of corruption in China?

Three economic correlates and two political correlates seem especially relevant to the case of China. First, greater economic development is associated with less corruption. This is a very robust relationship.[8] It seems to operate partly through the effect of political variables, particularly democratic institutions and media freedoms, rather than, for example, socioeconomic variables like urbanization or a more highly educated mass public. The causal pathway is probably from economic development to lower corruption. Second, competition achieved through markets and trade openness is associated with less corruption.[9] Third, greater state intervention in the economy, in the form of state ownership or bureaucratic red tape through many state-controlled permits and approvals, for example, is associated with more corruption.[10] As to political correlates, a greater number of political rights is associated with less corruption, but the relationship is complicated: small increases have little effect in democracies or in soft authoritarian states, but they have significant effect in more strongly autocratic polities.[11] Finally, and quite remarkably, I think, especially when considering implications for China, press freedoms are even more important than political freedoms in their association with less corruption.[12]

These correlates from cross-national research help to place China's corruption in perspective. China's coincidence of rapid growth and high corruption is unusual, although, as Wedeman shows, not unique or truly puzzling.[13] Accepting that all corruption is overdetermined, China's corruption nonetheless follows some more general patterns. Specifically, we should not be surprised to find widespread corruption in a nondemocracy where the state continues to play an important role in the economy, where market competition is tempered by political intervention, and where press freedoms are greatly limited. I return briefly to these correlates in my conclusion, where I consider prospects for China's anticorruption efforts.

Turning from correlates to measurement of corruption, the methodologies adopted to measure corruption in China differ from the subjective and experiential survey-based approaches used in most cross-national empirical research. Careful empirical research uses the revealed rate of corruption in enforcement statistics (e.g., cases of criminal corruption filed by procuratorates) as only a point of departure. Scholars adjust figures to take into account changes in definition of crimes and in enforcement intensity.[14] Both Guo and Wedeman go further.[15] They collect press accounts of corruption involving senior officials, code the cases, and subject the data to descriptive statistical analysis to tease out patterns. For example, Guo collects Chinese press accounts of 594 cases of corruption to determine latency periods (years between the corrupt act and its discovery) and to calculate cumulative corruption (stock of corruption cases). Wedeman collects accounts reproduced in LexisNexis. In addition to Guo's measures, Wedeman examines the emerging rate of corruption (the year that individuals who are subsequently caught actually committed the corrupt act). Despite the transparency and systematic nature of these efforts, the problem of bias in the data subjected to analysis remains fundamental.

There are also more indirect (and also imprecise) estimations that can inform our understanding of the magnitude of corruption in China. For example, Wang attempts to correct the understatement of incomes in the 2009 official National Bureau of Statistics household income survey.[16] He concludes that total hidden income in China amounts to about 30 percent of GDP, most of it in the hands of the top 10 percent of urban households. Even the simple report in *Zhejiang Online* of 1.2 million "naked officials" (i.e., officials with immediate family members residing overseas, sometimes as foreign nationals) in China in 2013 is somewhat informative, as this status is often associated with transferring corrupt gains out of China.[17]

Whatever the actual magnitude of corruption, it is certainly a serious political issue, because Chinese view it as widespread. Corruption is always found at (or near) the top of the "hot issues" troubling ordinary citizens, business executives, and government officials themselves, all polled routinely in recent decades.[18]

Historical Context

Corrupt practices were (obviously) not new to China in the 1980s. Scholars describe "commissions" and "managerial fees" in the Maoist era, used by industrial enterprises in relationships of supply, procurement, sales promotion, and contracting, for example.[19] Corruption was also not uncommon in the countryside, where production team leaders concealed grain or sold produce on the black market to boost collective consumption.[20] Both forms represent what Lu characterizes as "organizational corruption."[21] In the 1980s, however, there was an increase in the volume of corruption as well as the appearance of new forms of corruption. At the same time, the increased monetization of the Chinese economy made corruption more widely visible and accessible to more players.

Corruption in China in the 1980s was a policy outcome, the unintended consequence of economic reform policies.[22] Prominent examples are: arbitrage by officials taking advantage of the two-track pricing system, capture of rents by party and government agencies engaging in (sometimes illegal, sometimes only semilegitimate) business activities, predatory exactions by township and county governments, and asset stripping in state-owned enterprises.[23]

The New Challenge of Corruption

As is the case for the 1980s, there is a broad consensus in the literature that different types of economic reforms generated opportunities for different forms of corruption after the mid-1990s, forms that we do not find (or, at least, can hardly find) in the 1980s. Further, not only are the forms substantively different, but also corruption after the mid-1990s involves more senior officials and larger (real) sums than in the 1980s.

The new forms, senior players, and large sums probably all exacerbate the challenge to the regime, with new direct and indirect effects on regime legitimacy. Wedeman convincingly argues that the new forms present a bigger obstacle to economic development, compared to the "predatory plunder and petty corruption" of the 1980s.[24] Indirectly, then, as economic performance is a key prop for the regime's legitimacy, the challenge of corruption after the mid-1990s is greater than before. Directly, as the Chinese authorities unmask more corrupt senior officials, including three Politburo members (Chen Xitong, Chen Liangyu, and Bo Xilai, all since 1995), enjoying their illicitly gained assets worth fantastically large sums, it may do more to confirm mass public cynicism than to boost confidence in the anticorruption effort. In this regard, it is worth noting that the February 2013 meeting of the Central Discipline Inspection Commission (CDIC), the Communist Party's anticorruption agency, postponed a commitment to require officials to publicly disclose assets: apparently, on the basis of interviews with officials in Guangdong, a CDIC official warned his colleagues that authoritative disclosure of the impressive assets held by senior officials would lead to public anger and social unrest.[25]

I here adopt a two-step strategy to examine the new challenge of corruption. I begin with a broad description of the new forms of corruption we can identify, associating them with new economic reforms. Then, because it is impossible to ascertain empirically which forms are truly most common, I single out for more focused discussion some forms that seem to pose particularly serious challenges. Specifically, I narrow my focus to corruption involving senior officials and large sums; from this subset, I identify forms of corruption with qualitative features that seem to me to pose particularly serious challenges to good governance or regime legitimacy, or both, in China.

New Economic Reforms and New Forms of Corruption

There is a wide consensus among corruption scholars that the economic reforms that followed Deng Xiaoping's 1992 "southern tour" generated new forms of corruption; indeed, there is a wide consensus about which reforms are associated with which forms of corruption after the mid-1990s.[26]

Broadly, scholars distinguish between the mutually beneficial ("satisfied customer") exchanges between public officials and private businesspersons and nontransactive corruption, where officials prey on public resources. The forms of corruption that emerged in the 1990s were mostly of the former type, compared to the nontransactive corruption of the 1980s.

More specifically, a deepening of economic reform followed Deng's southern tour. Wedeman in particular (but other scholars agree) distinguishes three economic reforms that created opportunities for new corruption.[27] First, new reforms transferred control rights over state assets to economic interests. This includes the transfer of control of state-owned enterprises to enterprise managers and the transfer of land use rights to developers. The official management over this process has allowed officials to bargain with economic players for profit shares or kickbacks in exchange for control rights. Reform deepening has meant an increase in the value and scale of assets, accompanied by an increase in the seniority of officials involved in the transfer. Moreover, as most transfers have not secured property rights for economic players, the way is open for officials to continually press their demands. Second, although China has made progress in creating a regulatory structure for its new economy, there are still too many regulations and too many regulatory players, with too much discretion and with overlapping jurisdiction. This too is a breeding ground for official exactions from the private sector. The third area is the financial sector. Guo sees in fiscal and administrative decentralization the roots of new corruption in public investment and procurement as well as personnel appointments and promotions.[28] Wedeman focuses on the continued high state control over finances in a situation of capital scarcity and with career pressures for big infrastructural development.[29] This has implications for corruption. Access to credit in the hands of (or at least strongly influenced by) local government officials means that businesses have incentives to influence officials by various means, including bribery; government officials have means and incentives to make unauthorized loans as well as investments and to engage in profit-skimming. In the criminal code, this is reflected in corruption involving misappropriation of public funds.

Four Particularly Serious Challenges

As noted above, not only have new forms of corruption emerged in the 1990s, especially since the mid-1990s, but there is also a general consensus, even among Chinese researchers, that corruption now involves a greater number of more senior officials and (sometimes fantastically) larger sums, compared to the 1980s. Moreover, cases can now implicate hundreds of officials working collusively, sometimes headed by a generalist party leader.[30] Whether this amounts more broadly to a change in what Shleifer and Vishny call the "industrial organization of corruption" is unclear, however.[31] Efforts to estimate the magnitude and rate of corruption confront the usual measurement problems, but both Guo and Wedeman, using different data and different measures, argue that corruption among senior officials actually ceased to increase in the late 1990s, and may even have decreased.[32]

"Senior" officials and "large" sums are formal-legal categories. Senior officials are at the bureaucratic rank of county (division) or higher; since 1998, large sums involve at least 50,000 yuan for bribery or at least 100,000 yuan for misappropriation of public assets. Table 7.1 summarizes what a purposive sample of Chinese-language summary accounts identifies as serious forms of corruption, all involving senior officials and large sums, year by year, for roughly the past decade. To create the table, I chose Chinese-language sources that reviewed the year's corruption and focused on cases involving big sums and senior officials.[33]

I chose four forms of corruption for discussion here: sale of official positions, judicial corruption, land leasing and real estate profiteering, and financial corruption. I made the selection on qualitative grounds, with no claims here about relatively greater volume—although in Wedeman's presentation of cases involving senior officials and large sums (coded from the LexisNexis database), judicial corruption, financial corruption, and corruption in real estate also all figure very prominently in news stories in 2002–2009 (his most recently coded period).[34] More importantly, as discussed below, each of these forms as well as (indeed, especially) sale of official positions present what I judge to be particularly serious new challenges for the regime. Here, I am reflecting on the political challenges, which are quite separate from relative losses of state revenue.

1. *Sale of official positions.* The evident rise of buying and selling public offices reflects the recognition that public office can generate bribe revenues. Cases can involve senior officials in long office-selling chains, including sale of local Communist Party leadership offices. For example, in Heilongjiang Province, in a major case involving 265 officials, disclosed in 2002, the going rate was about $100,000 for municipal party leadership and about $40,000 for county party leadership.[35] Not surprisingly, judging from bribe prices, the most desirable offices are those where bribes are most readily available: chief executives of agencies in charge of public projects (e.g., transportation departments), leaders in regulatory and law enforcement agencies (e.g., judges, prosecutors, police chiefs), and first-in-command generalists (e.g., party committee secretaries).

The buying and selling of public offices is a particular challenge as it undermines the Chinese Communist Party organizational monopoly in personnel

Table 7.1. Common Forms of Corruption, 2002–2012: Cases Involving Big Sums and Senior Officials

Year	Form of Corruption
2002	Bribery Abuse of judicial discretion Abuse of discretion to embezzle funds Fund laundering through family business Illegitimate sources of funds
2003	Bribery Abuse of judicial discretion Sale and purchase of official positions Fund laundering through family business Illegitimate sources of funds
2004	Bribery Sale and purchase of official positions Embezzlement through fraudulent loans Fund laundering in corporate enterprises
2005	Bribery Sale and purchase of official positions Abuse of financial discretion in banking Embezzlement of state funds
2006	Bribery Nepotism, cronyism Real estate profiteering
2007	Bribery Abuse of approval discretion in medicines and medical equipment
2008	Bribery Real estate profiteering Illegitimate sources of funds
2009	Bribery Sale and purchase of official positions Embezzlement of state funds Illegitimate sources of funds
2010	Bribery Illegitimate sources of assets
2011	Bribery Real estate profiteering
2012	Bribery

See note 33 to this chapter for specific sources.

management, the linchpin of party political rule. The hierarchically struc-
tured *nomenklatura* system assigns to Communist Party committees, from
top to bottom, the authority to vet and select for promotion officials of even
moderate importance. Standards for evaluating performance are decided on
at the highest level. Officials and party committees are linked in a series of
dyads, with party committees holding personnel management authority
over all officials working one level down the bureaucratic and territorial hierarchy. With economic decentralization, where localities have broad powers to shape how they meet goals set in Beijing, hierarchically organized
party power to define what types of officials get along and ahead is crucial to
holding the system together. The buying and selling of offices is more than a
simple implementation failure. It eats away at party power at its core, essentially substituting an inefficient (given what must be fairly high transaction
costs) market for some underlying normative theory of the state implicit in
Beijing's standards for career advancement.

2. *Judicial corruption.* A specialized literature on Chinese judicial corruption has grown in recent years, fed partly by more (and more detailed)
press accounts of it.[36] Judicial corruption covers a wide range of activities,
but most common is bribe taking to influence court judgments. Other sorts
of corrupt conduct by judges and other judicial personnel include extortion,
excessive fees, and leaking confidential legal information. The crux of the
problem is that there is a very substantial amount of judicial discretion,
which produces weak accountability, while at the same time the judiciary is
not independent from the Communist Party. The dependence on the party
is substantive (i.e., courts and procurators report to the local party committee secretary of political-legal affairs); in addition, the party controls judicial
personnel appointments. Judicial discretion arises from the administrative
hierarchical ranking system: judges are appointed and promoted in administrative ranks (i.e., ministerial, bureau, division, section) and higher-ranking
judges have authority over lower-ranking judges.[37] More straightforward influences on judicial corruption have to do with funding and training. Only
recently has China introduced a judiciary examination system and a threshold education level of college for judges. Local governments control judicial
budgets, and Wang finds low government funding significantly correlated
with high judicial corruption.[38]

As Rose-Ackerman observes, judicial corruption is a particularly alarming form of corruption, as it discriminates against the scrupulous (and poor)
in a venue of last resort for many.[39] This is also the case in China, where the

number of economic and civil cases has increased dramatically. Judicial corruption reinforces a sense that rules don't matter, regardless of their proliferation and elaboration. It has broad application and high political salience, more so than, for example, violations of basic human rights in regime handling of political dissidence, which often goes unobserved by the Chinese mass public.

3. *Land leasing and real estate profiteering.* Fiscal reform in the 1990s has significantly increased revenues that local governments remit to the center, while maintaining or increasing local fiscal responsibilities (e.g., for social services and infrastructure construction). This change, and financial competition across provinces for domestic and foreign investment, has made land leasing crucial to increasing local government revenues.[40] At the same time, real estate profiteering through selective authorization of whether, to whom, and at what price to lease land has become a new opportunity for corruption.[41] Land leasing normally takes place in opaque negotiated transfers, not public bidding, but even the public land auctions are not immune to corrupt deals.[42] The Ministry of Land Resources surveyed sixteen cities in 2005 and discovered that half of the land used for development had been illegally acquired, pointing to official kickbacks and profit sharing.[43]

Corruption in land leasing is particularly serious because the authority to transfer land use rights is now nearly the only major resource that local governments have to boost revenues to fulfill new unfunded mandates from Beijing.[44] As discussed above, the regulatory infrastructure to make these transfers credible and lasting is not yet in place. This means that corruption in land leasing and real estate profiteering is likely to be a continuing challenge to good local governance. When officials exploit the opportunities created by government ownership and transfer rights over land, they pocket for themselves local revenues badly needed to provide for basic social welfare.

4. *Financial corruption.* Financial corruption, especially the misappropriation of public funds for interest-free capital for private investment, presents another new challenge for the regime. Officials in the state-monopolized financial institutions have the most opportunities to engage in this form of corruption, but officials in state enterprises, local governments, and state procurement agencies also misuse public funds as private assets. Funds are usually invested in the stock market or real estate, highly speculative areas that offer the possibility of quick returns.[45] Essentially, only failures are exposed: evident big losses of funds that were borrowed and then not returned over some period of time.

Financial corruption is largely the result of weak regulatory and monitoring mechanisms in financial institutions at a time when new opportunities for investment in real estate and stock markets have opened up. The form described above, where officials secure for themselves interest-free loans for speculative investment in property and stocks, diverts scarce capital from activities with greater potential to enhance social welfare and promote economic growth.

Anticorruption Efforts

Up until about 2002, China's anticorruption strategy alternated between routine anticorruption enforcement and intensive anticorruption campaigns. Routine enforcement is hindered by flawed institutional design. Party discipline inspection committees have broad jurisdiction that includes corruption, but they are functional departments under the leadership of party committees, which means they cannot effectively monitor "generalist leaders," such as party committee secretaries. Discipline inspection committees share anticorruption enforcement responsibilities with procuratorates. Strictly, the procuratorates are in charge of investigating and prosecuting criminal corruption; in practice, nearly all officials are Communist Party members, and discipline inspection committees have jurisdiction to investigate and impose penalties on party members engaging in a wide range of "inappropriate conduct"—with the consequence that milder party penalties often substitute for harsher punishment (including the death penalty) for criminal corruption. Flaws in routine anticorruption enforcement generated periodic anticorruption campaigns, which produced reporting peaks, confession peaks, and enforcement peaks—but their deterrent effect appears to have been weak: high proportions of new corruption cases involved acts committed not long after campaigns.[46]

In the past decade, however, leaders in Beijing have acknowledged fighting corruption is a long-term task, not a series of battles. The new anticorruption strategy privileges prevention and represents an institutional turn: it recognizes the need to change the incentives that structure corrupt acts. It has begun to target corruption-generating procedures and opportunities. For example, since 2002, State Council departments have abolished or reduced approval requirements on more than 2,000 items, and local governments have abolished or reduced approval requirements on more than 77,000 items.

The two numbers represent over half of approvals required before 2002. This is completely different from simply issuing rules and prohibitions, which are the core of an enforcement approach to corruption control.

The Xi Jinping-Li Keqiang administration that ascended to power in late 2012 has endorsed the institutional turn. Xi's admonition that power be restricted by "a cage of regulations" should be understood in this perspective, not as a simplistic call for more prohibitions. At the same time, the new administration has issued a raft of new prohibitions to promote official probity; these are simply rules, not new incentive structures. They may have some public relations appeal, but officials will undoubtedly find "workarounds" that, when exposed, will feed public cynicism.

In this regard, how should we view the retreat in February 2013 from measures to require officials to disclose their assets? On the one hand, it is a nontrivial failure: an asset disclosure rule is more than simply a rule, as it restructures incentives. Such a rule at least implicitly condones more intrusive monitoring, formally by anticorruption agencies, and informally by the mass public. More transparency of this sort is better than less. At the same time, without much fanfare, Li Keqiang has publicly pledged to further cut administrative approval items by at least one-third in the coming five years.[47] This action is likely to have much greater anticorruption effect than any asset disclosure rule, should such a rule be eventually passed. Removing administrative approval authority changes the rules of the game.

Here, of course, theory has slipped into the discussion. The argument implicit in the above perspective on China's anticorruption reforms privileges institutions, that is, self-enforcing arrangements that structure incentives to constrain players to act in certain ways. As it turns out, this perspective is not at odds with what we know empirically (and atheoretically) from the crossnational research I reviewed above. The economic and political correlates most relevant to China's challenge of corruption all have to do with weak incentive structures. A successful anticorruption effort calls for a strengthening of incentive arrangements.

Conclusion

In this regard, the institutional turn toward restructuring incentives to prevent corruption constitutes an important shift that should, in theory, eventually produce better results, even without a political reform that challenges the party monopoly on organized political power. At the same time, the prognosis for effective change should take into specific account what we have learned from a decade of cross-national empirical research on corruption. The state continues to play a comparatively major role in the economy, and the playing field is by no means nearly level, especially in critical sectors such as finance. Moreover, although a December 2010 White Paper on anticorruption measures welcomes mass public supervision of officials through the Internet,[48] this will probably continue to be limited to exposure of local and individual cases, as it is today. That is, the new administration has shown its discomfort with the tradeoffs of a free press that is "bad news" for corruption.

Scholars who have written about China's corruption differ in their assessment of the prospects for successful anticorruption reform, just as they differ in their views of the regime's sincerity in carrying out anticorruption measures. Sifting through roughly the same evidence, Yan Sun and Ting Gong are somewhat pessimistic, and Minxin Pei and Qinglian He[49] are strongly dismissive, for example. In contrast, Andrew Wedeman can probably be counted as cautiously (or conditionally) optimistic. It seems to me that the range of expert views reflects not only our efforts to piece together, attentive to fundamental problems of measurement and data, what is going on with corruption in China, but also, as with nonexperts, broader underlying nuances of difference in our views on Chinese politics.

If China's new leaders simply continue to muddle along, corruption will undoubtedly continue to pose a serious challenge to regime legitimacy. This amounts to a political challenge from an increasingly aware Chinese mass public. At the same time, dire predictions of regime collapse seem misplaced—or at least corruption is unlikely to be the direct source of serious regime instability. For one thing, authoritarian leaders generally have most to fear from elite (not mass) defections;[50] engaging in serious anticorruption reform (not corruption) would seem to be the greater challenge in this regard. From a comparative historical context, the most serious threat to (authoritarian or democratic) regime stability is economic crisis.[51] In this sense, to the extent that corruption undermines the economic growth that is an important prop of the regime, a failure of anticorruption reform does pose a daunting challenge to regime stability.

CHAPTER 8

Responsive Authoritarianism in Chinese Media

Daniela Stockmann

In most liberal democracies, commercialized and new media have been taken for granted, but in China and most other authoritarian states, the introduction of advertising and new media has represented a radical break from the past. Within the past thirty years, the Chinese state has undergone media reform that involves two key processes: the introduction of market forces in state media and the adoption of new communication technologies such as the Internet.

In introducing such reforms, China follows a general global trend toward media reform that has not been confined to democracies. This is significant because regime type and regulatory practices of the media industry have traditionally been regarded as linked to each other. In many nondemocratic states, the media used to be state-owned and financed with state subsidies. But since the late 1970s until the first decade of the twenty-first century, most authoritarian regimes have opened media markets and introduced new communication technologies that have posed great challenges to authoritarian leaders.[1] New and market-based media apparently served as a catalyst of the "Jasmine Revolutions" in the Middle East, reinvigorating the scholarly discussion on the consequences of new and market-based media for the continuation of authoritarian rule. This discussion has concentrated on the potential liberalizing role of the media in nondemocracies, and new and market-based media are often portrayed as forces that contribute to a free press and possibly democracy in authoritarian states. Only recently have scholars working on media in authoritarian regimes devoted more attention to the possibility that corporate and global media might function as a reactionary force that strengthens authoritarian rule.[2]

Here, I come to the conclusion that market-based and new media do indeed pose a major challenge to China's regime stability, but that the Chinese central leadership is currently able to cope with these challenges in ways that are beneficial to its rule. Chinese media remain embedded in the Chinese political system, and through this institutional infrastructure, the Chinese Communist Party can maintain the balance between liberalization and control, which has a stabilizing effect on the overall political system. In maintaining this balance, China resembles other one-party regimes that have a greater capacity to restrict information flows and thus can use market-based and new media to their advantage.[3]

The Institutional Context

As a Leninist political system, the Chinese state comprises territorial divisions at the center, province, city, county, township, and village levels. It is also composed of numerous government and Communist Party units (commissions, ministries, bureaus and departments) at the national level, which replicate themselves in a vertical chain through lower levels of government. Individual units receive administrative guidance from above, but they are also subject to the leadership of the local governments to which they belong.

Media outlets are integrated in this broader political structure at their level of government. For example, in order to obtain a license, all newspapers have to find a sponsor.[4] Through the means of the sponsor, state and party units can directly influence personnel appointment and dismissals of senior staff in newspapers. For example, the editor of a newspaper registered with the provincial-level All China Federation of Women is appointed by its sponsor, but needs to get approval from the local party authorities and then receive confirmation from the next higher party unit, the CCP Central Committee.[5] At the central level, directors (*shezhang*), editors-in-chief, deputy editors-in-chief, and editorial committee members of central party papers are included in *nomenklatura* lists for the appointment of cadres.[6] Those who are appointed are encouraged to be, but no longer required to be, party members.[7]

Licensing policies are implemented by the General Administration of Press and Publications (GAPP) (*xinwen chuban zongju*, formerly State Publication and Press Administration) and the State Administration for Radio, Film, and Television (SARFT) (*guangbo dianying dianshi zongju*). These institutions are responsible for drafting and enforcing regulatory press policies, including licensing, investigation, and prosecution of illegal media outlets; and plans exist as of March 2013 to combine them into one institution similar to the U.S. Federal Communication Commission (FCC). By making decisions about when, where, by whom, and how many media outlets can be founded, the CCP is able to determine the structural setup and organization of the media industry. Similar regulating bodies also exist in liberal democracies, especially in the area of media broadcasting, but in China the power of these institutions is supported by the absence of a media law that protects freedom of the press.

In the abstract, the constitution affirms the right of Chinese citizens to freedom of speech. However, laws and regulations impose content restrictions regarding such broad subjects as national security and state secrets.[8] Regulations governing newspapers continue to oblige newspapers to uphold the party principle, composed of three components: 1) the news media must accept the CCP's guiding ideology as its own; 2) media outlets must propagate the party's programs, policies, and directives; and 3) they must accept the CCP's leadership and stick to the party's organizational principles and press policies.[9]

Apart from the above state administrative bodies, the CCP also established Propaganda Departments (PD) (*xuanchuanbu*) under CCP party committees at every level of government. This institution is at the heart of the Chinese propaganda system. The PD is a very secretive body, and its internal structure and decision-making process is not entirely clear to outsiders. In general, the PD is in charge of guiding and planning China's ideological development, thus having leadership relations with a number of institutions relevant to propaganda works, including the GAPP and SARFT.[10] At the central level, the minister of the PD (currently Liu Qibao) usually also serves as a member of the Politburo, and it has become conventional since 1992 that he also serves as the deputy head of the Central Leading Group of Propaganda and Ideological Works, ranked second after the Leading Group head (currently Liu Yunshan), also a member of the Standing Committee of the Politburo, the most powerful policymaking body in the Chinese political system.[11]

News bureaus of the PD are involved in editorial control of media content.[12] In practice, journalists engage primarily in self-censorship, and overt censorship by the PD primarily takes place after publication; it involves a combination of standing rules, documents, and instructions from the party propaganda authorities, and informal norms and content regulations within newspapers. Instructions by the PD are binding, as most media outlets have lower administrative rank.[13] If a media outlet is found to have been engaged in unethical practices, such as carrying fake news, surreptitious advertising, or pornographic or politically problematic content, PD officials will get in touch with senior media staff and can, if several warnings do not suffice, resort to more severe measures affecting employment of staff members.

This basic institutional framework was established in the 1950s and was re-established after the Cultural Revolution. During the reform period, the CCP adjusted this institutional framework to maintain its capacity to guide media into playing a politically correct "main melody" (*zhu xuanlü*) in China's 1,918 newspapers, 9,867 periodicals, 169 radio stations, and 183 TV stations.[14]

In contrast to traditional media, the Internet developed as part of the telecommunications bureaucratic structure rather than the propaganda apparatus. This state administrative structure is composed of a large number of institutions involved in regulating and monitoring the Internet, and efforts have been made to decrease fragmentation by strengthening regulatory authority. The Ministry of Information Industry (MII), created in 1998 through a merger of the Ministry of Posts and Telecommunications and the Ministry of Electronic Industry, was put in charge of regulating the technological and industrial structures of the Internet as well as licensing of Internet service providers (ISPs). Conflict between the MII and SARFT over licensing of Internet and TV services led to the foundation of a new regulatory institution as coordinator, the State Council Information Management Commission (SCIMC) (*guowuyuan xinxhua guanli weiyuanhui*). A major institution involved in monitoring of Internet news and Bulletin Board Services (BBS) is the Internet Information Management Bureau, added to the State Council Information Office (SCIO) in 2000. This institution was also put in charge of directing party-state propaganda on the Internet, whereby the PD provides guidance.[15] However, various party and state agencies, ranging from the Ministry of Culture to the Ministry of Public Security and the Chinese military, have some jurisdiction over the Internet. To overcome this fragmentation and to coordinate, the State Leadership Group of Informatization (*guojia xinxihua lingdao xiaozu*), traditionally led by the premier and composed of major Politburo members and heads of commissions, ministries, party departments, and government agencies responsible for the communication and information industry, provides the highest and broadest oversight over the further development of the Internet.

Through the means of this sophisticated institutional framework, the party maintains the capacity to exert a very considerable amount of political control over the organization, personnel, and editorial content of traditional and new media. Within this sophisticated institutional framework, the CCP has decided to introduce market forces and new communication technologies to the media industry.

Current Challenges

Market-based media are often regarded as working hand in hand with new communication technology, posing a challenge to the continuation of authoritarian rule. CNN television reporting was said to have a signaling and accelerating effect on public protests in Eastern Europe in the late 1980s, playing a part in the breakdown of the Soviet Union.[16] Similarly, the Internet has been described as space for development of civil society and an alternative news agency that is able to subvert state control over the flow of information.[17] Numerous studies of the role of the media during democratization argued that criticism voiced in independent media outlets eroded the regime's legitimacy.[18] Greater diversity of information is also said to transform political culture and foster the emergence of a public sphere.[19]

Similarly, in China, numerous observers of Chinese media have noted that market-based and new media are posing a major challenge to the social and political stability of the party-state. This is so, because market-based and new media constitute the most autonomous information sources in China. Television tends to be the type of media most tightly controlled by the state, followed by radio broadcasting, newspapers, magazines, electronic papers delivered to mobile phones, the Internet, and cell phones. Within the social space in which China's most autonomous media operate, market-based and new media pose a challenge to social and political stability by constantly pushing the boundaries for news reporting and setting a new agenda for public discourse, thus undermining the ability of the state to control political messages, a prerequisite for effective guidance of public opinion. In addition, the interactivity that constitutes a key feature of new communication technologies such as the Internet has empowered citizens and facilitates organization among citizens.

Market-Based Media

Advertising appeared for the first time on Shanghai Television and in the Shanghai-based *Liberation Daily* [*Jiefang Ribao*] newspaper in 1979.[20] Similar initiatives soon followed in other localities, though the central government did not legalize advertising until a trial version of regulations on advertising management entered into force in 1982.[21] For a long time, policymakers did not make public statements about media marketization. It was not until 1992 that Liang Heng, an official responsible for newspaper management at the State Press and Publications Administration, acknowledged for the first time the commodity nature of the press and announced the imperative of "eventually pushing newspapers to the market."[22] After the Fourteenth Party Congress in 1992, the CCP proclaimed the increase of efficiency, reduction of government subsidies, cut of staff members, commercialization, and restructuring of the whole culture and arts sector as a policy goal.[23]

The decision to introduce market forces in media was not entirely voluntary. Budgetary constraints forced the state to cut media subsidies as early as 1978.[24] The previous system under which media outlets had been fully financed by the state had simply become unsustainable. The government's new approach was to pursue a path of experimenting with media marketization while at the same time maintaining the role of the media as a mouthpiece for the CCP and propaganda instrument with the broader goal to guide public opinion.

Media marketization in China is composed of three processes: deregulation, commercialization, and partial privatizion. Deregulation describes the process of diminishing intervention by the state media organizations; the government delegates greater authority over programming, personnel, and business decisions to lower levels in the broadcast and print administrative hierarchy, and increases the number of licenses for media outlets, facilitating growth.

Commercialization involves shifting the primary goal from serving the public (as defined by the state) toward earning profits. As part of media reform, the Chinese press was encouraged to obtain outside funding through advertising and increased sales. Today most media institutions finance themselves with advertising revenues, though some continue to receive indirect or small state subsidies.

Partial privatization further promoted this profit orientation. Since the late 1990s, shares in broadcasting and print media groups have been publicly traded on the stock market and, since 2002, investment in media groups has been permitted. Although restrictions remain on the share of nonstate investment in media outlets—such a share cannot exceed 49 percent—the trend toward private ownership is clear.

Today, the traditional news media differ with respect to their degree of deregulation, commercialization, and partial privatization: magazines tend to be more marketized than newspapers, and print media more marketized than broadcast media. Even within each of these media types there remain differences among media outlets. For example, newspapers that have been affected the least by media reform are often referred to as official (such as, for example, *People's Daily* or *Chongqing Daily*); at the opposite end of the spectrum are commercialized papers, which are leading in terms of media reform (such as, for example, *Beijing Times* or *Southern Weekly*). Newspapers in between the two extremes are called semiofficial (such as, for example, *Beijing Youth Daily* or *Beijing Evening News*). Since semiofficial and commercialized papers share many similarities in the eyes of journalists, they often refer to these two types as nonofficial papers.

The introduction of market forces in media requires the state to allow media a certain degree of autonomy in order to allow it to cater to audiences as a means to attract advertising and make a profit. Therefore, media marketization has provided editors and journalists with greater space for news reporting. Over time, the Propaganda Department has reduced the scope of its supervision so that media are allowed to compete freely in reporting on open topics, while PD authorities continue to watch closely over topics they consider threatening to the policies and goals of political leaders.

This opening of space leads to tensions between media practitioners and propaganda officials. Zhou He even describes these dynamics as a "tug of war."[25] Media practitioners see themselves under pressure between the state and the market. As one editor at a semiofficial paper in the *People's Daily* group put it: "you need to fundamentally serve the needs of the government, but also the needs of the market of readers, it's two kinds of pressures. If you lose your readers, don't you die? And if you publish in an unorganized manner (*luan deng*), don't you die as well?"[26] The dependency of newspapers on selling papers provides them with bargaining power when negotiating space with propaganda officials.

Tension between senior media staff and officials primarily arises when the Propaganda Department gives instructions to abstain from reporting. There are many examples of reporters "playing edge ball" (*da cabianqiu*), trying to push the boundaries of news reporting. A prominent case involves a joint editorial by thirteen newspapers, including *Chongqing Times*, advocating speeding up the reform of the household registration system. The editorial was published during the 2010 "two meetings" of the National People's Congress and the National Political Consultative Conference, about which the Central Propaganda Department and the Government Bureau of Internet Affairs had issued instructions to not "sensationalize or feature news articles that will create a major impact."[27] The Central Propaganda Department requested that the editorial should "be removed from the Internet" and that media should abstain from sensationalizing or featuring reports on the incident.[28]

As the state allows media to cater to the market, some reporters have started pushing against the state structure itself.[29] Hassid describes such reporters as advocate professionals who are committed to media independence and see themselves as advocates for the less-well-off.[30] When seeking opportunities, advocate journalists—often with the help of broader networks of social activists—engage in contentious politics at the boundaries. From the perspective of propaganda officials this creates trouble, as journalists are not always doing what they are told or find loopholes in the system.

By pushing the boundaries for news reporting, journalists are setting or changing the agenda for public discourse. Stories about the Chongqing nail house, Deng Yujiao, and Li Qiaoming, are just a few examples of "incidents" (*shijian*) that highlighted larger problems within Chinese society.[31] Once these stories were posted online, they were often picked up by nonofficial papers and other market-based media, and thus funneled to the center of attention of public discourse. As agenda-setters, traditional media are working closely together with new media: speedy spread of information online provides editors and journalists with arguments that the news has already become public and therefore needs to be covered in traditional media.

New Media

The Internet became available in China, first for scholarly use, then for popular use, in 1994–1995. At the time, the governmental ministries involved in the introduction of the Internet were largely focused on the Internet's potential economic benefits: relaxed control over domestic and international flows of information was seen as fostering initiative, innovation, and economic growth.

The Chinese Internet has grown at a rapid pace, representing a drastic jump from having 620,000 users back in 1997, when the China Internet Network Information Center (CNNIC) carried out its first survey, to overtaking the United States in 2008 as having the most Internet users in the world.[32] By March 2014, the number of Internet users in China had reached 618 million, constituting more than one quarter of the world's netizens. While impressive in size, Chinese Internet users only make up roughly 45 percent of the Chinese population, and are primarily located in the cities on the more developed east coast of China.[33]

While the Internet constitutes the most autonomous information source available to the Chinese, the state influences Internet sites to varying degrees, similar to traditional market-based media. Political institutions at all levels of government have increased their Internet presence, including new opportunities for citizens to submit letters and petitions online.[34] In comparison, online news Web sites are somewhat less controlled than governmental Web sites. Chinese netizens can obtain the news from two kinds of Web sites—those sponsored by traditional media outlets, such as Xinhuanet, and those not directly run by other news entities, such as Sina. The first kind are allowed to write their own articles and are, in fact, managed similarly to commercialized papers; the second kind are generally not allowed to write their own reports and tend to republish articles from nonofficial papers.[35]

Apart from these sources, netizens also use BBS chat forums, blogs, chats (such as MSN and QQ), Weibo (the Chinese version of Twitter) and WeChat (the Chinese version of WhatsApp) to obtain information about politics.[36] Bloggers are more likely to criticize the state compared to newspaper articles, which are often republished on online news Web sites.[37] Yet blogs also have a much smaller audience, percentage-wise. According to the randomly sampled national China Survey 2008, most netizens seek political information from the more tightly controlled official Web sites and online news Web sites; social media are not primarily used as sources of political information.[38]

These online social media play a particularly important role in setting the agenda in public discourse.[39] "Incidents" (shijian), such as the Chongqing nail house, Deng Yujiao, and Li Qiaoming mentioned earlier, are usually communicated in the most autonomous spaces for political discussion, such as BBS forums, the blogosphere, QQ discussion groups, and, more recently, Weibo and WeChat. These stories can quickly spread online and lead to the rise of what many Chinese officials and reporters call online public opinion. This is so because the size of the Chinese Internet facilitates "informational cascades" in which people take informational cues from the aggregate number of people who participate in political action.[40] When reporters of market-based media pick up these stories, they can become part of the broader public discourse covered in traditional media, pushing pressure on political leaders to show responsiveness.

In addition to the role of new media in setting the agenda for public discourse and therefore changing the political messages covered in Chinese media, new media also allow for immediate interaction between users. This so-called "interactivity" of computer-mediated communication (CMC) has enabled "cybercommunities" to form online virtual networks where social interactions take place between participants who share common ideas, interests, and hobbies so that a sense of community and belonging can develop. Cybercommunities have become one of the dominant features of China's Internet. These communities predominantly exist with respect to nationalist endeavors; marginalized groups, such as women, ethnic minorities, migrants, and peasants, are present as well as users enjoying leisure and entertainment activities.[41] These groups can "bond" and reinforce close-knit networks of people sharing similar backgrounds and beliefs, such as, for example, nationalist cybercommunities; they can also "bridge" groups and enable communication of people in disparate communities, such as, for example, migrant workers and their families.[42]

In doing so, social networks, such as Tianya, Strong Nation Forum (*Qiang Guo Luntan*), Sina Forum, Taobao, Weibo, and so forth can empower citizens and facilitate civic and political engagement and political action. Qiu has shown that the "information have-less" (e.g., migrant workers and rural groups) have found new methods to share access to the Internet via cybercafés and long-distance phone bars, creating opportunities to perceive that they have control over situations and to transcend social boundaries across class, regions, ethnicity, and gender, thus having the potential to strengthen feelings of empowerment and upward mobility.[43] In addition, China's NGOs rely heavily on the Internet to connect activists around the country.[44]

One key advantage of such social networks is that they facilitate speedy mobilization of collective action while reducing the risk of personal danger due to anonymity. Online forums and networks enable, for example, nationalist activists to organize petitions and protests.[45] Chinese media scholars and propaganda officials have become increasingly worried that such incidents of "public opinion crisis" facilitated by new media serve as catalysts for disagreement between citizens and the government, placing central and local officials under pressure to react.[46]

Of course, the state has not remained passive while facing these challenges. Before I move on to the state's response I would like to briefly comment on one common statement that I have frequently come across when talking to Chinese public officials, media practitioners, and communication scholars. Often, it is claimed that the Internet and market-based media have undermined the credibility of China's media by publishing fake information. It is true that stories appearing on online media are not easily verified, and marketized media outlets have published so-called "fake news," such as the case of the 2007 "fake dumpling case," when a report aired on Beijing television claiming that dumplings were sold filled with cardboard. However, as the most autonomous information sources, market-based and online media enjoy high levels of credibility among the Chinese public, because they are perceived as experts about the concerns of "ordinary people" that publish "real news," as opposed to propaganda.[47]

China's Attempt to Deal with the Challenge

China experts and media activists interpret the dynamics between state and media in two ways, one side stressing liberalization and prospects for democratization, the other emphasizing control and authoritarian resilience.[48] How can we make sense of these two assessments of the political consequences of Chinese media?

The answer I offer here is that both interpretations are right in part, but not as different as they seem at first glance. Media reform requires a certain degree of liberalization, because market-based media need to cater to audiences in order to make a profit, and new communication technologies are faster than propaganda officials in spreading information. But this increased social space places pressure on the authoritarian state. As a result, China is also constantly building up its capacity to control media, mostly through institutional infrastructures, in order to maintain a roughly uniform flow of political information. Therefore, China deals with the challenges posed by market-based and new media by both opening up social spaces in media and maintaining control through institutional mechanisms.

Liberalization

China undergoes fairly regular cycles. Major events can disrupt these cycles and lead to public opinion crises that are, of course, dependent on international and domestic events and less predictable. Each year China undergoes a cycle of tightening and loosening at around the time of the Spring Festival, followed by meetings of the National People's Congress and the National People's Political Consultative Conference in Beijing, called the "two meetings" (liang hui). During this time (usually between late January and March), reporting is more tightly controlled than toward the end of the year, when there is more room for criticism.[49]

In addition, space for news reporting tends to be more tightly restricted when there is change in political leadership. Leadership change is always a time of intra-elite competition, which increases the likelihood that leaders will suppress negative news about themselves, as was, for example, the case during the 2003 SARS crisis, or more recently during the 2012 Bo Xilai scandal. These periods are characterized by divided leadership, as power is passed on between different generations of leaders. If public officials fail to give clear signals about the center's policy stance because they are distracted by other issues or divided amongst themselves, such periods also provide opportunities for societal forces to mobilize.[50] Therefore, leadership successions are periods of heightened tension between state and societal forces in media, as the leaders are attempting to control the media and the media seek opportunities to cater to audiences.

Apart from these fairly regular annual and leadership cycles, there are some clear signs that the space for political information in Chinese media has significantly increased over time. Many topics that used to be taboo and could not be covered by reporters are now regularly covered in the news, though they remain sensitive, and reporters need to be careful about *how* they cover these stories. These changes are most visible with respect to information management during crisis situations. China's system of crisis communication was established in 1989, when regulations stipulated that media did not have the right to report as events unfolded and often were not permitted to cover incidents at all.[51] The SARS epidemic in 2003 led to important changes in the rationale for information management among Chinese leaders.[52] In 2007 an Emergency Response Law was put into effect, and it did not contain any explicit restrictions on reactions by the media in the case of an emergency, which had been required under the previous system.[53] After the 2008 Wenchuan (Sichuan) earthquake, it took the government only two hours to publicly acknowledge the severity of the disaster, and the State Council gave daily press conferences.[54] In contrast to the state's initial reaction after the SARS crisis, reporters were allowed to cover relief efforts, later inspiring vivid scholarly discussion among Chinese communication scholars and journalists about how to deal with the new challenges of disaster coverage. Similar openings have taken place with respect to reporting about protests since 2008, starting with the unrest in Tibet and the Chongqing taxi strike in the same year.[55]

At first glance, these observations differ from common accounts that stress the tightening of media control during the Hu-Wen administration. However, at the same time that they have opened up space for political information, Chinese leaders have also stepped up their efforts to keep advocate journalists and netizens on a tighter leash by adjusting the institutional infrastructure of control.

Control

The institutional context in which media remain embedded continues to serve as the "safety belt" of the CCP for tightening control over market-based and new media, when necessary. However, over time, the state has switched toward complementing these overt techniques of censorship with means that are less easily linked directly to propaganda officials. These new techniques are aimed at reducing tensions that arise after exerting control over media content by means of institutions. With respect to traditional media, the state has moved toward strengthening the legal system and fostering self-regulation among journalists as a possible alternatives to overt censorship by the PD. Similar trends are visible in other one-party states that have undergone media marketization, such as Tanzania or Kenya, for example.[56]

A common source of legal constraint for Chinese journalism is defamation litigation. In 2004, Chinese courts heard 5,195 defamation cases.[57] Media lose most defamation cases brought against them by officials, party-state entities, corporations, courts, and judges in response to critical coverage, most of the time leading to financial awards against the media.[58] This supervision by the courts has positive and negative effects on media reporting. On the one side, it increases media attention to collecting evidence to support stories and abstaining from fake news reporting, as in the case of the previously mentioned 2007 "fake dumpling case."[59] On the other hand, reporters are often unable to win defamation cases, even if they have collected evidence. To avoid financial risks, reporters refrain from publishing investigative or critical stories.[60] As the state is introducing courts as possible alternatives to editorial control by the PD, the CCP is shifting away from direct conflict between media practitioners and propaganda officials and toward conflict being managed by state administrators in the courtroom.

A second means by which the state is trying to reduce censorship tensions between public officials and journalists is to foster journalistic ethics. The key term here is "social responsibility," which, in the context of Chinese media, denotes attitudes and behavior in line with the goals and policies of state and party units. The PD is trying to tie ideas about social responsibility to ideas about truthfulness. In 2011, the Sixth Plenum of the Fifteenth Party Congress issued a decision regarding the deepening of reform of the cultural sector, which asked reporters to "uphold social responsibility and professional ethics, truthfully and accurately disseminate news information, be aware of committing mistakes, consciously refuse mistaken positions [*cuowu guandian*], and be determined to put an end to fake news."[61] Many reporters acknowledge that fake news reporting constituted a problem, as some papers invented stories or sensationalized existing stories to attract audiences, but the PD clearly also has some leeway in defining what constitutes truthful information, as in the case of defining the true number of deaths and injured by official statistics when Typhoon Saomai hit Fujian Province.[62]

In addition, social responsibility is tied to social stability and the party. Propaganda officials often justify their directives by citing social stability, even if news stories are not obviously related to mass incidents and protests, following such logic as "if the press breaks discipline, it might give rise to social disorder," or "if the news entails too much criticism, it might result in public outrage."[63] In doing so, they aim to convince editors and journalists that the only alternative to media management is social disorder and chaos and to motivate journalists to voluntarily conform to instructions. A scholar working closely with the *China Women's News Daily* [*Zhongguo Funübao*] stated: "journalists discuss some topics that the state (*guojia*) can resolve, but they won't place too much pressure on the government, because otherwise it will result in chaos (*luan*)."[64] An editor-in-chief of a central-level official paper noted, "When you run a newspaper, you can't avoid committing mistakes. You just don't want to give rise to too big problems for the country."[65] Fear of social disorder functions as an "empty dignifier," often drawing people with divergent opinions together behind editorial control over media content.[66]

While propaganda authorities are eager to convince journalists that socially responsible behavior requires self-censorship, some journalists have their own interpretation of what constitutes truthful and "safe" information. Due to the large size of the Chinese media sector, such contentious acts can create the impression that China "is like a pressure-cooker" on the verge of explosion.[67] However, on average, market-based media follow the official line of the government, and political information flows tend to be roughly uniform.[68]

Censorship of new media is primarily enforced by Web administrators in charge of monitoring Web content, by software that can censor keywords, and even by Internet commentators, also called "fifty-cent party members" (*wu mao dang*), because they are paid fifty cents for each message posted online that supports the party-state.[69] These means are not easily detected by netizens—fifty-cent party members do not reveal their state employment, and error messages that users receive online often hint at technical difficulties rather than censorship.[70] These means are significantly different from the ways in which traditional media are controlled.

Still, netizens find ways to circumvent state control, mocking censors by posting homonyms that sound like politically sensitive terms. For example, when the Central PD instructed Web sites to remove text and images supporting Google's decision to shift to Hong Kong, netizens referred to "ancient doves" (*guge*) instead of the firm's name.[71] Netizens' usage and re-interpretation of expressions challenged the monopoly of the party in formalizing the language through which it guides public discourse.[72]

Under China's responsive authoritarianism, liberalization and control are two sides of the same coin. To allow media to serve the goals of the party, the state needs to tolerate a certain degree of autonomy. Yet as media outlets compete for audiences, they also have incentives to widen their space. To synchronize media messages, the state reacts by gradually adjusting the institutions in charge of maintaining the balance between liberalization and control. As one editor put it: "we should not say that the PD is changing its management of the media. This change is brought about by the media as it forces the state to react."[73]

Responsiveness?

Officials have shown responsiveness to the pressure exerted by market- and Web-based media. After the 2008 Wenchuan earthquake, for example, authorities responded to media pressure by initiating official investigations and eventually acknowledging for the first time that poor construction of "tofu" school buildings may have led to collapses, thus accommodating popular views. Together with various government bodies, the State Council also launched a campaign to ensure that school buildings will be capable of withstanding natural disasters in the future.[74]

Such kinds of public opinion supervision (*yulun jiandu*) of Chinese media over the Chinese bureaucracy and courts can lead to adjusting decisions to meet popular demands. However, most of the time, these incidents result in the dismissal of officials, not in policy changes, as in the case of Sun Zhigang or the "tofu" buildings.[75] However, the populist rhetoric in which the center claims to be the protector of the common people is not just lip service paid to stay in power. In some cases, such as the "tofu" school buildings, the central government (cautiously) accommodated popular demands for better treatment of migrants and improved safety of school buildings, although this adjustment has been partial and arguably only temporary as the policy measures employed by the central government fail to address the roots of the problem—inequality, discrimination, and rampant corruption.[76]

We should be careful not to misinterpret this responsiveness of the Chinese state as a sign of democratization. Media reform has not brought about greater diversity in the political information available to most citizens. While there is room for criticism in Chinese media, and this criticism is voiced by people with diverse backgrounds, media avoid incorporating opposing views on an issue and fail to provide truly diverse information on politics.[77] Hua notes that media discussion about public opinion supervision remains trapped in a morality that precludes any questioning of the system.[78]

Nevertheless, to many Chinese, the greater influence of "ordinary people" on political decision making marks a democratization of the political system. When using the term *minzhu*, most Chinese do not have in mind a liberal democracy characterized by free, fair, and competitive elections as well as greater protection of civil liberties. According to the randomly sampled Asiabarometer survey, about 42 percent of Chinese could not explain what democracy was, but among those who had an idea, a large percentage associated the term with statements such as "government takes people's interest into consideration when making decisions," "government takes care of people's interest," or "government allows people to tell their opinions."[79] As Chinese public officials accommodate popular views, they may satisfy demands for such interpretations of democracy, focusing on greater influence by certain subgroups within Chinese society. However, they are also careful to avoid political diversification and blaming societal problems on the overall political system, which could serve as a catalyst for a breakdown of the current regime and the establishment of a new political system that could—but does not have to—resemble liberal democracy.

Conclusion

Under China's responsive authoritarianism neither the state nor the media emerge as the winner, although a balance between liberalization and control has had a stabilizing effect on the overall system. From the perspective of media practitioners, media marketization is associated with greater space for news reporting, which allows them to cater to audience demands. From the perspective of netizens, new communication technology gives ordinary people a voice in public discourse and new opportunities to connect and organize. By constantly pushing the boundaries set by the state, market-based and new media can also brand themselves as credible news products that media consumers evaluate positively.

From the perspective of public officials, market-based media function as a source of public opinion that allows the state to obtain societal feedback about its policies and political goals. Constant negotiation between media practitioners, netizens, and propaganda officials for societal space constitutes one mechanism through which the Chinese leadership learns about public opinion. And the credibility boost brought about by media marketization and new communication technology allows Chinese media to be more effective in disseminating information and guiding public opinion, particularly among potential troublemakers.[80]

Responsive authoritarianism in Chinese media requires the Chinese state to strike a balance between communicating information from society to the state, while simultaneously maintaining the capacity to disseminate the goals and policies of the government and guide public opinion. If propaganda officials can walk the fine line between liberalization and control, market-based and new media can be beneficial to the state.

This strategy is a risky endeavor on the part of the Chinese state because it could be planting the seeds of its own collapse. How much liberalization can responsive authoritarianism in media endure? In other words, where is the tipping point at which China may start losing the capacity to synchronize information flows? The precise moment is unpredictable and will usually only be recognized in retrospect.[81] However, a comparison of China with other one-party-states that have followed similar trends in the relationship between the state and market-based and new media reveals that that there is considerable leeway for the Chinese government before infrastructures start to crumble.[82] While media certainly pose a constant challenge to regime stability in China, media alone are unlikely to have the power to tip over the Chinese party-state in the near future.

CHAPTER 9

China's Law and Stability Paradox

Benjamin L. Liebman

Do robust legal institutions support or subvert efforts to maintain social stability in an authoritarian state? Over the past decade this question has become central to discussions concerning legal reform in China. In the 1980s and 1990s, China devoted extensive resources to constructing a legal system. In contrast, in the 2000s, the party-state's focus shifted toward emphasizing resolution of disputes outside the formal legal system, negotiated outcomes in the formal legal system, and flexible application of rules and procedures. Substantive legal reforms have continued in many important areas. Nevertheless, the Chinese party-state has relied heavily on institutions outside the formal legal system to manage increased instability.

This chapter examines recent trends in state attempts to maintain social stability and in the handling of individual disputes. My aim is to deepen existing understanding of the relationship between state efforts to maintain stability and legal reforms. Trends away from use of the formal legal system have been noted by scholars outside and inside of China.[1] Such developments are manifest in the renewed emphasis on mediation in the past decade,[2] in pressure on courts to resolve disputes in ways that do not result in escalation or appeal, in the embrace of populism in the legal system, and in extreme state concern with petitions and protest.[3] Inside the courts, concerns about stability often influence the handling of civil and criminal cases, with courts adopting flexible approaches to legal rules.[4] The concern with stability is also observable in pressure on defendants in a range of cases to settle before they get to court.[5] A range of nonlegal institutions focused on maintaining stability have gained prominence in the past decade.

My focus in this chapter is on a central question that I refer to as China's law and stability paradox. Having devoted extensive resources to constructing a legal system since reforms began in 1978, why has the party-state retreated from using law when faced with the perception of rising instability? The Chinese party-state devoted impressive resources to constructing its legal system between 1978 and 2003. The results have been significant: I have elsewhere described this period as perhaps the most rapid development of a legal system in world history.[6] China has made progress both in creating formal law and in training legal personnel to implement it. Yet the party-state has been reluctant to use law to address rising social conflict.

Examining China's law-stability paradox adds to existing literature in three areas. First, recognizing the tension between legal reform and state stability policy challenges common assumptions and arguments regarding the role legal reforms have played in China's "authoritarian resilience."[7] Embrace of legal reforms during the first two decades of reform fit well into the dominant description of governance in the 1990s: the attempt to create rules and procedures governing how the state acts and the attempt to differentiate legal from nonlegal actors. The past ten years challenge this narrative, suggesting not just a retreat from legal reform but from a rule-based model of authoritarian governance.

Second, analyzing recent trends in the framework of the law-stability paradox contributes to literature on China's model of an authoritarian legal system. A central insight that emerges is that China's stability and legal policies should not be analyzed in binary terms. The party-state's embrace of nonlegal mechanisms for resolving conflict may reflect distrust of law and fear of autonomous legal institutions. But such policies also suggest a continuation of historical approaches to resolving social conflict and attempts to align legal outcomes with popular demands. Statements from China's new leaders in 2013 regarding the importance of legal rules suggested that they may rethink their approach to managing instability. The Communist Party Central Committee's "Decision on Major Issues Concerning Comprehensively Deepening Reform" ("Decision"), issued in November 2013, sets forth some potentially important legal reforms. Examining the law-stability paradox, however, suggests that any greater reliance on law will occur within the contours of China's existing model of populist authoritarian justice.

Third, recent developments in China contribute to literature on the role law plays in managing conditions of uncertainty. Much writing on recent trends in the Chinese legal system portrays developments in China as reflecting leadership concerns that stronger legal institutions may threaten Communist Party control. In contrast, this chapter suggests that trends away from legal reform in the past decade also reflect ambivalence about the utility of law in managing a period of complex social transformation. China's law-stability paradox may be in part a manifestation of a phenomenon scholars have observed elsewhere: the possibility that rigid adherence to legal rules may deepen crises.[8] In China, distrust of law may reflect party-state concerns about being constrained in the face of perceived crisis and also a recognition of disconnect between legal rules and popular expectations.

Historical Context

China's embrace of legal reforms in the 1980s and 1990s is often attributed to three complementary goals.[9] First, the construction of a legal system was necessary for economic development and in particular to attract foreign investment. China's early legal reform efforts thus focused in significant part on creating a framework for a marketizing economy. Second, the embrace of law served to mark a break from China's recent past, most notably the chaos and violence of the Cultural Revolution. Legal reform signaled a shift away from the often arbitrary system of justice that had dominated since the early 1960s and toward a system that emphasized rules and social stability. Third, the construction of a modern legal system was linked to China's reemergence on the international stage: a modern legal system was understood as necessary if China was to become a global power.

Despite the importance of delineating a new era, legal reforms in the 1980s and 1990s also reflected a continuation of traditions rooted in China's revolutionary and prerevolutionary history. Three aspects of this tradition are of particular relevance for discussions of the relationship between stability and law. First, legal developments in the first two decades of reform emphasized both experimentation and flexibility. Legal rules were designed to facilitate, not constrain, party-state policy. A debate begun in the Jiangxi Soviet between those who embraced legal rules and those who emphasized the importance of flexibility continued throughout this period. Rigid adherence to legal rules remained rare and disfavored, and substantive outcomes continued to dominate over concerns about procedure.

Second, legal reform did not resolve or eliminate longstanding tension between the goals of populism and professionalism, although for much of the period it appeared that professionalism was in the ascendancy. The idea that law and the legal system should be responsive to the mass line was never eliminated, even as the concept of the mass line shifted to reflect new institutional realities. Governance by campaign likewise continued to play an important role, both inside and outside of the legal system. This was evidenced most clearly in periodic "strike hard" anticrime campaigns. But it also arose in popular campaigns designed to educate officials and ordinary people about law and in sporadic efforts to implement law in a range of areas, including enforcement of civil judgments, intellectual property, and environmental law.

Third, no fundamental differentiation between legal and nonlegal actors developed. The state devoted extensive resources to formal training of legal personnel, culminating in the requirement in 2002 that all judges and procurators pass the national bar exam. The state also worked to improve technical legal capacity across a range of legal institutions, including people's congresses, administrative bodies, courts, and procuratorates. Nevertheless, judges and other legal professionals remained part of the party-state administrative apparatus. Judges, procurators, and justice bureau personnel developed functional expertise but never became fundamentally distinct from other party-state actors.

A range of other party-state actors, most notably party political-legal committees, the official media, and letters and visits offices, continued to play important roles in resolving disputes. Sometimes this was done by these institutions on their own, in other cases through direct intervention in the legal system. Within the courts, adjudication came to be used to resolve the majority of cases, but mediation both inside and outside of the courts remained prevalent and important. The legal system had developed and changed, but in important respects it had not changed as much as many hoped or perceived. Such trends reflected practical realities: flexibility remained an important governance tool, in particular when tensions arose between the goals of economic development and stability. But such an approach also reflected a continuation of revolutionary-era distrust of differentiation among institutions.[10]

China's Law and Stability Paradox

The Hu-Wen regime came to power in 2003 against the backdrop of concerns about inequality and instability. Many liberals within the Chinese legal community greeted the new leadership with optimism. For a brief period their optimism appeared well founded, with the dramatic Sun Zhigang case in 2003 leading to the abolition of the "Custody and Repatriation" detention system, increased focus on accountability of government officials following the SARS crisis, a flurry of discussion and litigation aimed at enforcing the rights enshrined in the Chinese Constitution, and the addition to the constitution of a provision on the protection of human rights in 2004.[11] Legal developments in the Hu-Wen era, however, soon shifted in a different direction. Instead of increased evolution toward a Western model, legal reform in the 2000s focused elsewhere: on populism in the legal system, on eliminating potential sources of unrest, and on strengthening of institutions that resolve disputes outside the formal legal process or before they reach court.

Many such new policies were directly linked to the party-state's efforts to address a perceived rise in instability and conflict in China. Media and scholarly accounts described a surge in petitioning and protest in the early part of the 2000s, in particular the phenomenon of petitioners traveling to Beijing to seek redress from central authorities. The party-state's initial response to this new wave of grievances was accommodation. Beginning in 2007, however, the party-state shifted toward an emphasis on preventing disorder at all costs. As a result, local authorities took increasingly coercive measures to quell discontent and to block the raising of grievances to Beijing.[12]

Surprisingly little scholarship has addressed whether China became less stable in the 2000s, or has even defined what "social stability" means in China. The most important metric of social stability appears to be reports of protest and "mass incidents." Such reports are far from comprehensive, however, and largely come from media accounts. China in the 2000s appeared more unstable in part because new media technologies made information about unrest more widely available. Scholars have questioned whether an increased volume of protest necessarily equates to greater instability or is a threat to regime survival.[13] It would also be a mistake to equate the rise of protest to lack of trust in the party-state: the willingness of many to petition and protest may in fact reflect trust in central authorities.[14] Regardless of whether China in fact became less stable during the 2000s, it is clear that the central party-state became increasingly concerned with threats to stability during the period.

The term "social stability" in China is often understood to refer specifically to incidents of protest or social conflict. Yet the phrase has come to cover a much broader swath of activity and discourse, including online discussions of high-profile issues and any conduct that the party-state views as a potential threat to its authority or legitimacy, including corruption, group litigation, and virtually any publicly discussed controversial topic. In short, social instability in China refers both narrowly to acts of protest and also broadly to conduct that party-state officials view as having the potential to create unrest or to challenge the party-state's power.

Stability Concerns in the Formal Legal System

Within the legal system, the clearest evidence of the party-state's obsession with social stability has been the reemphasis on mediation. Renewed attention to mediation began initially with a focus on land disputes, but soon spread to a wide range of contentious and noncontentious civil disputes. The 1980s and 1990s had witnessed a gradual growth in the volume of cases in the courts and in the percentage of cases resolved through adjudication, as opposed to court-supervised mediation. In the 2000s, judges came under pressure to resolve cases through mediation, with courts setting specific targets for the percentage of cases to be mediated. Mediation rates in some jurisdictions exceeded 80 percent.[15]

Mediation and the encouragement of dispute resolution outside the courts are not necessarily in tension with legality. In China, however, mediation is often coercive, with courts and officials exerting extreme pressure on parties to resolve their cases, and with legal rules playing limited roles in guiding outcomes. In major disputes, mediation is often handled through "grand mediation" (*da tiaojie*) led by local party leaders, with courts just one of many actors at the table, and with parties and their families coming under extreme pressure to settle their cases.[16]

Renewed focus on mediation was a direct result of the focus on stability, as courts concluded that mediated cases were less likely to result in petitions or protest than were adjudicated cases. The policy also reflected broader policy shifts, most notably the renewed use of revolutionary concepts of "justice for the people" (*sifa weimin*) and the Ma Xiwu adjudication method of the 1940s, which emphasized judges resolving disputes immediately, on the spot, and in line with popular views.[17] The renewed attention to mediation also reflected recognition that the legal system's ability to resolve contentious social issues such as land disputes was limited.

Most writing on the increased importance of mediation in the 2000s has focused on civil cases. The trend also extended to administrative suits against the government and to criminal cases. The 1989 Administrative Litigation Law stated that mediation was not permitted in administrative cases except administrative compensation proceedings, an apparent attempt to reduce the possibility of coercive mediation. To some degree negotiation and mediation were always parts of administrative litigation, despite the legal ban. In the 2000s, courts increasingly engaged in reconciliation and mediation in administrative cases, and in 2006 official court policies for the first time authorized the practice.

In criminal cases many courts have also sought to resolve cases through negotiated outcomes. The trend is most clear in minor crime cases involving first-time offenders, most notably fight, theft, and traffic crime cases. In some jurisdictions, defendants in such cases who compensate their victims or pay restitution typically receive suspended sentences, meaning no jail time.[18] Yet the trend also exists in more serious cases. One factor determining why some defendants prosecuted for major crimes such as murder avoid execution appears to be whether the defendant (or his or her family) pays compensation and "obtains the understanding of the victim's family."[19]

The emphasis on suspended sentences in routine criminal cases reflects the national policy of "balancing leniency and severity," which encourages leniency so as to mitigate the hard edge of Chinese criminal practice.[20] But it also derives from concerns about social stability: judges note that criminal cases are a frequent source of petitions and protest from both victims' and defendants' families. Judges comment that cases resolved through negotiation and compensation are far less likely to result in escalation than are cases that lack such agreements. Whether negotiated outcomes actually produce stability is, however, unclear: criminal cases continue to be a primary source of complaints concerning the courts, in particular from victims' families suspicious that defendants will avoid punishment through backroom deals.

Concerns about social stability also affect how judges interpret and apply the law. In tort cases, most notably medical disputes, it is routine for judges to adjust outcomes to ensure that aggrieved litigants receive compensation, even if there is no formal legal basis for doing so. Judges comment that in cases that have the potential to impact social stability they often adopt flexible interpretations of the law in order to ensure that aggrieved individuals receive compensation.[21] This flexibility appears particularly common in labor disputes,[22] those involving corporate dissolution and bankruptcy (where layoffs are a risk), and tort cases. Courts in China are often innovative, breaking new legal ground. But such innovation is directed toward pacifying litigants and avoiding escalation.[23] Innovative judging helps insulate courts and judges from criticism, not increase courts' authority.

The effect of state policy emphasizing social stability is also manifest in courts' extreme sensitivity and high level of responsiveness to petitioning. China's petitioning system has longstanding historical roots, both in the early years of the People's Republic and in imperial times. In the late 1990s and 2000, a surge of petitions relating to courts and litigation gave rise to the term "litigation-related petitioning" (*shesu xinfang*). The phrase refers both to petitions directly to the courts and to petitions to Letters and Visits Bureaus and other state entities regarding the courts. At its peak in 1999 the Supreme People's Court (SPC) reported more than ten million petitions filed with the courts.[24] Officially reported numbers subsequently fell dramatically as the SPC instructed lower courts to reduce the volume of complaints and adjusted counting methodologies.[25] By 2011 the official reported number of petitions was fewer than one million per year.[26] Nevertheless, the effects of petitioning on the courts remain significant, as reflected both in courts' responsiveness to petitioners and in court internal evaluation standards.

Courts remain extremely responsive to petitioners, in particular those who threaten or engage in escalation by petitioning to Beijing. Courts, like local governments, continue to send personnel to Beijing to intercept petitioners. Courts often arrange direct payments to petitioners to convince them to stop petitioning. Sometimes such payments come from court or government finances; in other cases the court may pressure a defendant, in particular a corporate defendant, to pay compensation in addition to any already awarded at trial.[27] One study of court-related petitioning found that nearly half of those who went to Beijing to complain about the courts in one northeast municipality received some direct benefit, most often direct cash payments.[28] Some courts have offered petitioners apartments to convince them to stop petitioning. In the run-up to the 2008 Olympics, one court in central China provided color televisions to petitioners to convince them not to go to Beijing. Petitioning often leads courts to rehear already final cases through formal rehearing procedures. Most Western writing on petitioning portrays the petitioning system as nonresponsive to grievances absent collective action or escalation. In contrast, evidence from the courts suggests that even individual petitioners often receive direct benefits.

Petitioning is effective because courts and individual judges continue to be evaluated in part based on the volume of petitions relating to their cases. In the mid-2000s many courts began to consider whether judges' cases had resulted in petitions (regardless of the substantive correctness of such decision) in making determinations regarding promotion and annual bonuses.[29] Judges' obligations are captured in the slogan "decide the case and resolve the matter" (*anjie shiliao*). A judge who does her or his job properly not only reaches a correct decision but also handles the case in a way that results in no escalation. At the national level, the SPC continues to rank lower courts based on the number of petitions to Beijing. Although official reports show a sharp decline in the volume of litigation-related petitions, judges say that the time spent managing or preventing petitioning has not decreased.

Concerns about stability have also meant that courts either refuse to accept or are not permitted to hear a wide range of potentially sensitive cases. These have included numerous claims resulting from high-profile disasters, including the Wenchuan earthquake, the Wenzhou high-speed rail accident, and the melamine-contaminated milk scandal. Courts in some cases have also refused to accept cases on a wide range of issues linked to social unrest such as land disputes. Courts lack authority to accept many sensitive cases and refuse to accept such cases even when they do have such authority.

The 2000s also saw a broader emphasis on populism in and party oversight over the legal system. The term *populism* in the Chinese legal system includes a range of external factors that affect legal institutions, including media oversight and protest. Appeals to populism often mix with party efforts to assert oversight over the courts. The blending of populism and party oversight was captured most clearly in the promotion of the "three supremes" by then SPC president Wang Shengjun: the supremacy of the party's business, the supremacy of popular interests, and the supremacy of the constitution and law.[30]

Many efforts to emphasize populism in the legal system are linked to the belief that the legal system is a source of popular discontent. Under the banner of "an active judiciary" (*sifa nengdong zhuyi*), courts have been instructed to seek out and consider popular views, to provide assistance to those in need, and to serve the interests of the "general situation."[31] The courts' renewed emphasis on holding hearings in the countryside, on including people's assessors alongside judges, and on welcoming People's Congress oversight of the courts, are all practices that had appeared out of favor by the early 2000s.

This appeal to populism was explicitly linked with rejection of foreign legal models and concepts, in particular judicial independence.

Renewed emphasis on populism was not entirely pernicious. Such efforts were designed in part to reduce the disconnect between ordinary people and a legal system viewed by many as increasingly serving the interests of the well connected. Having failed to boost popular confidence through professionalization, courts tried to be more responsive to public demands. Courts made serious efforts to make it easier for litigants to use the courts. In some provinces, most notably Henan, appeals to populism were accompanied by efforts to increase transparency. Beginning in 2009, courts in Henan were instructed to place most of their decisions online, an effort aimed at reducing wrongdoing by judges and increasing confidence in the legal system. More recently, the SPC has likewise called for courts nationwide to make judgments available online.

Stability concerns affect other legal actors as well. Procurators and the police mediate many routine criminal cases. Procurators have also come under pressure from petitioners to file rehearing requests. Yet perhaps the most significant effect of social stability concerns has been encouraging legal institutions, including courts, police, procurators, and judicial bureau officials to work together. These efforts were a retreat from modest steps toward role differentiation that began in the 1990s. As a report in *Caijing* noted, resolution of disputes inside and outside the courts is being unified, and courts are being asked "to take a broader role in social management."[32] Thus, for example, one court in Shanxi reported that judges have joined other party and government entities to engage in "social stability risk evaluation" activities, designed to obtain information about and eliminate potential sources of instability before they arise.[33]

Outside of formal dispute resolution, social stability concerns mean that the "shadow of the law"[34] remains weak. Thus, for example, fear of protest is often the most important determinant of settlements in medical disputes, with defendants at times paying more through settlement than they would potentially pay in court.[35] Similar trends have appeared in labor disputes and in other areas likely to result in unrest. In a system in which stability counts above all else, defendants appear far more concerned about the risks of escalation than the costs of paying out compensation.

Many within the Chinese academic community have pointed out that the emphasis on stability maintenance produces a vicious circle in the legal system. Courts face incentives to prevent escalation and protest, but official responsiveness to petitioning and protest appears to result in more unrest. Senior officials in the legal system, and likely those outside the legal system, are aware of this manifestation of the law-stability paradox, whereby formal law and the authority of legal institutions are undermined by a short-term desire to achieve normatively desirable outcomes. From the outside, the system makes little sense, requiring the state either to continue to be responsive to the threat of unrest or to engage in greater repression to prevent escalation. Yet the paradox remains, with courts and other actors in the legal system coming under extreme pressure to avoid unrest, often by ignoring legal rules.

Nonlegal Institutions

The deemphasis on judicial resolution of disputes in the 2000s occurred alongside the strengthening of other party-state institutions that promote stability. Perceiving rising instability in the 2000s, central authorities invested extensive resources in a range of party-state institutions outside the legal system that were designed to reduce instability and resolve disputes. Officials from party stability offices often take on primary roles in addressing social instability, at times instructing courts and procuratorates regarding the appropriate handling of sensitive cases, or directly intervening to resolve disputes. Details of the overlapping roles of these institutions are often unclear and there is significant variation in the structure and function of such organizations at the local level. My goal in this section is to describe the general trend of the party-state's increased reliance on such institutions. The prominence of party-state stability institutions suggests that central authorities remain ambiguous in their views of the utility of using formal legal institutions to address social conflict.

At the national level, the party's Central Political Legal Committee (*zhengfa weiyuanhui*) (PLC) has long been recognized as the most important party entity overseeing and coordinating actors in the legal system, including the police, procuratorates, courts, and justice bureaus. In the 1990s, two additional overlapping bodies were created at the central level: the Central Commission for Comprehensive Management of Public Security (*zhongyang shehui zhian zonghe zhili weiyuanhui*) and the Central Stability Maintenance Leading Small Group (*zhongyang weihu wending gongzuo lingdao xiaozu*) (LSG). In 2011, the Central Commission for Comprehensive Management of Public Security was renamed the Central Commission for Comprehensive

Social Management (*zhongyang zonghe zhili weiyuanhui*) (CCSM). Although the Central Commission for Comprehensive Management of Public Security was created in the early 1990s, it (and its successor, the CCSM) rose to prominence in the 2000s.[36]

The CCSM is distinct from the PLC. The CCSM describes itself as a party and government coordination body that includes representatives from forty-nine different party and state departments and organizations. It thus includes not only representatives of the police, courts, procuracy, and judicial bureaus, but also representatives of institutions ranging from party organizations such as the Central Disciplinary Commission, Organization Department, and Propaganda Department to government ministries such as the Ministry of Education, Ministry of Justice, and Ministry of Public Health. It appears that virtually every central party entity, ministry, and ministry-level organization is represented on the CCSM.[37] The full CCSM meets a few times a year, although the schedule does not appear fixed.

Despite the formal separation from the PLC, in practice there is significant overlap. The CCSM has a broader mandate than the PLC and includes representatives from a wider range of departments and institutions. Nevertheless, the functional office and working staff of the CCSM are located within the PLC in the Stability Maintenance Coordination Office (*zonghe zhili weiyuanhui bangongshi* or *zongzhiban*) (SCO). The overlapping nature of the work of the PLC and the CCSM is reflected in their joint website, www.chinapeace.org.cn.

The CCSM system appears focused on developing policies aimed at maintaining social stability, generally referred to as "reform of social management." During his time as chair of both the CCSM and of the PLC, former Politburo Standing Committee member Zhou Yongkang explained that the CCSM's responsibilities were varied and wide ranging. They include prevention of juvenile crime, overseeing NGOs, school safety, managing the Internet, fighting crime, developing policy and legislation, and overseeing China's household registration system.[38] Although the CCSM lacks formal powers, its Web site describes the committee as having the power to coordinate the work of various arms of the government, to supervise and assess other party-state entities' work on social management, and to conduct research and submit proposals relating to social management. CCSMs and SCOs at the national and local levels have significant influence, both because they tend to be headed by senior officials, generally the head of the political-legal committee, and because they operate with discretion within the PLCs.

The second relatively new stability organization is the LSG, created in 1998. China has over the years maintained numerous "leading small groups" that focus on particular issues. Although the exact reasons for the creation of the LSG are unclear, the LSG likewise appears to have gradually expanded in importance, shifting its focus from perceived acute threats such as cults and terrorism to social unrest.[39] Local "stability small groups" were mostly created later, generally in the mid-2000s.[40] Like the CCSM, the LSG exists outside the PLC, but its working office and staff are located within the PLC in the Stability Maintenance Office (*weiwenban*) (SMO).[41] The structure is repeated at the provincial and municipal level, although some provincial and local SMOs are located within Letters and Visits Offices, not PLCs. At the local level, LSGs are often headed by party secretaries, with political-legal committee heads serving as deputy directors.[42] SMOs are closely tied to the police; at the national level the SMO has generally been headed by a former deputy minister of public security.

In contrast to the general work of CCSMs and SCOs, the work of LSGs and SMOs at each level is more directly focused on responding to specific incidents of unrest, dissuading and restraining petitioners, and dispute resolution. One of the few detailed reports on the operation of the SMO noted that it was responsible for general policies regarding social stability, propaganda work relating to social stability, assisting and overseeing the resolution of contradictions and disputes at the local level, assisting and leading the management of all types of mass incidents at the local level, and assisting and overseeing management of major cases and mass incidents.[43] More recently, SMOs have also become responsible for evaluating risks to social stability "for all important programs and policies" and have instructed all other work units and departments to engage in a social stability risk evaluation prior to undertaking significant new policies.[44] SMOs also have oversight power over other party-state entities, with the power to issue "yellow cards" to and public criticisms of entities or individuals who are perceived as failing to prevent social unrest or who are responsible for particular incidents.

The dual structure of stability organizations is generally replicated at the provincial and local levels, with provincial and local governments maintaining their own CCSMs, SCOs, LSGs, and SMOs. In practice, however, it appears that much of the work of these entities merges together. This is particularly the case at the township and street levels, where the work of SMOs, SCOs, petitioning offices, and justice bureaus are often combined into "Comprehensive Stability Maintenance Centers."[45] The goal of such efforts is to

resolve disputes through mediation as soon as they arise.[46] Thus, for example, Guangdong reported that each of its 1,504 township and street committees had established comprehensive stability maintenance and petitioning
centers, with 17,000 full-time and many more part-time staff. Guangdong
also reported that local Comprehensive Stability Maintenance Centers were
resolving 95 percent of all petitions and more than 60 percent of all labor
disputes through mediation.[47] Reports from local authorities likewise describe the roles played by local stability organizations in resolving disputes.[48]
In some areas, local Stability Maintenance and Petitioning Centers have been
explicitly tasked with the goal of achieving "zero petitioning and zero litigation."[49] Local stability offices coordinate their efforts with public security
officials but also sometimes have their own personnel to use in responding
to mass incidents.

New offices assigned with the task of maintaining stability (sometimes
with new personnel, sometimes with personnel reassigned from other positions) have also been created in a range of other party-state entities, including major state-owned enterprises and universities. Responsibilities of such
offices largely mirror stability organizations in other party-state entities,
with corporate stability offices explicitly instructed to coordinate with local
party and state institutions.[50]

Details of the work performed by the varied organizations assigned to
manage stability, including SMOs and SCOs, are only sometimes available.
Nevertheless, two aspects of their work are clear. First, the resources that
have been devoted to the range of stability maintenance organizations over
the past decade have been extraordinary.[51] Faced with rising social instability, authorities at each level of the party-state have poured resources into
offices and organizations operating outside the formal legal system dedicated to maintaining stability. Second, in many cases stability maintenance
officials have extensive roles, ranging from the power to intercept and detain
individual petitioners; to making payments to petitioners to settle grievances; to hiring private security companies to intercept, detain, and return
petitioners to their home jurisdictions;[52] to directly coordinating and overseeing mediation of disputes. These roles are executed with no formal legal
authority.

Outside the formal work of the SMOs, SCOs, and other offices assigned
to manage stability, concerns about stability have come to influence virtually
all aspects of officials' work, the result of the creation of a "single veto" system
for individual officials. Under the system, failure to deal properly with a single

incident of unrest can veto any chance of promotion, regardless of the quality of other work performed.[53] Such policies also provided incentives for repression, evidenced most clearly in the "black jails" that were created to detain petitioners without any legal process.

Legal reform did not stop in the Hu-Wen era. Reforms continued in many areas, with important new laws governing labor, torts, and criminal procedure. Reforms to the criminal law and to review procedures in capital cases resulted in a significant decline in the volume of executions. Courts continued to emphasize the training of judges. Nevertheless, the 2000s brought deepening distrust of law and legal institutions, a shift away from formal legal procedures and institutions, and investment in a range of nonlegal stability maintenance organizations. It is impossible to know whether state stability efforts succeeded: would there have been more or less unrest without such efforts? The reliance on new institutions may have in part reflected concerns that the legal system lacked the ability to handle a rise in claims.[54] In some areas, most notably labor disputes following the enactment of the Labor Contract Law in 2007, a surge in the volume of disputes tested courts' ability to adapt.

Yet the institutional capacity of the courts appears to be a weak explanation in other areas, including high-profile tort cases where courts were not permitted to handle cases. The total number of civil cases accepted by China's courts increased from 4.8 million in 2003 to 7.2 million in 2011.[55] Most of the increase came in the later portion of the Hu-Wen decade. The problem facing courts, however, is not just that many disputes are kept out of the formal legal system; it is that even when disputes enter the formal system, courts often are under pressure to issue decisions that take account of a range of nonlegal factors.

What changed in the Hu-Wen era? Rising social unrest brought a perceived need for rapid political responses. The color revolutions of the early 2000s and the Arab Spring of 2011 heightened concerns that legal reforms threatened party-state leadership. Perceived public distrust in formal legal institutions led to greater emphasis on populism and informal dispute resolution. In important respects, however, little changed. Commitment to both reform and stability has characterized legal development for much of the PRC's history. In the 2000s concerns about stability gained a more prominent role. The lack of differentiation between legal and nonlegal institutions has deep revolutionary and prerevolutionary roots. Flexibility has been a key part of both political and legal policy since the earliest days of the PRC.

Courts in China have always been responsible for a wide range of tasks other than adjudicating disputes and work under the leadership and direct guidance of PLCs and other party institutions. The creation of new institutions and the realignment of incentives for officials to address perceived crises has long been a characteristic of PRC governance. Indeed the claim that the party-state has invested in a range of new nonlegal institutions in order to address instability presumes a distinction between such institutions that has largely been inapplicable in China.

One consequence of official emphasis on eliminating all potential sources of instability is that many ordinary grievances and disputes are transformed into negotiations and disputes with the state. Internal contradictions thus become external contradictions. The problem is not only that the party-state is focusing too heavily on stability and treating routine signs of discontent as evidence of crisis. The problem may also be that the party-state has put too much emphasis on responding to public demands, a phenomenon I have referred to elsewhere as the "overresponsive state."[56] The party-state's selective responsiveness—and the lack of rules or guidelines dictating when grievances are addressed—is itself an important source of unrest.

Prospects for Reform

Since coming to power in late 2012, Xi Jinping has embraced the concept of "rule of law China" (*fazhi zhongguo*). Xi has called for greater emphasis on the legal system and has stressed the importance of raising popular trust in legal work.[57] Official media have echoed such calls and have devoted extensive attention to the importance of law as a primary tool for resolving disputes and regulating government behavior. Some in the legal community have viewed the emphasis on "rule of law China" as a sign of a significant new commitment to strengthening law; others have interpreted such statements as an opening to push for deepening legal reforms.

The Third Plenum's Decision in November 2013 announced multiple potentially important reforms. Most notable was the closure of the widely condemned reeducation through labor system, which allowed the police to sentence individuals to three years in detention without judicial review. The Decision emphasized the importance of human rights, the constitution, and judicial independence, and called for renewed efforts to rein in corruption. The decision also called for reexamination of the role of court adjudication committees,[58] expansion of legal aid, greater emphasis on transparency in the courts, elimination of the use of torture, addressing and avoiding wrongful convictions, and reducing the number of crimes subject to the death penalty. The Decision provides only a general framework for reform. Nevertheless, it has been interpreted by some within China as evidence of renewed commitment to legal reform. Serious efforts are also being made to implement the revised criminal procedure law, which became effective on January 1, 2013. Reports have also circulated suggesting that party officials are investigating former Politburo Standing Committee Zhou Yongkang, the person most closely associated with the stability-at-all-costs approach of the 2000s. Some have viewed such reports as a sign that party-state leaders are serious about reducing abuses committed in the name of stability and are committed to greater use of formal legal institutions to address social conflict.

Yet proposed reforms have come alongside renewed focus on stability, reflected in the announced creation of a new "National Security Commission" under the direct leadership of Xi Jinping. The exact structure and role of the commission and its relationship to existing bodies such as the PLC, the CCSM, and the LSG remains unclear. It is clear, however, that the new commission signals continued and deepening commitment to addressing perceived external and internal threats to security and stability.

Proposed legal reforms are also not likely to have much significance for individuals the state views as threats. This has been made clear by the reemergence of party-state concerns that legal reform could be used to challenge the authority of the party-state. Reports have noted bans issued by party officials on the discussion of topics such as "judicial independence" and "constitutionalism" in the media and in universities.[59] A number of prominent legal activists were detained in the second half of 2013, suggesting that the boundaries of politically permissible activities were shrinking even as party-state leaders were calling for renewed focus on law. Xi Jinping has also reemphasized the role of mass line ideology, raising questions about the significance of proposed reforms. There are signs that many individuals who would previously have been sentenced to reeducation through labor, including drug users and prostitutes, are being detained through other forms of arbitrary detention. Xi's "rule of law China" will likely continue to include the explicit embrace of populism, rejection of Western models, and the reliance on a range of legal and nonlegal actors to address social conflict.

For example, one likely consequence of renewed emphasis on fighting corruption is increased authority for party discipline commissions. Reports have suggested that Politburo Standing Committee member Wang Qishan, the new head of the Central Disciplinary Commission, has been given authority over the legal system. Rather than reflecting deeper commitment to following legal rules and procedures, increased power for discipline commissions suggests a continuation of the longstanding practice of using nonlegal actors to address perceived threats to stability and party legitimacy.

Increased reliance on party discipline authorities reflects China's law-stability paradox. Legal institutions are likely too weak to address extensive problems that threaten stability and the legitimacy of party rule. Reliance on traditional tools of party control may be a short-term necessity. Yet relying on party institutions, be it the PLCs, stability organizations, or discipline commissions, also reinforces the secondary role played by legal actors, and in so doing may make rule-based solutions more difficult in the long run. Legal institutions are not trusted to resolve perceived crises or major problems. As a result, legal institutions are not given the space or authority necessary to become stronger.

New attention to reforming the legal system appears unlikely to lead to radical changes either to how the party-state views law or how it manages instability and crisis. The precise content of "rule of law China" remains unclear. But it is clear that the "rule of law" central party-state officials have embraced means something very different than that sought by liberals in China. Evidence from the past decade makes clear that China's political-legal system is focused on conflict elimination, not protection of individual rights.

Much writing on recent legal developments in China views the deemphasis on law in the past decade as reflecting rising distrust of law and legal institutions among China's top leadership. Such distrust has clearly increased in the past decade. Yet viewing recent developments only in terms of central leadership authority is a mistake. Recent literature also suggests decreased levels of belief among ordinary people that the legal system can protect their interests.[60] The choice by many to seek redress outside the legal system is rational given the incentives local authorities face to prevent protest. Such choices also may reflect rising popular views that the legal system largely favors the politically and economically connected.[61] Communist Party officials are not the only constituency who distrust law: ordinary people likewise recognize the difficulty of using legal rules to protect their interests. The challenge for any serious efforts to strengthen the role of law in addressing social conflict is not only to realign incentives that local officials face in ways that encourage them to follow legal rules. The challenge is also to convince those most likely to engage in acts of unrest or resistance that the legal system can protect their interests.

Conclusion

China's law-stability paradox reflects tension between the party-state's interest in short-term stability and the long-term need for a rule-based system. Recent scholarship has observed trends against institutionalization and the continuing importance of revolutionary approaches to governance.[62] Crisis management continues to dominate, even within a system that has invested in the creation of new institutions to facilitate rule-based dispute resolution. Many recent developments in the legal system have historical roots: the lack of differentiation between legal and nonlegal actors, the party-state's reliance on flexible approaches to law, and the creation of new institutions to address perceived threats to stability and legitimacy. Facing uncertainty and rapid change, China's leadership has relied on familiar techniques of social management and control. China's party-state appears to view law as one of many tools in its governance toolkit, not as an overarching answer to the many problems the party-state confronts.

Reliance on nonlegal institutions also reflects weaknesses in formal legal institutions. Courts in China are playing roles in an expanding range of substantive areas. But they continue to serve more as forums for the airing of grievances than as institutions for resolving legal uncertainty. Courts also appear trapped in a cycle of popular distrust. Because legal institutions are not trusted, individuals frequently seek recourse outside the legal system. The lack of trust, from party officials and the public, also means that legal institutions are not given the authority to act that might allow them to increase public confidence.

Yet the law-stability paradox also reflects uncertainty about the party-state's own legitimacy and about the proper role of law in managing a time of unprecedented change. The central party-state has linked its legitimacy to outcomes and has perpetuated the idea of central officials being "father and mother officials" who are responsive to the grievances of ordinary people. In so doing, the party-state has created a dynamic in which it believes it must respond to complaints that threaten to escalate into unrest, even when doing so violates legal norms. Law in China operates in the shadow of protest, with legal issues transformed into political questions—the opposite of de Tocqueville's observation about the United States that "scarcely any political question arises . . . that is not resolved, sooner or later, into a judicial question."[63] Strengthening the role law plays in regulating Chinese society and citizen-state interactions requires not only boosting legal institutions but also altering the ways in which the party-state conceives of its own legitimacy.

China's law-stability paradox may also be a sign of ambiguity within China about the appropriate role of law in managing a society engaged in unprecedented social transformation. Although official rhetoric has emphasized the role that law can play in ensuring stability, evidence from the past decade suggests that top leadership perceives law as constraining efforts to maintain social stability. Developments in China suggest an inability to confront the trade-off between short-term stability maintenance goals and the long-term stability that many in China argue would follow from deeper embrace of legal rules and procedures.

Recent literature on the Western financial crisis has noted the ways in which excessive reliance on formal rules can constrain actors in a way that deepens crisis.[64] China's leadership may not have explicitly embraced such reasoning. But elements of China's approach to managing instability, in particular the continued desire to be able to move rapidly and flexibly, have parallels to proposals by those in the West who argue that excessive reliance on legal rules can at times exacerbate a crisis. The problem is not that China has created safety valves for managing unrest outside the legal system. The problem is that China has not created rules governing when and how such safety valves should be used.

China's embrace of nonlegal solutions to instability in the 2000s was likely the product of short-term political calculations and traditional policy approaches to managing conflict, not long-term concern about the constraining force of law. Nevertheless, implicit in this approach was also recognition that rigid adherence to legal rules risked further unrest, in particular in a society in which respect for legal norms and processes is not deeply rooted and in which popular ideas of justice are at times in tension with legal rules. The threat of instability in China comes not only from local officials who ignore the law; it comes from the disconnect between popular expectations regarding the obligations of the state to look after its citizens and the reality on the ground, and also between popular conceptions of justice and formal written law. Recognizing parallels between official concerns about excessive reliance on rules in China and emerging theories on how legal systems should (or should not) respond to uncertainty suggests that the law-stability paradox that emerged in China in the 2000s was not merely a reactive attempt to maintain party-state control, but also reflected deeper questions about the role law plays in managing change and uncertainty.

CHAPTER 10

China's Military Modernization: Many Improvements, Three Challenges, and One Opportunity

Andrew S. Erickson

China has exploited key technological and military operational trends to address its core security interests relatively efficiently, and with increasing effectiveness, to the potential detriment of the interests of its neighbors and the United States. Yet, despite this remarkable advancement, it confronts three mounting challenges moving forward, as well as one major opportunity.

1) While China's land borders with all nations save India and Bhutan are settled, its major island and maritime claims in the "Near Seas" (Yellow, East, and South China Seas) remain unresolved.

2) Further increasing military capabilities to address conflicting claims is efficient technologically but may trigger negative reactions regionally and undermine China in both military and nonmilitary respects.

3) Developing long-range combat capabilities such as world-class deck aviation requires significant advances in hardware, software, organization, and integration. Achieving these reforms would be unprecedented in difficulty. Prioritizing requisite resources may be difficult given diffuse objectives amid proliferation of competing priorities.

4) China's one great security opportunity lies in the fact that the vast majority of its growing overseas interests may be addressed through a

combination of more easily achievable low-end military capabilities, nonmilitary dimensions of national power, and cooperation with other nations, particularly the United States.

This chapter begins by examining People's Liberation Army (PLA) development and key dynamics. It then discusses the three aforementioned major challenges facing China and its military before explaining how the PLA might enhance its ability to address them. It concludes by considering the potential for China to address its overseas security interests by enhancing cooperation with the militaries of the United States and other nations.

Overview

Beyond continued improvements within existing parameters, there are three major interrelated spectra along which the nature and scope of the PLA's development can be measured, as outlined in Table 10.1. The first is distance from China's homeland. For now, the PLA is focused most strongly on nearby areas where it enjoys geographic and physics-based advantages; further away, it suffers from physics-based limitations and vulnerabilities. The second is jurisdiction, which influences the nature and scope of presence, deterrence, or conflict. The PLA is focused on addressing outstanding territorial and maritime claims on China's periphery, where it requires stand-alone capabilities, but does not need major combat capabilities for the global commons because it can take advantage of the U.S. provision of security there. The third is operational disposition, which affects capabilities and options regarding force employment. The PLA continues to rely on overlapping

Table 10.1. Key Dimensions of PLA Progress

Variable	Spectrum	Implication
Distance	Homeland vs. abroad	Physics-based advantages/ limitations/vulnerabilities
Jurisdiction	Sovereign territory/claims vs. commons	Degree/nature/scope of presence/deterrence/conflict
Operational disposition	Overlap vs. integration	Capabilities and options regarding use of force

capabilities clustered primarily in mainland China and radiating with diminishing intensity from there. It enjoys many workarounds to maximize capabilities and minimize limitations. To project power under contested conditions far away, it could not rely on such a patchwork of potent but uneven components, but would have to develop far more sophisticated, integrated capabilities. The PLA will likely continue to progress along these spectra, but doing so is far more difficult than strengthening existing approaches. It will be arduous, time-consuming, and expensive.

Asymmetric Focus

China has astutely harnessed the proliferation of asymmetric technologies to its benefit, with special relevance to the Near Seas and their immediate approaches. China's evolving platforms and weaponry suggest a strategy consistent with Beijing's focus on Taiwan and other outstanding claims there. Since World War II, the United States has helped to secure and maintain the global commons—key media used by all but owned by none. Initially, this involved the sea and air; more recently, it has come to include the space and cyberspace dimensions. For a long time to come, the United States will remain the only nation capable of operating in multiple places simultaneously in the global commons, thanks to continued superiority in long-range precision strike, power projection, and nonmilitary operations support capabilities.

In order to further its interests, however, Beijing wishes to impose controversial territorial notions on the portions of these commons that adjoin its territorial waters and airspace, and to do so is developing "counterintervention" capabilities designed specifically to dissuade U.S. and allied military intervention in any related scenarios. Such an approach purposely avoids matching U.S. forces directly and instead privileges operations optimized for a relatively narrow range of contingencies and missions.

Regional and U.S. Reactions

While increasingly dependent on China economically, China's Near Seas neighbors increasingly fear its military development and its intentions because aspects of its behavior alarm them. They therefore seek closer cooperation with other powers, particularly the United States. For their part, U.S. policymakers worry that China has become increasingly capable of exploiting the aforementioned asymmetric trends to undermine America's preeminent position in world affairs. In Washington's view, in the Near Seas themselves, and possibly beyond them over time, China is working to carve out a sphere of strategic influence within which freedom of navigation and other important international system-sustaining norms do not apply.

China is already capable of engaging in some form of counterintervention operations within and around the Near Seas, assisted in part by its land-based Second Artillery Force (SAF), as well as in other types of longer-range operations: precision strike, space, and global cyber espionage activities. This counterintervention challenge threatens U.S. naval platforms, but is far more than just a Chinese navy-based threat. It could already be difficult for the United States to handle kinetically with its current approaches, and the situation appears to be worsening rapidly. The United States may not have years to develop new countermeasures and prepare to address the most difficult aspects of the problem. There is even a concern that China could eventually become an East Asian hegemon. Since its postwar ascent to superpower status, Washington has strongly opposed any Eurasian state's efforts to dominate the region. This remains the case, and a rising China chafes increasingly at what it perceives as U.S.-led containment.

Short-Range Advantages, Long-Range Challenges

While China's comprehensive national power may continue to increase rapidly, growth may, alternatively, slow or even falter. China is already facing increasing headwinds and constraints. These negative factors could manifest themselves even as China challenges the dominance of U.S., allied, and friendly forces increasingly via asymmetric means, especially in the Near Seas.

Demographic challenges, economic problems, and even resulting political instability could combine with rising nationalism to motivate Chinese leaders to adopt more confrontational military approaches, particularly regarding unresolved claims. If this is the case, the era in which China poses the greatest potential to challenge its neighbors and U.S. regional interests may have already begun. Assuming that high-intensity kinetic conflict can be avoided given shared U.S. and Chinese interests, China's greatest challenge to the interests of its neighbors and the United States might thus be the already-unfolding strategic competition, friction, pressuring, and occasional crises on, under, and over the Near Seas.

Far Seas Opportunities

In keeping with President Hu Jintao's broad 2004 directives to safeguard China's national security in all domains while supporting economic development and world peace—which his successor Xi Jinping has yet to alter visibly—beyond the Near Seas and their immediate approaches, China's expansion of military power projection is proceeding only at a very limited level of intensity and does not pose a serious problem for the United States or China's neighbors. As a growing great power, it is widely expected that China will increase its presence in this realm, and in many respects it is welcomed. The United States continues to have many viable options to address any problems that might emerge in this area, at least regarding a high-intensity kinetic conflict. Chinese forces themselves are highly vulnerable to precisely the same types of asymmetric approaches that they can employ to great effect closer to China's shores. Given this, there is substantial room for cooperation beyond the Near Seas. China's increasing overseas interests and capabilities allow it to contribute in unprecedented ways. In the maritime domain, China appears to be cautiously open to U.S. ideas about defending common trade routes, and is willing to take advantage of U.S. security guarantees.

Historical Context

To understand where China is coming from strategically, and where it may be going, it is necessary to consider key historical dynamics.

National Security Interests

China has historically pursued three core grand strategic goals: "first and foremost, the preservation of domestic order and well-being in the face of different forms of social strife; second, the defense against persistent external threats to national sovereignty and territory; and third, the attainment and maintenance of geopolitical influence as a major, and perhaps primary, state."[1] This prioritization of objectives offers enduring explanatory power for PLA development. Unlike Imperial and Nazi Germany, the Soviet Union, and other states that overextended themselves for ideological reasons, China has consistently addressed core objectives foremost, and only pursued lesser priorities as resources and circumstances have permitted.

Since 1949, this prioritization may be depicted as the disturbance formed when a stone hits water, with Chinese Communist Party (CCP) leadership continuity a sphere of foremost concern, resting on a steep cone of party-state institutions; domestic stability of core ethnic majority Han areas next as a pronounced indentation; homeland security and retention of borderlands after that as the first of a series of ever-diminishing concentric ripples; and addressing unresolved territorial and maritime claims a more distant, still largely unrealized objective. Only since rapprochement, Deng's reforms and Four Modernizations, the Soviet Union's collapse, and China's subsequent rise in economic and overseas influence has another major layer of security concerns been addressed in substantive depth: China's growing extraregional interests and its expatriates' security and welfare. Finally, while China has always pursued some form of international influence as a great power, it has far greater ability to do so now that it has made progress on more immediate concerns such as the ability to exert influence on its maritime periphery.

The Influence of Geography Upon PLA Development

The stone hitting water metaphor corresponds well to the physical dimensions of PLA development. China's overall military capabilities remain limited in geographic reach, and the PLA has yet to develop fully the wide range of platforms, weapons systems, supporting infrastructure, and integration capabilities needed for large-scale, high-intensity power projection far beyond its immediate maritime periphery and lengthy land borders. Close to home, PLA capabilities are rapidly reaching a very high level. However, they are making much slower progress, from a much lower baseline, further away. The major exceptions to this diffusion-gradient pattern occur in cyberspace, in which physical distances are meaningless, and space, in which China's capabilities are more evenly distributed, and hence more global, in nature. For the most part, China is prioritizing Near Seas defenses, with "Far Seas" (i.e., beyond-Near-Seas) capabilities a very distant second.

China's emerging military development pattern clearly reflects its relative prioritization of security concerns. Its military capabilities may be expressed using a series of concentric circles, or "range rings," with the most advanced, potent, and numerous platforms and weapons systems concentrated on China's shores, in its territorial waters and airspace (up to twelve nautical miles from its shores), and in its claimed exclusive economic zone (EEZ), which potentially includes even southern reaches of the South China Sea. To this, on November 23, 2013, China added over the East China Sea what may be the first of multiple air defense identification zones (ADIZs). Here, China's capabilities are advancing rapidly. It is building capabilities to accomplish its primary military task: "winning local wars under informatized conditions," in which information-based systems play a critical role.[2]

PLA development thus far has been focused largely on achieving forces capable of coercing Taiwan and counterintervention capabilities to prevent Taiwan from declaring independence, in part by developing credible capabilities to thwart U.S. forces should Washington intervene; it is applying this approach throughout the Near Seas. The PLA's current order of battle is based primarily on the world's foremost array of land-based, mobile, conventionally armed missiles; diesel submarines armed with cruise missiles, torpedoes, and sea mines; and improving variants of surface ships and aircraft outfitted with increasingly capable missiles. Though already formidable in firepower, it remains sized and shaped primarily for defending claims on China's disputed maritime periphery. Far Seas operations applications may face limitations because of the smaller portfolio of capabilities with which missile operations can be combined. Quality remains prioritized over quantity.

Scope and intensity of PLA development should not be confused. China is seeking to further its core interests by pursuing an asymmetric approach. Using a side-by-side comparison of all Chinese and American forces as the key metric, as is sometimes done by those who would minimize the PLA's significance, is only relevant if one assumes that the pertinent scenario is a Cold War-style Sino-American global conflict—a virtual impossibility, fortunately. Rather, to assess relevant scenarios, one must compare the actual assets that relevant militaries could deploy, which must done in the context of their missions and geopolitical constraints.

Feeding and Arming the Dragon

Beijing is developing its military much as Deng developed China's market economy: by initiating modernization in the most promising and strategic areas, followed by less-developed, less-crucial areas. China's development of a modern strategic arsenal is part of a comprehensive and costly—though gradual, long-term, and cost-effective—military modernization. Quantity of platforms, weapons systems, and personnel is being held even or reduced while quality is being rapidly increased and integration and training are being steadily improved.

China's FY2014 defense budget is roughly $132 billion. Even if actual spending exceeds that official figure significantly, China's defense spending is second only to that of the United States—albeit several hundred billion dollars less. This already gives China sufficient funding to develop formidable military capabilities for use on its immediate periphery and in its general region, but not to develop a global force like that of the United States.

Lower Chinese labor and material costs increase purchasing power substantially in certain areas, thereby enabling China to afford considerable capabilities even if official budgets reflect more and more of actual spending. Beijing is investing heavily in science, technology, research and development (R&D), and education in order to facilitate its military modernization. China's defense industry, while still uneven in efficiency and quality of output, is improving steadily. Together, these factors enable steady increases in overall PLA capabilities, with particularly rapid progress in selected areas such as missiles, submarines, warships, and electronic warfare, and with particularly strong application to the Near Seas and their immediate approaches. Cyber and, to some extent, space capabilities are important exceptions to this overall geographic pattern of prioritization, concentration, and capability decreasing sharply with distance.

As part of a larger process of creating expanding "pockets of excellence," China has made great progress in developing certain strategic weapons. For example, increasingly secure second-strike capabilities offer nuclear deterrence, and China boasts the world's only long-range anti-ship ballistic missile.

China is also one of the few nations actively developing and testing counter-space and hypersonic weapons technologies.

Current Challenges

Unresolved Claims, Regional Blowback

Great power balancing and contention, largely ended in Western Europe and North America, is alive and well in Asia. China distinguishes between its present domestic and regional focus and the earlier actions of European powers, which seized overseas colonies and otherwise used military force coercively far beyond their homelands. Close to its own continental homeland, however, it is assertive like few nations today. Regarding present territorial and maritime claims, Beijing is unyielding—and has increasing options to support its position. China has settled its previously extensive land border disputes with all thirteen of its continental neighbors save India and Bhutan. By contrast, it has not resolved territorial and maritime claims completely with *any* of its eight maritime neighbors—a striking disparity.

In 2011, when asked by the author to explain this disparity, an expert at the Chinese Academy of Social Science's Center for Chinese Borderland History and Geography stated that China's pre-1949 treaties had to be honored vis-à-vis continental neighbors such as Russia. By this logic, because no other states judged such agreements to be unfair, Beijing had no redress. However, while Beijing resents all "unequal" treaties that it was forced to sign during the Century of Humiliation, its approach appears to vary based on strategic cost-benefit analysis. It relinquished claims to vast territories in order to obtain security, maritime focus, commerce, and technology deemed essential for development. For instance, Beijing quietly concluded comprehensive border negotiations with Moscow in 1987–2004—thereby effectively reinforcing multiple concessions from previous periods of weakness, including the 1858 Treaty of Aigun, which effectively transferred over one million km^2 of territory to Russia. While the expert failed to address the 1895 Sino-Japanese Treaty of Shimonoseki/Maguan directly, Beijing maintains that the 1945 Potsdam Declaration mandated return of all territories seized by Japan. Beijing thus perceives no treaty restrictions vis-à-vis maritime neighbors. Instead, it offers them "joint development," but claims all sovereignty for itself—ignoring sovereign claims deeply rooted in popular sentiment from its counterparts and coercing them when they respond.

From Beijing's perspective, these disputes stem from failure to recognize China's rightful interests, including the preeminent regional power status that it is now regaining as it overcomes historical injustices. China's Near Seas claims encompass an area of substantial economic activity and resource extraction, transit, and processing for China. For these reasons, the Near Seas and their immediate approaches absorb the bulk of Chinese strategic focus and military deployment, and will likely continue to do so for the foreseeable future.

Central to China's territorial concerns is Taiwan's status; Beijing does not accept the fact that while Washington does not support Taiwan's independence, it nevertheless seeks to ensure that islanders are not coerced militarily or forced to relinquish their democratic system. Mainland China maintains that Taiwan must commit to a process of reunification by an unspecified time in the future, and Beijing insists that it will intervene militarily if necessary to prevent Taipei from declaring independence. Because the PRC remains unable to realize reunification with Taiwan, but insists on pursuing its "One China" principle, Taiwan's status remains Beijing's single greatest military development driver. The issue may intensify when China's economic and military power has increased to the point where Beijing feels more able to assert its interests.

Despite recent improvements in cross-Strait relations, China's leaders are likely to continue to expend considerable energy and resources on preparations to coerce Taiwan because they worry about national strength and territorial integrity, CCP popular legitimacy, and succession politics. The majority of current foreign military analyses suggest that, particularly because of the island's inherent geographic advantages, China lacks the capability to conduct a successful amphibious invasion of Taiwan, particularly if the United States elected to intervene. A missile and air strike campaign combined with an air and naval blockade, by contrast, could devastate Taiwan's military capability and economy while affording China a defensive position. Because submarines and strikes from attack aircraft employing standoff munitions, missiles, and mines are integral to the Joint Blockade Campaign, one of several major potential operations which the PLA trains to execute, the significant PRC buildup of these armaments has altered the military balance in the mainland's favor. Current force balances suggest that, *absent American assistance*, Taiwan is likely already unable to prevent the PLA from attacking it with missile strikes or pressuring it with a blockade. The PLA is more capable of imposing a blockade than an amphibious invasion, and with greater speed. In a worst-case scenario, such capability might encourage Chinese decision makers to force Taiwan to stop whatever Beijing perceives as having started the war before U.S. assistance could arrive. Moreover, the PLA has increasing ability to make any U.S. intervention in such a conflict extremely costly.

Other potential sources of Sino-American friction include disagreement surrounding the Senkaku/Diaoyu Islands, covered by the U.S.-Japan Security Treaty based on Tokyo's administration of them; disputed areas in the South China Sea; and unintended incidents involving Chinese and foreign government platforms above, on, or under China's claimed EEZ, including in its ADIZ. The last might occur during U.S. surveillance missions, which occur in international waters and airspace but which Beijing opposes. China's 2013 decision to consolidate four of its five major maritime law enforcement agencies under its State Oceanic Administration facilitates fine-tuning of Near Seas pressure, and frees PLA Navy (PLAN) forces to focus farther afield.

China has EEZ and continental shelf disputes in the Yellow Sea with South Korea and in the East China Sea with Japan, as well as island disputes with Japan. In the South China Sea, while China has cooperated with Vietnam in delimiting maritime claims in the Beibu/Tonkin Gulf, Beijing retains significant disputes with Hanoi and all its other neighbors. The PRC has sovereignty (territory)·disputes with Taiwan, Vietnam, Malaysia, the Philippines, and perhaps Brunei. It has jurisdiction (sea zones and accompanying resources) disputes with all of the former parties as well as Indonesia.

Given the South China Sea's status as a resource-rich, heavily transited portion of the global maritime commons, with portions abutted and claimed by many nations, it is likely to be the most strategically central and contested of the Near Seas. Discussions with unofficial Chinese interlocutors by the author in Beijing in 2011–2012 further suggest a hierarchy of Chinese interests, in which South China Sea islands and surrounding waters constitute a "core interest"—a term that has been avoided in official statements. By this logic, the EEZ is China's "vital interest." China has "important interests" in freedom of navigation in the high seas. All territorial integration is a core issue, but, in the view of China's leadership, safeguarding Beijing's core interest in the South China Sea islands is different from safeguarding China's interests in the "big three" sensitive areas—Xinjiang, Tibet, and Taiwan.

Despite its persistence in its South China Sea claims and use of a "nine-dashed line" on all official maps, Beijing offers no definitive official basis for these claims, instead allowing official and semi-official interlocutors to draw selectively on as many as four different legal arguments—sovereign waters, historic waters, island claims, and security interests—apparently to maximize claims while dismissing the contradictions therein.

This is part of a larger pattern in which China is attempting to lead a small minority of roughly 23 of 192 UN member states in promoting revisionist and inconsistent interpretations of the UN Convention on the Law of the Sea (UNCLOS) in order to prohibit undesired operation of foreign military platforms in its claimed EEZ and the airspace above it, including in its ADIZ. From Washington's perspective, Chinese prohibition of military operations in virtually the entire South China Sea would undermine freedom of navigation in some of the world's most important shipping and energy lanes, as well as set a precedent for the 38 percent of the world's oceans potentially claimed as EEZ areas to be similarly restricted—even by nations that lack the capacity to maintain order there in the face of substate threats. The United States is therefore working with interested members of the Association of Southeast Asian Nations (ASEAN), not to adjudicate regional maritime claim disputes—which it does not do as a matter of policy—but rather to ensure that these nations are not unduly pressured by China.

Recent U.S. offers to support ASEAN members in efforts to "multilateralize" discussion of disputes over South China Sea claims, and Beijing's angry responses, threaten to make this a particular zone of tension in the future. Since June 2011, Beijing appears to have improved its regional relations by implementing a more measured approach to managing, though not to settling, claims. It remains uncertain whether this merely represents a temporary response to changes in the regional security environment and adjustment following previous overreaching. Even now, PLAN-affiliated voices continue to express positions at odds with this peaceful approach, with some going so far as to advocate surgical strikes to reclaim reefs and waters occupied by the Philippines and Vietnam to end intractable problems once and for all, teach the smaller nations a lesson to warn others, and show them their place strategically.

While China safeguards all substantive and symbolic aspects of its own sovereignty vigorously, its neighbors perceive a double standard. A key example occurred in the aftermath of North Korea's March 26, 2010, sinking of South Korean corvette ROKS *Cheonan* (PCC-772) on South Korea's side of the Koreas' de-facto maritime boundary, killing forty-six sailors; and in its November 23, 2010, shelling of South Korea's Yeonpyeong Island, killing two marines and two civilians. Instead of condemning Pyongyang's behavior, which contravened UN and other international norms, Beijing treated both sides equally, hosted Kim Jong-il for a state visit afterward, called for calm, and thwarted meaningful UN sanctions. With the Kim Jong-un regime seeking to demonstrate its military credentials and engage in "shakedown diplomacy" to demand foreign aid, Beijing will likely face further charges of abetting an irresponsible actor.

Given China's increasingly assertive rhetoric and reliance on nationalism as a source of party legitimacy amid possible economic and social challenges, it is unlikely to become more positive or conciliatory in the near future. To some, this represents the partial abandonment of nearly three decades of pragmatic, modest, and extremely effective policies instituted by Deng Xiaoping, who encapsulated them with the slogan "Keep cool-headed to observe, be composed to make reactions, stand firmly, hide our capabilities and bide our time, never try to take the lead, and be able to accomplish something." In 2009, Hu Jintao revised Deng's dictum partially to "uphold (*jianchi*) keeping a low profile and bide [our] time, while actively (*jiji*) getting something accomplished."[3] Where many of China's neighbors were recently attracted by its impressive "soft power" approach, they are now increasingly concerned and seek U.S. support as a "hedge" against Chinese irredentism.

U.S. Counterpressure

Beyond safeguarding its homeland and defending its allies, the United States' fundamental strategic objective remains the defense of the international system, in part through securing the global commons. Following the U.S.-led effort to construct this system throughout the Cold War, this now consists of maintaining the existing system. In order to preserve its ability to do so in an era of disruptive new technologies and domestic resource constraints, Washington is now prioritizing its Asia-Pacific presence and working to enhance its diplomatic and military approaches thereto. As National Security Advisor Thomas Donilon has emphasized, the United States is engaging in "strategic rebalancing" by "turning our attention to Asia and resources to Asia, mindshare, if you will, and policy attention to Asia."[4] Then-Secretary of State Hillary Clinton referred to this same transition as a "strategic pivot."[5] President Obama is determined to prioritize the region so as to "allocate the resources necessary to maintain a strong military [and] security presence in Asia."[6] In what President Obama himself terms a "broader shift," he recently declared: "I have . . . made a deliberate and strategic decision—as a Pacific nation, the United States will play a larger and longer-term role in shaping this region and its future. . . . I have directed my national security team to make our presence and mission in the Asia Pacific a top priority. As a result, reductions in U.S. defense spending will not . . . come at the expense of the Asia Pacific. . . . we will allocate the resources necessary to maintain our strong military presence in this region."[7]

In the diplomatic realm, Washington is strengthening cooperation with friends, allies, and partners regionwide. This involves initiatives such as pursuing free trade agreements like that with Korea in 2011 and the Trans-Pacific Partnership. In the security realm specifically, in keeping with its concept of defense of the global system, the United States is emphasizing that it will not let smaller nations be bullied. In July 2010, for instance, Secretary Clinton declared at the ASEAN Regional Forum in Hanoi that Washington would not support unilateral military efforts to change the South China Sea status quo. In her words, "the United States helped shape a regionwide effort to protect unfettered access to and passage through the South China Sea, and to uphold the key international rules for defining territorial claims in the South China Sea's waters."[8] More recently, in December 2013, Secretary of State John Kerry visited Vietnam and the Philippines to help dispel growing impressions that distractions in Washington and the Middle East were undermining the Asia-Pacific rebalance. This followed cancellation the previous month of President Obama's trip to the region due to the partial U.S. government shutdown. Kerry delivered promises of aid, maritime-focused security assistance, and opposition to the unproductive manner in which China had announced its ADIZ.[9]

In the military realm, the United States is enhancing capability and interoperability with its Asian treaty allies. Secretary Clinton termed these alliances "the fulcrum for our strategic turn to the Asia-Pacific."[10] President Obama's November 2011 visit to Australia featured an announcement of an agreement that gives U.S. Navy and Marine Corps personnel permanent and constant access to existing facilities in Darwin. A higher tempo of visits by U.S. forces, particularly rotations of Marines, will further enhance the already substantial interoperability of the U.S. and Australian armed forces and facilitate their ability to respond to regional nontraditional security challenges.

Cooperation with allies such as Japan, South Korea, and Australia will expand, particularly in anti-submarine warfare (ASW) and integrated air and missile defense. The United States is increasing counterterrorism training and ship visits in the Philippines and humanitarian and disaster relief networking in Thailand. By 2025, broad area maritime surveillance aerial vehicles may be stationed in those nations to facilitate maritime domain awareness. In Singapore, the United States is stationing Littoral Combat Ships. This, or a similar platform, will likely be the predominant U.S. small combatant in 2025. The sovereign U.S. territory of Guam, together with an evolving network of bases and places including Japan, Singapore, and Australia, will support American force projection in-theater, while Diego Garcia will serve as a similar linchpin in the Indian Ocean.

The United States is also improving its doctrine to improve interservice coordination and countermeasures to asymmetric weapons and operational approaches. Developing and implementing an Air-Sea Battle Concept (ASBC) is central to this effort "to sustain U.S. freedom of action."[11] This evolving approach was initiated in September 2009 to preserve the ability to assure access wherever it might be challenged. From Washington's perspective, this makes its application a question of which countries, if any, might be willing to threaten the functioning and integrity of the global commons by threatening the use of force to achieve parochial objectives. How best to operationalize ASBC and maintain its effectiveness on limited budgets amid rising asymmetric challenges is currently the subject of considerable debate. The most likely near-term application of ASBC is not China but Iran. Even here, it is premature to assume where, if anywhere, the doctrine might be applied; the United States developed Air-Land Battle explicitly to use against the Soviet military, but instead used it against the Iraqi military in the first Gulf War. Yet, in Beijing's view, ASBC is clearly aimed at China, as part of a hostile U.S. containment policy. Elements of this discussion worry Chinese analysts immensely, although it must be emphasized that not even U.S. analysts know the complete picture of ASBC yet, thus rendering all public analyses speculative to some extent.

Making a Virtue of Overseas Limitations

Although concerns about Taiwan's status have played a large role in driving Chinese defense spending since at least the mid-1990s, the PLA's interests have expanded as China's reliance on foreign resources, trade, and shipping lanes continues to rise. Taiwan President Ma Ying-jeou's March 2008 election and his government's cross-Strait policies have greatly reduced the risk of conflict. Now, with cross-Strait relations stable and China continuing to grow as a global stakeholder, the PLA is supplementing its previous approach. Further afield, in the Western Pacific and the Indian Ocean, aside from long-range missiles that offer little in the way of escalation control, China has not developed high-intensity military capabilities. Instead, it has been projecting power in the form of recent peacetime deployments.

Beijing could already augment power projection, but doing so substantially under contested conditions would require far greater investment in nuclear-powered submarines, deck aviation, auxiliary platforms, overall force structure, and training. Such preparations would be visible to outside observers for the most part; thus far there are few indications that China is moving substantially in this direction. For now, at least, these developments suggest increasing capabilities, if not intentions, for the PLA to further common security objectives. Indeed, China's military is training increasingly with its foreign counterparts.

Long-Range Dissipation

The PLA may be moving very gradually toward the Far Seas in some respects, but there remain many highly visible milestones that it has yet to reach. For now, it appears that China is building toward that kind of a force incrementally and in an evolutionary way that prioritizes Near Seas defense. This is not truly a case of China developing two different militaries to fulfill two different sets of missions, since some platforms and weapon systems can contribute in both areas—but there is definitely a multilayered pattern to PLA development. Many vehicles and armaments are primarily relevant in one area or the other. Cherry-picking the characteristics of either of these layers or levels to characterize PLA/maritime power overall fundamentally misrepresents its critical dynamics.

On one hand, it is a mistake to exaggerate the scope of intense build-up: China is simply not moving to develop a blue water power-projection navy at the same rate that it is deploying shorter-range platforms and weapon systems such as missiles. While China commissioned its first aircraft carrier, *Liaoning*, on September 25, 2012, it will be years before its deck aviation capabilities are relevant in combat against militaries more capable than those of its vulnerable South China Sea neighbors. China is starting from a very low baseline in this extremely complex and difficult warfare area. On the other hand, it is equally misguided to suggest that restraint and limitations in the Far Seas is or will be matched by similar restraint in the Near Seas.

Nor will such a transition be swift or easy. Close to home, China can employ numerous workarounds to compensate for ongoing military weaknesses. Such approaches are impossible further away. Likewise, as Chinese forces venture further afield and deploy increasingly symmetric capabilities in order to do so effectively, they become vulnerable to the same physics-based limitations that they are targeting so efficiently in foreign platforms close to China. *Liaoning*, for instance, is vulnerable to the same attacks as any other high value unit—and then some, given its immature capabilities and defense systems. More broadly, as China starts to field forces that play the same game as the United States, they will have to assume the same risks wherever the game is played. It is certainly advantageous to do so under the umbrella of Chinese missiles, but the options for defeat are many. Even if technological and other advances ameliorate these challenges to some extent, the strategic coherence that focus on outstanding territorial claims generates likely cannot be replicated overseas.

Systemic Slowdown?

In the coming decade, motley systemic factors will further reinforce geographical influences on PLA development. China has risen at a rate beyond even its leaders' expectations over the past three decades, and a power shift is afoot in the international system. The unipolar system that persisted from 1991 to roughly 2008 has dissipated. Based on its remaining potential for inland development, China could very well continue to expand its economy a rate that the United States, Japan, and Europe would envy. The U.S. National Intelligence Council forecasts that China will become the world's largest economy by GDP in 2022 as measured by purchasing power parity, which it deems likely to be the strongest indicator of "fundamental economic strength," or "sometime near 2030" by market exchange rates.[12] The International Institute for Strategic Studies goes so far as to predict that Chinese defense spending might surpass that of the United States as early as 2025.[13]

For all its efforts to guide national development and claims of exceptionalism, however, China is not immune to larger patterns of economics and history. As such, it will likely not be able to avoid the S-curve-shaped growth slowdown that so many previous great powers have experienced, and that so many observers believe the United States and its allies are undergoing today. Factors likely to slow China's growth include an aging population, shifts in manufacturing, pollution, corruption, chronic diseases, water shortages, rising middle-class expectations, and growing domestic security spending. China is encountering these headwinds at a much earlier stage in its development than the United States and earlier great powers, thanks in part to its late modernization, dramatic internal disparities, and such governmental choices as the one child policy.

Within its military, China is likewise susceptible to many of the challenges earlier-developed militaries have faced. In addition to a future slowdown in Chinese economic growth, potential dynamics include a variety of factors that increase costs and technological requirements, thus yielding diminishing returns for each additional RMB. These factors include rising salaries and benefits, as well as other entitlements—particularly as growing numbers of retiring officers enjoy the state's greater generosity.

By developing and deploying new military technologies, China is raising the bar for regional arms competition, forcing it to spend more on advanced systems in order to narrow the gap with the United States and Japan. In a worst-case scenario, this could risk pricing China out of some of the asymmetric "market niches" that it currently enjoys. Ironically, by focusing so clearly on relatively low-cost asymmetric weapons capabilities, China has inadvertently published an attractive counterintervention playbook, inspiring rivals to undermine China's own capabilities. For example, in the contested Near Seas, Japan, Taiwan, and Vietnam in particular may increasingly deploy missiles, naval mines, and torpedoes to hold PLA assets at risk. Vietnam's ongoing submarine purchases from Russia are a prime example. China can already exploit its geographical proximity by deploying many overlapping forces to attempt to defeat and overwhelm such approaches. Further afield, removed from the possibility of cobbling together such stopgap alternatives, China is far from being able to defend its forces effectively if they face such challenges from a capable power such as India.

For the near future, the United States is likely to remain a dominant force in areas of Chinese interest. In Wang Jisi's analysis, legal traditions, social values, technological-institutional innovations, and civil society underwrite America's competitive edge and will keep it the world's sole superpower for the next twenty to thirty years at least.[14] For all these reasons, it is extremely premature to project a global power transition in which China eclipses U.S. power and influence overall. Nevertheless, both America's present fiscal challenges and China's rise and regional interests are undeniable realities. From the perspective of U.S. interests, stability, and access to the global commons, then, the greatest risk would appear to be any Chinese efforts to either exploit a "strategic window of opportunity," during which Washington has not yet resolved its domestic challenges and Beijing has not yet been slowed down by its own, or pursue outstanding claims to divert attention from domestic problems. Either way, the primary arena for this strategic competition is likely to be the Near Seas and their immediate approaches, not further from China.

An Uphill Battle: Grappling with Greater Challenges

China will likely continue to pursue overall improvements, seek to consolidate major Near Seas gains, and enhance Far Seas capabilities as possible; some Near Seas-Far Seas disparities will persist. Beijing's leaders understand these realities and are accordingly pragmatic. China's overseas interests will continue to grow, but it will not address them with the unilateral military focus that it devotes to the Near Seas. Rather, it is likely to pursue a diverse approach, parlaying economic strength into diplomatic and commercial carrots, engaging in low-end military deployments to strengthen influence and address common goals in parallel—if not fully integrated—with foreign militaries, and developing targeted capabilities to rescue its citizens overseas and suppress nonstate threats.

This is the default approach. Making rapid progress in these areas, and/or shifting significantly to a more externalized power-projection military, would demand major improvements in: (1) hardware, (2) software, (3) organization, and (4) integration.

Improving Hardware

Today, because of Western, particularly American, export controls, China is typically only able to directly acquire military technology from suppliers in

Russia, Ukraine, and—in some respects—Israel. Nevertheless, a full range of licit and illicit acquisition approaches, including purchases of multifarious dual-use technology available on the international market, has greatly facilitated many aspects of PLA development. Talented young engineers and technical experts, many with educational and work experience abroad, are greatly facilitating this advance. China may finally be implementing substantive defense reforms at the central government and enterprise levels, albeit slowly, and with limitations. Beijing promotes critical technologies development through major state research and development funding programs.

Some view repeated reorganizations as proof that China's defense industrial base remains problematic. Despite recent progress, China still loses talented individuals to coastal enterprises, foreign multinationals, and emigration. Elements of China's scattered research institutions jealously guard information and resources while relying on government subsidies or focusing disproportionately on immediately profitable products. Remaining obstacles to reform include employment goals, bureaucratic competition, and local interests. Concern about social instability resulting from shedding redundant workers is exacerbated by the location of many defense firms in China's impoverished hinterlands. And mastering some apex technologies, such as aeroengines, requires technological breakthroughs that will be challenging even for China's increasingly capable defense industry.

Nevertheless, in many respects, China's military has made the most progress, and enjoys the most potential for absolute gains, in hardware. China today is able to devote resources and launch defense industrial programs with unrivaled flexibility, particularly as fiscal challenges and evolution of priorities by societal aging constrain the rate at which the United States, its key allies, and other advanced nations propel the leading edge of military technology. Only the United States is pursuing so many military shipbuilding and aircraft programs simultaneously. Much resource investment may incur some redundancy and inefficiency, and China may still struggle with high-end innovation, but it is increasingly able to develop and acquire the systems it needs to assert itself vis-à-vis the Near Seas.

China's economy is growing fast enough to support the ever-increasing cost of advanced platforms and weapons at essentially a constant defense burden. Since the cost of modern weapons and platforms increases faster than inflation almost by definition, this has tremendous implications for supporting R&D. It offers freedom to innovate rapidly that the United States and other Western countries lack. Military R&D without the burden of legacy systems could lead China to field a truly surprising capability that presents a real challenge to the ability of the U.S. Navy to operate in the area. In that case, China might not have to overtly exploit a window of U.S. vulnerability, but simply produce something that calls into question the U.S. ability to operate in the region, and thereby undermines regional confidence in the United States. China is investing in new military capabilities that could lead to an unexpected capability that changes the ways of war fundamentally.

"Software" Reforms

While hardware has progressed rapidly in many respects, "software," in the form of professionalism, education, and training, has lagged, leaving PLA capabilities less than the sum of their parts. Certainly, these problems are widely recognized and receive increasing attention. Xi Jinping has accorded realistic training unprecedented emphasis. Moreover, thanks to China's geographic proximity and numerous means of compensating for quality and coordination with quantity, education and the ability for services to engage jointly in operations may be far more important for Far Seas operations than the Near Seas campaigns that remain the PLA's focus.

Overcoming Embedded Organizational Inefficiency

Intimate connections to CCP rule and legitimacy make China's remaining military organizational challenges the most difficult and least likely to be readily addressed. Optimized for party control, the PLA's command structure is suboptimal for interagency coordination and real-time crisis decision making, especially for geographically distant crises.

There have been no major changes in civil-military relations of late. CCP pronouncements stipulate that the PLA will remain a party army for the foreseeable future. This system has the benefit of maintaining political consensus and avoiding rash decisions, but, as compared with Western military systems with complete civilian leadership and a single chain of command, it suffers from two major challenges that are aggravated by the requirements of modern warfare. First, it is sometimes difficult to clearly divide responsibilities under the unified party committee leadership. Second, it may be difficult to decide which decisions are sufficiently important to forward to the party committee. This might slow the deployment of troops into combat situations and limit their ability to react quickly to changing conditions once there.

China's vast territory, diverse populations, and complex geography, with attendant transportation and logistics challenges, initially necessitated a regional approach to national defense that imposed centralized control on decentralized operations. Since February 1949, the PLA has employed a geographically delineated system of "military regions," which encompass military units permanently allocated to them. The military region structure may be increasingly ill suited to military missions with which PLA is likely to be charged, and may gradually evolve into a more externally oriented structure. Based on a proposal unveiled at the Third Plenary Session of the Eighteenth CPC Central Committee that "We must intensify the reforms and readjustment of the structure and makeup of the military" and "We must set off down the reform path which involves a joint operational command structure with Chinese characteristics," state media reported on January 3, 2014, that China would "establish a joint operational command system 'in due course'."[15] Two days later, China's Ministry of National Defense Information Office dismissed this and even more ambitious foreign media characterization as "groundless," referencing its own November 28, 2013, briefing—regarded as the official answer on this issue.[16] In this briefing, spokesman Yang Yujun had confirmed that the PLA "carried out active explorations." He added: "Based on the spirit of the relevant decisions by the central authorities, for the next step, once there has been sufficient study and verifications, we will intensify the reforms at the appropriate time and take the road of joint operational command structure reforms with Chinese characteristics."[17] Apparently the "gun" does not want to be perceived as being out ahead of party guidance, particularly on such a bureaucratically complex, sensitive matter.

Meanwhile, growing Chinese external interests demand gradual reduction of the ground forces' still-preeminent power, but such a change faces considerable organizational resistance and corresponding competition among the other three services and one branch. Each strives to develop in new domains, and can claim vital capabilities. With the most external geopolitical orientation and operations, the PLAN would seem to have an edge in budget claims. Moving from its current Near Seas-specific three-fleet structure toward a two-ocean Pacific and Indian Ocean navy would demand more and better vessels. Yet the PLA Air Force is striving to control China's burgeoning military space assets, a globe-spanning capability vital to supporting modern informatized warfare. The Second Artillery Force, too, seeks space responsibilities. Interservice rivalry is likely to be exacerbated by factors that constrain PLA budget growth or reduce purchasing power of existing monies.

A partial de facto solution to the de jure problem of organizational inefficiency may be offered by missions further afield wherein unintended consequences of organizational exigencies can nevertheless address existing problems. Gulf of Aden antipiracy missions, for instance, have elevated the PLAN's role and autonomy. In addition to forcing experience under realistic conditions that might be impossible for risk-averse forces to obtain otherwise, the nature of such operationally complex Far Seas operations encourages a decentralized approach, common to major world navies, but new to China.

Integration

Assuming that the aforementioned requirements can be achieved in practice, the key to realizing advanced overseas combat capabilities will be integrating forces and their supporting elements effectively. Such integration has long been central to American warfare; the PLA is exploring an analogous approach theoretically under the rubric of "information systems-based systems operations."[18] Such movement toward "jointness" and integration emphasizes variable-distance operations in variable spatial dimensions (not only surface and subsurface but also air and space), at variable times (e.g., peacetime, crisis, and wartime). Under this rubric, the PLAN would be charged with "form[ing] maritime operations systems," with aircraft carriers at the core: "employing information systems to permeate, fuse and connect weapons systems can accomplish operational effectiveness that far exceeds what a single weapon such as an aircraft carrier can accomplish. At the same time, this integration can reduce the risks of a single weapon such as an aircraft carrier."[19] It remains to be seen to what extent the PLA can realize this ambitious approach in practice, and whether evolving ways of warfare might render carriers too vulnerable to fulfill the central role that they have played for decades in the U.S. Navy.

Conclusion: Embracing the One Opportunity?

Despite "new historic missions" and gradual progress overseas, PLA development remains focused close to home, with a geographically informed hierarchy of priorities whose focus and intensity diminishes with distance. To further key national interests, rectify perceived historical injustices and territorial division, and regain its status as preeminent regional power, China is developing counterintervention capabilities to carve out a zone of exceptionalism in the Near Seas—not just for countering U.S. intervention, but also to deter, coerce, or defeat potential regional adversaries. The PLA already boasts formidable capabilities vis-à-vis the areas most important to China, but progress further afield will be arduous.

To further its own interests, as well as those of its allies and partners, the United States is attempting to prevent Chinese regional exceptionalism by maintaining a strong Asia-Pacific presence through rebalancing its forces. Even assuming that the requisite technical, operational, and financial challenges can be surmounted, some worry that by developing further capabilities and emphasizing them for deterrence purposes, Washington might in fact make matters worse strategically. As Sr. Capt. Li Jie, Naval Research Institute, emphasizes, "We have to follow closely [America's] future development and find out their intention. We will then go from there to come up with the appropriate weapons and new strategies to hit at their Achilles' heel."[20] Chinese interlocutors in particular warn that American assertiveness risks creating a new "Cold War" and conflict with China. Employing typical phrasing, Ministry of National Defense spokesman Geng Yansheng denounced recent U.S. initiatives in Australia as "all a manifestation of a Cold War mentality."[21]

Rhetorically, this is overblown. Given substantial economic relations and shared security interests in the vast majority of the global commons, neither side is engaged in what can be properly termed a "Cold War." Both sides have significant concerns, however, and in some ways the situation is more volatile and challenging than the latter stages of the actual Cold War. Among a wide variety of arms control agreements, Moscow signed the Intermediate-Range Nuclear Forces Treaty with Washington; Beijing, as a nonsignatory, has developed the world's foremost substrategic (in-range) missile force—a strategic tool. The Soviet Union did not pursue constant global cyber espionage against U.S. government and commercial targets, as Beijing is doing today. Moscow never had the espionage successes that China apparently has in theft of proprietary technology and corporate intelligence. So, while China's positive global contributions and strong regional focus appear to preclude a Soviet-style approach at this time, its military rise nevertheless presents a significant challenge for its neighbors and the United States.

Bilateral relations more generally, and state visits by civilian leaders, are more positive, but military-military relations remain constrained. As Avery Goldstein points out, "Sino-American crises that could erupt in the near future, while China remains militarily outclassed by the United States, present distinctive dangers."[22]

Washington believes it is working to preserve an international system that has benefitted the vast majority of nations, including China. Only by maintaining and demonstrating strength can the United States preserve strategic stability in this promising but volatile region. Beijing, acutely attuned to perceived changes in relative power, probes and pressures unremittingly when it perceives weakness, but moderates, however reluctantly, when it encounters strength. Indeed, as Joseph Nye points out, "After the 2008 financial crisis, many Chinese expressed the mistaken belief that the [United States] was in terminal decline, and that China should be more assertive— particularly in pursuing its maritime claims in the South China Sea—at the expense of America's allies and friends."[23] Now, with Washington's focus on the Asia-Pacific restored, Beijing has adjusted in a more positive direction once more.

Of course, budgetary uncertainties cloud Washington's rebalancing. Some believe that the United States cannot forever sustain its primacy and should seek a compromise and accommodation with China, especially regarding China's EEZ. These are serious issues that cannot be dismissed lightly: sound bites are no substitute for ship numbers. In any case, the United States has long invited, and continues to invite, China to cooperate in the defense and development of the global system. The Pentagon's East Asia Strategy Review, which emphasizes the integration of China into the international system through trade and exchange, "has guided American policy since 1995," in Nye's judgment.[24] "China has prospered as part of the open and rules-based system that the United States helped to build and works to sustain," Secretary Clinton emphasizes,[25] arguably more so than any other nation. Indeed, no other nation has done more than the United States to facilitate China's post-1978 development.

There is simply no need for the two great powers to enter into a conflict that would damage both severely. The fundamental question is how China can continue to develop while supporting and shaping—but not disrupting— the international system. Washington welcomes the former trajectory, but will not accept the latter. It is making preparations to ensure that it will continue to have the wherewithal to ensure that it does not occur. This is not a new "Cold War," but rather a positive effort to shape a stable and productive twenty-first-century world in which the United States remains actively engaged while China continues peaceful development. The key to achieving this goal would be for the United States and China to maximize cooperation in the Far Seas while minimizing friction and managing crises in the Near Seas. Can such a primarily cooperative approach be achieved, or is managing competition the best that can be done?

CHAPTER 11

Things Fall Apart: Maritime Disputes and China's Regional Diplomacy

M. Taylor Fravel

China is a geographically challenged state, with numerous neighbors on land and at sea. As Samuel Kim once noted, China is a "G-1," a country without real or natural allies.[1] Although it has security relationships with Pakistan and North Korea, these countries, on balance, are liabilities and do little to enhance China's security. As a result, China's relationships with neighboring states, especially those adjacent to its land and sea borders, have played a central role in China's foreign policy during the Mao era and after. When relations with these states have been poor, China has been more prone to encirclement, as great powers can gain additional sources of leverage over China by improving ties with China's neighbors. By contrast, when relations with these states have been good, China has increased its autonomy, which limits the ability of other great powers to constrain China's behavior and allows China to concentrate on domestic imperatives such as economic growth.

One central feature of China's diplomacy since the end of the Cold War has been the steady engagement of its neighbors, improving ties with almost all these states. Under the rubric of "omni-directional diplomacy," China normalized ties with estranged neighbors, engaged newly independent states, and improved ties with major states like India and Japan. Such diplomatic success was achieved despite the presence of contentious issues between China and many of its neighbors, especially over disputed territory. In some cases, the resolution of territorial disputes has created a foundation for improved ties.[2] In other cases, the significance of these disputes has been downplayed to allow for the development of deeper political and economic relations.[3]

Today, however, China's successful engagement of its periphery has begun to unravel as China has affirmed and asserted its claims in maritime disputes in the East and South China Seas. These actions have revealed the limits of China's "good neighbor policy" of the 1990s and most of the 2000s. As a stronger China seeks to defend what it views as its territorial and maritime interests, it threatens the security of its neighbors, who grow increasingly wary of China's long-term intentions. As a result, China's neighbors are balancing against Beijing, externally by improving ties with the United States and other major powers in the region, and internally by strengthening their own military and especially naval capabilities. In turn, the influence of the United States in the region has grown, creating (from China's perspective) the potential specter of balancing coalitions, at least in the security realm.

China has responded in several different ways to this new situation on its periphery. To repair ties with its neighbors and improve its position in the region, China has pursued periods of moderation in its maritime disputes, worked to immunize broader bilateral relations with neighbors from these disputes, and moved to improve ties with the United States to decrease Washington's role in these disputes. Nevertheless, these actions do not appear to be working because they fail to address concerns about Chinese intentions that these disputes generate—concerns exacerbated by perceptions of growth of Chinese power, especially its military capabilities.

This chapter is organized as follows. The first section reviews the importance of China's periphery in China's grand strategy and foreign policy. The second examines how China's defense of its maritime claims has harmed ties with many of its East Asian neighbors, who are now taking actions to enhance their ability to resist China in these disputes, by both strengthening ties with the United States and by investing in greater military capabilities. The third section discusses how China has sought to respond to the worsening of ties with its maritime neighbors in the region.

The Centrality of Regional Diplomacy

Among great powers, past and present, China enjoys a uniquely complex regional security environment. China has fourteen neighbors on land and eight at sea. China's land border runs more than 22,000 kilometers, while its coastline extends approximately 14,500 kilometers. The sheer number of neighbors, in culturally distinctive subregions, would pose a daunting diplomatic challenge for any country. But China's situation is even more complicated, given the characteristics of its periphery: four neighbors—Russia, India, Pakistan, and North Korea—possess nuclear weapons, while others—such as Japan, South Korea, and Taiwan—could easily develop the bomb if they chose to do so. Some of China's neighbors could be described as potential failed states characterized by great uncertainty about their own domestic political stability, including North Korea and Afghanistan, as well as other states in Central Asia. Two neighbors, India and Russia, possess two of the largest ground forces in the world in addition to nuclear weapons. Others, including Japan and India, field modern and capable navies. Finally, the United States maintains formal alliances with five states in the region, including three of China's maritime neighbors (South Korea, Japan, and the Philippines). Through these alliances, the United States maintains a substantial military presence in East Asia, including 180 ships and approximately 2,500 aircraft as part of the U.S. Pacific Command (PACOM).[4]

Based on these characteristics, managing ties with its immediate neighbors plays a central role in China's foreign policy. As a group and individually, these states can harm Chinese interests. First, the large number of neighbors on land and at sea means that China can easily face conflicts or challenges to its interests simultaneously along different vectors, or what Chinese strategists describe as "strategic directions" (*zhanlue fangxiang*).[5] As a result, China can face strategic pressure in different areas and, historically, has feared being encircled and contained by other powers.[6] Second, the large number of neighbors suggests that China has to work even harder than other great powers to maximize its autonomy in its own backyards. China's geographic circumstances can facilitate the formation of balancing coalitions that can coalesce to limit Chinese freedom of maneuver in the region. China's neighbors also serve as sources of influence or leverage over China that powers from outside the region (or stronger powers within the region) can exploit to constrain China's autonomy. They can do this directly, by using China's neighbors as bases for forward-deployed troops, or indirectly, by supporting these countries in their own conflicts with China. Third, with many neighbors, many more opportunities for conflict exist on China's periphery than for most other great powers. As a result, China can be more easily dragged into regional entanglements that divert its national resources from other priorities, especially economic development.

Perhaps unsurprisingly, maintaining good ties with its immediate neighbors advances important Chinese interests. The first is the prevention of encirclement by potentially hostile states, including preventing the formation of coalitions that can form to balance Chinese power. The second is maximizing strategic autonomy and freedom of maneuver, both with its immediate neighbors and with great powers that might otherwise try to use their own ties with China's neighbors to constrain China. Third, good ties with neighboring states are a prerequisite for maintaining a "peaceful and stable external environment" and the absence of armed conflict on China's borders within which to pursue economic growth. Conflicts along China's borders can not only increase the presence and thus potential influence of other great powers, creating a strategic challenge, but may also directly involve China.

Although maintaining good ties with neighboring states played a role in China's "Bandung" era foreign policy in the 1950s, these ties have become even more important after the demonstrations and massacre in Tiananmen Square in June 1989. Since then, China has pursued an "omni-directional diplomacy" (*quanfangwei waijiao*) premised on maintaining good relations with the largest number of states, both to compensate for its lack of natural allies and to hedge against America's dominant position in the international system.[7]

China's post-Tiananmen engagement of the Asian region began with the rapid normalization of diplomatic relations with the neighboring and other regional states. Between 1989 and 1992, China established diplomatic relations or normalized ties with Laos, Vietnam, South Korea, Indonesia, and Singapore. China also quickly established formal diplomatic relations with all the successor states of the collapsed Soviet Union on its land border (Russia, Kazakhstan, Kyrgyzstan, and Tajikistan). As a part of this process, China resolved outstanding territorial disputes with Russia, Laos, Vietnam, Kazakhstan, Kyrgyzstan, and Tajikistan, and entered into military confidence-building measures with India and the Soviet successor states in Central Asia.[8]

A rise in tensions over the disputed Spratly Islands in the South China Sea in the early to mid-1990s, however, limited the pace of China's regional engagement after Tiananmen. Along with the rapid growth of China's economy toward the end of the 1990s, fears arose among China's smaller neighbors and other states in the region about China's ambitions.[9] China addressed these concerns in several ways. First, it moderated its approach to the disputed Spratly Islands and ultimately signed a code of conduct declaration with the Association of Southeast Asian Nations (ASEAN) in 2002.[10] Second, it turned to multilateral institutions to reassure states in the region about China's intentions. This process started with a deepening of China's substantive engagement with ASEAN, culminating in the establishment of a number of formal dialogue mechanisms in the late 1990s and a free-trade agreement in 2002.[11] China also played a leading role in the establishment of the Shanghai Cooperation Organization, a group focused on Central Asia that now includes six members, five observer states, and three dialogue partners. Third, China increased its economic interactions with these states and sometimes signed attractive free-trade agreements to demonstrate how China's rise would benefit the region as a whole economically.[12] Fourth, China has actively pursued strategic partnerships with states in the region, especially the most powerful ones, including Russia, India, and Japan.[13]

China developed several slogans to characterize this diplomatic engagement of its neighbors. Overall, it has been described as the "good neighbor policy" (*mulin zhengce*). The goals have been described as "becoming friends and partners with neighbors" (*yulinweishan, yilinweiban*) and building an "amicable, tranquil, and prosperous neighborhood" (*mulin, anlin, fulin*). By the middle of the 2000s, China's ties with most of its neighbors were viewed as an unparalleled success. Economic and political ties deepened, while contentious disputes over territory were either resolved or sidelined. Many observers trumpeted China's "charm offensive" and the rise of China's "soft power."[14] All of this occurred under the rubric of "peaceful rise" and "peaceful development," or the claim that China's rise could be different than past great powers.

Maritime Disputes and the End of Good Neighborliness

China's "win-win" approach toward its neighbors, however, has begun to unravel. In East Asia, China's ties with many (but not all) of its neighbors have deteriorated since roughly 2008. The proximate cause has been China's assertion of its territorial claims, which brings it into direct conflict with its neighbors. The structural cause has been the continued growth of the Chinese economy and the continued success of China's military modernization efforts, which casts a long shadow over China's actions in its territorial disputes. As a result, China's neighbors have sought to improve ties with the United States, as China's actions created a powerful rationale for Washington to remain engaged and enmeshed in the region.

The deterioration of China's ties with many neighbors is not the product of a new policy or strategy toward the region. Instead, it has occurred because a stronger and more capable China has acted to defend what it believes to be important or vital interests being challenged by other states. The dynamics of the concept of the "security dilemma" illuminate why China's "good neighbor policy" has begun to unravel. According to this concept, the dilemma exists because one state's efforts to increase its own security usually decrease the security of other states.[15] Given the uncertainty created by anarchy in the international system, even if one state enhances its military power for what that country sees as defensive reasons, other states are likely to view the same actions as offensive and threatening, resulting in security competition characterized by mistrust, suspicion, and spirals of tension. In this view, security is zero-sum, where one side's gain can only come at the expense of another. Such spirals are especially likely when a state increases its defense spending significantly and acquires force projection capabilities, two features of China's current military modernization effort.[16]

The dynamics of the security dilemma are especially pernicious in territorial disputes, which are zero-sum conflicts over the ownership of land or the exclusive jurisdiction over maritime space. Territorial disputes by definition are unstable and prone to negative spirals of instability associated with the security dilemma. States in such disputes are especially sensitive to perceived challenges to their claims by other states. Any action by one state to strengthen its own claim creates strong incentives for other states to respond. Such incentives are especially powerful because of the public nature of claims in territorial disputes and because international law requires states to actively assert and defend their claims.[17]

As territorial disputes escalate, states that feel threatened will act to protect their interests. Most states in disputes with China have adopted different types of balancing responses designed to check or counter China's growing capabilities. As described by Kenneth Waltz, a state can undertake internal balancing measures to increase its own capabilities, especially its military capabilities.[18] In addition, a state can seek to aggregate its capabilities with other states facing a similar threat. Historically, such external balancing has involved the formation of alliances, but can also include the strengthening of existing alliances and the establishment of other types of security cooperation.

The South China Sea

In the South China Sea, China's pursuit and defense of its maritime claims has worsened ties with many states in Southeast Asia. China's behavior has created opportunities for the United States to deepen its ties with states in the region and sparked efforts by regional states to strengthen their own naval capabilities. Japan and India have likewise become more engaged in Southeast Asia, expressing support in various forms and ways for states opposing China in the South China Sea.

Background

Conflict in the South China Sea revolves around competing claims to territorial sovereignty and maritime jurisdiction. Claims over maritime jurisdiction include not just the scope of claims, but also their content, such as the navigation rights of military vessels.

In the South China Sea, the territorial sovereignty of two groups of islands and reefs is contested. The first is the Paracel Islands, which are claimed by China and Vietnam (along with Taiwan). China has controlled the Amphitrite Group since the mid-1950s and consolidated control over the entire archipelago after a brief clash with South Vietnam over the Crescent Group in 1974.[19] The second is the Spratly Islands, which consist of roughly 230 features, including several small islands, coral reefs, and shoals. Vietnam, China, and Taiwan claim sovereignty over all these land features. The Philippines claims fifty-three of these features, while Malaysia claims twelve. All of the claimant states occupy some of the islands and features that they claim.[20]

Claims to maritime jurisdiction involve exclusive rights to water space. In particular, they involve whether states have the exclusive right to exploit resources that are contained in the water column or seabed with a two hundred-nautical-mile exclusive economic zone (EEZ) or an extended continental shelf. Vietnam, the Philippines, Malaysia, and Brunei base their claims to maritime rights in the South China Sea from their coasts. Indonesia asserts maritime rights from Natuna Island. China, however, bases its claims to maritime rights on sovereignty over the Paracels and Spratlys. Yet most (but not all) of the features in the Spratlys would not qualify as islands under article 121(3) of the United Nations Convention on the Law of the Sea (UNCLOS), and thus cannot serve as the basis for a claim to an EEZ, much less an extended continental shelf. In addition, ambiguity surrounds China's claims to maritime jurisdiction for other reasons. For many decades, Chinese maps have shown a "nine-dashed line" enclosing most of the waters in the region. Yet the Chinese government has never defined what the line does—or does not—mean.[21] Commentary by Chinese scholars and analysts suggest that China may seek to claim some sort of historic rights to the resources contained within the line.[22]

Growing Tensions

In the South China Sea, tensions caused by maritime disputes between China and other claimants, especially Vietnam and the Philippines, have increased substantially in the past few years. One key turning point was a deadline set by a UN body tasked with assessing claims to extended continental shelves. Diplomatic tensions over maritime rights increased in the weeks before the May 2009 deadline for submissions to the UN Commission on the Limits of the Continental Shelf (CLCS).[23] If a territorial or maritime dispute exists, however, then the commission's rules dictate that it "shall not consider and qualify a submission made by any of the States concerned in the dispute."[24] As a result, all claimants in the South China Sea had strong incentives to challenge the continental shelf submissions where sovereignty or maritime rights claims overlapped. Accordingly, China and the Philippines both objected to Vietnam's submission and to the joint Vietnamese-Malaysian submission. All the claimants then issued claims and counterclaims.[25]

Even though the May 2009 deadline for submissions had been established ten years earlier, its impending arrival significantly increased the competition over maritime rights in the South China Sea. By submitting claims to the commission, many regional states formally expanded the exclusive maritime jurisdiction that they claimed beyond a two-hundred-nautical-mile EEZ from their coastlines, thereby increasing the intensity of competition over maritime rights. Previously, these states had either not stated that they would claim extended continental shelf rights or had not clearly delineated the size of the continental shelf that they claimed. In addition, in the letters submitted to the CLCS, states not only contested each other's claims to maritime rights but also each other's claims to territorial sovereignty over the Paracel and Spratly Islands. Finally, China's first diplomatic letter challenging Vietnam and Malaysia's submissions included a map of the region that depicted the Paracel and Spratly Islands along with the now infamous nine-dashed line.[26] Although the Chinese note did not mention the line, Vietnam and other claimants viewed the map as an expansion of China's claims.

In the eyes of other claimants, Chinese actions reinforced the view that China seeks control over the entire South China Sea. In 2009, China detained over four hundred Vietnamese fishermen who had ventured into the waters around the Paracel Islands, which China controls. In 2011, China harassed seismic survey vessels contracted by Vietnam and by the Philippines. In one incident, a ship from the China Marine Surveillance force, a maritime law enforcement agency under the State Oceanic Administration, severed the towed sonar cable on a Vietnamese-contracted seismic survey vessel operating roughly one hundred miles from the Vietnamese coast.[27] In June 2012, the China National Offshore Oil Company invited foreign oil companies to bid on exploration blocks that overlapped with existing Vietnamese blocks within the two-hundred-nautical-mile EEZ from its coast.[28]

Another incident in 2012 indicated that China's approach had become more assertive. In early April, a Philippine naval ship was dispatched to investigate reports of fishing boats inside Scarborough Shoal, a coral reef approximately 135 miles from the Philippines and 543 miles from China. Although Philippine personnel searched the boats, which were harvesting giant clams and other marine animals in violation of Philippine law, two patrol ships from the China Marine Surveillance force under the State Oceanic Administration arrived on the scene and blocked the entrance to the shoal, thus preventing the arrest of the fishermen.[29] A standoff ensued, as both sides used government ships to demonstrate their sovereignty over the shoal and jurisdiction over the adjacent waters. When the standoff ended in mid-June 2012, China had achieved effective control over the shoal and adjacent waters. In addition to blocking access to the shoal, China also tried to coerce the Philippines by quarantining imported bananas, a key Philippine export, and halting Chinese tour groups.

Although China's engagement with ASEAN has been a hallmark of its regional diplomacy in the 2000s, China's active defense of its territorial claims has damaged China's ties with this organization and the region more generally. In keeping with its goal of pursuing bilateral and not multilateral talks over the territorial and maritime jurisdiction disputes, China has tried (and mostly failed) to keep the South China Sea and the broader issue of maritime security from the agenda of meetings of the ASEAN Regional Forum (ARF) and from the East Asian Summit (EAS). In 2010, more than half of the members of the ARF, including most of the claimants in the South China Sea, publicly expressed concern about the disputes, breaking many years of silence on the issue in the forum. In response, Foreign Minister Yang Jiechi responded harshly, stating at one point, "China is a big country and other countries are small countries and that is just a fact."[30] In July 2012, China used its influence over Cambodia, then holding the ASEAN chair, to prevent references to specific disputes in the South China Sea from being included in an ASEAN joint communiqué. When agreement could not be reached about how to characterize the disputes in the South China Sea, Cambodia exercised its power as chair and decided that, for the first time in forty-five years, no communiqué would be issued.[31] In other words, China's meddling posed a threat to ASEAN unity as a whole. Finally, during a China-ASEAN meeting in October 2012, Vice Foreign Minister Fu Ying chastised ASEAN states for "internationalizing" the dispute by raising the issue with nonclaimant states. Fu also outlined how China expected these states to behave in the future: that there should no multilateral talks, no discussion with other major powers like the United States, no media interviews to bring publicity to the dispute, and no action at the United Nations.[32]

Regional Responses

From the perspective of China's regional diplomacy from the mid-1990s to the mid-2000s, China's hard-nosed actions in the South China Sea have been counterproductive, worsening ties with its neighbors. First, China's image has been harmed by what a Philippine official described as its "dictatorial" approach in the South China Sea. In the Philippines, a public opinion survey taken in May 2012 during the Scarborough standoff indicated that "net trust" in China had dropped by 46 percent, to negative 36 percent.[33] Following the cable-cutting incident in May 2011, Vietnamese held anti-Chinese protests over the South China Sea for twelve weeks, until finally halted by

the government. Even Singapore, normally a state China counts as a friend
in East Asia, publicly called on China in 2011 to clarify its claims in the South
China Sea because of its concern about growing tensions in the region.[34]
Indonesia, a state reluctant to openly confront China diplomatically, sub-
mitted a *note verbale* to the United Nations to protest Chinese claims in
Indonesian waters.[35] As discussed in the following section, Vietnam and the
Philippines have also taken steps to improve maritime cooperation with
Japan.

Second, regional states have engaged in external balancing by seeking to
improve security ties with other states, especially the United States. Perhaps
the most noteworthy has been the improvement in Vietnamese-United States
relations. In the past few years, the two countries have been moving toward
the formal establishment of a "comprehensive partnership." Defense ties
have blossomed, to include annual port calls, exchanges, and, in 2011, a
memorandum of understanding (MoU) for advancing bilateral defense cooperation.[36] Similarly, the United States and the Philippines further deepened their security relations. In November 2011, the two countries signed
the Manila Declaration to reaffirm their mutual defense treaty on its sixti-
eth anniversary.[37] In April 2012, the two countries held a "2 + 2" ministerial,
including foreign affairs and defense chiefs for the first time. The meeting
outlined a series of strategic objectives and included a detailed action plan,
parts of which focused on maritime security (including strengthening maritime security capabilities and maritime domain awareness).[38]

Regional states have engaged India and Japan, as I will discuss in the next
section. Again, Vietnam has been the most active in this regard. As India has
invested in Vietnam's offshore oil and gas fields, it is a natural partner for
Hanoi. Although India announced its "Look East" policy in the early 1990s,
military and maritime cooperation with Vietnam has increased in the last
five years. In addition to dialogues and exchanges, the two countries now
conduct joint military exercises. In June 2013, for example, four Indian Navy
ships visited Vietnam and conducted joint exercises with the Vietnamese
Navy in the South China Sea.[39]

Third, states in the region have begun to increase their spending on
defense to enhance their own maritime capabilities, or internal balancing.
Vietnam has been the most active in this regard. In addition to increasing its
defense budget from roughly 2 percent of GDP in 2004 to 2.5 percent of GDP
in 2010,[40] Vietnam has also purchased advanced equipment, primarily from

Russia, including twenty Su-30MMK Flanker fighter aircraft, six Kilo-class submarines equipped with antiship missiles, and four *Gepard*-class frigates also armed with advanced Russian antiship missiles.[41]

The East China Sea

In the East China Sea, China's pursuit and defense of its maritime claims has worsened ties with Japan. China's behavior has created opportunities for the United States to strengthen its alliance with Japan and sparked efforts by Japan to enhance its own military capabilities.

Background

Management of China's claims in the East China Sea have posed similar problems for China's relations with a key neighbor in Northeast Asia, Japan. China and Japan contest the sovereignty of the Senkaku/Diaoyu Islands. They also disagree about where to delimit maritime jurisdiction in the East China Sea, primarily in waters north of the disputed islands. Japan maintains that a median line should be drawn between the coasts of the two states, while China claims that its maritime jurisdiction extends beyond two hundred nautical miles, to where its continental shelf ends at the Okinawa Trough.

Growing Tensions

Tensions over both disputes simmered on a low boil during the mid-2000s. At the time, the China National Offshore Oil Company was developing a series of gas fields in the Xihu Trough. Wells for one of the fields were drilled only several miles away from the median line claimed by Japan, prompting concerns in Japan that China would siphon natural resources that Japan claimed as its own. To address these concerns, the two countries reached an informal agreement on natural gas development in the East China Sea in June 2008.[42] In December 2008, however, two vessels from the China Marine Surveillance force crossed into the territorial waters around the islands in an apparent bid to scuttle the gas field agreement. This marked the first time that Chinese government ships had entered what Japan views as its sovereign territorial waters around the islands.

The situation deteriorated in September 2010, when a Chinese fishing vessel entered the territorial waters around the islands and rammed Japanese Coast Guard vessels to evade capture. After the boat and crew were detained, Japan decided to indict the captain for violating a number of domestic laws. China objected to this move, which was seen as an exercise of Japan's sovereignty over the islands and an escalation of the dispute. Over the following two weeks, China's reaction was harsh. The Ministry of Foreign Affairs in Beijing summoned the Japanese ambassador multiple times, often in the middle of the night. Official delegations and visits to Japan were postponed. While in New York for a meeting at the United Nations, Premier Wen Jiabao offered strong and pointed remarks against Japan, stating that China would take "further measures" and Japan would bear "all the responsibility for consequences" if the captain was not released immediately and unconditionally.[43] Finally, a shipment of rare earth metals used to manufacture a variety of electronics to Japan was apparently postponed, indicating that China would punish Japan economically until the captain was released.[44]

After the September 2010 incident, China increased the presence of its civilian maritime law enforcement agencies in the waters around the islands. Vessels from the Bureau of Fisheries Administration sailed to the islands approximately once a month. Most of the time, they loitered in waters beyond Japan's twelve-nautical-mile territorial waters around the islands. On three occasions, however, Chinese government ships did enter into these waters: August 2011 (two vessels from the Bureau of Fisheries Administration), March 2012 (one CMS vessel), and July 2012 (three vessels from the Bureau of Fisheries Administration).

China's harsh reaction to the detention of the fishing captain and the increased presence of Chinese government ships near the disputed islands had two negative consequences. First, it worsened China's image in Japan. According to an annual survey conducted by the Japanese government, the percentage of respondents who reported feeling an affinity toward China dropped from 38.5 percent in 2009 to 20 percent in 2010.[45] Second, events in the East China Sea underscored the value of the alliance with the United States to Japanese who had been questioning its utility. In the late 2000s, Japanese politicians had called on the United States to reaffirm publicly that

Article 5 of the US-Japan Mutual Defense Treaty covered the Senkaku/ Diaoyu Islands. In October 2010, Hillary Clinton became the first secretary of state in several decades to publicly reaffirm the U.S. commitment.[46]

In April 2012, the conservative governor of Tokyo, Shintaro Ishihara, launched a public campaign to purchase three of the disputed islands owned by a private Japanese citizen. Ishihara claimed that the central government was not doing enough to protect the islands, an argument which resonated easily because of the increased presence of Chinese government ships near the islands after the 2010 ramming incident. After millions of dollars were raised, Prime Minister Yoshihiko Noda faced a tough decision: whether to let the islands fall into the hands of an unpredictable and nationalist politician or buy the islands to control their use and development. Noda announced his decision to purchase the islands on July 7, 2012, which, unfortunately, was the anniversary of the 1937 Marco Polo Bridge incident that commemorates Japan's bid to conquer China in World War II. Even though Noda argued that central government ownership would be stabilizing, China opposed the move, which was seen as not only an exercise of sovereignty over the islands, but also as strengthening Japan's claim by bringing more of the islands under the direct control of the Japanese government.

In early September, the sale of the islands was completed. China reacted with even greater vigor than in 2010 to register its opposition and to demonstrate that it contested Japan's sovereignty over the islands. First, China issued a government statement announcing the drawing of baselines for demarcating territorial waters around the islands, a legal act that affirmed its claim. Second, China began to dispatch patrols of China Marine Surveillance vessels within twelve nautical miles of the islands, an act undertaken to challenge Japan's sovereignty and administrative control not just on maps but also on the water. Between September 2012 and December 2013, Chinese vessels entered the territorial waters around the islands seventy-four times and maintained a near continuous presence in the contiguous zone just beyond the territorial waters.[47] Third, anti-Japanese protests were permitted to occur for several days throughout the country. These were probably the largest antiforeign protests since 1989, with demonstrations reportedly in eighty-five cities.[48] Fourth, Foreign Ministry officials began to use increasingly harsh language. At one point, a senior member of the ministry described Japan's purchase of the three islands "like an atomic bomb dropped on China."[49] Fifth, during the protests, some Japanese factories and companies were vandalized. Moreover, sales of Japanese cars in China (which protestors had targeted) plummeted by more than 50 percent.[50]

Japan Responds

China's actions in the East China Sea have been counterproductive, harming ties with a key neighbor. First, as mentioned above, China's actions harmed its image in Japanese eyes. Although affinity for China improved in 2011 to 26.3 percent, it plummeted to the lowest level in several decades in 2012, 18 percent.[51] As slogans used by the Chinese protestors called for the annihilation of Japan (*jianmie riben*), such low levels of affinity are understandable. Nevertheless, Chinese leaders have sought to maintain a stable, nonhostile relationship with Japan, a position that is now untenable. At the same time, Japanese affinity for the United States rose to 84.5 percent in 2012, the highest levels on record, up from 78.9 percent in 2009.[52]

Second, Japan has engaged in external balancing against China in two ways. To start, Japan has moved to further strengthen its alliance with the United States. Toward this end, on several occasions in 2010 and 2012, Japan sought and received public and high-level affirmations from American officials that Article 5 of the US-Japan Mutual Defense Treaty covered the Senkaku/Diaoyu Islands. In addition, the islands appear to be playing a greater role in defense planning. In January 2013, working-level talks on revising the U.S.-Japan defense guidelines, the operational core of the alliance, began in response to China's increased activities in the East China Sea.[53] In March 2013, the United States and Japan updated plans to defend the islands from attack.[54] In June 2013, the two countries held unprecedented amphibious exercises, dubbed "Dawn Blitz," off the coast of California.

In addition, Japan has strengthened ties with other states in an effort to balance China's growing maritime capabilities. In June 2012, Japan and India held their first bilateral naval exercise in waters near Tokyo.[55] In January 2013, Japan and India held their first maritime affairs dialogue, which included diplomatic and military officials. Japan has also engaged the Philippines, holding maritime dialogues in 2011 and 2013.[56] Japan has agreed to donate ten patrol boats to the Philippine Coast Guard in order to strengthen its maritime capacity. In June 2013, Tokyo pledged even greater support for Manila. Japanese Defense Minister Itsunori Onodera stated that the two countries "agreed that we will further co-operate in terms of the defense of remote islands."[57] Finally, in April 2013, Japan and Vietnam announced that they would hold maritime security talks in May 2013 focused on China's assertiveness and Japan's possible support for strengthening Vietnam's maritime capacity.[58]

Third, Japan has also engaged in limited internal balancing. The new Abe government, elected in December 2012, pledged to increase Japan's defense budget for the first time in eleven years. In December 2013, Japan announced that defense spending would increase by 2.2 percent in the 2014 fiscal year, the largest increase in two decades.[59] The Maritime Self Defense Forces has moved to expand the size of its submarine fleet by extending the service life of existing boats and building new Soryu-class submarines and new destroyers. The Ground Self Defense Forces have also sought to bolster their presence in the southern tip of the Ryukyus, on Yonaguni Island, and may create a new amphibious force to focus on seizing and controlling islands.[60]

China's Response to Its Regional Challenge

Whether China has formulated a response to the worsening of ties with its neighbors remains unclear. Several Chinese policy responses to the deterioration of relations with states on its periphery can be identified, but none appears as if it will be able to reverse the decline in bilateral relations with many of its maritime neighbors.

First, especially in the South China Sea, China has sought—at times—to moderate how it defends its claims. The first phase of moderation occurred from roughly mid-2011 until the standoff over Scarborough Shoal in April 2012. First, in the summer of 2011, China's top leaders, including President Hu Jintao and Premier Wen Jiabao, reaffirmed the late Deng Xiaoping's guiding principle for dealing with China's maritime conflicts of "setting aside disputes and pursuing common development." Second, China reached agreements with other claimant states with the aim of managing tensions, promoting dialogue, and facilitating eventual dispute resolution. In addition to a July 2011 agreement with ASEAN on guidelines for implementing the code of conduct declaration, China reached a much more substantial agreement with Vietnam in October 2011 over basic principles for resolving maritime disputes that stress using international law. Third, China's top leaders have held high-level meetings with their counterparts to improve broader bilateral relationships. Philippine President Benigno Acquino and Vietnamese

Communist Party General Secretary Nguyen Phu Trong visited Beijing in August and October 2011, respectively. Likewise, Vice President Xi Jinping traveled to Vietnam in December 2011 as part of a Southeast Asian tour. Fourth, authoritative Chinese-language media, such as the *People's Daily* in mid-2011, began to underscore the importance of a cooperative approach in the South China Sea. Such articles were written largely to explain policy decisions to domestic readers, especially those working within party and state bureaucracies. Fifth, China engaged other claimants by establishing a three-billion yuan (476-million U.S. dollar) China-ASEAN Maritime Cooperation Fund (November 2011), hosting several workshops on oceanography and freedom of navigation in the South China Sea (December 2011), and hosting a meeting with senior ASEAN officials to discuss implementing the 2002 code of conduct declaration (January 2012). Finally, China halted the more assertive behavior that attracted so much adverse attention between 2009 and 2011. Vessels from the Bureau of Fisheries Administration have detained and held only two Vietnamese fishing vessels since late 2010 (with the last detention occurring in March 2012).[61] Patrol ships from China Marine Surveillance (or the newly established China Coast Guard) have not interfered in Vietnamese or Philippine hydrocarbon exploration activities since May 2011. More generally, China has not obstructed related exploration activities, such as Exxon's successful drilling of an exploratory well in Vietnamese waters claimed by China in October 2011.[62]

After the standoff at Scarborough Shoal, however, China returned to a more assertive approach. In addition to acquiring effective control over the reef and surrounding waters, China adopted other unilateral actions designed to strengthen its position in the South China Sea. Most importantly, China announced in June 2012 that the administrative status of the Paracel and Spratly Islands would be upgraded from a county-level office to one of three prefectural-level cities (*dishiji*) in Hainan Province. In July 2012, as discussed above, China used its influence over Cambodia to prevent Vietnam and the Philippines from inserting references to their specific disputes with China in the ASEAN joint communiqué.

By the end of 2013, China appeared to have begun another period of moderation in the South China Sea. In April 2013, China announced that it wanted to restart stalled talks with ASEAN over a binding code of conduct.[63] In June 2013, China and ASEAN announced that "consultations" on a code of conduct would be held in September.[64] Talks were held in September, as planned, and further talks have been scheduled for Spring 2014.[65] Earlier, China had avoided such talks, stating "conditions were not ripe." At the same time, China has sought to pursue a more balanced approach with Vietnam. In early June 2013, defense ministries in each country agreed to establish a hotline between their navies.[66] In mid-June, during President Sang's visit to China, Vietnam and China agreed to establish a hotline between fisheries departments in addition to resuming talks on the demarcation of the mouth of the Tonkin (Beibu) Gulf and pursuing a political settlement in the South China Sea.[67] In October 2013, Vietnam and China established a joint working group to explore development projects in disputed waters, and the group held its first meeting in January 2014.[68]

Consistent with a return to moderation in the South China Sea, China's top leaders signaled the importance of improving ties with Southeast Asia and limiting the potential for the territorial and maritime claims to harm ties with these countries. During a meeting on maritime affairs at the end of July 2013, Xi Jinping indicated that China might pursue a more moderate approach. Xi affirmed Deng Xiaoping's guidance for managing offshore island disputes of "setting aside disputes and pursuing joint development" while also underscoring the need to coordinate "rights defense" in the maritime domain with the maintenance of regional stability.[69] In September and October 2013, Xi Jinping and Li Keqiang both conducted tours of the region before attending APEC and EAS meetings, respectively. Taken together, they visited half of the members of ASEAN and four of the five claimants in the South China Sea: Indonesia, Malaysia, Thailand, Vietnam, and Brunei. During these bilateral visits and at the APEC and EAS meetings, China sought to deepen relations with the region that had been harmed by the escalation of these disputes. Finally, in October, China's top leaders held an unprecedented meeting on regional diplomacy, which was attended by all seven members of the Politburo Standing Committee and lasted for two days.[70] The main theme of the speech was the importance of "maintaining a stable external environment," which, by implication, had been harmed by disputes that had arisen with many neighbors. Notwithstanding new fishing rules issued by the Hainan's legislature, China appeared poised as of early 2014 to prevent the further escalation of tension in the South China Sea.[71] Nevertheless, the October meeting on regional diplomacy was premised on defending China's sovereignty and contained no indication that China would alter its position on the maritime disputes at the heart of increased frictions in the past few years.

Nevertheless, both periods of moderation in the South China Sea have focused on managing how China pursues its claims and not efforts to settle or resolve the underlying disputes. As a result, tactical pauses that increase stability are possible, but other states in these disputes will likely remain fearful of Chinese intentions, unless actions are taken by which China might "tie its hands" by, for example, offering a clear but limited definition of the nine-dashed line. Otherwise, these states will continue to have strong incentives to strengthen their security ties with the United States, thus undermining a key objective in China's regional policy.

In the East China Sea, China has not adopted a more moderate approach toward Japan since September 2012. The most that could be said is that China has moderated the frequency of patrols within the territorial waters of the disputed Senkaku/Diaoyu Islands. As demonstrated in Figure 11.1, Chinese government ships have entered the territorial waters around the islands between three and eight times per month. Nevertheless, the situation remains deadlocked, as Japan refuses to accede to China's demand that Tokyo acknowledge the presence of a dispute over the islands. As a result, the situation remains brittle and prone to spikes in tension. In October 2013, for example, Japan stated that it would shoot unidentified drones over the islands following the flight of a Chinese drone in September roughly one hundred kilometers north of the islands. In November 2013, perhaps in response to Japan's stance on drones as well as a desire to increase pressure on Japan, China announced the establishment of an East China Sea Air Defense Iden-

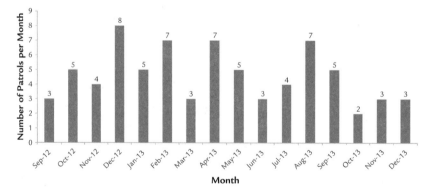

Figure 11.1. Chinese government patrols within the territorial waters of the Senkaku/Diaoyu islands.
Source: Japan Coast Guard, http://www.kaiho.mlit.go.jp/senkaku/index.html.

tification Zone. The *People's Daily* described the difference between the East China Sea and South China Sea in January 2014 as "tension in the east, stability in the south" (*dongjin nanwen*).[72]

China's second policy response to the escalation of tensions has been an effort to prevent these maritime disputes from harming overall relations with other countries. Although China has pursued this approach in the past in many disputes, including with India today, it has nevertheless become more challenging under the shadow of growing Chinese military capabilities, especially naval power. China perhaps has been most successful with Vietnam, where exchanges and interactions between the Communist Parties of the two countries have continued at a rapid pace and at high levels despite the presence of these disputes. As discussed above, Vietnamese President Sang's June 2013 trip to Beijing reflected a concerted effort to prevent the various maritime disputes between China and Vietnam from affecting overall political relations. Likewise, to commemorate two decades of engagement with ASEAN, China in November 2012 launched a campaign to underscore the importance of the China-ASEAN relationship, which was designed to demonstrate to all states in the region how they have gained— and can gain—from China's rise, while also hinting at what they might lose if they continue to counter China. Whether efforts to separate economics from politics are successful, however, would depend on the degree to which China asserts and defends its claims in maritime disputes. Given the disparity in power between China and most ASEAN states and the asymmetric economic relationships, however, such arguments may fall on deaf ears.

The situation with Japan in the East China Sea is more difficult to assess. According to recent analysis, the Chinese-Japanese economic relationship has remained robust since the purchase of the islands in September 2012, and trade has effectively been delinked from politics.[73] Nevertheless, following Prime Minister Abe's visit to the Yasukuni Shrine in December 2013, China may decide to increase economic pressure on Japan as well. In early 2014, it remains too soon to tell.

Third, since early 2012, China has embarked on an effort to strengthen ties with the United States. A turning point may have occurred in February 2012, when then Vice President Xi Jinping called on the United States and China to develop a "new type of great power relationship," a slogan that has since gathered steam over the following year.[74] The most important driver is arguably the policy of rebalancing to Asia that senior U.S. officials and President Obama articulated in 2011. Nevertheless, improved ties with the United

States would aid China's regional policy by raising the costs for the United States of increasing its support for those states in maritime disputes with China (lest future ties with China be harmed) and reducing the potential of a counterbalancing coalition forming over maritime issues or perhaps more broadly. In this way, China seeks to drive a wedge between the United States and those states in the region with which it has direct maritime conflicts. Regional states may also be deterred by improved U.S.-China ties from seeking further security assistance from the United States.

Whether any of these efforts will be successful and allow China to repair frayed ties with its neighbors remains uncertain. Despite the periods of moderation discussed above, it remains unclear whether China recognizes that its policies have backfired, reducing its security and not improving it. Although territorial disputes are inherently interactive, and China has been at times reacting to the actions of others, China's public rhetoric places all blame on opposing states. States in disputes with China are blamed for their provocations, while the United States is blamed for encouraging these states to resist China with provocative acts. Such rhetoric may not reflect the private views of Chinese policymakers. If such rhetoric does, however, it indicates what Luttwak describes as "great power autism" and low odds of China taking the steps needed to reassure states in the region and decrease the value of strong ties with the United States.[75] If China does not acknowledge that its policies have backfired, then relations with neighboring states will only continue to deteriorate.

In addition, the moment for China to reassure its neighbors over maritime claims may have passed. The past few years have witnessed impressive displays of China's growing maritime capabilities. In 2005 and 2006, Chinese government ships from the China Marine Surveillance force began regular patrols in China's claimed EEZ.[76] In 2008, the PLA Navy began long-distance training exercises in the East and South China Seas, exercises whose frequency and scope only continue to increase.[77] China's Navy now regularly conducts long-distance exercises in the Western Pacific, which require that PLAN vessels transit through the Japanese home islands. Although such actions are consistent with international norms, they underscore the change in Chinese capabilities that is occurring in the region. Under these conditions, and given China's assertive actions, uncertainty about China's intentions are likely to linger for a long time to come. Because these states have other interests at stake with China, especially in the economic realm, the opportunity for improved ties despite the presence of these disputes remains. Nevertheless, it requires a sustained engagement by Beijing and a tacit agreement by all claimants to decrease the assertion of their claims. In recent years, the episodes of moderation have been fleeting.

Why China has been unable to do more to prevent any further deterioration of ties with its maritime neighbors begs an important question. The intensification of China's maritime disputes occurred during a once-in-a-decade leadership transition in which the majority of leaders on the Politburo were replaced. As a result, Chinese leaders face strong domestic incentives not to appear weak in their interactions with other states, especially in disputes concerning sovereignty. Relatedly, Chinese leaders may believe that it is important to stand firm when faced with what they view as challenges to China's claims, especially during this period of political transition.[78] In the case of Japan, historical memory further increases the need to be seen as not making concessions, especially when sovereignty is at stake.

Conclusion

China's relations with its immediate neighbors play a central role in China's foreign policy. Good relations with neighbors enhance China's autonomy, while poor relations can restrict China's freedom of maneuver by increasing the influence of major powers along China's periphery. From the mid-2000s, and especially from 2010, the intensification of maritime disputes in East Asia involving China has raised serious questions about China's position in the region. Intensification of these disputes create strong incentives for states opposing China to balance externally by seeking the support of other states (especially the United States) and to balance internally by increasing their own naval capabilities. Regional states seek to balance against China not just because of the immediate conflicts over territorial sovereignty and maritime jurisdiction but also because of fears about how a stronger China will behave in the region in the future.

To date, China's active defense of its claims in maritime disputes in the East China Sea and the South China Sea has harmed ties with opposing states and increased the attractiveness of the United States for others in the region. This poses a clear challenge to China's foreign policy, which from the early 1990s to the mid-2000s sought to improve ties with all of its neighbors, to create space for China's development, and to limit the influence of major powers in the region. If current trends persist, and tensions in existing territorial disputes continue to spiral upward, worsening ties with neighboring states will further increase the value of a strong U.S. presence for others in the region and incentives for states to work together to balance against China in the maritime domain. Over time, this could accelerate polarization of the region and create a much more competitive environment that would ultimately harm Chinese interests more than it advances them. As the more powerful state in these maritime disputes, China needs to undertake proactive action to restore stability.

CHAPTER 12

China's Challenges: Volatility in China–U.S. Relations

Robert Sutter

The Sino-American relationship continues to twist and turn. Since the beginning of this decade, developments have seriously challenged the pattern of pragmatic U.S.-Chinese engagement that prevailed for much of the previous decade. Most importantly, Sino-American relations have become more competitive and tense in the Asia-Pacific, along the rim of China, long the primary focus of PRC foreign relations.

The Barack Obama government in its first term stressed a new "pivot" to Asia, focusing particularly on military initiatives as a means to compete more effectively with China for regional influence. In his second term President Obama has taken steps to modify policies and seek moderate management of differences, notably during an informal summit with the Chinese president in June 2013.

Chinese President Xi Jinping also has welcomed top-level meetings. He has committed China to pursuing careful management of Sino-American differences within an emerging framework of a "new type of great power relationship." However, I argue here that a serious challenge on the part of China involves managing its newly assertive stance on territorial disputes along China's rim. Chinese leaders reflect a strong nationalistic trend in China that calls for using growing Chinese military, security, economic, and political capabilities to exert pressure and coerce neighbors that challenge Chinese territorial claims. Although we have little concrete information on the private calculus of Chinese leaders, it is plausible and arguably probable that Chinese officials—including senior officials—share the nationalistic orientation seen commonly in broader elite and public opinion in China. In fact, Xi Jinping has been at the center of the new Chinese determination to take a harder stance in order to protect Chinese territorial claims. Xi's second in command, Premier Li Keqiang, and other senior leaders are explicit in insisting that there is no contradiction between China's continued emphasis on practicing the norms of "peaceful development" and its recent unprecedented use of the impressive array of growing Chinese security forces, as well as increased economic and political leverage, in order to coerce and intimidate disputants of Chinese claims in the East China Sea and the South China Sea.[1]

As I will discuss here, Chinese behavior has remained tougher against perceived affronts of its territorial claims for two years. Xi and Li signaled a partial pause in the tough public approach when they led efforts in September and October 2013 to emphasize the positive and soft-pedal differences with Southeast Asian countries over China's extraordinary claims regarding the South China Sea. However, these efforts stumbled with China's surprise initiation in late November of an Air Defense Identification Zone over disputed East China Sea territories that raised angst throughout the region and in the United States about Beijing's more demanding and assertive approach to territorial disputes.[2] While often portraying their actions as reactive and defensive, top leaders have employed strong and expanding Chinese security, economic, and political capabilities to change the status quo in the disputed seas. In doing so, they have the firm backing of specialist and popular commentators that reflect a strongly nationalistic Chinese sentiment that in turn is echoed and reinforced by senior leaders, including President Xi and Premier Li, and presumably represents the preferred orientation of at least some and probably many of these leaders.

The Obama government continues to assert that it opposes unilateral changes in the East China Sea and the South China Sea. Such rhetoric rings hollow to many of China's Asian neighbors, who see China's growing fleet of maritime security forces, fishing armadas, naval forces, and other ever-strengthening tools being used continuously in ways that change the situation in these contested waters. Leaders meeting in shirtsleeves probably won't solve this problem. This chapter avers that domestic politics over sovereignty and security issues pose a major challenge China's leaders face in endeavoring to adopt a more moderate and constructive stance toward the United States over these sensitive issues. Against this background, it is unclear if the Obama government will further modify its pivot and dilute its opposition to unilateral changes in the status quo in seas near China for the sake of greater cooperation with Beijing. A more likely outlook is increased Sino-American tension that hopefully still can be managed without U.S.-China confrontation or conflict.

Competition Challenges Engagement in 2012

Growing Chinese-U.S. divergence and competition in Asia headed the list of issues in 2012 that challenged and tested the abilities of Chinese and American leaders to manage their differences, avoid confrontation, and pursue positive engagement. Senior Chinese and U.S. leaders stayed in close contact with one another in an avowed effort to search for a "new type of great power relationship" which would avoid conflict and manage tensions as China's rising power and expanding interests rub against American interests, policies, and practices. Nevertheless, competition for influence along China's rim and in the broader Asia-Pacific region exacerbated an obvious security dilemma in this sensitive region featuring China's rising power and America's reaction, shown notably in the two sides' respective military build-ups.

The Republican presidential primaries in 2012 saw sharp and often hyperbolic attacks on Chinese economic and security policies. Governor Mitt Romney emerged from the pack as the party's nominee, supporting tough trade and security measures to protect U.S. interests against China. President Obama joined the fray with harsh rhetoric not seen in his presidential campaign in 2008. Calling China an "adversary," he highlighted his administration's reengagement with countries in the Asia-Pacific region as a means to compete with China in security, economic, and other terms.[3]

Chinese media and officials condemned the so-called China bashing seen in the American presidential and congressional election campaigns. The Chinese leaders remained firm in deflecting American pressure on the value of China's currency and broader trade practices and strongly rebuffed U.S. efforts to get China's cooperation in dealing with some sensitive international issues, notably the conflict in Syria. China continued efforts supporting close ties with the new North Korean leadership, despite the latter's repeated provocations.[4]

As discussed in greater detail below, concurrent with the increased competition between the United States and China for influence in the Asia Pacific, China resorted to extraordinary demonstrations of state power, short of direct use of military force, in response to perceived challenges by U.S. allies, the Philippines and Japan, regarding disputed territory in the South China Sea and the East China Sea. Chinese commentary accused the United States of fostering neighboring countries to be more assertive in challenging China's claims as part of alleged American efforts to contain China under the rubric of the Obama government's enhanced engagement with the Asia-Pacific region. Top Chinese leaders countered American-supported efforts for dealing with the disputed claims and also highlighted regional trade arrangements that excluded the United States in order to undermine American-led efforts to advance U.S. interests through a trans-Pacific trade pact.[5]

At the start of 2012, developments led to what leading specialists Kenneth Lieberthal and Wang Jisi characterized as pervasive and deeply rooted distrust between the two governments.[6] By the end of the year, leading specialist David Shambaugh joined other commentators in concluding that the overall U.S.-China relationship had become "more strained, fraught and distrustful." Intergovernmental meetings meant to forge cooperation are becoming "more pro-forma and increasingly acrimonious," he said; the two sides "wrangle" over trade and investment issues, technology espionage and cyber hacking, global governance challenges like climate change and Syria, nuclear challenges like Iran and North Korea, and their security postures and competition for influence in the Asia-Pacific.[7]

Cooperation and Moderation

On the other side of the ledger in 2012 were Sino-American developments and circumstances arguing for continued pragmatism on both sides in seeking to manage escalating competition and other differences without major incident. The overall trend of resilient and positive U.S.-China engagement continued. Among instruments serving to moderate the Sino-American frictions, the wide range of official Chinese-American exchanges through an array of over seventy bilateral dialogues continued and made significant progress in several areas. They also provided mechanisms for dealing with contentious issues and advancing common ground between the two countries.[8]

The so-called Taiwan issue—historically the leading cause of friction between the United States and China—has remained on a recent trajectory of easing tensions. Taiwan's election in January 2012 and the victory of incumbent President Ma Ying-jeou validated the moderate continued approach to cross-strait relations, foreshadowing closer engagement along lines welcomed by both Beijing and Washington.[9]

Despite pervasive Sino-U.S. distrust, there also were episodes demonstrating notable cooperation and seeming trust building between the two powers. Chen Guangcheng, the prominent Chinese civil rights activist, in April 2012 escaped house arrest and fled from his home province to Beijing, where he eventually took refuge in the U.S. Embassy. Talks between U.S. officials and Chinese officials led to a deal to safeguard Chen and his family and provide Chen with medical treatment. Chen subsequently changed his mind and sought to go to the United States with his family. In the media spotlight, he appealed for American support. Intensive renewed U.S.-Chinese talks concurrent with the annual Security and Economic Dialogue between top American and Chinese department leaders then underway in Beijing resulted in a second deal where Chen and his family were allowed to leave for the United States on May 19.[10]

Meanwhile, the Obama government has endeavored since late 2012 to stress its interests in sustaining broader and deeper American engagement with the Asia-Pacific region on the one hand, while on the other hand playing down emphasis in the recent past on American security and military moves that add directly to the growing security dilemma with China.[11]

Specialists on both the American and Chinese sides seemed to agree that effectively managing differences through a process of constructive engagement remains in the interests of both countries:[12]

- Both administrations benefit from positive engagement in various areas.
- Both administrations see that the two powers have become so interdependent that emphasizing the negatives in their relationship will hurt the other side but also will hurt them.

- Both leaderships are preoccupied with a long list of urgent domestic and foreign priorities; in this situation, one of the last things they would seek is a serious confrontation in relation with one another.

The Challenge Ahead: The Troubling Mix of Territorial Disputes and Chinese Domestic Politics

The Obama government's reengagement in Asia ran up against rising Chinese assertiveness and coercive and intimidating actions to protect and advance Chinese sovereignty and security interests in disputed territories along China's rim. The Chinese actions have been influenced and strongly supported by a broad and patriotic elite and public base that viewed the U.S. activism as a justification. In effect, the U.S. and Chinese initiatives represented the most important challenge or test of the durability of cooperative Sino-American engagement for 2012, and the testing continued throughout 2013.

As noted above, the Obama government has modified its Asian reengagement, charting a course to improve U.S. relations throughout the region, helping to deter China from aggressive actions while avoiding serious friction in relations with China. It has eschewed confrontation with China about other serious disputes, amid American domestic opinion that remains critical of China but preoccupied with other issues and wary of serious negative consequences of confrontation or conflict with China.

Much less certain is whether or not and to what degree the Xi Jinping government intends to deal pragmatically with the United States. Xi participated in the decision making behind Chinese behavior in 2012, which showed a pattern of exploiting incidents in nearby seas and thereby resulted in a pattern of continued expansion of Chinese control of contested territories and territorial rights through extraordinary use of coercion and intimidation short of direct application of military force. The fact that the United States has done little and that few others, with the exception of Japan, seem willing or able to take strong actions in the face of the Chinese advances adds to reasons why domestic decision makers and broader Chinese elites and public opinion are said to see the Chinese advances as victories for China. Their sense of triumph has led some prominent specialists in China and abroad to anticipate further Chinese expansion at the expense of U.S. allies and associates.[13]

If continued, such Chinese actions are likely to be seen as a direct Chinese test of U.S. resolve as a regional security guarantor under the rubric of the Obama government's "rebalancing" policy in the Asia-Pacific. They are likely to provoke a confrontation between a more assertive China and a reengaging United States. Thus, it is argued here that the willingness and ability of China's leaders to curb recent assertiveness represents a key indicator of whether or not U.S.-Chinese relations will remain on a path of pragmatic engagement with leaders on both sides carefully managing differences to avoid confrontation and conflict.

Context: How Domestic Politics Have Complicated China–U.S. Ties

The record of the Sino-American relationship since the opening of positive engagement under Mao Zedong and Richard Nixon shows that more often than not domestic politics have served as a serious obstacle or protracted drag that has complicated progress in cooperation between the two governments. The initial opening was driven by overlapping strategic interests on the part of Chinese and American rulers amid deep differences and diverging aspirations and interests among their respective people and elites. It is hard to image two societies more different in interests and international outlook than the United States and China at the start of the normalization of their relations in the early 1970s.[14]

Nixon's strategic retreat from Asia and alignment with China against the expanding Soviet Union was broadly accepted in the United States as a needed pragmatic adjustment. However, there was strong domestic resistance to the sacrifice of American ties to Taiwan, which Nixon pledged to Chinese leaders, but that were kept secret for many years from Congress, the media, and the American public by U.S. leaders fearing disruptive American domestic reaction. Meanwhile, as Americans engaged more deeply with China, American popular and elite opinion remained value-laden, pursuing the promotion of U.S. norms to "change" China in ways very much at odds with those supported by leaders and prevailing opinion in China.

In China, the life-and-death struggle for power during the Cultural Revolution involved strong leadership differences over the opening to the United States that were prominent in the ascendance and ultimate downfall and death of Defense Minister Lin Biao and the arrest of the Chinese military high command coincident with the planning of Nixon's initial visit to China. The sparse official media coverage of international affairs during the Cultural Revolution registered continued debate after Lin's fall that seemed to reflect strong elite differences on how accommodating and cooperative China should be in engagement with the United States. Chinese strong-man leaders Mao Zedong and Deng Xiaoping were generally dominant in Chinese foreign policymaking during their tenures. They were in a better position than their U.S. counterparts in dealing with domestic elite and public opinion. Notably, they employed the growing foreign affairs apparatus and massive propaganda system of China in order to condition opinion among the millions of CCP members and general Chinese public in directions supporting the Chinese leaders' preferred foreign policy.

The progress in relations came to an abrupt halt at the end of the 1980s.[15] The brutal crackdown on student-led demonstrators in Tiananmen Square in 1989 had a sharp and negative impact on American public opinion, the Congress, the media, and various interests groups that endures up to the present. The concurrent collapse of international Communism and the demise of the Soviet Union ended the strategic rationale for improving U.S. relations with China, opening the way to an outpouring of diplomatic, economic, and political pressure amid barrages of invective that showed leaders and elites and public opinion in China how hostile Americans were prepared to be in confronting the policies and practices of the Chinese party-state.

Chinese leaders deepened ongoing Chinese foreign policy, education, and propaganda efforts to strengthen Chinese patriotism in ways that would underline differences with the United States and protect the one-party state from U.S.-led pressure and attack. They sought to preserve beneficial economic and other substantive ties, but the experience with Americans after Tiananmen underlined an already strong inclination in China to view the United States negatively. The United States notably was seen to be seeking to change China's political system, to continue and strengthen support for Taiwan, to sustain a leadership position in Asia at odds with Chinese interests, and to foster American world leadership in directions challenging aspirations for a multipolar world providing greater opportunity for Chinese interests. Whatever trust had been built up between the two governments in the previous two decades seemed shattered beyond repair.

The road back to more cooperative engagement and pragmatism has been difficult. A major catalyst was the Taiwan Straits crisis of 1995–1996, featuring nine months of periodic live-fire Chinese military exercises around Taiwan in reaction to the visit to the United States of the Taiwan president in 1995. The tension didn't end until the United States deployed two aircraft carrier battle groups to the Taiwan area to face-off with the Chinese military in the area.

Seeking, among other things, to avoid a repetition of the dangerous crisis over Taiwan, the Clinton administration shifted to a stance of much more disciplined and positive engagement with China. Bargaining with China proved difficult, as both sides registered little mutual trust as they required concrete concessions before moving relations forward. And the American government was subjected to repeated challenges, often with partisan motives from domestic opponents, especially in the Congress.

After the intervention of U.S. aircraft carriers in 1996, the determined and impressive Chinese military buildup opposite Taiwan was based on the assumption that Chinese forces needed to be strong enough to deter Taiwan's moves toward independence and to deter or delay American military intervention in the event of a military conflict between China and Taiwan. American military planning and preparations became more focused on dealing with China's growing military challenges, deepening the U.S.-China security dilemma in the Asia-Pacific.

The lack of mutual trust and the fact that domestic pressures would not allow serious Sino-American differences to be dealt with through accepted international norms was graphically illustrated following the American bombing of the Chinese embassy in Belgrade during the U.S.-led war against Serbia over the Kosovo issues in 1999. Resorting to tactics used periodically in the course of China's Revolution in the twentieth century, but far removed from international norms, widespread mob violence usually orchestrated and channeled by Chinese authorities attacked and destroyed American diplomatic properties amid a massive official propaganda campaign that included authoritative media charges equating the United States with Nazi Germany, and Bill Clinton with Adolph Hitler.[16]

The George W. Bush administration's initially tougher policies toward China were more in line with American congressional and media opinion than Clinton's pursuit of a "strategic partnership" with the Communist regime still viewed negatively by the majority of Americans. In response, Chinese leaders Jiang Zemin and Hu Jintao saw China's interests best served by giving higher priority to reassuring and accommodating the United States; they reacted with notable restraint to Bush's pronouncements on Taiwan, missile defense, Iraq, and North Korea. They sought to positively engage the

United States and stabilize U.S. relations as part of efforts to promote a positive "strategic opportunity" that would facilitate China's continued modernization and "peaceful development" in the first two decades of the twenty-first century. As Bush's government and the United States became preoccupied with the war on terrorism and the conflicts in Afghanistan and Iraq, the U.S. government sought China's cooperation, notably in dealing with North Korea's nuclear weapons program. The United States and China also worked together to insure that moves toward greater self-determination of Taiwan by its president Chen Shui-bian would be constrained. They demonstrated in the process common Sino-American interests in avoiding conflict in the Taiwan Strait despite the strengthening of military forces of both sides in the area.[17]

The Obama administration endeavored to build on the positive U.S.-China engagement developed under Bush. Candidate Obama eschewed the harsh campaign criticism of China typical of recent U.S. presidential campaigns. China loomed large in his efforts to seek international cooperation in dealing with the world financial crisis and recession, proliferation of weapons of mass destruction, climate change, and terrorism.[18] The results were disappointing to the American government. On the one hand, the Hu Jintao government was unwilling to take steps regarding these international issues apart from those that would directly benefit Chinese development. On the other hand, the Chinese government seemed to see the solicitous Obama government approach at a time of major American economic weakness and preoccupation with the problems of stabilization and military withdrawal from Southwest Asia as an opportunity to press the Americans on a broad range of longstanding and recent Sino-American differences. The Chinese government exerted greater pressure on the Obama administration on issues of U.S. arms sales to Taiwan and U.S. policy toward Tibet. It threatened to curb investment in U.S. government securities and its reliance on the U.S. dollar in international transactions. Chinese civilian security ships harassed U.S. Navy surveillance ships operating in international waters along China's rim as China complained that such military activities were illegal within China's claimed exclusive economic zone—a distinct but minority interpretation of international law not followed by the U.S. government.

The tougher Chinese posture toward the United States was part of an overall pattern of greater assertiveness and truculence from China seen during 2009–2010. The cause of the shift is still debated among specialists, but

Chinese domestic public and elite opinion seemed to support strongly the tougher stance. The more truculent stance emerged in somewhat erratic ways and reflected the stated preferences of representatives of a variety of institutions and groups active in an ongoing domestic debate in China about the appropriate course of Chinese foreign policy in the twenty-first century. Some officials and commentators argued in favor of stronger efforts to defend longstanding Chinese territorial claims and other interests, while others supported continuing past efforts designed to reassure China's neighbors and the United States.[19]

Specifically, in addition to the actions against the United States noted above, Chinese officials and commentaries at this time supported stronger actions in defense of territorial claims in the South China Sea, the East China Sea, and along the border with India. Chinese leaders went to great lengths to consolidate closer relations with North Korea during a sensitive time of leadership succession. In the process, they turned a blind eye to Pyongyang's egregious attacks on South Korea that resulted in the sinking of a South Korean Navy ship, killing forty-six sailors, and an artillery barrage, killing four, including two civilians, and wounding others. When the United States and South Korea reacted to the ship sinking with military exercises in the Yellow Sea involving a U.S. aircraft carrier, China publicly warned that such action was a threat against China, a notable escalation in its reaction to such exercises.[20]

In the face of greater Chinese assertiveness and growing concerns by U.S. allies and other governments in the Asia-Pacific region about the intentions of a rising China, the Obama government became more directly involved in the ASEAN Regional Forum, the East Asian Summit, and other multilateral groups as part of broader efforts at enhanced engagement in the region. Initially harsh attacks by Chinese officials and official commentary against the American policies and practices subsided by late 2010. The period before and immediately after President Hu Jintao's visit to Washington in January 2011 saw authoritative affirmation of the reassurances that the Chinese had been making toward the United States for the past decade.[21] Unfortunately, the reassurances were not sustained and, in 2012, China engaged in a well-coordinated defense of its interests, involving multifaceted coercive actions often beyond the scope of international norms. The actions focused on U.S. allies and had clear implications for U.S. interests, and the ongoing Obama government strengthened engagement with Asia. The

Chinese actions seemed to receive the full support of Chinese elite and public opinion, which favored stronger measures in foreign relations, notably relations with the United States.

Territorial Disputes, Chinese Domestic Politics, and China–U.S Relations

Political scientist Robert Putnam reminds officials and observers concerned with international affairs that successful negotiation and other interaction between two governments requires that arrangements reached mesh well with the interests not only of the government officials concerned with international dynamics, but with the interests of the domestic stakeholders in each society.[22]

As noted above, the domestic foundation of positive engagement between the United States and China has often been seen as weak since the engagement process began over forty years ago. Because of the emotional reaction to the Tiananmen crackdown and the concurrent collapse of the strategic rationale for U.S. accommodation with China as a result of the decline and collapse of the Soviet Union, American domestic forces pressed for a hard line against China. The results for U.S.-China relations were deep mutual distrust and strengthening of Chinese popular and elite worldviews that focused on major differences with the United States, the need for greater Chinese power, and the resolve to preserve and advance Chinese interests in the face of expected American resistance and opposition.

Recent developments during the tenure of the Obama government show the influence of Chinese domestic politics and various stakeholders in influencing a hardening in China's positions on sensitive issues that call into question the durability of the positive engagement between the two countries prevalent in the first decade of this century. The hardening seems broadly in line with an overall mind-set among elite and popular opinion in China that has been strengthened by patriotic image building by the Chinese authorities for over twenty years. The implications of these domestic Chinese determinants on Chinese foreign policy and behavior are seen as much more serious today than in earlier decades. In particular, today's Chinese leaders are viewed as much weaker than Mao Zedong and Deng Xiaoping, who could call upon party, government, and other resources to mobilize domestic opinion in line with their preferred foreign policy courses. Current Chinese leaders tend to be seen as unable to stand up to domestic forces and popular and elite opinion favoring stronger measures to defend China's international claims and interests. Meanwhile, as noted at the outset of this chapter, it is plausible and arguably probable that top Chinese decision makers share the nationalistic orientation seen commonly in broader elite and public opinion in China. The result forecasts Chinese actions that could easily further exacerbate the security dilemma between the United States and China along the rim of China. Stronger and more assertive Chinese actions could eventually compel the Obama government, now endeavoring to moderate its enhanced engagement with Asia in ways that avoid conflict with China, to engage in an "action-reaction" dynamic that increasingly precludes positive U.S.-Chinese engagement.[23]

Patterns of Chinese Assertiveness

Chinese assertiveness resumed in 2012 and persisted through 2013, as China took action to defend its disputed claims in the South China Sea and the East China Sea.[24]

Round One

The first round of Chinese assertiveness over territorial issues beginning in 2012 involved the South China Sea. Chinese authorities used impressive and extraordinary demonstrations of China's security, economic, administrative, and diplomatic powers to have their way in the South China Sea.

- China employed its large and growing force of maritime and fishing security ships, targeted economic sanctions out of line with international norms and WTO rules, and repeated diplomatic warnings to intimidate and coerce Philippine officials, security forces, and fishermen to respect China's claims to the disputed Scarborough Shoal.
- China showed stronger resolve to exploit more fully contested fishing resources in the South China Sea with repeated announced deployments of one of the world's largest (32,000-ton) fish-processing ships to the area, and the widely publicized dispatch of fleets of

fishing boats supported by supply ships in disputed South China Sea areas.

- China created a new, multifaceted administrative structure backed by a new military garrison that covered wide swaths of disputed areas in the South China Sea. The coverage was in line with China's broad historical claims depicted in Chinese maps with a nine-dashed line encompassing most of the South China Sea. The large claims laid out in Chinese maps also provided justification for a state-controlled Chinese oil company to offer nine new blocks in the South China Sea, which were far from China but very close to Vietnam, for foreign oil company development. Against this background, little was heard in Chinese commentary of the more moderate explanation of Chinese South China Sea territorial claims made by the Chinese foreign ministry spokesperson on February 29, 2012, who said that China did not claim the "entire South China Sea," but only its islands and adjacent waters.

- Chinese authorities later prompted some alarm in the South China Sea when provincial authorities announced that Chinese maritime police patrols would board and hold ships carrying out illegal activities in the claimed Chinese areas of the South China Sea. And Vietnam and the Philippines as well as Taiwan joined India and other countries in condemning new Chinese passports that showed the South China Sea and other disputed areas along the rim of China as Chinese territory.

- China advanced cooperative relations with the 2012 ASEAN chair, Cambodia, thereby insuring that, with Cambodia's cooperation, South China Sea disputes did not receive prominent treatment in ASEAN documents in the annual ASEAN Ministerial Meeting in April and later ASEAN-related meetings in November. A result was strong division in ASEAN on how to deal with China, which resulted in unprecedented displays of ASEAN disunity at those meetings.

Chinese officials and official Chinese media commentaries endeavored to set limits on and compartmentalize their treatment of South China Sea disputes. Their public emphasis remained heavily on China's continued pursuit of "peaceful development" and cooperation during meetings with Southeast Asian representatives and those of other concerned powers, including the United States. Thus, what emerged was a Chinese approach that has continued up to the present, which has two general paths.

1. One path shows South China Sea claimants in the Philippines, Vietnam, and others in Southeast Asia, as well as their supporters in the United States and elsewhere, how powerful China has become in disputed South China Sea areas; how China's security, economic, administrative, and diplomatic powers are likely to grow in the near future; and how Chinese authorities could use those powerful means in intimidating and coercive ways short of overt military force in order to counter foreign "intrusions" or public disagreements regarding Chinese claims.

2. Another path forecasts ever closer "win-win" cooperation between China and Southeast Asian countries, ASEAN, and others, including the United States. It focuses on burgeoning China-Southeast Asian trade and economic interchange and is premised on treatment of South China Sea and other disputes in ways that avoid public controversy and eschew actions challenging or otherwise complicating the extensive Chinese claims to the area. In this regard, China emphasizes the importance of all concerned countries to adhere to efforts to implement the 2002 Declaration of the Conduct of the Parties in the South China Sea (DOC). It duly acknowledges recent efforts supported by ASEAN to reach the "eventual" formulation of a code of conduct (COC) in the South China Sea, implying that the process of achieving the latter may take some time.

In sum, China set forth an implicit choice for the Philippines, Vietnam, other Southeast Asian disputants of China's South China Sea claims, ASEAN, and other governments and organizations with an interest in the South China Sea, notably the United States. On the one hand, based on recent practice, pursuit of policies and actions at odds with Chinese claims in the South China Sea would meet with more demonstrations of Chinese power along the lines of first path, above. On the other hand, recent Chinese leaders' statements and official commentary indicate that others' moderation and/or acquiescence regarding Chinese claims will result in the mutually beneficial development seen in the second path. The Philippines, Vietnam, and other disputants of Chinese claims do not seem to be in an advantageous position in the face of Chinese power and intimidation. ASEAN remains divided on how to deal with China. And, options of the United States and other concerned powers to deal effectively with the new situation of greater muscle in Chinese policies and practices regarding the South China Sea, short of use of military force, remain to be determined.

Round Two

The second round of Chinese assertiveness on sensitive sovereignty and security issues came with the more widely publicized and still ongoing dispute with Japan over the Diaoyu/Senkaku Islands.[25] Even more so than in the recent case in the South China Sea, China's response to a perceived affront by Japan involved a variety of extralegal measures sharply contrary to international norms. They included, in particular, trade sanctions and failure to provide security of Japanese people and property in China. As large demonstrations emerged in over one hundred Chinese cities fostered by well-orchestrated publicity efforts of Chinese authorities, the security forces tended to stand aside as agitated Chinese demonstrators destroyed Japanese properties and manhandled Japanese citizens. The displays of violence were eventually mildly criticized by Chinese official media commentary, but the publicity organs of China were full of support of Chinese peoples' "righteous indignation" against Japan as the widespread violence spread throughout the country. Meanwhile, the Chinese authorities deployed maritime security forces and took legal steps that showed Japan and other concerned powers that the status quo of Japan's control of the islands had changed amid continued challenge from China employing security forces and other means short of direct use of military force.

Popular and elite opinion in China reacted positively to the Chinese actions in the South China Sea and the East China Sea. Some Chinese officials and media also viewed approvingly the reaction of the United States, which was seen as less willing in 2012–2013 to confront China on such assertive actions than in the period of disputes in 2010. Chinese media flagged with prominent headlines President Obama's reassurance to Prime Minister Wen Jiabao in Phnom Penh on November 20, 2012, that the United States "will not take sides on disputes" in the seas bordering China. A specialist in the Chinese Foreign Ministry-affiliated think tank highlighted approvingly a "more cautious" U.S. approach toward territorial disputes in the region.[26]

In sum, Chinese elite and public opinion embraced the argument that China's tough stance has been successful. Incoming leaders, including Xi Jinping and Li Keqiang, closely identified with the firm stance protecting Chinese sovereignty and security. Unlike the debates and various policy options stressed in Chinese commentary during the period of assertiveness in 2009–2010, the Chinese approach toward the disputed seas in 2012–2013 has been effectively coordinated and implemented without signs of debate or disagreement, even though the Chinese actions involved extraordinary use of coercion, intimidation, and extralegal means well beyond the pale of international norms said to be respected by the Chinese government.

Will Xi Jinping Curb Chinese Assertiveness?

Given the Obama government's repeated signals since November 2012 that it intends to carefully moderate its engagement policies in ways that avoid overt friction with China, it is argued here that the main uncertainty we currently face in forecasting U.S.-Chinese relations involves the ability and willingness of the Xi Jinping government to deal pragmatically with the United States. In particular, the strong and deeply rooted popular and elite public opinion supporting firmer measures at odds with American interests and those of many Chinese neighbors makes it harder to predict that the incoming Xi government will respond positively and pragmatically to the Obama government overtures in ways that will ease the security dilemma along China's rim and other Sino-American tensions.

Meanwhile, tensions among China and other claimants to disputed territory and natural resource claims in the South China Sea and the East China Sea seem likely to continue and rise.[27] Confrontations between Chinese and other claimants' government maritime security vessels, fishing ships, and oil survey vessels have been accompanied by repeated protests, economic and diplomatic sanctions and threats, and popular demonstrations in the respective countries. China has strongly pressured the Philippines to halt an arbitration case Manila initiated before a UN tribunal challenging China's South China Sea claims. China's abruptly announced air defense identification zone over disputed East China Sea territories confronted Japan and its ally, the United States, who reacted strongly, along with U.S. allies South Korea and Australia, while other regional commentators worried about implications for stability throughout the maritime periphery of China. The need to exploit the energy along with fishing resources in the contested seas is growing. Vietnam and the Philippines see oil exploitation in the South China Sea as particularly important for their development. China also has demonstrated stronger efforts than in the past to exploit the oil and gas resources in the South China Sea areas claimed by others and in the East China Sea in areas claimed by Japan.[28]

The rising tensions in the nearby seas continue to involve China-U.S. relations. Chinese commentators claim that Japan and the Philippines, formal allies of the United States, and Vietnam, a state building closer military ties with the United States, have been emboldened and supported by the United States in their confrontations with China. The rise in protests and disputes over the contested seas is linked with the Obama government's engagement with Asia-Pacific countries. Some Chinese commentators view the United States as manipulating the conflicts in the nearby seas in order to complicate China's neighboring relations and ascendance to Asian leadership. Meanwhile, popular and elite opinion is seen by Chinese and foreign commentators to compel Beijing to adopt tough positions regarding the South China Sea and the East China Sea and related issues with the United States.[29]

Foreign specialists judge that a good deal of the impetus for popular and elite pressure for a tough Chinese approach on these territorial issues rests with the type of nationalism that has been fostered with increased vigor by the Chinese authorities since the end of the Cold War and the collapse of international Communism. The patriotic discourse emphasizes that since the nineteenth century, China has been treated unjustly and its territory and related sovereign rights have been exploited by other powers. China remains in a protracted process, building power sufficient to protect what China controls and to regain disputed territory and rights. On the whole, the patriotic discourse leads to a sense of "victimization" by Chinese people and elites, who are seen as having greater influence on China's decision making on foreign affairs now that the strong-man politics of Mao Zedong and Deng Xiaoping have given way to a collective leadership more sensitive to nongovernment elites and popular views.[30]

The strong patriotism fostered by Chinese authorities has included extensive efforts to build an image of China as a righteous actor on the world stage, different from the other world powers, who are seen as selfishly following their own interests. Thus, for example, China's foreign policy is said to follow principled and moral positions that provide the basis for effective Chinese strategies in world affairs. Remarkably, such strategies are interpreted as insurance that China does not make mistakes in foreign affairs, an exceptional position reinforced by the fact that the PRC is perceived by the rest of the world as avoiding publicly acknowledging foreign policy mistakes or apologizing for its actions in world affairs. Undoubtedly, some Chinese foreign policy officials and specialists privately disagree with the remarkably righteous image of Chinese foreign relations, but many officials, including top leaders, seem to agree with China's prevailing foreign policy line. In any event, no authoritative commentator criticizes the official orthodoxy of Chinese patriotism and strong self-righteousness that is broadly accepted by elite and public opinion. Whatever criticism elites and public opinion register against Chinese foreign policy tends to focus on China being too timid and not forceful enough in dealing with foreign affronts.[31]

In contrast, many of China's neighbors and foreign specialists see a moral, principled, and benign approach as the exception rather than the rule in the zigzags of the often violent foreign relations of the PRC through much of its sixty years. This has been the case particularly in neighboring areas. In the post-Cold War period, China has tried to reassure neighboring leaders who well remember the violence and threatening Chinese practices of the past. China's recent behavior in the South China Sea and in the East China Sea has been seen by neighbors as intimidating and truculent, recalling past Chinese efforts at intimidation and coercion. Part of the problem in Chinese efforts at reassurance is that Chinese elite and popular opinion shows almost no awareness of past Chinese violence and excesses, and therefore has little appreciation of the reasons behind the suspicion and wariness of many neighboring governments, and of the main outside power in the region, the United States. Regarding the latter, one other practice seen throughout the history of PRC foreign relations, and supported by the strong patriotic discourse in China, has been to register strident opposition to efforts by outside powers to establish and sustain positions of influence and strength around China's periphery. Such moves, by the United States, but also by the Soviet Union in the past and Japan and India up to the present, are repeatedly seen by Chinese authorities as well as supporting elite and public opinions in grossly exaggerated terms of threat to China, involving a revival of Cold War "containment" or other schemes.

Thus, the broad implication of Chinese elite and popular opinion being strongly influenced, not only by patriotic discourse emphasizing China being victimized by other powers, but by a unique and strong sense of morality and righteousness in foreign affairs, is that China views whatever problems it faces with neighbors and other concerned powers as being caused solely by others. Accordingly, it has little patience with the complaints of other claimants or with calls by others for China to compromise on sensitive issues involving sovereignty and security in nearby Asia.

Outlook and Some Options

Looking ahead, there is plenty of evidence to support a scenario of continuation of China's assertive advances into disputed nearby territories. Recent Chinese policies and practices have the support of important domestic stakeholders, broad elite and public opinion, and probably many senior officials. At the same time, such Chinese actions seem likely in the future to become a direct test of U.S. resolve as a regional security guarantor under the rubric of the Obama government's engagement policy in the Asia-Pacific. Thus, an eventual confrontation between a more assertive China and an engaging United States seems more likely.

The likely continued serious tensions in the nearby disputed seas add to a long list of unresolved and often draining and daunting challenges the new Chinese leadership faces in domestic and foreign affairs. In East Asia, the most important arena of contemporary Chinese foreign relations, the Xi Jinping leadership faces considerable difficulty in managing tensions in the Korean Peninsula in addition to issues in the nearby seas. Arguably, the Chinese authorities now face three ongoing "hot spots" (the Korean Peninsula, the East China Sea, and the South China Sea), and each involves in one way or the other a deepening and potentially dangerous Chinese security dilemma with the United States, and broader Chinese competition for regional leadership with the American superpower. Managing this array of problems would have been difficult for past strong Chinese leaders Mao Zedong and Deng Xiaoping, who preferred modified united front approaches that allowed China to focus on the "main" target or enemy, reducing tensions with others so as to gain leverage in dealing with the top priority issue.[32]

The ability of the much weaker Xi Jinping to pull back from some disputes in order to focus on the most important one almost certainly is less than that of a Mao or Deng. Realistically speaking, Xi appears in no position to run against the prominent rising tide of uniquely self-righteous elite and public opinion in China that has been conditioned to see China as repeatedly treated unjustly by nefarious foreign powers in the past and as blameless in disputes with others. Indeed, he may strongly agree with such opinion.

Meanwhile, some put the onus on the Obama government to go further in accommodating Chinese concerns over its "rebalancing" policy. In their view,[33] it is up to America to reduce the security dilemma and competition with China posed by the United States pursuing actively closer ties with a full range of regional countries and multilateral organizations, ranging from India in South Asia to Japan and South Korea in Northeast Asia, and including all of Southeast Asia and many of the Pacific Island countries and Australia and New Zealand.

Of course, defenders of the Obama policies counter that such one-sided reassurance not only risks being seen as appeasement at home and weakness abroad, but it works against a wide range of U.S. interests not involving China.[34] And they also could argue that accommodating the uniquely myopic and self-righteous Chinese view of regional and world affairs has a variety of negative consequences for the international order deemed important by Americans and much of the rest of the world. In particular, China has become the world's second power, with a broad and fast-growing international involvement. This rising superpower promises to be an extremely disruptive regional and global element if it continues to resort to the kinds of gross violations of international norms seen in its response to perceived affronts to Chinese interests.

Considering the above, perhaps the best that can be expected in future China-U.S. relations is for the Xi Jinping leadership to follow Xi's summit meeting with Barack Obama by responding in kind to the Obama government's redefinition of the recent engagement policy in ways that reduce overt competition with China. Such a course holds the promise of at least some reduction of China-U.S. tensions over the Asian hot spots, and may help to reduce the intensity of clashing interests of the Asian powers involved in these disputes. The benefit for China of such a course would be reduced risk of confrontation with the United States and its very negative implications for Chinese interests. It also would reduce publicity about the regional hot spots, which could increase the freedom of action of experienced Chinese foreign policy practitioners to use more nuance and moderation in seeking Chinese goals without the distracting demands for strong defense of Chinese interests by aroused Chinese elite and public opinion.

Conclusion

Domestic politics have long been the source of serious obstacles or protracted drag on forward movement in Sino-American relations. There was an enormous and profound gap between the domestic elites and public of the two countries as Nixon and Mao began the process of normalization of relations. At various times, leaders on both sides took measures to force forward relations between the two societies, though high-level negotiations remained focused on searches for strategic and economic advantage.

Whatever progress was made in bridging the gap between the two countries was shattered with the Tiananmen crackdown and the resulting sharp negative turn in American attitudes toward the Chinese authorities and their policies and practices. Trust between the leaders and people of the two countries was overwhelmed by strident and abusive American invective and accompanying pressure against Chinese policies and practices as well as by bitter Chinese counterattacks on the United States and its policies and practices as the world's "hegemon." Concurrent efforts by the Chinese government deepened as an orthodoxy among the Chinese elite and public offered a series of worst-case views of the United States amid a uniquely self-absorbed and self-righteous Chinese worldview.

The most serious contemporary challenge flowing from volatile U.S.-Chinese relations is the impact of Chinese domestic politics and how they prompt and support more assertive Chinese policies against the United States and U.S. allies and associates in the Asia-Pacific. Under prevailing conditions, Chinese assertiveness is likely to continue over territorial disputes along China's rim and other issues that eventually will worsen the security dilemma between the two countries.

Options to deal with this potentially dangerous trend include the United States further modifying its engagement approach in ways that play down competition with China. The U.S. government already has taken several steps in this direction since late 2012; some experts place the onus on the United States to take much greater additional steps to reassure China. Another option is for the newly installed Xi Jinping government to take steps to moderate Chinese demands and educate Chinese elite and public opinion with a more realistic view of disputes along China's rim and the intentions and role of the United States. Such a posture would allow for greater Chinese flexibility in dealing with regional disputes, seeking mutual compromise and avoiding confrontations that in recent years have seen China react in extraordinarily disruptive ways, going far beyond the limits of accepted international norms.

Realistically speaking, the best that can be hoped for probably involves some positive Chinese response to the more moderate stance on China seen in recent pronouncements by leaders of the Obama government regarding engagement in Asia. The need for continued pragmatic engagement between China and the United States is well recognized by experts on both sides. Domestic politics on the American side have not pushed U.S. officials toward confrontation with China; domestic politics in China are aroused in ways that tend to demonize American intentions. It is argued here that the immediate course of U.S.-Chinese relations is closely linked with how the Xi Jinping government meets this domestic Chinese challenge.

NOTES

Chapter 1. China's Challenges: Reform-Era Legacies and the Road Ahead

1. For accounts and assessments of the changing nature of elite politics in reform era China, see, generally, Richard Baum, *Burying Mao: Chinese Politics in the Age of Deng Xiaoping* (Princeton, N.J.: Princeton University Press, 1994); Joseph Fewsmith, *Elite Politics in Contemporary China* (Armonk, N.Y.: M.E. Sharpe, 2001); David Shambaugh, "The Dynamics of Elite Politics during the Jiang Era" *China Journal* 45 (2001): 101–11; Cheng Li, "The New Bipartisanship Within the Chinese Communist Party," *Orbis* 49, no. 3 (2005): 387–400.

2. Some of the fallen designated or apparent successors were deemed politically unreliable and attacked for policies or views at odds with those of the top leader or leaders (Liu Shaoqi in 1966, Hua Guofeng in 1981, Hu Yaobang in 1987, Zhao Ziyang in 1989). Others were alleged to have been involved in plots to usurp power (Lin Biao in 1971, Jiang Qing and her close associates in 1976).

3. For accounts that discuss the possibility of an unsettled succession to Deng, see Lowell Dittmer, "Patterns of Elite Strife and Succession in Chinese Politics," *China Quarterly* 123 (1990): 405–30; and Richard Baum, "China After Deng: Ten Scenarios in Search of Reality," *China Quarterly* 145 (1996): 153–75. The timing of Deng's decision to sack Hu Yaobang is contested. Some secondary sources present accounts that suggest Deng may have grown disillusioned with Hu early in the fall of 1986 and planned to replace him even before he was accused of mishandling the response to student demonstrations in December 1986. See Baum, *Burying Mao*, 436 n. 2; and, especially, Yang Mingwei, "Deng Xiaoping yu Li Xiannian, Chen Yun mishang 'jiaoban' jie Hu Yaobang cizhi neimu," *Renminwang*, December 26, 2011. Pending the declassification of CCP archives, the best evidence currently available confirms only Deng's growing anger in December and his determination to dismiss Hu in January.

4. The numerical designation of each generation is used to define cohorts of Communist Party leaders in China. The first generation included revolutionaries who

assumed leadership positions in 1949 with the founding of the People's Republic of China (PRC) (for example, Mao Zedong and Zhou Enlai). The second generation included the immediate successors to this cohort, many of whom were younger participants in the Communist revolution (for example, Deng Xiaoping and Chen Yun). The third generation was composed of those whose political careers were forged mainly after the PRC was founded (for example, Zhao Ziyang, Li Peng, and Jiang Zemin). The fourth generation included mainly those whose careers were launched later and whose trajectory was interrupted by the upheavals of the Cultural Revolution (for example, Hu Jintao and Wen Jiabao). The fifth generation includes those whose young lives and early training were complicated by the instability of the Cultural Revolution, but who resumed their education and began to build their careers during the reform era initiated in 1979 (for example, Xi Jinping and Li Keqiang). Especially since Deng Xiaoping stepped aside in the early 1990s, each generation's preeminent leader has been defined by his filling three top positions—General Secretary of the Chinese Communist Party, Chairman (President) of the Chinese State, and Chairman of the Party's Central Military Commission (CMC).

5. During the last years under Hu, Xi Jinping had clearly emerged as his likely successor. In addition to a resume that included serving as governor of Fujian Province, party leader in Zhejiang and Shanghai (posts of the type that matter for rising to the top, but the equivalent of which several other members of the upper elite had held), Xi also (and more importantly) held the position of vice president, and was one of just two members of his "generation" (along with Li Keqiang) who were on the Politburo Standing Committee (PSC) selected after the Seventeenth Party Congress. Still, even as the legacy of personal rather than institutionalized politics diminishes, it has not been entirely absent from elite politics. In 1997, in order to sideline a political competitor, Jiang Zemin pushed through a rule on retirement age (at 67 still eligible for promotion, at 68 obliged to retire) that required his rival, Qiao Shi, to step down. And despite retiring from other posts in 2002–2003, Jiang held onto his position as chair of the CMC, yielding it to General Secretary and President Hu Jintao only in 2004. Hu himself owed his position in large measure to the fact that Deng Xiaoping, before withdrawing from public life, had personally anointed him as Jiang's future successor and thereby put Hu on track to be named to formal posts that have become regular stepping stones to the top leadership position. More recently, Xi Jinping, although assuming all three key top posts according to the increasingly institutionalized procedures, did have to cope with an apparent attempt at an irregular challenge to the orderly succession process from Bo Xilai. Yet, the response to Bo's gambit and Xi Jinping's immediate succession to all three top posts (avoiding a repetition of Jiang Zemin's delayed retirement from the CMC chairmanship) both suggest that the CCP elite has been growing ever more committed to institutionalizing stable procedures for succession.

6. The literature on the routinization of charisma, and the trend toward institutionalized or bureaucratic leadership in postrevolutionary regimes builds on the insights of Weber. See Max Weber, Hans Heinrich Gerth, and C. Wright Mills, *From Max*

Weber: Essays in Sociology (New York: Oxford University Press, 1958), chaps. 9 and 10; Richard Lowenthal, "Development vs. Utopia in Communist Policy," in *Change in Communist Systems*, ed. Jeremy R. Azrael and Chalmers A. Johnson (Stanford, Calif.: Stanford University Press, 1970), 33–116; and Kenneth Jowitt, *New World Disorder: The Leninist Extinction* (Berkeley: University of California Press, 1992).

7. See, for example, Cui Hongjian, "China Under Xi Jinping—Scope and Efforts to Deepen Reform," China Institute of International Studies, December 27, 2013, http://www.ciis.org.cn/english/2013-12/27/content_6575550.htm; Cheng Li and Ryan McElveen, "Can Xi Jinping's Governing Strategy Succeed?" Brookings Institution, September 26, 2013, http://www.brookings.edu/research/articles/2013/09/26-xi-jinping-china-governing-strategy-li-mcelveen; and François Godemont, "China at the Crossroads," European Council on Foreign Relations, Apr. 2012, http://www.ecfr.eu/page/-/ECFR53_CHINA_ESSAY_AW.pdf.

8. See, for example, Zachary Keck, "Xi Jinping: China's Most Powerful Leader Since Deng and Mao?" *The Diplomat*, August 5, 2013 "Every Move You Make: Xi Jinping Has Made Himself the Most Powerful Leader since Deng Xiaoping," *The Economist*, November 16, 2013.

9. For accounts of economic reforms, their origins, and their impact, see Barry Naughton, *The Chinese Economy: Transitions and Growth* (Cambridge, Mass.: MIT Press, 2007); Yasheng Huang, *Capitalism with Chinese Characteristics* (New York: Cambridge University Press, 2008); Susan L. Shirk, *The Political Logic of Economic Reform in China* (Berkeley: University of California Press, 1993); David Zweig, "China's Political Economy," in *Politics in China: An Introduction*, ed. William A. Joseph (New York: Oxford University Press, 2010), 192–221.

10. In the decades since China opened to the outside world, scholarship about the Maoist years has led to a more accurate understanding of the costs of mistaken policies and disruptive politics. Major episodes such as the Great Leap Forward (1958–1961) and the Cultural Revolution (1966–1976), the consequences of which were obscured by a veil of official propaganda and secrecy, were exposed as disasters of epic proportions after Mao's death. The Chinese Communist Party itself formally reversed its verdict on these events when it published the Resolution on CCP history in June 1981, though its reassessment was partial and incomplete. Chinese and foreign scholars in subsequent years have relied on ever more extensive empirical research (including interviews with those who lived through the experience, and Chinese documents that had previously been unavailable) to provide a clearer understanding of what had happened. For prominent recent examples, see Yang Jisheng, *Tombstone: The Great Chinese Famine, 1958–62* (New York: Farrar Strauss and Giroux, 2012); and Joseph Esherick, Paul Pickowicz, and Andrew Walder, *The Chinese Cultural Revolution as History* (Stanford, Calif.: Stanford University Press, 2006).

11. See Martin King Whyte, "The Social Sources of the Student Demonstrations in China, 1989," in *Revolution: Theoretical, Comparative and Historical Studies*, ed. Jack A. Goldstone (Fort Worth, Tex.: Harcourt Brace , 1994), 180–93.

12. See data on China from the World Bank, Washington, D.C., http://data.world bank.org/country/china.

13. For examples of assessments and criticisms at the end of the Hu era and discussions of agendas for post-Hu reform, see Matt Schiavenza, "Was Hu Jintao a Failure?" *The Atlantic*, March 13, 2013; Tom Orlik, "Charting China's Economy: 10 Years Under Hu," *Wall Street Journal*—China Realtime Report, November 16, 2012/; Kerry Brown, "What did Hu Jintao and Wen Jiabao do for China?" *BBC News*, March 13, 2013; William H. Overholt, "Reassessing China: Awaiting Xi Jinping," *Washington Quarterly* 35, no. 2 (Spring 2012): 121–37; and World Bank and Guo wu yuan fa zhan yan jiu zhong xin (China), "China 2030: Building a Modern, Harmonious, and Creative High-Income Society," 2013, http://www.worldbank.org/content/dam/Worldbank /document/China-2030-complete.pdf.

14. With a weak and, indeed, weakening social welfare safety net, citizens faced strong incentives to save a very large fraction of their rising incomes to ensure they had the personal resources to pay for the high costs of housing, education, health care, and retirement. With few practical alternatives available to investors, China's households deposited their expanding wealth in savings accounts, despite receiving interest that was fixed at artificially low rates. Swelling accounts and low interest paid to savers enabled national and local officials to rely on banks, rather than direct tax revenues, to finance investments that boosted China's growth rates.

15. On society and aspects of social change during the reform era (and especially on issues of inequality), see generally Deborah S. Davis and Wang Feng, eds., *Creating Wealth and Poverty in Post-Socialist China* (Stanford, Calif.: Stanford University Press, 2008); Elizabeth J. Perry and Mark Selden, eds., *Chinese Society: Change, Conflict and Resistance*, 2nd ed. (New York: Routledge, 2003); Zai Liang and Zhongdong Ma, "China's Floating Population: New Evidence from the 2000 Census," *Population and Development Review* 30, no. 3 (2004): 467–88; Cindy Fan, *China on the Move: Migration, the State, and the Household* (New York: Routledge, 2008); Martin King Whyte, *The Myth of the Social Volcano: Perceptions of Inequality and Distributive Injustice in Contemporary China* (Stanford, Calif.: Stanford University Press, 2010); Martin King Whyte, Jennifer Adams, Arianne Gaetano, and Lei Guang, eds., *One Country, Two Societies: Rural-Urban Inequality in Contemporary China* (Cambridge, Mass.: Harvard University Press, 2010); Theresa Wright, *Accepting Authoritarianism: State-Society Relations in Reform-Era China* (Stanford, Calif.: Stanford University Press, 2010).

16. On legal reform and development in reform era China (also relevant to the political issues discussed in the following subsection), see, generally, Stanley B. Lubman, *Bird in a Cage: Legal Reform After Mao* (Stanford, Calif.: Stanford University Press, 1999); Randall P. Peerenboom, *China's Long March Toward the Rule of Law* (New York: Cambridge University Press, 2002); Margaret Y. K. Woo and Mary E. Gallagher, eds., *Chinese Justice: Civil Dispute Resolution in Contemporary China* (New York: Cambridge University Press, 2011); and Jacques deLisle, "Legalization Without Demo-

cratization in China Under Hu Jintao," in *China's Changing Political Landscape: Prospects for Democracy*, ed. Cheng Li (Washington, D.C.: Brookings Institution, 2009).

17. On political order and political reform in the reform era, see, generally, Jonathan Unger and Lowell Dittmer, eds., *The Nature of Chinese Politics: From Mao to Jiang* (Armonk, N.Y.: M.E. Sharpe, 2002); Kenneth G. Lieberthal, *Governing China: From Revolution Through Reform*, 2nd ed. (New York: Norton, 2004), chaps. 4–7; Barry Naughton and Dali L. Yang, eds., *Holding China Together: Diversity and National Integration in the Post-Deng Era* (New York: Cambridge University Press, 2004); Li, *China's Changing Political Landscape*; Minxin Pei, *China's Trapped Transition: The Limits of Developmental Autocracy* (Cambridge, Mass.: Harvard University Press, 2006); and William A. Joseph, ed., *Politics in China: An Introduction*, 2nd ed. (New York: Oxford University Press, 2014).

18. See, generally, John Pomfret, "After Tiananmen, How Did the Communists Stay in Power?" *Washington Post*, June 7, 2009. For pessimistic takes on the regime's post-Tiananmen political stature and prospects, see Francis Fukuyama, "The End of History," *National Interest* (Summer 1989). For the view that problems of the general type that helped lead to Tiananmen persisted as mortal perils to the regime a decade later, see Gordon G. Chang, *The Coming Collapse of China* (New York: Random House, 2001). For a more optimistic thought experiment about a longer-term transition to democracy, see Bruce Gilley, *China's Democratic Future* (New York: Columbia University Press, 2004).

19. See Suisheng Zhao, "Deng Xiaoping's Southern Tour: Elite Politics in Post-Tiananmen China," *Asian Survey* 33, no. 8 (August 1993): 739–56.

20. Nicholas D. Kristof, "China Sees 'Market Leninism' as Way to Future," *New York Times*, September 6, 1993; Andrew Nathan, "Authoritarian Resilience," *Journal of Democracy* 14, no. 1 (2003): 6–17; Li, "The New Bipartisanship."

21. Minxin Pei, "Is CCP Rule Fragile or Resilient?" *Journal of Democracy* 23, no. 1 (2012): 27–41; Cheng Li, "The End of the CCP's Resilient Authoritarianism?" *China Quarterly* 211 (2012): 595–623; Andrew J. Nathan, "China Since Tiananmen: Authoritarian Impermanence," *Journal of Democracy* 20, no. 3 (2009): 37–40.

22. On China's foreign policy and engagement with the international system during the reform era, see, generally, Elizabeth Economy and Michel Oksenberg, eds., *China Joins the World* (New York: Council on Foreign Relations, 1999); Andrew J. Nathan and Andrew Scobell, *China's Search for Security* (New York: Columbia University Press, 2012); Robert G. Sutter, *Chinese Foreign Relations: Power and Policy Since the Cold War* (Lanham, Md.: Rowman & Littlefield, 2012); Suisheng Zhao, ed., *Chinese Foreign Policy: Pragmatism and Strategic Behavior* (Armonk, N.Y.: M.E. Sharpe, 2004); and Evan S. Medeiros, *China's International Behavior: Activism, Opportunism, and Diversification* (Santa Monica, Calif.: RAND, 2009).

23. See Aaron L. Friedberg, "The Future of U.S.-China Relations: Is Conflict Inevitable?" *International Security* 30, no. 2 (Fall 2005): 7–45; Friedberg, *A Contest for Supremacy: China, America, and the Struggle for Mastery in Asia* (New York: Norton,

2011); Avery Goldstein, *Rising to the Challenge: China's Grand Strategy and Interna-tional Security* (Stanford, Calif.: Stanford University Press, 2005); Richard K. Betts, "Wealth, Power, and Instability: East Asia and the United States After the Cold War," *International Security*18, no. 3 (Winter 1993/94): 34–77; John J. Mearsheimer, *The Trag-edy of Great Power Politics* (New York: Norton, 2001); Thomas J. Christensen, "Foster-ing Stability or Creating a Monster? The Rise of China and U.S. Policy Toward East Asia," *International Security* 31, no. 1 (Summer 2006): 81–126; Michael D. Swaine, *America's Challenge: Engaging a Rising China in the 21st Century* (Washington, D.C.: Carnegie Endowment for International Peace, 2011).

24. On China's peaceful rise, see Bijian Zheng, "China's 'Peaceful Rise' to Great-Power Status," *Foreign Affairs* 84, no. 5 (2005): 18–24; Goldstein, *Rising to the Chal-lenge;* M. Taylor Fravel and Evan S. Medeiros, "China's New Diplomacy," *Foreign Affairs* 82, no. 6 (November-December 2003): 22–35; and Joshua Kurlantzick, *Charm Offensive: How China's Soft Power Is Transforming the World* (New Haven, Conn.: Yale University Press, 2007).

25. See Michael D. Swaine, "Perceptions of an Assertive China," *China Leadership Monitor* 32 (May 11, 2010): 1–19; Swaine, "China's Assertive Behavior—Part One: On 'Core Interests'," *China Leadership Monitor* 34 (Winter 2011): 1–25; Swaine and M. Taylor Fravel, "China's Assertive Behavior, Part Two: The Maritime Periphery," *China Leadership Monitor* 35 (Summer 2011): 1–34; Alastair Iain Johnston, "How New and Assertive Is China's New Assertiveness?" *International Security* 37, no. 4 (April 1, 2013): 7–48; Jacques deLisle, "Troubled Waters: China's Claims and the South China Sea," *Orbis* 56, no. 4 (2012): 608–42.

26. Some in the United States, however, were critical of the Obama administra-tion's articulation of a policy of strategic reassurance toward China in the run-up to his November 2009 state visit to Beijing. See Kelley Currie, "The Doctrine of 'Strategic Reassurance': What does the Obama Formula for U.S.-China Relations Really Mean?" *Wall Street Journal*, October 22, 2009.

27. See David Barboza and Chris Buckley, "China Plans to Reduce the State's Role in the Economy," *New York Times*, May 24, 2013.

28. "President Xi Promises to Shake off GDP Obsession in Promoting Officials," *Xinhuanet*, June 29, 2013.

29. For English and Chinese versions of the Sixty-Point Decision, see "CCP Cen-tral Committee Resolution Concerning Some Major Issues in Comprehensively Deepening Reform," *China Copyright and Media: The Law and Policy of China's News and Entertainment Media*, November 15, 2013, http://chinacopyrightandmedia.word press.com/2013/11/15/ccp-central-committee-resolution-concerning-some-major -issues-in-comprehensively-deepening-reform/; "Xi Jinping ren Zhongyang Quanmian Shenhua Gaige Lingdao Xiaozu Zuzhang," *Xinhuanet*, December 30, 2013.

30. "Xi Stresses Vitality and Order in Rule of Law," *Xinhuanet*, January 8, 2014; Jerome A. Cohen, "Struggling for Justice: China's Courts and the Challenge of Re-

form," *World Politics Review*, Jan. 14, 2014; Chun Feng, "Is the Rule of Law Coming to China?" *Diplomat*, September 10, 2013.

31. Some have suggested a link between the imminent launch of a new wave of potentially destabilizing economic and social reforms in late 2013 and the CCP's renewed efforts to strengthen its political hand. Document No. 9 was apparently approved on April 22, 2013, with its contents briefed to selected individuals in positions of leadership throughout China, but not widely circulated. However, word about the "seven nos" or "seven don't speaks" quickly spread among China's attentive public. In September 2013, a U.S.-based Chinese-language magazine published what it claimed was the document's text. For the story and the English translation, see "Document 9: A ChinaFile Translation. How Much Is a Hardline Party Directive Shaping China's Current Political Climate?" *ChinaFile*, November 8, 2013, http://www.chinafile.com/document-9-chinafile-translation. On the political restrictions articulated as seven dangerous political topics to guard against, see Chris Buckley, "China Takes Aim at Western Ideas," *New York Times*, August 19, 2013. On new rules governing social media that would punish Internet users whose posts attracted broad attention for content deemed slanderous, see Josh Chin, "China Tightens Grip on Social Media," *Wall Street Journal*, September 9, 2013.

On the critique of Western values such as constitutionalism, see Yang Xiaoqing, "A Comparative Study of Constitutional Governance and the People's Democratic System," *Seeking Truth*, May 21, 2013; and "Constitutional Governance Is an Evasion That Negates China's Development Road," *Global Times*, May 22, 2013. On the crackdown on Xu Zhiyong and other advocates for more radical legal-constitutional reform, see "China: Nationwide Arrests of Activists, Critics Multiply," Human Rights Watch, August 30, 2013; Andrew Jacobs, "Rights Advocate in China Is Indicted over Role in Campaign Against Corruption," *New York Times*, December 13, 2013.

Chapter 2. Poverty and Inequality

This work was supported by the United Kingdom's Economic and Social Research Council [grant numbers ES/J012629/1, ES/J012688/1]. Information on how to access research materials is available at the project webpages: http://www.gla.ac.uk/schools/socialpolitical/research/sccr/research/.

1. World Bank, "Poverty and Equity," http://povertydata.worldbank.org/poverty/country/CHN (accessed March 27, 2013).

2. "The Gini index measures the extent to which the distribution of income (or, in some cases, consumption expenditure) among individuals or households in an economy deviates from a perfectly equal distribution. The Gini index measures the area between the Lorenz curve and the hypothetical line of absolute equality, expressed as a percentage of the maximum area under the line. A Gini index of zero represents

perfect equality and 100, perfect inequality." OECD, Glossary of Statistical Terms, http://stats.oecd.org/glossary (accessed March 27, 2013).

3. Tony Killick, "Responding to Inequality" (Inequality Briefing Paper 3, Overseas Development Institute, London, March 2002). In support, Killick cites World Bank, *The Quality of Growth* (New York: Oxford University Press, 2000); International Fund for Agricultural Development, *Rural Poverty Report, 2001* (Oxford: Oxford University Press, 2001); N. Birdsall and J. Londono, *Asset Inequality Does Matter: Lessons from Latin America* (Washington, D.C.: Inter-America Development Bank, 1997); and K. Deininger and P. Olinto, *Asset Distribution, Inequality and Growth* (Washington, D.C.: World Bank, 2000).

4. Daron Acemoglu and James A. Robinson, *Economic Origins of Dictatorship and Democracy* (Cambridge, UK: Cambridge University Press, 2006). In support, they cite Edward N. Muller and Mitchell A. Seligson, "Inequality and Insurrections," *American Political Science Review* 81, no. 2 (1987): 425–51. See also Alberto Alesina and Roberto Perotti, "Income Distribution, Political Instability, and Investment," *European Economic Review* 40, no. 6 (June 1996): 1203–28.

5. Cheng Li, "China in Revolution and War," Memorandum to the President (Washington, D.C.: Brookings Institution, 2013).

6. Martin K. Whyte, *The Myth of the Social Volcano: Perceptions of Inequality and Distributive Justice in Contemporary China* (Stanford, Calif.: Stanford University Press, 2010).

7. Richard Wike, "China Inequality Causes Unease—Pew Survey," *BBC News*, October 16, 2012, www.bbc.co.uk/news. More recent surveys follow the Global Financial Crisis, however, and it is likely that people whose incomes have fallen (when over the last thirty years average incomes have risen sustainedly) are more dissatisfied with inequality. Economic crisis has been found elsewhere to have increased political instability and the likelihood of a political coup. See Stephan Haggard and Robert R. Kaufman, *The Political Economy of Democratic Transitions* (Princeton, N.J.: Princeton University Press, 1995); Mark J. Gasiorowski, "Economic Crises and Political Regime Change: An Event History Analysis," *American Political Science Review* 89, no. 4 (December 1995): 882–97; Adam Przeworski, Michael Alvarez, Jose A. Cheibub, and Fernando Limongi, "What Makes Democracy Endure?" *Journal of Democracy* 7, no. 1 (January 1996): 39–55.

8. See also M. Feldstein, "China's Biggest Problems Are Political, Not Economic," *Wall Street Journal*, August 2, 2012. In the longer term, public attitudes will also be important. Inequality may be perpetuated by reducing social trust and cohesion that in turn increases toleration of inequality. See Robert Andersen and Meir Yaish, "Public Opinion on Income Inequality in 20 Democracies: The Enduring Impact of Social Class and Economic Inequality" (Discussion Paper 48, GINI Project, European Commission, 2012).

9. James K. Galbraith and George Purcell, "Inequality and State Violence: A Short Report," in *Inequality and Industrial Change: A Global View*, ed. James K. Galbraith

and Maureen Berner (New York: Cambridge University Press, 2001), 202–11. Boix argues *democratic* transition is more likely when inequality is low. Carles Boix, *Democracy and Redistribution* (Cambridge, UK: Cambridge University Press, 2003).

10. Deborah Davis and Wang Feng, "Creating Wealth and Poverty in Post-Socialist China: An Overview," in *Creating Wealth and Poverty in Post-Socialist China*, ed. Deborah Davis and Wang Feng (Stanford, Calif.: Stanford University Press, 2009), 3–19.

11. John Dixon, *The Chinese Welfare System, 1949–1979* (New York: Praeger, 1981).

12. Dixon, *The Chinese Welfare System, 1949–1979*.

13. Davis and Wang, "Creating Wealth and Poverty in Post-Socialist China."

14. China's urban Gini index was an extremely low 22.7 as late as 1988 according to Davis and Wang, "Creating Wealth and Poverty in Post-Socialist China."

15. Dixon, *The Chinese Welfare System, 1949–1979*.

16. Guan Xinping, "Poverty and Antipoverty Programs in Rural China Since the Mid-1980s," *Social Policy & Administration* 29, no. 3 (1995): 204–27.

17. Heike Holbig, "Remaking the CCP's Ideology: Determinants, Progress, and Limits under Hu Jintao," *Journal of Current Chinese Affairs* 38 no. 3 (2009): 35–61.

18. "Guanyu zai quanguo jianli chengshi jumin, zuidi shenghuo baozhang zhidu de tongzhi" [Notice concerning setting up a national urban resident minimum livelihood guarantee system], September 2, 1997, in State Council and Ministry of Labor and Social Security, ed., *Shehui baozhang: changyong zhengce fagui* [Social security: frequently used policies and regulations] (Beijing: Falü chubanshe, 1999), 285–87.

19. Dorothy J. Solinger, "*Dibaohu* in Distress: The Meagre Minimum Livelihood Guarantee System in Wuhan," in *China's Changing Welfare Mix: Local Perspectives*, ed. Beatriz Carrillo and Jane Duckett (London: Routledge, 2011), 36–63.

20. Meng Xin, Robert Gregory, and Youjuan Wang, "Poverty, Inequality and Growth in Urban China, 1986–2000," *Journal of Comparative Economics* 33 (2010): 710–29.

21. "Shiye baoxian tiaoli" [Unemployment insurance rules], January 22, 1999, in State Council, *Shehui baozhang*, 219–25. See also Jane Duckett and Athar Hussain, "Tackling Unemployment in China: State Capacity and Governance Issues," *Pacific Review* 21, no. 2 (2008): 211–29.

22. "Guanyu shenhua qiye zhigong yanglao baoxian zhidu gaige de tongzhi" [Notice concerning deepening enterprise employee old age insurance system reform], March 1, 1995, in State Council, *Shehui baozhang*, 81–91; "Guowuyuan guanyu jianli chengzhen zhigong jiben yiliao baoxian zhidu de jueding" [State Council decision concerning the creation of an urban employee basic health insurance system], December 12, 1998, in State Council, *Shehui baozhang*, 156–60.

23. Major 1990s poverty reduction initiatives were set out in the 8–7 program (begun in 1994), and the five-year plans.

24. "One Trillion Yuan Spent on Western Infrastructure," *Xinhuanet*, September 6, 2006.

25. Party Central Committee and State Council, "Guanyu jinyibu jiaqiang nong-cun yiliao weisheng gongzuo de jueding" [Decision concerning further strengthening

rural health work], October 19, 2002, http://www.gov.cn/gongbao/content/2002/content 61818.htm (accessed March 29, 2013).

26. Ka Ho Mok, "Education Policy Reform," in *The Market in Chinese Social Policy*, ed. Linda Wong and Norman Flynn (Basingstoke, UK: Palgrave, 2001).

27. Emily Hannum and Jennifer Adams, "Beyond Cost: Rural Perspectives on Barriers to Education," in *Creating Wealth and Poverty in Post-Socialist China*, ed. Davis and Wang.

28. Jane Duckett, *The Chinese State's Retreat from Health: Policy and the Politics of Retrenchment* (London: Routledge, 2011).

29. Ya Ping Wang, *Urban Poverty, Housing and Social Change in China* (London: Routledge, 2004).

30. Jane Duckett, "State, Collectivism and Worker Privilege: A Study of Urban Health Insurance Reform," *The China Quarterly* 177 (March 2004): 155–73.

31. Yoel Kornreich, Ilan Vertinsky, and Pitman B. Potter, "Consultation and Deliberation in China: The Making of China's Health-Care Reform," *China Journal* 68 (July 2012): 176–203.

32. World Bank, *China: Public Services for Building the New Socialist Countryside* (Washington, D.C.: World Bank, 2007).

33. Philip H. Brown, Alan de Brauw, and Yang Du, "Understanding Variation in the Design of China's New Cooperative Medical System," *China Quarterly* 198 (June 2009): 304–29.

34. See "Zhongguo jiaoyu shishang de lichengbei: quanmian shishi chengxiang mianfei yiwu jiaoyu" [A milestone in China's education history: Fully implement urban and rural free compulsory education], *Xinhuanet*, July 31, 2008.

35. Q. Gao and F. Zhai, "Anti-Poverty Family Policies in China: A Critical Evaluation," *Asian Social Work and Policy Review* 6 (2012): 122–35.

36. "New Push for Wider Pension Coverage," CCTV.com, March 13, 2013, http://english.cntv.cn/program/newshour/20130313/104376.shtml (accessed April 1, 2013).

37. Wanchuan Lin, Gordon G. Liu, and Gang Chen, "The Urban Resident Basic Medical Insurance: A Landmark Reform Towards Universal Coverage in China," *Health Economics* 18(IS2), (2009): S83–S96.

38. Party Central Committee and State Council, *Guanyu shenhua yiyao weisheng tizhi gaige de yijian* [Opinions on deepening Medical and Health System Reform], April 6, 2009.

39. M. C. Dorfman, R. Holzmann, P. O'Keefe, D. Wang, Y. Sin, and R. Hinz, *China's Pension System* (Washington, D.C.: World Bank, 2013).

40. Wen Jiabao, "Guanyu dangqian nongye he nongcun gongzuo de jige wenti" [Concerning some problems in current agricultural and rural work], *Renmin ribao* [People's Daily], January 20, 2006. See also Wen Jiabao, "Zhongguo nongye he nongcun de fazhan daolu" [China's agricultural and rural development path], *Nongmin ribao* [Farmers' Daily], January 17, 2012; Wen Jiabao, "Government Work Report on 5 March 2007 to the 5th Meeting of the 10th National People's Congress," *Renmin ribao*,

March 18, 2007; Wen Jiabao, "Government Work Report on 5 March 2008 to the 1st Meeting of the 11th National People's Congress," *Renmin ribao*, March 20, 2008.

41. For the text of the Plan in Chinese, see http://www.gov.cn/2011lh/content _1825838.htm (accessed September 3, 2013).

42. The poverty reduction trend has been sustained overall, but was fastest in the early 1980s. Poverty rose briefly in the late 1980s and late 1990s, only to fall again. See World Bank, *From Poor Areas to Poor People: China's Evolving Poverty Reduction Agenda* (Beijing: World Bank, 2009).

43. United Nations, *Millennium Development Goals Report 2012* (New York: United Nations, 2012).

44. "China Raises Poverty Line by 80 Percent to Benefit over 100 Million," *Xinhua-net*, November 29, 2011.

45. "Life at the Bottom of the Middle Kingdom," *The Economist*, December 2, 2011.

46. The World Bank calculates the dollar-based benchmark in purchasing power parity. It measures consumption, rather than income. See "Life at the Bottom of the Middle Kingdom."

47. Although scholarly research does sometimes distinguish "absolute poverty" or deprivation from other poverty (often called "relative poverty"), leading poverty researcher Peter Townsend has argued that "both poverty and subsistence are relative concepts and . . . can only be defined in relation to the material and emotional resources available at a particular time to the members either of a particular society or different societies." Peter Townsend, "The Meaning of Poverty," *British Journal of Sociology* 16 (2010): 85–86.

48. This is the approach used across most of Europe. See Jonathan Cribb, Robert F. Joyce, and David Phillip, "Living Standards, Poverty and Inequality in the UK: 2012," *IFS Commentary* C124 (London: Institute for Fiscal Studies, 2012).

49. A large body of research has explored the perpetuation of poverty in deprived communities. Classic early studies include Oscar Lewis, *Five Families: Mexican Case Studies in the Culture of Poverty* (New York: Basic Books, 1959); Michael Harrington, *The Other America* (New York: Touchstone, 1962).

50. UNDP and ILO, "Policies for Poverty Reduction in China" (New York: UNDP and ILO, 2000).

51. See World Bank, *World Development Report 2001* (Washington, D.C.: World Bank, 2001).

52. For more information, see the CHIP Web site, http://www.icpsr.umich.edu /icpsrweb/ICPSR/series/243 (accessed July 10, 2013).

53. UNDP and ILO, "Policies for Poverty Reduction in China."

54. World Bank, Gini Index data, http://data.worldbank.org/indicator/SI.POV .GINI (accessed March 27, 2013). According to the World Bank, whereas the poorest 20 percent of the population accounted for 8 percent of national income in 1990, and the richest 20 percent accounted for 41 percent, by 2005, the poorest 20 percent accounted

for only 5 percent of national income and the richest 20 percent for 48 percent of national income. World Bank, "Poverty and Equity," http://povertydata.worldbank.org /poverty/country/CHN (accessed March 27, 2013).

55. *People's Daily* reported the retrospective figures as 47.9 in 2003, 47.3 in 2004, 48.5 in 2005, 48.7 in 2006, 48.4 in 2007, 49.1 in 2008, 49.0 in 2009, 48.1 in 2010, and 47.7 in 2011. "Gini Coefficient Release Highlights China's Resolve to Bridge Wealth Gap," *People's Daily Online*, January 22, 2013, http://english.people.com.cn/90778/8101702 .html (accessed February 24, 2013).

56. Reuters, "Zhongguo 2010 nian jiating shouru jini xishu yuan gao yu shijie junzhi–jigou" (China's 2010 household income Gini coefficient is far higher than the world average—organization), December 10, 2012.

57. Figures for the United States and United Kingdom from OECD, http://stats .oecd.org (accessed September 4, 2013).

58. UNDP, International Human Development Indicators, http://hdr.undp.org /en/data/explorer (accessed March 27, 2013).

59. B. Li, "Floating Population or Urban Citizens? Status, Social Provision and Circumstances of Rural-Urban Migrants in China," *Social Policy & Administration* 40, no. 2 (2006): 174–95.

60. "Taking the Higher Ground for Hukou Reform," Caixin Online, March 8, 2013.

61. Killick, *Responding to Inequality*.

62. World Bank, *From Poor Areas to Poor People*.

63. "New Push for Wider Pension Coverage"; Yang Yao, "Doubts Raised About Pension System," *China Daily*, February 23, 2013.

64. Christine P. W. Wong, "Can the Retreat from Equality Be Reversed?" in *Paying for Progress in China*, ed. Vivienne Shue and Christine P. W. Wong (London: Routledge, 2007), 12–28.

65. See Yang Xiao, "Jiejue pinfu chaju de sikao" [Thoughts on solving inequality], *Guangming ribao*, June 7, 2011, 5.

66. "New Poverty Line Poses New Challenges," *China Daily*, June 25, 2012.

67. Xi Jinping, "Jinjin weirao jianchi he fazhan zhongguo tese shehuizhuyi xuexi xuanchuan guanche dang de shibada jingshen—zai shibajie zhonggong zhongyang zhengzhiju diyi ci jiti xuexi de jianghua" [Firmly maintain and develop the study and promotion of socialism with Chinese characteristics and grasp the spirit of the 18th Party Congress—speech at the first collective study time of the 18th Party Central Committee Politburo], November 17, 2012, http://www.scspc.gov.cn/. China's leaders often prefer not to discuss problems but to focus positively on how they are providing a solution. Rather than dwelling on the problem of "social instability," for example, Hu Jintao and Wen Jiabao have promoted "social harmony." Similarly, we found from a systematic search of leaders' speeches in *People's Daily* between 2000 and 2013 that they did not discuss "inequality," but did often urge improvements in "equity" or "equity and justice" (*gongping zhengyi*).

68. See Li Keqiang, "Xuexi dang de shibada jingshen, cujin jingji chixu jiankang fazhan he shehui jinbu" [Study the spirit of the Party's 18th Congress, promote sustainable healthy economic development and social progress], *Renmin ribao*, November 21, 2012.

69. Li Keqiang, "Yong gaige de zuida hongli rang guangda renmin shouyi" [Use the greatest dividends of reform to allow all the people the greatest benefit], *Xinhuanet*, January 6, 2013.

70. "Premier Li Outlines Top Tasks of China's New Cabinet," *Xinhuanet*, March 17, 2013 .

71. "Premier Li Outlines Top Tasks of China's New Cabinet."

72. Lyu Chang and He Dan, "China to Increase Efforts to Alleviate Poverty," *China Daily*, March 25, 2013.

73. CCP, "Guanyu quanmian shenhua gaige ruogan zhongda wenti de jueding" [Decision on fully deepening the reform on some major issues], November 16, 2013.

74. See Xi Jinping, "Guanyu 'Zhonggong zhongyang guanyu quanmian shenhua gaige ruogan zhongda wenti de jueding' de shuoming" [Commentary on the Chinese Communist Party Centre's decision concerning fully deepening reform on some major issues], *Renmin ribao*, November 16, 2013, 1.

75. "Shibada yilai 18 wei shengbuji guanyuan bei chachu" [Since the 18th Party Congress, 18 provincial and ministerial level cadres have been investigated], *Renminwang*, December 30, 2013.

76. Central Commission for Discipline Inspection, "Dang de shiba da yilai jijian jiancha jiguan chaban anjian gongzuo zongshu" [Summary of the cases investigated and dealt with by discipline and supervision organs since the 18th Congress of the Chinese Communist Party], http://www.ccdi.gov.cn/xwyw/201401/t20140109_16730 .html (accessed January 14, 2014).

77. Carl Riskin, "Has China Reached the Top of the Kuznets Curve?" in *Paying for Progress in China*, ed. Shue and Wong, 29–45.

78. Carl Riskin and Qin Gao, "Market Versus Social Benefits: Explaining China's Changing Income Inequality," in *Creating Wealth and Poverty in Post-Socialist China*, ed. Davis and Wang.

Chapter 3. Migration, *Hukou*, and the Prospects of an Integrated Chinese Society

I thank Zhen Li, Lei Lei, and Bo Zhou for research assistance, and Deborah Davis, Emily Hannum, and Avery Goldstein for constructive comments/suggestions on earlier versions of this chapter.

1. There is a large body of literature on China's migrant population. See Kam Wing Chan, "The Household Registration System and Migrant Labor in China: Notes on a Debate," *Population and Development Review* 36, no. 2 (2010): 357–64; Yu Chen,

"Occupational Attainment of Migrants and Local Workers: Findings from a Survey of Shanghai's Manufacturing Sector," *Urban Studies* 48, no. 1 (2011): 3–21; Cindy C. Fan, *China on the Move: Migration, the State, and the Household* (New York: Routledge, 2008); Dorothy J. Solinger, *Contesting Citizenship in Urban China: Peasant Migrants, the State, and the Logic of the Market* (Berkeley: University of California Press, 1999); Zai Liang and Michael J. White, "Internal Migration in China, 1950–1988," Demography 33, no. 3 (1996): 375–84; John Jiles and Ren Mu, "Elderly Parent Health and the Migration Decision of Adult Children: Evidence from Rural China," *Demography* 44, no. 2 (2007): 265–88; Peiling Li, ed., *Migrant Workers: The Socioeconomic Analysis of Migrant Workers in China* (Beijing: Social Science Publishing House, 2003); Ken Roberts, "China's 'Tidal Wave' of Migrant Labor: What Can We Learn from Mexican Undocumented Migration to the United States?" *International Migration Review* 31, no. 2 (1997): 249–93; Jianfa Shen and Nanhong Nora Chiang, "Chinese Migrants and Circular Mobility: Introduction," *China Review* 11, no. 2 (Fall 2011): 1–10; and Ran Tao, "Achieving Real Progress in *Hukou* Reform," *East Asia Forum* (February 8, 2010), http://www.eastasiaforum.org/2010/02/08/achieving-real-progress-in-chinas-*hukou* -reform/. For more popular portrayals of China's migrant population, see Michelle Dammon Loyalka, *Eating Bitterness: Stories from the Front Lines of China's Great Urban Migration* (Berkeley: University of California Press, 2012) and Peter Hessler, *Country Driving: A Journey Through China from Farm to Factory* (New York: Harper-Collins, 2010).

2. Chan, "The Household Registration System and Migrant Labor in China"; Jun Han, *Research Strategic Problems of Migrant Workers in China* (*zhongguo nong min gong zhanlue wenti yanjiu*) (Shanghai: Shanghai Yuandong Press, 2009).

3. Xiaowei Zang, "Age and the Cost of Being Uyghurs in Urumchi," *China Quarterly* 210 (2012): 419–34.

4. In this chapter, I use the terms *migrant workers* or *floating population* interchangeably to refer to individuals who live in locations where they do not have local household registration (*hukou*) status.

5. For details, see Xinhuanet, March 17, 2013, http://news.xinhuanet.com/2013lh /2013-03/17/c_115053973.htm (accessed April 6, 2013).

6. The full text of the 1954 Chinese Constitution is available from http://china .findlaw.cn/info/guojiafa/xffl/95747.html (accessed March 23, 2013).

7. Qingwu Zhang, *Hukou Migration and Floating Population* (*hukou qianyi yu liudong renkou luncong*) (Beijing: Public Security University Editorial Office, 1994).

8. Fei-ling Wang, *Organizing Through Division and Exclusion: China's* Hukou *System* (Stanford, Calif.: Stanford University Press, 2005) and Xiaogang Wu and Donald J. Treiman, "Household Registration and Social Stratification in China," *Demography* 41, no. 2 (2004): 363–84.

9. Liang and White, "Internal Migration in China, 1950–1988."

10. Rose Li, "Migration to China's Northern Frontier, 1953–82," *Population and Development Review* 15 (1989): 503–30.

11. Thomas Bernstein, *Up to the Mountains and Down to the Villages: The Transfer of Youth from Urban to Rural China* (New York: Columbia University Press, 1997).

12. Fan, *China on the Move.*

13. Zai Liang, "Foreign Investment, Economic Growth, and Temporary Migration: The Case of Shenzhen Special Economic Zone, China," *Development and Society* 28, no. 1 (1999): 115–37.

14. Zai Liang and Zhen Li, "Internal Migration in China: Socio-demographic Characteristics and Its Development Implications" (presentation at United Nations Population Division, New York, December 3, 2012).

15. Nansheng Bai and Song Hongyuan, *Return Home or Go to the City? A Study of Return Migration in Rural China* (Beijing: China Finance Economics Press, 2002).

16. In 1994, an official from the Shenzhen Labor Bureau (*laodong ju*) noted that Shenzhen needed to recruit migrant workers from Henan Province that year. Author's interview conducted in July 1994 in Shenzhen.

17. Xiaotong Fei, *Rural Development in China: Prospect and Retrospect* (Chicago, Ill.: University of Chicago Press, 1989).

18. The full text of China's tenth five-year plan is available at http://www.people .com.cn/GB/historic/0315/5920.html (accessed June 4, 2013).

19. Feng Wang, "The Breakdown of a Great Wall: Recent Changes in Household Registration System in China," in *Floating Population and Migration in China: The Impact of Economic Reform*, ed. T. Sharping (Hamburg: Institute of Asian Studies, 1997), 149–65.

20. Kam Wing Chan, "The Chinese *Hukou* System at 50," *Eurasian Geography and Economics* 50, no. 2 (2009): 197–221. For details on Chongqing's 2010 *hukou* reform, see http://news.xinhuanet.com/politics/2010-08/15/c_12447839.htm (accessed April 6, 2013).

21. Yiu Por Chen and Zai Liang, "Educational Attainment of Migrant Children: The Forgotten Story of China's Urbanization," in *Education and Reform in China*, ed. Emily Hannum and Albert Park (New York: Routledge, 2007), 117–30, in-text quote on page 117.

22. Chengrong Duan and Yang Ge, "Research on the Left Behind Children in China," *Population Research* 29, no. 1 (2008): 12–19.

23. John Bryant, "Children of International Migrants in Indonesia, Thailand, and the Philippines: A Review of Evidence and Policies," UNICEF Innocenti Research Center Working Paper 2005-05, http://www.unicef-irc.org/publications/381; Yao Lu and Donald Treiman, "Migration, Remittances, Educational Stratification Among Blacks in Apartheid and Post-Apartheid South Africa," *Social Forces* 89, no. 4 (2011): 1119–43.

24. Jingzhong Ye and Pan Lu, *Differentiated Childhoods: Children Left Behind in Rural China* (Beijing: Social Science Academic Press, 2008).

25. Jim Yardley, "Rural Exodus for Work Fractures Chinese Family," *New York Times*, December 21, 2004, A2.

26. Mao Nie, Lei Li, and Li Huajun, *The Sad Village: Reflections on China's Left Behind Children* (Beijing: People's Daily Press, 2008); Yidong Qiu, *The Story of Left Behind Middle School Students* (Beijing: Children Press, 2008).

27. Hilary Whiteman, "Deaths in Dumpster Expose Plight of China's Street Kids," *CNN*, November 22, 2012.

28. Jingzhong Ye and James Murray, eds., *Left Behind Children in Rural China* (Beijing: Social Science Academic Press, 2005) and Ye and Pan, *Differentiated Childhoods*.

29. Ye and Pan, *Differentiated Childhoods*.

30. Ming Wen and Danhua Lin, "Child Development in Rural China: Children Left Behind by Their Migrant Parents and Children of Nonmigrant Families," *Child Development* 83 (2011): 120–36.

31. Fieldwork in Jintang County, July 2010. School officials also mentioned these left behind children are likely to smoke, and to smoke a good brand of cigarettes to show their unique social status (money from their parents).

32. Yao Lu, "Education of Children Left Behind in Rural China," *Journal of Marriage and Family* 74 (2012): 312–41.

33. Ye and Pan, *Differentiated Childhoods*.

34. Sara S. McLanahan and Gary Sandefur, *Growing up with a Single Parent* (Cambridge, Mass.: Harvard University Press, 1997).

35. Shaoqing Lu and S. L. Zhang, "A Marginalized Basic Education," Ford Foundation Research Report, Beijing, June 2001.

36. Things have certainly gotten better for migrant schools over the years. One migrant-sponsored school in Fuzhou has recently received a license from the Education Bureau of Fuzhou City. This means the school can issue graduation certificates. The school principal told me his school now receives financial subsidies to cover student tuition. As a result, the tuition burden from migrant children has been significantly reduced. Interview with school principal, June 24, 2012.

37. Lin Guo and Zai Liang, "Schooling and Migration in China," in *Education in China: Educational History, Models, and Initiatives*, ed. Qiang Zha (Great Barrington, Mass.: Berkshire Publishing, 2013).

38. State Council, "Several Issues About Solving Migrant Workers' Problems" [*guo wuyuan guanyu jiejue nong min gong wenti de ruogan yijian*], March 27, 2006, http://www.gov.cn/jrzg/2006-03/27/content_237644.htm; Zai Liang, Lin Guo, and Chengrong Duan, "Migration and the Well-Being of Children in China," *The Yale-China Health Journal* 5 (2008): 25–46.

39. Emily Hannum and Albert Park, eds., *Education and Reform in China* (New York: Routledge, 2007); Wen Li, Albert Park, and Sangui Wang, "Schooling Equity in Rural China," in Hannum and Park, *Education and Reform in China*, 27–44.

40. Details are available from http://college.gaokao.com/school/tinfo/1/result/1/1/ (accessed April 6, 2013).

41. Hunan Province sends the largest number of migrants to Guangdong Province.

42. This interregional inequality in access to higher education was also manifested in interviews with migrants in Beijing. One of the study subjects in Lee's ethnographic work said "If you gave special favor to students from impoverished places, we will have no complaints. But Beijing students already have the best schools and yet they need lower scores to enter colleges. All because of *hukou* divisions." Ching Kwan Lee, "From Inequality to Inequity: Popular Conceptions of Social (In)justice in Beijing," in *Creating Wealth and Poverty in Postsocialist China*, ed. Deborah S. Davis and Wang Feng (Berkeley, Calif.: University of California Press, 2009), 221.

43. Liang and Li, "Internal Migration in China."

44. Shan Wu, Chou Chengxia, and Song Yue, "Remove *Hukou* Restriction and Fighting for the Right of Migrant Children," *World Journal Magazine,* April 22, 2012, 54–56.

45. Rumor has it that Zhang Qianfan of Peking University gave failing "grades" to Beijing and Shanghai's policy on this.

46. The requirement of three-year enrollment in the social security program may be quite restrictive. Many migrant workers are not willing to participate in the program because if they return to their hometown a portion of their social security will not be returned to them. This is another issue facing migrant workers: that is, their social security benefits are not portable.

47. To curb rising housing prices, several cities in China have used *hukou* as a condition for real estate purchase. In Beijing, non-Beijing *hukou* residents must have a five-year tax-paying record to be eligible for the purchase of housing. See new regulations for Beijing http://zhengwu.beijing.gov.cn/bmfu/bmts/t1155210.htm (accessed June 4, 2013).

48. Wu and Treiman, "Household Registration and Social Stratification in China."

49. Lei Lei and Zai Liang, "Schooling, Work, and Idleness Among Migrant Children in China" (paper presented at Annual Meeting of the American Sociological Association, Boulder, Colo., August 17–20. 2012).

50. Chan, "The Household Registration System and Migrant Labor in China."

51. Julia Kwong, "Educating Migrant Children: Negotiations Between the State and Civil Society," *China Quarterly* 180 (2004): 1073–88.

52. Wei Chen, "Not Only for College Exam, but Respect and Rights" (*buzhi shi gaokao, haiyou zunyan he quanli*), *World Journal,* March 31, 2013, 62–63.

53. The complete Document from the Third Plenum of the Eighteenth CCP Central Committee can be found at http://cpc.people.com.cn/n/2013/1115/c64094-23559163 .html (accessed January 17, 2014).

54. The full report of this CCP Central Committee meeting in December 2013 can be found at http://finance.people.com.cn/n/2013/1214/c1004-23841511.html (accessed January 17, 2014).

55. These issues are clearly related to urban poverty and inequality, which are discussed extensively in the chapter by Jane Duckett and Guohui Wang in this volume.

Also see Bob Davis and Tom Orlik, "China Seeks to Give Migrants Perks of City Life," *Wall Street Journal*, March 6, 2013, A12.

56. In addition to education, the next two issues involving migrant workers' well-being in cities are likely to be affordable housing and minimum support (*dibao*). Both will have major fiscal consequences for local governments. However, if migrant workers pay enough of their share of taxes, they cannot justifiably be denied access to either benefit.

Chapter 4. China's Demographic Challenges: Gender Imbalance

An earlier version of this chapter was presented at the "China's Challenges: The Road Ahead" conference at the Center for the Study of Contemporary China, University of Pennsylvania, April 25–26, 2013. I thank Deborah Davis and Baochang Gu for their comments.

1. Ansley Coale, and Judith Banister, "Five Decades of Missing Females in China," *Demography* 31, no. 3 (1994): 459–79.

2. United Nations Population Fund (UNFPA), *Sex Imbalances at Birth: Current Trends, Consequences and Policy Implications* (Bangkok, Thailand: UNFPA Asia and the Pacific Regional Office, 2012).

3. James Lee and Wang Feng, "Malthusian Models and Chinese Realities: The Chinese Demographic System 1700–2000," *Population and Development Review* 25, no. 1 (March 1999): 33–65; D. E. Mungello, *Drowning Girls in China: Female Infanticide since 1650* (Lanham, Md.: Rowman & Littlefield, 2008). Michelle T. King. *Between Birth and Death: Female Infanticide in Nineteenth-Century China* (Stanford, Ca.: Stanford University Press 2014).

4. John Bongaarts, "The Implementation of Preferences for Male Offspring," *Population and Development Review* 39, no. 2 (2013): 185–208; Cedric H. Bien et al., "High Adult Sex Ratios and Risky Sexual Behaviors: A Systematic Review," *PLoS ONE* 8, no. 8 (August 13, 2013): e71580. doi:10.1371/journal.pone.0071580.

5. UNFPA, *Sex Imbalances at Birth*.

6. Susan Greenhalgh, "Patriarchal Demographics? China's Sex Ratio Reconsidered," *Population and Development Review* 38, no. 1 (February 2013): 130–49; Christophe Guilmoto, "The Sex Ratio Transition in Asia," *Population and Development Review* 35, no. 3 (September 2009): 519–49; Dudley L. Poston, and Li Zhang, 2009. "China's Unbalanced Sex Ratio at Birth: How Many Surplus Boys Have Been Born in China since the 1980s?" in *Gender Policy and HIV in China: Catalyzing Policy Change*, ed. Joseph D. Tucker et al. (Dordrecht, NL: Springer, 2009), 57–69.

7. G. William Skinner, "Family Systems and Demographic Processes," in *Anthropological Demography: Toward a New Synthesis*, ed. David I. Kertzer and Thom Fricke (Chicago: University of Chicago Press, 1997), 53–95.

8. Sex-selective behaviors do not necessary imply a gender bias, and could exist in a nonpatrilineal family system. For example, as Pollard and Morgan document, fami-

lies with two children of same sex are more likely to have a third child than families with two children of opposite sexes in the United States. Michael S. Pollard and S. Philip Morgan, "Emerging Parental Gender Indifference? Sex Composition of Children and the Third Birth," *American Sociological Review* 67, no. 4 (2002): 600–13.

9. Although the sex of existing children is related to the sex of future children, its overall effect is very small at the population level. John Bongaarts and Robert G. Potter, *Fertility, Biology, and Behavior: An Analysis of the Proximate Determinants* (New York: Academic Press, 1983).

10. Sex-selective migration could also affect sex ratio at a population level.

11. Ansley Coale, *The Demographic Transition*, vol. 1 (IUSSP Liege International Population Conference, Liege: IUSSP, 1973), 53–72; Kingsley Davis and Judith Blake, "Social Structure and Fertility: An Analytic Framework," *Economic Development and Cultural Change* 4, no. 3 (April 1956): 211–35.

12. Peter McDonald, "Explanations of Low Fertility in East Asia: A Comparative Perspective," in *Ultra-Low Fertility in Pacific Asia: Trends, Causes and Policy Issues*, ed. Gavin Jones, Paulin Tay Straughan, and Angelique Chan (London: Routledge, 2009), 23–39; Baochang Gu and Krishna Roy, "Sex Ratio at Birth in China, with Reference to Other Areas in East Asia: What We Know," *Asia-Pacific Population Journal* 10, no. 3 (1995): 17–42; Chai Bin Park and Nam-Hoon Cho, "Consequences of Son Preference in a Low-Fertility Society: Imbalance of the Sex Ratio at Birth in Korea," *Population and Development Review* 21, no. 1 (March 1995): 59–84.

13. Kusum, "The Use of Pre-Natal Diagnostic Techniques for Sex Selection: The Indian Scene," *Bioethics* 7 (2/3): 149–65.

14. Guilmoto, "The Sex Ratio Transition in Asia"; UNFPA, *Sex Imbalances at Birth*.

15. Susan Greenhalgh, "Fertility as Mobility: Sinic Transitions," *Population and Development Review* 14, no. 4 (December 1988): 629–74.

16. Yong Cai, "China's Below-Replacement Fertility: Government Policy or Socioeconomic Development?" *Population and Development Review* 36, no. 3 (September 2010): 419–40; Zhenzhen Zheng et al., "Below-Replacement Fertility and Childbearing Intention in Jiangsu Province, China," *Asian Population Studies* 5, no. 3 (2009): 329.

17. Kuifu Yang, Liang Jimin, and Zhang Fan, eds., *Zhongguo Renkou Yu Jihuashengyu Dashi Yaolan* (Beijing: China Population Press, 2001).

18. In 1952, the Chinese government issued an internal regulation, the "Interim Restrictions on Birth Control and Induced Abortion," that limited induced abortion to situations involving threats to the mother's life. The 1952 regulation was abolished in 1957, and replaced with a much more relaxed version that permitted induced abortion during the first trimester of pregnancy. The regulation was further relaxed to permit later abortions in 1964.

19. Ministry of Health, China (MOH), *China Health Statistical Yearbook* (Beijing: Peking Union Medical College Press, 2000–2012).

20. Hongbin Li, Junjian Yi, and Junsen Zhang, "Estimating the Effect of the One-Child Policy on the Sex Ratio Imbalance in China: Identification Based on the

Difference-in-Differences," *Demography* 48, no. 4 (November 2011): 1535–57; Wei Zhu et al. "China's Excess Males, Sex Selective Abortion, and One Child Policy: Analysis of Data from 2005 National Intercensus Survey," *BMJ: British Medical Journal* 338, no. 7700 (April 18, 2009): 920–23.

21. Feng Wang, Yong Cai, and Baochang Gu, "Population, Policy, and Politics: How Will History Judge China's One-Child Policy?" *Population and Development Review* 38 (Supplement, 2013): 115–29.

22. Baochang Gu et al., "China's Local and National Fertility Policy at the Twentieth Century," *Population and Development Review* 33, no. 1 (2007): 129–47.

23. Yong Cai and William Lavely, "Child Sex Ratios and Their Regional Variation," in *Transition and Challenge—China's Population at the Beginning of the 21st Century*, ed. Zhongwei Zhao and Fei Guo (Oxford: Oxford University Press, 2007), 108–23; Daniel Goodkind, "Child Underreporting, Fertility, and Sex Ratio Imbalance in China," *Demography* 48, no. 1 (February 2011): 291–16.

24. Coale and Banister, "Five Decades of Missing Females in China."

25. Had Coale and Banister extended their analysis to an earlier time period, say the 1920s, they would have found that the proportion of missing was somewhat lower than in 1936–1940.

26. The one child policy was announced in the "Open Letter to All Members of the Chinese Communist Party and of the Chinese Communist Youth League," published in *People's Daily,* September 25, 1980.

27. Zongtang Liang, "On Population," *Shanxi People's Press*, 1983. That the rise of gender imbalance is a possible "side effect" of the one child policy was acknowledged in the "Open Letter" in 1980.

28. Coale and Banister, "Five Decades of Missing Females in China"; Terence H. Hull, "Recent Trends in Sex Ratios at Birth in China," *Population and Development Review* 16 (1990): 63–83; Yi Zeng et al., "Causes and Implications of the Recent Increase in the Reported Sex Ratio at Birth in China," *Population and Development Review* 19, no. 2 (June 1993): 283–302.

29. Sten Johansson and Ola Nygren, "The Missing Girls of China: A New Demographic Account," *Population and Development Review* 17 (1991): 35–51; Zeng et al., "Causes and Implications of the Recent Increase in the Reported Sex Ratio at Birth in China."

30. Young Cai and William Lavely, "China's Missing Girls: Numerical Estimates and Effects on Population Growth," *The China Review* 3 (2003): 13–29; Goodkind, "Child Underreporting, Fertility, and Sex Ratio Imbalance in China."

31. Yongping Li, "Sex Selective Abortion's Effect on Sex Ratio at Birth," *Renkou Yanjiu* (1993), 21–25. In Chinese.

32. Junhong Chu, "Prenatal Sex Determination and Sex-Selective Abortion in Rural Central China," *Population and Development Review* 27, no. 2 (2001): 259–81.

33. Ansley Coale, and Paul George Demeny with Barbara Vaughan, *Regional Model Life Tables and Stable Populations*, 2nd ed. (New York: Academic Press, 1983).

34. This reversal was not uniform across regions. Gender parity in infant mortality has persisted in some areas, while in others, female mortality exceeds male by 80 percent or more.

35. Baochang Gu and Yi Xu, "Discussion on Sex Ratio at Birth in China," *Zhongguo Renkou Kexue* (1994): 41–48; M. Giovanna Merli, "Underreporting of Births and Infant Deaths in Rural China: Evidence from Field Research in One County of Northern China," *China Quarterly* (1998): 637–55; M. Giovanna Merli, and Adrian E. Raftery, "Are Births Underreported in Rural China? Manipulation of Statistical Records in Response to China's Population Policies," *Demography* 37, no. 1 (February 2000): 109–26.

36. Cai and Lavely, "China's Missing Girls."

37. Yong Cai, "China's New Demographic Reality: Learning from the 2010 Census," *Population and Development Review* 39, no. 3 (September 2013): 371–96.

38. Kam Wing Chan, "Measuring the Urban Millions," *China Economic Quarterly* (March 2009): 21–26.

39. These 1 percent surveys are sometimes referred as mini-censuses.

40. Cai, "China's New Demographic Reality."

41. Ibid.

42. Weimin Zhang and Hongyan Cui, "Preliminary Assessments of 2000 Census Data," *Renkou Yanjiu* 4 (2002): 25–35.

43. Coale and Demeny, *Regional Model Life Tables and Stable Populations.*

44. UNFPA's estimate of missing girls in China is based on the United Nations Population Division's population projection for China. The corresponding total for the age range in Table 4.1 is less than twenty million.

45. Dudley L. Poston, Eugenia Conde, and Bethany DeSalvo, "China's Unbalanced Sex Ratio at Birth, Millions of Excess Bachelors and Societal Implications," *Vulnerable Children and Youth Studies* 6, no. 4 (2011): 314–20.

46. Goodkind "Child Underreporting, Fertility, and Sex Ratio Imbalance in China"; Monica Das Gupta, Woojin Chung, and Li Shuzhuo, "Evidence for an Incipient Decline in Numbers of Missing Girls in China and India," *Population and Development Review* 35, no. 2 (2009): 401–16; Mikhail Lipatov, Shuzhuo Li, and Marcus W. Feldman, "Economics, Cultural Transmission, and the Dynamics of the Sex Ratio at Birth in China," *Proceedings of the National Academy of Sciences of the United States of America* 105, no. 49 (December 9, 2008): 19171–76.

47. National Bureau of Statistics of China. "Ma Jiantang Taking Questions Concerning the Communique on Major Figures of the 2010 Population Census." In *Major Figures on the 2010 Population Census of China* (July 2011).

48. Two provinces, Jiangxi and Henan, stand out in the 2010 census with suspiciously large discrepancies between the short form and long form. For example, in the 2000 census, Henan's SRB is 114.7 in the short form, but 130.3 in the long form, and Jiangxi's SRB is 118.5 in the short form and 138.0 in the long form. Similar discrepancies are also observed in the 2010 census data, but at a much smaller scale. Even with those

discrepancies, the overall patterns shown in Figure 4.5 remain the same whether the long-form or short-form data are used in the analysis.

49. Woojin Chung and Monica Das Gupta, "The Decline of Son Preference in South Korea: The Roles of Development and Public Policy," *Population and Development Review* 33, no. 4 (December 2007): 757–83.

50. Rachel Murphy, Ran Tao, and Xi Lu. "Son Preference in Rural China: Patrilineal Families and Socioeconomic Change," *Population and Development Review* 37, no. 4 (2011): 665–90.

51. Isabelle Attané, "The Demographic Impact of a Female Deficit in China, 2000–2050," *Population and Development Review* 32, no. 4 (December 2006): 755–70; Nicholas Eberstadt, "The Global War Against Baby Girls," *The New Atlantis* 33 (Fall 2011): 3–18; Christophe Guilmoto, "Skewed Sex Ratios at Birth and Future Marriage Squeeze in China and India, 2005–2100," *Demography* 49, no. 1 (February 2012): 77–100; Poston and Zhang, "China's Unbalanced Sex Ratio at Birth"; Mara Hvistendahl, Unnatural Selection: Choosing Boys over Girls, and the Consequences of a World Full of Men (New York: Public Affairs, 2011); Catherine Tucker and Jennifer Van Hook, "Surplus Chinese Men: Demographic Determinants of the Sex Ratio at Marriageable Ages in China," *Population and Development Review* 39, no. 2 (2013): 209–29.

52. Yong Cai and Feng Wang, "From Collective Synchronization to Individual Liberalization: (Re)emergence of Late Marriage in Shanghai" (paper presented at the Annual Conference of the Population Association of America, 2012, San Francisco, Calif.); Cameron Campbell and James Lee, "Social Mobility from a Kinship Perspective: Rural Liaoning, 1789–1909," *International Review of Social History* 48, no. 1 (2003): 1–26; Feng Wang and Quanhe Yang, "Age at Marriage and the First Birth Interval: The Emerging Change in Sexual Behavior Among Young Couples in China," *Population and Development Review* 22, no. 2 (June 1996): 299–320.

53. Martin King Whyte, ed., *One Country, Two Societies: Rural-Urban Inequality in Contemporary China* (Cambridge, Mass.: Harvard University Press, 2010).

54. Greenhalgh, "Patriarchal Demographics?"

55. Scott J. South and Katherine Trent, "Imbalanced Sex Ratios, Men's Sexual Behavior, and Risk of Sexually Transmitted Infection in China," *Journal of Health and Social Behavior* 51, no. 4 (December 2010): 376–90; Tucker et al., eds., *Gender Policy and HIV in China*; Valerie Hudson and Andrea den Boer, *Bare Branches: The Security Implications of Asia's Surplus Male Population* (Cambridge, Mass.: MIT Press, 2004); Avraham Y. Ebenstein and Ethan Jennings Sharygin, "The Consequences of the 'Missing Girls' of China," *World Bank Economic Review* 23, no. 3 (January 2009): 399–425.

Chapter 5. Policy Model and Inequality: Some Potential Connections

Albert Keidel and other conference participants provided useful comments on an earlier draft.

1. From http://english.caijing.com.cn/2013-01-18/112445259.html.

2. See the news report on the various Gini estimates by independent academics, http://www.bloomberg.com/news/2012-12-09/china-s-wealth-gap-soars-as-xi-pledges -to-narrow-income-divide.html.

3. It should be noted that an independent research project, China Household Income Project (CHIP), has produced Gini estimates far closer to the NBS estimates. However, CHIP follows the NBS sampling frame.

4. Martin Whyte, *Myth of the Social Volcano: Perceptions of Income Inequality and Distributive Injustice in Contemporary China* (Stanford, Calif.: Stanford University Press, 2010).

5. Benjamin M. Friedman, *The Moral Consequences of Economic Growth* (New York: Vintage, 2010).

6. Albert Keidel, *China's Economic Fluctuations: Implications for its Rural Economy* (Washington, D.C.: Carnegie Endowment for International Peace, 2008).

7. Daron Acemoglu and James A. Robinson, "The Political Economy of the Kuznets Curve," *Review of Development Economics* 6, no. 2 (2002): 183–203.

8. The findings are widely reported in the media. See http://www.bloomberg.com /news/2012-12-09/china-s-wealth-gap-soars-as-xi-pledges-to-narrow-income-divide .html.

9. Ximing Wu and Jeffrey M. Perloff, "China's Income Distribution, 1985–2001," *Review of Economics and Statistics* 87, no. 4 (2005): 763–75.

10. Sylvie Demurger, Martin Fournier, and Shi Li, "Urban Income Inequality in China Revisited (1988–2002)," *Economics Letters* 93, no. 3 (2006): 354–59.

11. Hongbin Cai, Yuyu Chen, and Li-An Zhou "Income and Consumption Inequality in Urban China: 1992–2003," *Economic Development and Cultural Change* 58, no. 3 (2010): 385–413.

12. Wu and Perloff, "China's Income Distribution, 1985–2001."

13. Dwayne Benjamin, Loren Brandt, and John Giles, "The Evolution of Income Inequality in Rural China," *Economic Development and Cultural Change* 53, no. 4 (2005): 769–824.

14. Wu and Perloff, "China's Income Distribution, 1985–2001."

15. Ravallion, "A Comparative Perspective on Poverty Reduction in Brazil, China and India," World Bank Policy Research Paper No. 5080 (2009); Azizur Rahman Kahn and Carl Riskin, "China's Household Income and Its Distribution, 1995 and 2002," *China Quarterly* 182 (2005): 356–84.

16. Cai, Chen, and Zhou, "Income and Consumption Inequality in Urban China: 1992–2003."

17. Benjamin, Brandt, and Giles, "The Evolution of Income Inequality in Rural China."

18. Bjorn Gustafsson and Shi Li, "Income Inequality Within and Across Counties in Rural China 1988 and 1995," *Journal of Development Economics* 69, no. 1 (2002): 179–204.

19. Gustafsson, and Li, "Income Inequality Within and Across Counties."

20. Benjamin, Brandt, and Giles, "The Evolution of Income Inequality in Rural China."

21. Cai, Chen, and Zhou, "Income and Consumption Inequality in Urban China: 1992–2003."

22. Ibid.

23. Khan and Riskin, "China's Household Income and Its Distribution, 1995 and 2002."

24. See, for example, Tianlun Jian, Jeffrey D. Sachs, and Andrew M. Warner, "Trends in regional inequality in China," *China Economic Review*, 7, No. 1, (1996): 1–21, Sylvie Demurger, Martin Fournier and Shi Li, 2006, "Urban Income Inequality in China Revisited (1988–2002)," *Economics Letters*, 93, No. 3, (2006): 354–359. ; C. Cindy Fan and Mingjie Sun (2007) "Regional Inequality in China, 1978–2006," *Eurasian Geography and Economics* 48, no. 1 (2007): 1–20

25. Ravi Kanbur and Xiaobo Zhang, "Fifty Years of Regional Inequality in China: A Journey Through Central Planning, Reform, and Openness," *Review of Development Economics* 9, no. 1 (2005): 87–106.

26. C. Cindy Fan and Mingjie Sun, "Regional Inequality in China, 1978–2006," *Eurasian Geography and Economics* 48, no. 1 (2007): 1–20.

27. Ravallion, "A Comparative Perspective on Poverty Reduction in Brazil, China and India."

28. I have documented these policy changes and evolution elsewhere, including Yasheng Huang, *Capitalism with Chinese Characteristics: Entrepreneurship and State During the Reform Era* (New York: Cambridge University Press, 2008); and Yasheng Huang, "How Did China Take Off?" *Journal of Economic Perspectives* 26, no. 4 (2012): 165–91.

29. Khan and Riskin, "China's Household Income and Its Distribution."

30. Benjamin, Brandt, and Giles, "The Evolution of Income Inequality in Rural China."

31. Gustafsson and Li, "Income Inequality Within and Across Counties."

32. See Huang, *Capitalism with Chinese Characteristics* and "How Did China Take Off?"

33. Meijun Qian and Yasheng Huang "Political Institutions, Entrenchment, and the Sustainability of Economic Development", Working Paper, National University of Singapore Business School, 2012.

34. Kellee S. Tsai, *Back Alley Banking: Private Entrepreneurs in China* (Ithaca, N.Y.: Cornell University Press, 2005); Franklin Allen, Jun Qian, and Meijun Qian, "Law, Finance and Economic Growth in China," *Journal of Financial Economics* 77, no. 1 (2005): 57–116.

35. This is from a speech given by Chen Muhua in 1987, cited in Huang, *Capitalism with Chinese Characteristics*.

36. From a speech given by Han Lei in 1984, cited in Huang, *Capitalism with Chinese Characteristics.*

37. Huang, "How Did China Take Off?" 166.

Chapter 6. China's Contemporary Challenges: Rebalancing

1. All the national income and expenditure data in this paper, including those used in Figures 6.1 and 6.2, are the most recent official data. The source is National Bureau of Statistics (NBS), *Zhongguo Tongji Zhaiyao 2013* [China Statistical Abstract 2013] (Beijing: Zhongguo Tongji, 2013), expenditure side data, 33–35; sources of growth (Figure 6.2), 36; real consumption growth, 37; and GDP calculated from the production side, 19.

2. In economists' terms, the incremental capital/output ratio in China was 4 throughout the 1990s and 2000s. That implies that, on average, 10 percentage points of investment yields an additional 2.5 percentage points of growth.

3. The need for investment is argued by Justin Lin, and perhaps also Bert Keidel. For reporting on the views of Justin Lin, see Andrew Moody and Lyu Chang, "Pumping up Power of Consumption: China's Solution or Pitfall?" *China Daily*, June 20, 2013, pp. 1, 6.

4. Jun Zhang, "Zhu Rongji Might Be Right: Understanding the Mechanism of Fast Economic Development in China," *The World Economy* 35 (December 2012): 1712–32.

5. World Bank, World Development Indicators. Online Database. Access at http://databank.worldbank.org/data/.

6. Feng Lu, "Consolidation or Stimulation? Remarks on China's macro-economic situation and policy," US-China Economics Dialogue, Beijing, June 19, 2013.

7. For a good collection of academic articles on the subject, see the 2011 special issue of *China Economic Review,* and especially the article by the leading proponents of this view, Cai Fang and Du Yang, "Wage Increases, Wage Convergence, and the Lewis Turning Point in China," *China Economic Review* 21 (2011): 601–10.

8. China 2010 Census, Summary Volume, Table 3-1, "Population by Age and Gender" (Beijing: National Bureau of Statistics, 2012).

9. So Hanxue, "Jiuye yali douceng; Renshebu gezhi yanchi tiuxiu jihua" [Employment pressure has sharply increased; the Ministry of Labor and Social Security has set aside plans to raise the retirement age], *Zhongguo Jingyingbao* [China Business Journal], June 24, 2013, A3.

10. National Bureau of Statistics of China, "Statistical Communiqué of the People's Republic of China on the 2012 National Economic and Social Development," February 22, 2013.

11. Nicholas Lardy, *Sustaining China's Economic Growth After the Global Financial Crisis* (Washington, D.C.: Peterson Institute, 2012).

12. Xiao Ping and Zhang Muxia, "Shekeyuan zhuanjia cheng difang zhengfu fuzhai zongliang rengzai kekong fanwei" [An expert from the Chinese Academy of Social Sciences says the overall scope of local government indebtedness is still in the controllable range], *Renmin Ribao* [Overseas Edition], May 21, 2010.

13. Ibid.

Chapter 7. The Challenge of Corruption

I thank Daisy Bui Ying Chung for excellent research assistance with this chapter.

1. Transparency International, "Corruption Perceptions Index 2012," http://cpi.transparency.org/cpi2012/results/ (accessed April 1, 2013).

2. Transparency International, "Government Defence Anti-Corruption Index 2013," http://government.defenceindex.org/report (accessed February 25, 2013).

3. Andy Xie, an economist at Morgan Stanley Dean Witter, gave an estimate of 2–3 percent of GDP. See Rowan Callick, "East Asia and the Pacific," in *Global Corruption Report 2001*, ed. Robin Hodess, Jessie Banfield, and Toby Wolfe (Berlin: Transparency International, 2001), 10–21. Hu Angang estimated losses at about 15 percent, but his study includes the underground economy, tax evasion, and inefficient but legal regulatory activities of the state. See his "Fubai: zhongguo zui da de shehui wuran" [Corruption: China's biggest social pollution], in *Zhongguo: tiaozhan fubai* [China: Fighting against corruption] (Hangzhou: Zhejiang renmin chubanshe, 2001), 34–66.

4. See, for example, discussions in John A. Gardiner, "Defining Corruption," *Corruption and Reform* 7, no. 2 (1993): 111–24; Susan Rose-Ackerman, *Corruption and Government: Causes, Consequences, and Reform* (Cambridge, UK: Cambridge University Press, 1999), 91–110; Michael Johnston, *Syndromes of Corruption: Wealth, Power, and Democracy* (Cambridge, UK: Cambridge University Press, 2005), 10–13.

5. Daniel Treisman, "What Have We Learned About the Causes of Corruption from Ten Years of Cross-National Empirical Research?" *Annual Review of Political Science* 10 (2007): 211–44.

6. Treisman, "What Have We Learned About the Causes of Corruption?" 222.

7. Ibid.

8. Paolo Mauro, "Corruption and Growth," *Quarterly Journal of Economics* 110, no. 3 (1995): 681–712; Alberto Ades and Rafael Di Tella, "Rents, Competition, and Corruption," *American Economic Review* 89, no. 4 (1999): 982–93; Rafael La Porta et al., "The Quality of Government," *Journal of Law, Economics, and Organization* 15, no. 1 (1999): 222–79; Daniel Treisman, "The Causes of Corruption: A Cross-National Study," *Journal of Public Economics* 76, no. 3 (2000): 399–457.

9. Wayne Sandholtz and William Koetzle, "Accounting for Corruption: Economic Structure, Democracy, and Trade," *International Studies Quarterly* 44, no. 1 (2000): 31–50; Wayne Sandholtz and Mark M. Gray, "International Integration and National Corruption," *International Organization* 57, no. 4 (2003): 761–800; John Gerring and

Strom C. Thacker, "Political Institutions and Corruption: The Role of Unitarism and Parliamentarism," *British Journal of Political Science* 34, no. 2 (2005): 295–330.

10. Ades and Di Tella, "Rents, Competition, and Corruption"; Treisman, "The Causes of Corruption."

11. Treisman, "What Have We Learned About the Causes of Corruption?"

12. Alicia Adsera, Carles Boix, and Mark Payne, "Are You Being Served? Political Accountability and Quality of Government," *Journal of Law, Economics, and Organization* 19, no. 2 (2003): 445–90; Aymo Brunetti and Beatrice Weder, "A Free Press Is Bad News for Corruption," *Journal of Public Economics* 87, nos. 7–8 (2003): 1801–24.

13. Andrew Wedeman, *Double Paradox: Rapid Growth and Rising Corruption in China* (Ithaca, N.Y.: Cornell University Press, 2012).

14. Melanie Manion, *Corruption By Design: Building Clean Government in Mainland China and Hong Kong* (Cambridge, Mass.: Harvard University Press, 2004); Wedeman, *Double Paradox*.

15. Yong Guo, "Corruption in Transitional China: An Empirical Analysis," *China Quarterly*, no. 194 (2008): 349–64; Wedeman, *Double Paradox*.

16. Xiaolu Wang, "Analysing Chinese Grey Income," *Credit Suisse Expert Insights* (August 6, 2010), http://www.scribd.com/doc/35832909/CreditSuisse-Expert-Insights -20100806 (accessed April 23, 2013).

17. Cited in *South China Morning Post* (Hong Kong), March 5, 2013.

18. Minxin Pei, "Corruption Threatens China's Future," *Carnegie Endowment for International Peace Policy Brief*, no. 55 (2007): 1–7.

19. See, for example, Dorothy J. Solinger, *Chinese Business Under Socialism: The Politics of Domestic Commerce* (Berkeley, Calif.: University of California Press, 1984); Wojtek Zafanolli, "A Brief Outline of China's Second Economy," in *Transforming China's Economy in the Eighties*, vol. 2, *Management, Industry and the Urban Economy*, ed. Stephen Feuchtwang, Athar Hussain, and Thierry Pairault (Boulder, Colo: Westview Press, 1988), 138–55.

20. Anita Chan and Jonathan Unger, "Grey and Black: The Hidden Economy of Rural China," *Pacific Affairs* 55, no. 3 (1982): 452–71.

21. Xiaobo Lu, "Booty Socialism, Bureau-Preneurs, and the State in Transition: Organizational Corruption in China," *Comparative Politics* 32, no. 3 (2000): 273–94.

22. See discussion in Ting Gong, *The Politics of Corruption in Contemporary China: An Analysis of Policy Outcomes* (Westport, Conn.: Praeger, 1994).

23. Gong, *The Politics of Corruption in Contemporary China*; Ting Gong, "Jumping into the Sea: Cadre Entrepreneurs in China," *Problems of Post-Communism* 43, no. 4 (1996): 26–34; Ting Gong, "Forms and Characteristics of China's Corruption in the 1990s: Change with Continuity," *Communist and Post-Communist Studies* 30, no. 3 (1997): 277–88; Xiaobo Lu, "The Politics of Peasant Burden in Reform China," *Journal of Peasant Studies* 25, no. 1 (1997): 113–38; Yan Sun, "Reform, State, and Corruption: Is Corruption Less Destructive in China Than in Russia?" *Comparative Politics* 32, no. 1 (1999): 1–20; Andrew Wedeman, "Budgets, Extra-Budgets, and Small Treasuries:

Illegal Monies and Local Autonomy in China," *Journal of Contemporary China* 9, no. 25 (2000): 489–511; X. L. Ding, "The Illicit Asset Stripping of Chinese State Firms," *China Journal*, no. 43 (2000): 1–28; Jane Duckett, "Bureaucrats in Business, Chinese Style: The Lessons of Market Reform and State Entrepreneurialism in the People's Republic of China," *World Development* 29, no. 1 (2001): 23–37.

24. Wedeman, *Double Paradox.*

25. *South China Morning Post*, April 15, 2013.

26. See, for example, Gong, "Forms and Characteristics of China's Corruption in the 1990s"; Ting Gong, "Corruption and Local Governance: The Double Identity of Chinese Local Government in Market Reform," *Pacific Review* 19, no. 1 (2006): 85–102; Chengze Simon Fan and Herschel I. Grossman, "Incentives and Corruption in Chinese Economic Reform, *Policy Reform*, no. 4 (2001): 195–206; Yan Sun, *Corruption and Market in Contemporary China* (Ithaca, N.Y.: Cornell University Press, 2004); Yong Guo, "Jingji zhuangui zisheng fubai jihui de weiguan jizhi yanjiu: cong 594 ge fubai yao an zong dechu de jielun" [The micro-mechanism by which the economic transition breeds corruption: conclusions from a study of 594 cases involving senior officials], *Jingji shehui tizhi bijiao* [Comparative economic and social systems], no. 5 (2006): 53–59; Guo, "Corruption in Transitional China"; Wenhao Cheng, "An Empirical Study of Corruption Within China's State-Owned Enterprises," *China Review* 4, no. 2 (2004): 55–80; Xiaogang Deng, Lening Zhang, and Andrea Leverentz, "Official Corruption During China's Economic Transition: Historical Patterns, Characteristics, and Government Reactions," *Journal of Contemporary Criminal Justice* 26, no. 2 (2010): 72–88; Wedeman, *Double Paradox.*

27. Wedeman, *Double Paradox.*

28. Guo, "The micro-mechanism by which the economic transition breeds corruption."

29. Wedeman, *Double Paradox.*

30. See, for example, Jiangnan Zhu, "Why Are Offices for Sale in China? A Case Study of the Office-Selling Chain in Heilongjiang Province," *Asian Survey* 48, no. 4 (2008): 558–79.

31. Andrei Shleifer and Robert W. Vishny, "Corruption," *Quarterly Journal of Economics* 58, no. 3 (1993): 599–617.

32. Guo "Corruption in Transitional China"; Wedeman, *Double Paradox.*

33. Specific sources for Table 7.1: Ceng Yabo and Li Weibin, "Yu shi ju jin hua fanfu—2002 nian zhongguo fanfu redian zongshu" (Advancing with anticorruption: summary of 2002 Chinese anticorruption hot issues), *Zhongguo jiaoyu bao* (China Education News), 2003 at http://www.jyb.cn/gb/2003/02/28/zy/5-shzk/1.htm; Qian Qiao and Ba Shi, "2002 zhongguo fanfu jufeng" (2002 China's anticorruption hurricane), *Zhongguo gongwuyuan* (Chinese Public Servant), no. 1 (2003): 47–50; "2002 zhongguo fanfu da qi di" (Chinese anticorruption discoveries in 2002), *Qingdao xinwen wang* (Qingdao News), 13 March 2003, at http://www.qingdaonews.com/big5/content /2003-03/13/content_1097225.htm; He Yan, "2003 nian zhong jiwei chachu de shi

ming fubai gaoguan" (Ten corrupt senior officials investigated by the Central Commission for Discipline Inspection in 2003), *Jinri Hainan* (Hainan Today), no. 1 (2004): 37–38; Shan Gong, "2003 nian zhongguo fan fubai huimou" (Looking back on China's anticorruption in 2003), *Gongchandang ren* (Communists), no. 10 (2004): 40–41; Chong Gu, "2004 nian luoma gaoguan da puguang" (Exposing senior officials sacked in 2004), *Zhengfu fazhi* (Government Legal System), no. 4 (2005): 4–6; Lin Shuangchuan and Xue Kai, "2004 nian fubai tuxian 'san duo' tedian" (2004 Corruption highlights characteristics of "three two manys"), *Lianzheng liaowang* (Good Governance Outlook), no. 1 (2005): 10; Ling Chuan, "Cong luoma gaoguan kan fubai xin yanbian—dui 2004 nian bufen tanguan fubai an de fenxi" (Seeing new evolution of corruption from sacked senior officials—analysis of corruption cases in 2004), *Renmin zheng tan* (People's Political Scene), no. 1 (2005): 32–33; Chen Zewei, "Zhongguo chachu 13 ming sheng bu guanyuan" (China investigates 13 provincial and ministerial officials), *Jilin renda* (Jilin People's Congress), no. 2 (2006): 42; "2005 nian zhongguo shi da anjian" (China's ten biggest cases in 2005), *Renmin Gong'an* (People's Public Security), no. 2 (2006): 7; Yi Wen, "2005 nian zhongguo fazhi lanpishu fanfu pian: fubai zhongshengxiang" (2005 China's bluebook on rule of law, anti-corruption chapter: corruption in all phases), *Jilin renda* (Jilin People's Congress), no. 2 (2006): 40–42; Wei Yahua, "2006 nian zhongguo jiu da fangdichan fubai an" (2006 China's nine top real estate corruption cases), *Shichang liaowang* (Market Outlook), no. 12 (2006): 46–49; "2005 nian fubai da yao'an pandian" (Inventory of major corruption cases in 2005), *Zhongguo shenpan* (China Trial), no. 1 (2006): 38–39; Ceng Yabo and Cao Yong, "'Fanfu 2006' zhuanti baodao zhi er: gongzhong re yi shi da fubai shijian" ("Anticorruption 2006" cover story 2: hot public discussion of top ten corruption cases), *Minzhu yu fazhi* (Democracy and the Legal System), no. 1 (2007): 11–14; "2006 nian zhongguo 10 da fan fubai xinwen" (2006 Chinese top ten anticorruption news items), *Lianzheng Liaowang* (Good Governance Outlook), no. 1 (2007): 6–7; "2008 fan fubai 10 jian dashiji" (Ten major anticorruption events in 2008), *Lianzheng Liaowang* (Good Governance Outlook), no. 1 (2009): 16–17; Luo Shui, "2006 fanfa shi da an zhangxian zhongguo juexin" (Top ten anticorruption cases in 2006 highlight China's determination), *Huanghe. Huangtu. Huangzhong ren* (Yellow River. Yellow Soil. Yellow Race), no. 1 (2007): 39–41; Wu Liguo, "2006 fubai anjian jing ping" (2006 corruption cases detailed assessment), *Zhongguo jingmao dao kan* (China Economic and Trade Herald), no. 1 (2007): 46–49; Research Center of Central Commission for Discipline Inspection, "2007 Zhongguo fanfu changlian jianshe dashi" (Chinese anticorruption and good governance building major events in 2007), *Zhongguo jiancha* (Supervision in China), no. 1 (2008): 16–20; Xu Aiping and Lao Yan, "2007 nian fanfu changlian da pandian" (Review of anticorruption cases in 2007), *Zhengfu fazhi* (Government Legal System), no. 1 (2008): 8–10; Yuan Shixiang, "2008 nian dianxing fubai anjian yanjiu" (A study of typical corruption cases in 2008), *Shanghai dang shi yu dangjian* (Shanghai party history and construction), no. 8 (2009): 28–30; "2009 nian shi da fanfu dianxing anjian" (Top ten typical anti-corruption cases in 2009), *Bingtuan jianshe* (Army construction), no. 2 (2010):

34–35; "2009 nian fan fubai 10 jian dashi" (Ten major anticorruption events in 2009), *Gongchandang ren* (Communists), no. 2 (2010): 48–49; Li Yousheng and Lu Yicai, "Zhongyang fanfu zai liangjian 'liang ge meiyou' qiao jingzhong" (Center hones in on anticorruption again: "two nothings" sound the alarm), *Jizhe guancha* (Reporters Notes), no. 1 (2010): 4–7; Ceng Yabo, "2010 nian zhongguo shi da tese tanguan" (2010 top ten featured corrupt officials), *Zhengfu fazhi* (Government Legal System), no. 1 (2011): 36–37; Ye Mao, "2010 nian fubai yao'an zaishen" (2010: retrial of serious corruption cases), *Lianzheng liaowang* (Good Governance Outlook), no. 1 (2011): 20–23; Ye Mao, "2010 nian shi da fanfu xinwen" (Top ten anti-corruption news in 2010), *Lianzheng liaowang* (Good Governance Outlook), no. 1 (2011): 24–25; *Zhongguo fanfu chang lian jian she bao gao* (Report on construction of China's anti-corruption) (Beijing: Shehui kexue wenxian chubanshe, 2012); "2011 niandu dianxing xingshi anjian" (2011 typical criminal cases), *Fazhi zixun* (Legal Information), no. 1 (2012): 25–35; "2011 zui ju biaoben yiyi de fanfu 'dapian'" (A sample of representative anticorruption "blockbusters" in 2011), *Sichuan dang de jianshe* (Sichuan Party Construction), no. 2 (2012): 52–53.

34. Wedeman, *Double Paradox*.

35. Zhu, "Why Are Offices for Sale in China?"

36. Good examples are Ting Gong, "Dependent Judiciary and Unaccountable Judges: Judicial Corruption in Contemporary China," *China Review* 4, no. 2 (2004): 33–54; Ling Li, "The 'Production' of Corruption in China's Courts: Judicial Politics and Decision Making in a One-Party State," *Law and Social Inquiry* 37, no. 4 (2012): 848–77; Yuhua Wang, "Court Funding and Judicial Corruption in China," *China Journal* 69 (2013): 43–63.

37. Gong, "Dependent Judiciary and Unaccountable Judges."

38. Wang, "Court Funding and Judicial Corruption in China."

39. Rose-Ackerman, *Corruption and Government*.

40. Meina Cai, "The Political Economy of Landlocked Development in China," (Ph.D. dissertation, University of Wisconsin-Madison, 2012).

41. Gong, "Forms and Characteristics of China's Corruption in the 1990s."

42. See Hongbin Cai, J. Vernon Henderson, and Qinghua Zhang, "China's Land Market Auctions: Evidence of Corruption" (National Bureau of Economic Research Working Paper #15067, June 2009).

43. Pei, "Corruption Threatens China's Future."

44. Cai, "The Political Economy of Landlocked Development in China."

45. Sun, "Reform, State, and Corruption"; X. L. Ding, "Systemic Irregularity and Spontaneous Property Transformation in the Chinese Financial System," *China Quarterly* 163 (2000): 655–76.

46. Manion, *Corruption By Design*.

47. *South China Morning Post*, March 18, 2013.

48. State Council Information Office, "White Paper on China's Efforts to Combat Corruption and Build a Clean Government," December 2010, http://news.xinhuanet.com/english2010/china/2010-12/29/c_13669383.htm (accessed February 25, 2013).

49. He Qinglian. 1997. *Zhongguo de xianjing* [China's pitfall]. Hong Kong: Mirror Books.

50. For example, Svolik finds that among all authoritarian leaders who held power for at least a day between 1946 and 2008 and lost power by nonconstitutional means, more than two-thirds were removed by regime insiders. See Milan W. Svolik, *The Politics of Authoritarian Rule* (Cambridge, UK: Cambridge University Press, 2012).

51. Barbara Geddes, "What Do We Know About Democratization After Twenty Years?" *Annual Review of Political Science* 2 (1999): 115–44.

Chapter 8. Responsive Authoritarianism in Chinese Media

1. By authoritarian regime or state I refer to political systems that are neither characterized by free, fair, and competitive elections, nor politically liberal. In 2001, 71 out of 192 countries in the world could clearly be classified as authoritarian, 17 were ambiguous. See Larry J. Diamond, "Elections without Democracy: Thinking About Hybrid Regimes," *Journal of Democracy* 13, no. 2 (2002).

2. For a detailed summary of this discussion, see Daniela Stockmann, *Media Commercialization and Authoritarian Rule in China*, Communication, Society, & Politics Series (New York: Cambridge University Press, 2013).

3. Citations and empirical evidence for this argument, if not specifically mentioned here, have been published in Stockmann, *Media Commercialization and Authoritarian Rule in China*.

4. There are some exceptions to this rule. For instance, *Beijing Times* in the People's Daily group would have the right to circulate nationally, but only circulated in Beijing as of 2005. *Southern Weekend* managed to circulate nationally, though registered with the Southern Daily Group (*Nanfang Baoye*) at the Guangdong provincial level.

5. On the early PRC roots of this system, see Franklin W. Houn, "Chinese Communist Control of the Press," *Public Opinion Quarterly* 22, no. 4 (Winter 1958–59): 435–48.

6. John P. Burns, "Strengthening Central CCP Control of Leadership Selection: The 1990 Nomenklatura," *China Quarterly* 138, (June 1994): 458–91; Chan Hon, "Cadre Personnel Management in China: The Nomenklatura System, 1990–1998," *China Quarterly* 179, (September 2004): 703–34.

7. Anne-Marie Brady, *Marketing Dictatorship: Propaganda and Thought Work in Contemporary China* (Lanham, Md.: Rowman & Littlefield, 2008).

8. See, for example, Baoshou Guojia Mimi Fa [Law on protecting state secrets], 1998, art. 20 (stating that media publications and broadcasts shall not reveal state secrets); and Criminal Law of the People's Republic of China, 1997, art. 398 (barring divulgence of state secrets). See also Benjamin J. Liebman, "Watchdog or Demagogue? The Media in the Chinese Legal System," *Columbia Law Review* 101, no. 1 (2005).

9. Liebman, "Watchdog or Demagogue?; Yuezhi Zhao, *Media, Market, and Democracy in China: Between the Party Line and the Bottom Line* (Urbana: University of Illinois Press, 1998).

10. Brady, *Marketing Dictatorship.*

11. David L. Shambaugh,"China's Propaganda System: Institutions, Processes, and Efficacy," *China Journal* 57 (January 2007): 25–58.

12. In principle, sponsors also have the responsibility to engage in postpublication monitoring. However, none of the existing works mention whether and how much this has been practiced.

13. The central PD does not have authority to issue binding orders to central party papers such as the *People's Daily* or the *Guangming Daily*. See Guogang Wu, "Command Communication: The Politics of Editorial Formulation in the People's Daily," *China Quarterly* 137 (1994); Zhao, *Media, Market, and Democracy in China.*

14. Data relate to 2012, retrieved from the GAPP and National Bureau of Statistics Web sites at www.gapp.gov.cn and www.stats.gov.cn (accessed January 16, 2014).

15. Brady, *Marketing Dictatorship*; Yuezhi Zhao, *Communication in China: Political Economy, Power, and Conflict* (Lanham, Md.: Rowman & Littlefield, 2008).

16. Samuel Huntington, "Democracy's Third Wave," in *The Global Resurgence of Democracy*, ed. Larry J. Diamond and Marc F. Plattner (Baltimore, Md.: Johns Hopkins University Press, 1996), 3–25.

17. See for example, Philip N. Howard, *The Digital Origins of Dictatorship and Democracy: Information Technology and Political Islam* (New York: Oxford University Press, 2010).

18. See, for example, Gary D. Rawnsley and Ming-Yeh T. Rawnsley, "Regime Transition and the Media in Taiwan," in *Democratization and the Media*, ed. Vicky Randall (London: Frank Cass, 1998), 106–24; Chappell Lawson, *Building the Fourth Estate: Democratization and the Rise of a Free Press in Mexico* (Berkeley: University of California Press, 2002); Ayo Olukotun, "Authoritarian State, Crisis of Democratization and the Underground Media in Nigeria," *African Affairs* 101, no. 404 (July 2002): 317–42.

19. See, for example, Lance W. Bennett, "The Media and Democratic Development: The Social Basis of Political Communication," in *Communicating Democracy: The Media and Political Transitions*, ed. Patrick H. O'Neil (Boulder, Colo.: Lynne Rienner, 1998), 195–206; Dale F. Eickelman and Jon W. Anderson, *New Media in the Muslim World: The Emerging Public Sphere*, 2nd ed., Indiana Series in Middle East Studies (Bloomington: Indiana University Press, 2003).

20. Cao dates the first advertisement after the Cultural Revolution back to January 4, 1979, in the *Tianjin Daily* (*Tianjin Ribao*), twenty-four days before advertising appeared on Shanghai Television. Peng Cao, *Zhongguo Baoye Jituan Fazhan Yanjiu* [Research on the development of Chinese Newspaper groups] (Beijing: Xinhua Chubanshe, 1999). However, this information conflicts with most other sources. See Junhao Hong, "The Resurrection of Advertising in China: Developments, Problems, and Trends," *Asian Survey* 34, no. 4 (1994); and Chunlei Hu, "Zhongguo Baoye Jingji

Fazhan Jin 20 Nian Chengjiu" [The achievement of the Chinese newspaper industry in the course of the past 20 years], in *Zhongguo Baoye Nianjian* [China Newspaper Industry Yearbook] (Beijing: Zhonghua Gongshang Lianhe Chubanshe, 2004).

21. Conversation with Shen Yuanyuan, expert on Chinese regulation of advertising, December 8, 2011.

22. Zhao, *Media, Market, and Democracy in China*, 50.

23. Brady, *Marketing Dictatorship*.

24. Zhao, *Media, Market, and Democracy in China*.

25. Zhou He, "Chinese Communist Press in a Tug of War: A Political Economy Analysis of the Shenzhen Special Zone Daily," in *Power, Money, and Media: Communication Patterns and Bureaucratic Control in Cultural China*, ed. Chin-chuan Lee (Evanston, Ill.: Northwestern University Press, 2000), 112–51.

26. Interview with a male editor of a semiofficial and an official paper, Beijing, April 2005.

27. "What Chinese Censors Don't Want You to Know," *New York Times*, March 21, 2010.

28. "What Chinese Censors Don't Want You to Know"; and International Federation of Journalists (IFJ), "Zhongguo Xinwen Ziyou 2010" [Press freedom in China in 2010], 91 See http://asiapacific.ifj.org/en/pages/ifj-asia-pacific-reports (accessed July 20, 2012).

Zhang Hong, the editor of the online edition of *Economic Observer* and the author of the editorial was fired. The editor-in-chief and a vice editor-in-chief of *Economic Observer* received reprimands that could negatively affect his promotion. Editors-in-chief of the other twelve newspapers were admonished by the PD. See also "Shei Jiaomie Jinnian 'Lianghui' Diyi Xinwen Redian" [Who poured and killed this year's "two meetings" number one news?], http://www.chinainperspective.com/ArtShow.aspx ?AID=5727 (accessed December 21, 2011).

29. A similar negotiation takes place in other parts of the cultural sector, as described by Stanley Rosen, "Is the Internet a Positive Force in the Development of Civil Society, a Public Sphere, and Democratization in China?" *International Journal of Communication* 4 (2010).

30. Jonathan Hassid, "Four Models of the Fourth Estate: A Typology of Contemporary Chinese Journalists," *China Quarterly* 208 (December 2011): 813–32.

31. The Chongqing nail house already existed when I was doing fieldwork in 2005. Yang Wu, a local martial arts hero, and his wife, Wu Ping, refused to leave their house after the local government sold the right to use the land to a private developer. The developer dug a more than ten-meter-deep ditch around the house, leaving a small island with a "nail house" on top without water and electricity. In 2007 the photograph was posted online. Eventually, the dispute was settled, resulting in a new home as compensation for the couple. See also Qiang Xiao, "The Rise of Online Public Opinion and Its Political Impact," in *Changing Media, Changing China*, ed. Susan Shirk (Oxford, UK: Oxford University Press, 2011).

Deng Yujiao used to be a waitress at the "Fantasy Pleasure City" entertainment complex in Hubei Province, and was raped by three men and stabbed two of them in a struggle. Originally charged with the murder of a local government official, she escaped punishment after the story leaked into the Internet and was published widely in the media. See Benjamin J. Liebman, "Changing Media, Changing Courts," in *Changing Media, Changing China*, ed. Shirk.

Li Qiaoming was arrested for cutting down trees in Yunnan and died in police custody. Police claimed he received severe brain injuries after running blindfolded into a wall while playing hide-and-seek. In response to online pressure, Yunnan's deputy propaganda chief Wu Hao allowed the creation of an "online investigations committee," allegedly because he had been a *Xinhua* reporter himself. See China Media Project, www.cmp.hku.hk (accessed August 8, 2009).

32. Jack Linchuan Qiu, *Working-Class Network Society: Communication Technology and the Information Have-Less in Urban China* (Cambridge, Mass.: MIT Press, 2009).

33. For more details see China Network Information Center (CNNIC) http://www.cnnic.net.cn/hlwfzyj/ (accessed April 2, 2014).

34. Kathleen Hartford, "Dear Mayor: Online Communications with Local Governments in Hangzhou and Nanjing," *China Information* 19, no. 2 (2005): 217–60.

35. See "Provisions on the Administration of Internet News and Information Services" issued by the State Council Information Office and Ministry of Information Industry in September 2005, http://www.chinaitlaw.org (accessed May 31, 2007). See also Daniela Stockmann, "What Information Does the Public Demand? Getting the News During the 2005 Anti-Japanese Protests," in *Changing Media, Changing China*, ed. Shirk.

36. Since its launch in 2009, Weibo has had a strong impact on Chinese journalism, as it allows people to follow reporters, providing new insight into audience attention to stories. It also has further increased access to information and the speed in which information is transmitted, thus placing further pressure on traditional media for greater transparency in reporting.

37. Ashley Esarey and Qiang Xiao, "Digital Communication and Political Change in China," *International Journal of Communication* 5 (2011): 298–319.

38. The China Survey 2008 was a project of the College of Liberal Arts at Texas A&M University, in collaboration with the Research Center for Contemporary China (RCCC) at Peking University. The survey question primed people to think about sensitive information by asking about "political information," and may have underestimated the importance of social media. The results were: 21.5% accessed government Web sites, 19.4% Web sites of social organizations, 68.6% online news Web sites, 20.3% BBS, 14.6% blogs, and 16.6% chats. See http://thechinasurvey.tamu.edu/html/home.html (accessed April 2, 2014).

39. Qian Gang and David Bandurski, "China's Emerging Public Sphere: The Impact of Media Commercialization, Professionalism, and the Internet in an Era of Transition," 38–76; Xiao, "The Rise of Online Public Opinion and Its Political Impact," both in Shirk, ed., *Changing Media, Changing China*.

40. Susanne Lohmann, "Collective Action Cascades: An Informational Rationale for the Power in Numbers," *Journal of Economic* Surveys 14, no. 5 (December 2002): 655–84.

41. Jens Damm, "Cybercommunities," in *Internet in China: Online Business, Information, Distribution, and Social Connectivity*, ed. Randy Kluver and Ashley Esarey (Great Barrington, Mass.: Berkshire, 2013).

42. Ibid.

43. Qiu, *Working-Class Network Society*.

44. Guobin Yang, "The Internet and Civil Society in China: A Preliminary Assessment," *Journal of Contemporary China* 12, no. 36 (August 2003): 453–75; *The Power of the Internet in China: Citizen Activism Online* (New York: Columbia University Press, 2009).

45. See, for example, James Reilly, *Strong State, Smart State: The Rise of Public Opinion in China's Japan Policy* (New York: Columbia University Press, 2012).

46. Stockmann, "What Information Does the Public Demand?"

47. Stockmann, "What Information Does the Public Demand?"; Stockmann, *Media Commercialization and Authoritarian Rule in China*.

48. See, for example, Brady, *Marketing Dictatorship*; Zhao, *Communication in China: Political Economy, Power, and Conflict*; Esarey and Xiao, "Digital Communication and Political Change in China"; Gang and Bandurski, "China's Emerging Public Sphere."

49. See Brady, *Marketing Dictatorship*.

50. Joseph Fewsmith and Stanley Rosen, "The Domestic Context of Chinese Foreign Policy," in *The Making of Chinese Foreign and Security Policy in the Era of Reform, 1978–2000*, ed. David M. Lampton (Stanford, Calif.: Stanford University Press, 2001), 151–87; Reilly, *Strong State, Smart State*.

51. Lidan Chen, "Open Information System and Crisis Communication in China," *Chinese Journal of Comunication* 1, no. 1 (April 2008): 38–54.

52. Due to its concurrence with leadership succession and the "two meetings," the Propaganda Department initially instructed the Chinese media to synchronize the news and provide one identical perspective, followed by instructions to abstain from reporting the outbreak. In the absence of information, rumors started to spread, facilitated by new communication technologies, such as the Internet and SMS messages. Even after the government decided to release information, many still believed that the government still disguised the real situation. Brady, *Marketing Dictatorship*; Chen, "Open Information System and Crisis Communication in China."

53. Chen, "Open Information System and Crisis Communication in China." Handbooks for journalistic training from 2004 still strictly forbade reporting in the case of natural disasters or other cases of national emergency. In contrast, Central PD restrictions regarding the 2010 Yushu earthquake demanded positive coverage on April 15. On August 6, 2010, the Central PD asked that media must be in line with

official information. IFJ, "Zhongguo Xinwen Ziyou 2010" [press freedom in China in 2010].

54. Ni Chen, "Institutionalizing Public Relations: A Case Study of Chinese Government Crisis Communication on the 2008 Sichuan Earthquake," *Public Relations Review* 35 (September 2009): 187–98; Dennis Lai Hang Hui, "Research Note: Politics of Sichuan Earthquake, 2008," *Journal of Contingencies and Crisis Management* 17, no. 2 (2009): 137–40.

55. By the end of the two meetings in 2008, media covered protests in Tibet. See, for example, *CCTV*, March 16, 2008; *People's Daily,* March 17, 2008; *Beijing Youth Daily,* March 22, 2008; *Caijing,* March 24, 2008; *Sina,* April 15, 2008. On the Chongqing taxi strike, see Stockmann, *Media Commercialization and Authoritarian Rule in China.*

56. Stockmann,*Media Commercialization and Authoritarian Rule in China.*

57. Benjamin J. Liebman, "The Media and the Courts: Towards Competitive Supervision?" *China Quarterly* 208, (December 2011): 833–50.

58. Interviews with a male lawyer and a male journalist of commercialized paper (Beijing, June 2005). See also Liebman, "The Media and the Courts." On court cases involving the media, see Haitao Liu, Jinxiong Zheng, and Rong Shen, *Zhongguo Xinwen Guansi Ershi Nian, 1987–2007* [Twenty years of Chinese news lawsuits, 1987–2007] (Beijing: Zhongguo Guangbo Dianshi Chubanshe, 2007).

59. Liebman, "The Media and the Courts."

60. Ashley Esarey, "Speak No Evil: Mass Media Control in Contemporary China," in *Freedom House Special Report* (February 2006) 1–12. See http://www.freedomhouse .org/sites/default/files/inline_images/Speak%20No%20Evil-%20Mass%20Media %20Control%20in%20Contemporary%20China.pdf (accessed July 2, 2014)

61. "Zhongyang Guanyu Shenhua Wenhua Tizhi Gaige Zhundong Shehui Zhuyi Wenhua Da Fazhan Da Fanrong Ruogan Zhongda Wenti de Jueding" [Central Committee decision concerning the major issue of deepening cultural system reforms, promoting the great development and prosperity of socialist culture], *Xinhua,* October 26, 2011.

62. Gang and Bandurski, "China's Emerging Public Sphere."

63. Similarly, the Central Committee Decision cited above states that news organizations should strengthen public opinion supervision, promote the emphasis of the party and the state, reflect the existing problems of the masses, protect the benefit of the people, be close to the relationship between the party and the masses, and promote social harmony, linking ideas associated with opening of social space to promotion of the party line, social stability, and positive political outcomes.

64. Interview with a female professor of communication (Beijing, May 2005).

65. Interview with a male editor-in-chief of an official paper (Beijing, March 2005).

66. Kevin Latham, "Nothing but the Truth: News Media, Power and Hegemony in South China," *China Quarterly* 163 (September 2000): 633–54. The CCP did not have to

invent such arguments. The Chinese saying "great disorder under heaven" *(tian xia da luan)* refers to the end of dynastic cycles associated with natural disasters, protests, and invasion by foreign tribes. Lung-Kee Sun, *Zhongguo Wenhua De Shenceng Jiegou* [The deep structure of Chinese culture] (Guangxi: Guangxi Shifan Daxue Chuban-she, 2004), 438–39. By explaining that the only alternative to the current political system is social disorder, the PD aims to improve compliance among media practitioners.

67. Reilly, *Strong State, Smart State*, 34–35.

68. Stockmann, *Media Commercialization and Authoritarian Rule in China*.

69. David Bandurski, "China's Guerrilla War for the Web," *Far Eastern Economic Review* 171, no. 6 (July 2008). www.feer.com.

70. Rebecca MacKinnon, "China's Censorship 2.0: How Companies Censor Bloggers," *First Monday* 2 (2009).

71. On PD instructions, see IFJ, "Zhongguo Xinwen Ziyou 2010" [Press freedom in China in 2010].

72. Michael Schoenhals, *Doing Things with Words in Chinese Politics: Five Studies* (Berkeley: Institute of East Asian Studies, University of California, 1992).

73. Interview with a male editor of a semiofficial paper (Beijing, June 2005).

74. See reporting regarding the earthquake in *Xinhua*, May 23, 2008; *Beijing Youth Daily*, July 8, 2008, *New York Times*, September 8, 2008.

75. Xiaoling Zhang, "Reading Between the Headlines: SARS, Focus, and TV Current Affairs Programmes in China," *Media, Culture & Society* 28, no. 5 (September 2006): 715–37; Yuezhi Zhao and Wusan Sun, "Public Opinion Supervision: The Role of the Media in Constrainting Local Officials," in *Grassroots Political Reform in China*, ed. Elizabeth J. Perry and Merle Goldman (Cambridge, Mass.: Harvard University Press, 2007), 300–24; Liebman, "The Media and the Courts: Towards Competitive Supervision?"

76. Melanie Manion, *Corruption by Design: Building Clean Government in Mainland China and Hong Kong* (Cambridge, Mass.: Harvard University Press, 2004); Zhao and Sun, "Public Opinion Supervision"; Qiu, *Working-Class Network Society*.

77. See, for example, Zhang, "Reading Between the Headlines: SARS, Focus, and TV Current Affairs Programmes in China"; Stockmann, *Media Commercialization and Authoritarian Rule in China*.

78. Xu Hua, "Morality Discourse in the Marketplace: Narratives in the Chinese Television News Magazine Oriental Horizon," *Journalism Studies* 1, no. 4 (December 2000): 637–47.

79. Tianjian Shi and Jie Lu, "The Shadow of Confucianism," *Journal of Democracy* 21, no. 4 (October 2010): 123–30.

80. Stockmann, *Media Commercialization and Authoritarian Rule in China*.

81. Timur Kuran, "Now Out of Never: The Element of Surprise in East European Revolutions of 1989," *World Politics* 44, no. 1 (October 1991): 7–48; Adam Przeworski, *Democracy and the Market: Political and Economic Reforms in Eastern Europe and*

Latin America, Studies in Rationality and Social Change (New York: Cambridge University Press, 1991).

82. Stockmann, *Media Commercialization and Authoritarian Rule in China.*

Chapter 9. China's Law and Stability Paradox

1. Carl Minzner, "China's Turn Against Law," *American Journal of Comparative Law* 59, no. 4 (Fall 2011): 935–84; Benjamin L. Liebman, "A Return to Populist Legality? Historical Legacies and Legal Reform," in *Mao's Invisible Hand*, ed. Sebastian Heilmann and Elizabeth Perry (Cambridge, Mass.: Harvard University Asia Center Press, 2011): 269–313; Donald C. Clarke, "Jiang Ping: 'China's Rule of Law Is in Full Retreat,'" *Chinese Law Prof Blog*, March 2, 2010, http://lawprofessors.typepad.com/china_law_prof_blog/2010/03/jiang-ping-chinas-rule-of-law-is-in-full-retreat.html.

2. Minzner, "China's Turn Against Law."

3. Benjamin L. Liebman, "A Populist Threat to China's Courts?" in *Chinese Justice: Civil Dispute Resolution in Contemporary China*, ed. Margaret Y. K. Woo and Mary E. Gallagher (Cambridge, UK: Cambridge University Press, 2011), 269–313; Liebman, "A Return to Populist Legality?"

4. Benjamin L. Liebman, "Leniency in Chinese Criminal Law? Everyday Justice in Henan," *Berkeley Journal of International Law* (forthcoming).

5. Yang Su and Xin He, "Street as Courtroom: State Accommodation of Labor Protests in South China," *Law & Society Review* 44, no. 1 (March 2010): 157–84; Benjamin L. Liebman, "Malpractice Mobs: Medical Dispute Resolution in China," *Columbia Law Review* 113 (January 2013): 181–264.

6. Benjamin L. Liebman, "Legitimacy Through Law in China?" PBS, *Wide Angle* Discussion Guide, June 1, 2009, http://www-tc.pbs.org/wnet/wideangle/files/2009/04/legitimacy-through-law-in-china.pdf (accessed March 7, 2013).

7. Andrew J. Nathan, "Authoritarian Resilience," *Journal of Democracy* 14, no. 1 (January 2003): 6–17.

8. Katharina Pistor, "A Legal Theory of Finance," Journal of Comparative Economics 41, no. 2 (2013): 315–330.

9. I survey this period in more detail elsewhere. See Liebman, "A Return to Populist Legality?"

10. Xi Chen, "China at the Tipping Point? The Rising Cost of Stability," *Journal of Democracy* 24, no. 1 (January 2013): 57–64.

11. The debate at the time gave rise to the concept of "governance according to the constitution," and was not limited to discussion among lawyers or academics. The Standing Committee of the Politburo also for the first time engaged in collective study of the Constitution.

12. Lianjiang Li, Mingxing Liu, and Kevin J. O'Brien, "Petitioning Beijing: The High Tide of 2003–2006," *China Quarterly* 210 (June 2012): 313–34; Susan Trevaskes,

"The Ideology of Law and Order," in *China Story Yearbook 2012*, ed. Geremie R. Barmé (Canberra: Australian National University, 2012), 67–86.

13. Peter Lorentzen, "Regularized Rioting: Permitting Public Protest in an Authoritarian Regime," *Quarterly Journal of Political Science* 8, no. 2 (April 2013): 127–58.

14. Li, Liu, and O'Brien, "Petitioning Beijing."

15. Liebman, "A Return to Populist Legality?"; Minzner, "China's Turn Against Law."

16. Minzner, "China's Turn Against Law."

17. Liebman, "A Return to Populist Legality?"

18. Liebman, "Leniency in Chinese Criminal Law?"

19. Ibid.

20. Susan Trevaskes, "The Shifting Sands of Punishment in China in the Era of 'Harmonious Society'," *Law & Policy* 32, no. 3 (July 2010): 332–61.

21. Benjamin L. Liebman, "Malpractice Mobs: Medical Dispute Resolution in China," *Columbia Law Review* 113 (January 2013): 181–264.

22. Yang and He, "Street as Courtroom."

23. Liebman, "Malpractice Mobs."

24. *Zhongguo falü nianjian* [China Law Yearbook], 2000 (Beijing: Law Yearbook of China Press 2000).

25. The most dramatic drop in officially reported figures came from 2001 to 2002, when official statistics reported a drop from 9.1 million petitions to 3.6 million petitions (China Law Yearbook, 2001 and 2002). This drop almost certainly resulted from new methods for counting petitions. The number of petitions to the courts again peaked in 2004, at more than four million, before gradually declining over the remainder of the decade.

26. *Zhongguo falü nianjian* [China Law Yearbook], 2011.

27. Liebman, "A Populist Threat to China's Courts?"

28. Wang Ying, "Zhuanxingqi de zhongguo fayuan yu xinfang: shesu xinfang wenti shizheng yanjiu" [Chinese courts and petitioning in a time of transition: empirical research into the question of litigation-related petitioning] (Ph.D. dissertation, Qinghua University, 2010).

29. Liebman, "A Populist Threat to China's Courts?"

30. Liebman, "A Return to Populist Legality?"

31. Wang Shengjun, "Wang Shengjun: Fahui shenpan zhineng qianghua nengdong sifa" [Wang Shengjun: Develop adjudication quality in order to strengthen an active judiciary], *Fazhi ribao*, June 20, 2009; Wang Shengjun, "Chongfen fahui sifa nengdong zuoyong: baozhang jingji pingwen jiao kuai fazhan" [Increase the role of an active judiciary to guarantee stable and rapid economic development], *People's Court Newspaper*, January 6, 2010.

32. Xu Kai and Li Weiao, "Weiwen jiqi" [The machinery of stability preservation], *Caijing*, June 6, 2011, *Duihua* translation, June 8, 2011, http://www.duihuahrjournal.org/2011/06/translation-machinery-of-stability.html.

33. Ibid.

34. Alexis de Tocqueville, *Democracy in America,* ed. Phillips Bradley (New York: Knopf, 1946), 1: 140.

35. Liebman, "Malpractice Mobs."

36. Multiple factors appear to have contributed to this increased prominence: increased unrest, the role played by Luo Gan and Zhou Yongkang, who served as heads of the PLC and CCSM and as members of the Politburo Standing Committee from 2003 to 2007 and from 2007 to 2013, and increased knowledge of the CCSM due to greater media coverage.

The CCSM's name change was a reflection of the organization's growing importance and responsibility: one official report explained that the change reflected the CCSM's increased responsibility, leadership force, membership, and work institutions. "Zhongyang shehui guanli zonghe zhili weiyuanhui bangongshi fuzeren da jizhewen" [Central commission for comprehensive management of social stability work office representative replies to journalists' questions], *Renmin Ribao,* October 9, 2011.

37. "Zhongguo chang'an wang," China Peace, http://www.chinapeace.org.cn/ (accessed March 31, 2013).

38. "Zhou Yongkang zhuchi zhaokai zhongyang shehui guanli zonghe zhili weiyuanhui diyici quanti huiyi" [Zhou Yongkang chairs the opening of the first full meeting of the central commission on comprehensive social management], *Hebei China Peace,* March 28, 2013. The CCSM has established five subdivisions, or "small groups," targeting specific areas and reflecting primary areas of concern: railroad security and protection, management of floating populations, assistance and education of released convicts, prevention of juvenile crime, and public security in and near schools. Each of the small groups is situated at a specific ministry or party organization: the Ministry of Railroads, Ministry of Public Security, Ministry of Justice, Party Youth League, and Ministry of Education. "Zhongyang shehui zhi'an zonghe zhili weiyuanhui jianjie" [Brief introduction to the central commission for the comprehensive management of pubic security], *People Net,* July 17, 2007.

39. The relationship between the creation of the LSG and leadership concerns about the Falun Gong in the late 1990s is unclear. Although some have suggested that the initial creation of the LSG was a direct response to the Falun Gong, the actual creation of the office predates the Falun Gong's dramatic protests in 1999. A separate office, the 610 Office, also exists within many PLCs and explicitly focuses on the Falun Gong.

40. " 'Nanfeng Chuang' zazhi fengmian zhuanti: 09 nian weiwen xin siwei" ['Southern Window' magazine cover topic: thoughts on stability maintenance in 2009], *Southern Window,* April 13, 2009.

41. Some online reports state that the SMO is located in the Ministry of Public Security. In conversations, however, numerous officials and scholars stated that it is in the PLC.

42. Chengdu Stability Leading Small Group, "Guanyu tiaozheng 2011 nian weihu shehui wending gongzuo lingdao xiaozu de tongzhi" [Notice regarding the adjust-

ment of the 2011 social stability leading small group], *Chengdu Government*, April 30, 2011.

43. "'Nanfeng Chuang' zazhi fengmian zhuanti."

44. "Zhongyang weiwenban zhaokai quanguo shehui wending fengxian pinggu gongzuo zuotanhui," [Central Stability Maintenance Office opens National Social Stability Risk Evaluation Work Meeting], *Feng Huang Net*, September 13, 2012; Ministry of Health, "Weishengbu guanyu jianli weisheng xitong zhongda shixiang shehui wending fengxian pinggu jizhi de zhidao yijian (shixing)" [Ministry of Public Health guiding views (for trial implementation) regarding the social stability risk evaluation system for major projects in the public health system], January 5, 2011, http://www .moh.gov.cn/mohbgt/s3589/201101/50484.shtml; Harbin High and New Technology Industrial Development Zone, "Ha kaifaqu zhongda quntixing shijian yuce he yufang jizhi" [Harbin development zone mechanism for prediction and prevention of significant group incidents], May 21, 2008, http://www.kaifaqu.com.cn/zwgk/detail.jsp ?urltype=news.NewsContentUrl&wbnewsid=41653&wbtreeid=1059.

The importance of the social stability risk evaluation system was also highlighted in documents issued at the Eighteenth Party Congress in 2012. Official reports noted that such efforts were being undertaken in response to concerns about an increase in unrest, petitions, and mass incidents, in particular those concerning rural land takings, urban demolition and relocation, reform of state enterprises, and litigation. "Shiba da baogao jiedu—wei shenme yao jianli jianquan zhongda juece shehui wending fengxian pinggu jizhi." [Explanation of report from the 18th Party congress— Why establish the comprehensive social stability risk evaluation system for major policies?] *Xinhuanet*, February 18, 2013. The system appears to have been created in 2011 or early 2012. "Zhongyang weiwenban zhaokai quanguo shehui wending fengxian pinggu gongzuo zuotanhui" [Central stability maintenance office opens national social stability risk evaluation work meeting], *Feng Huang Net*, September 13, 2012.

45. Baocheng Chen, "China 'Stability' Agency Rises in Stature," *Caixin Online*, September 27, 2012; "China Seeks Soft Approach for Social Stability," *Xinhuanet*, February 26, 2011.

46. Chen, "China 'Stability' Agency Rises in Stature."

47. "Guangdong gouzhu zongzhi xinfang weiwen liti wangluo" [Guangdong establishes a solid and comprehensive social management, petitioning and stability network], *People Net*, May 26, 2010. Many staff counted as full-time staff were likely reassigned from or also engaged in other work. Nevertheless, the report provides a sense of the comprehensive nature of local stability work. Another manifestation of renewed emphasis on social stability and on resolving disputes before they escalate has been the resources devoted to neighborhood committees, with many staff becoming full-time employees for the first time.

48. "Gongshang jiufen 90 fenzhong tiaojie jiean" [Workplace injury disputes resolved through mediation in ninety minutes], *Nan Fang Net*, May 31, 2009; "Liang Weifa: Zongzhi Xinfang Weiwen Zhongxin yao chengwei jiejue jiufen an de 'zhongdian

zhan'," [Liang Weifa: Comprehensive stability center is going to become the 'terminus' for solving disputes], *Nan Fang Net*, November 6, 2009.

49. "Wuping xian: yi chuangjian 'Wusong wufang cunju' wei zhuashou zhuoli tuijin shehui maodun huajie" [Wuping County: creating "zero litigation and zero petitions villages and streets" in order to focus and push forward the resolution of contradictions in society], *Fujian Court Net*, April 18, 2012.

50. "Jituan gongsi 2011 nian xinfang weiwen gongzuo huiyi jingshen chuanda tigang" [Notes transmitting the spirit of the group companies' stability and petitioning work meeting 2011], *China Guodian*, September 13, 2011; "Huaneng chuanda guanche zhongyang qiye weihu wending gongzuo huiyi jingshen" [China Power transmits the spirit of the meeting regarding implementing stability work at central enterprises], *China Power*, March 26, 2007; "Jinmei jituan bushu qiye weiwen gongzuo" [Jinfeng Coal Chemical Industry Company arranges stability maintenance work], *Shanxi Jinfeng Coal Chemical Industry Co., Ltd.*, March 1, 2013, http://www.jfmh.cn/news_xx.asp?cn_id=3254.

51. Chen Xi, "China at the Tipping Point?"; Trevaskes, "The Ideology of Law and Order."

52. Xu and Li, "The Machinery of Stability Preservation."

53. Central Commission on Comprehensive Management of Public Security, "Zhongyang shehui zhian zonghe zhili weiyuanhui guanyu shixing shehui zhian zonghe zhili yipiao foujue quanzhi de guiding (shixing)" [Central commission on comprehensive management of public security regulation on the implementation of the system of a one-vote veto system for public security management (for trial implementation)], January 13, 1992, http://www.chinabaike.com/law/zy/bw/0972/1416708.html; Central Discipline Commission of the Communist Party, "Guanyu shixing shehui zhian zonghe zhili lingdao zeren zhi de ruogan guiding" [Certain provisions regarding implementation of the comprehensive public security management responsibility system for leaders], implemented November 14, 1993, http://law.people.com.cn/showdetail.action?id=2602698; Guizhou Commission on Comprehensive Management of Public Security, "Guizhou sheng shehui zhian zonghe zhili yi piao foujue quanzhi banfa (shixing)" [Guizhou Province methods on the comprehensive public security management one-vote veto system (for trial implementation)], implemented May 3, 1994, http://www.law-lib.com/law/law_view.asp?id=24394.

54. Li, Liu, and O'Brien make a similar argument regarding petitioning: finding that institutions lacked the capacity to handle a surge in complaints, the state retreated to oppression. Li, Liu and O'Brien, "Petitioning Beijing," 333.

55. China Law Yearbooks 2004–2012.

56. Liebman, "Malpractice Mobs."

57. Xi Jinping, "Xi Jinping: quanli tuijin pingan Zhongguo fazhi Zhongguo guoying duiwu jianshe" [Xi Jinping: Use Full Effort to Create an Excellent Team to Push Forward Peaceful China and Rule of Law], January 7, 2013, http://www.gov.cn/ldhd/2013-01/07/content_2306643.htm.

58. Court adjudication committees generally consist of senior judges and decide sensitive or difficult cases. The practice has been criticized because it results in cases being decided by judges who did not participate in the trial.

59. Raymond Li, "Seven Subjects Off Limits for Teaching, Chinese Universities Told," *South China Morning Post*, May 11, 2013; Li Qi and William Wan, "China's Constitution Debate Hits a Sensitive Nerve," *Washington Post*, June 3, 2013.

60. Mary E. Gallagher, "Mobilizing the Law in China: Informed Disenchantment and the Development of Legal Consciousness," *Law & Society Review* 40, no. 4 (December 2006): 783–816.

61. Yuen Yuen Ang and Nan Jia, "Perverse Complementarity: Political Connections and Use of Courts Among Private Firms in China," *Journal of Politics* (April 2013); Xin He and Yang Su, "Do the 'Haves' Come Out Ahead in Shanghai Courts?" *Journal of Empirical Legal Studies* 10, no. 1 (March 2013): 120–45.

62. Sebastian Heilmann and Elizabeth Perry, eds., *Mao's Invisible Hand: The Political Foundations of Adaptive Governance in China* (Cambridge, Mass.: Harvard University Asia Center, 2011).

63. de Tocqueville, *Democracy in America*, 1: 280.

64. Pistor, "Towards a Legal Theory of Finance."

Chapter 10. China's Military Modernization: Many Improvements, Three Challenges, and One Opportunity

The ideas expressed here are those of the author alone. He is indebted to Amy Chang, Gabriel Collins, Abraham Denmark, Peter Dutton, Bonnie Glaser, Thomas Henderschedt, Nan Li, and several anonymous individuals for useful comments on earlier drafts. Avery Goldstein, Michael Horowitz, and Michael Swaine furnished particularly valuable guidance and revision suggestions.

1. Michael Swaine and Ashley Tellis, *Interpreting China's Grand Strategy: Past, Present, and Future* (Santa Monica, Calif.: RAND, 2000).

2. Dennis J. Blasko, " 'Technology Determines Tactics': The Relationship Between Technology and Doctrine in Chinese Military Thinking," in Tai Ming Cheung, ed., *China's Emergence as a Defense Technological Power* (New York: Routledge, 2012), 61–88.

3. Bonnie Glaser and Benjamin Dooley, "China's 11th Ambassadorial Conference Signals Continuity and Change in Foreign Policy," the Jamestown Foundation *China Brief* 9, no. 22 (November 4, 2009).

4. "Press Briefing by Press Secretary Jay Carney, National Security Advisor Tom Donilon, and Deputy National Security Advisor for Strategic Communications Ben Rhodes," Press Filing Center, W Hotel Semniyak, Bali, Indonesia, November 19, 2011.

5. Hillary Clinton, "America's Pacific Century," *Foreign Policy*, October 11, 2011.

6. "Press Briefing by Press Secretary Jay Carney."

7. The White House, Office of the Press Secretary, "Remarks by President Obama to the Australian Parliament," Parliament House, Canberra, November 17, 2011.

8. Clinton, "America's Pacific Century."

9. Gregory B. Poling and Phuong Nguyen, "Kerry Visits Vietnam and the Philippines," Center for Strategic and International Studies, csis.org, December 19, 2013.

10. Clinton, "America's Pacific Century."

11. "CNO's Sailing Directions," http://www.navy.mil/cno/cno_sailing_direction _final-lowres.pdf.

12. *Global Trends 2030: Alternative Worlds* (Washington, D.C.: National Intelligence Council, 2012), http://www.dni.gov/files/documents/GlobalTrends_2030.pdf, 15.

13. International Institute for Strategic Studies, *The Military Balance 2013* (London: Routledge, 2013), 255–56.

14. Wang Jisi, "20 Niannei meiguo reng shi weiyi chaoji daguo" [America will still be the only superpower for the next 20 years], Huanqiu shibao [Global Times], August 2, 2011.

15. Yang Yi, "New Joint Command System 'On Way'," *Xinhua*, January 3, 2014.

16. Tao Shelan, "Zhongguo jun fang chengqing 'jianli lianhe zuozhan siling bu': Meiyou genju" [Chinese military clarifies "the establishment of a joint operational command": Unfounded], Zhongguo xinwen wang [China News Network], January 5, 2014.

17. Transcript of regular news conference by the PRC Ministry of National Defense at the Ministry of National Defense Information Affairs Office in Beijing on November 28, 2013; Chen Jie, "PLA to Carry Out Structural and Organizational Reform," *China Military Online*, November 29, 2013, http://eng.mod.gov.cn/DefenseNews/2013-11/29 /content_4477126.htm.

18. The seriousness with which this concept is being explored is indicated by the publication in dedicated sections of no fewer than four articles (2010, no. 4), eight articles (2010, no. 5), and seven articles (2011, no. 1) by researchers from across the PLA and defense industry in *China Military Science*, the PLA's premier academic journal.

19. Senior Colonel Lin Dong, "Jiyu xinxi xitong de junshi liliang tixi de fa zhan linian" [Development concepts on information systems-based military force systems], *China Military Science*, no. 1 (2011): 22.

20. Li Jie, "Qieji wu du konghai yiti zhan meijun yizhengshi duifu zhongguo!" ["Air Sea battle" not to be misread; U.S. forces starting to deal with China!], Huanqiu shibao [Global Times], January 12, 2012.

21. Brian Spegele, "China Sees 'Cold War' in U.S.'s Australia Plan," *Wall Street Journal*, December 1, 2011.

22. Avery Goldstein, "First Things First: The Pressing Danger of Crisis Instability in U.S.-China Relations," *International Security* 37, no. 4 (Spring 2013): 88.

23. Joseph S. Nye, "Obama's Pacific Pivot," Project Syndicate, December 6, 2011, http://www.project-syndicate.org/commentary/nye101/English.

24. Ibid.

25. Clinton, "America's Pacific Century."

Chapter 11. Things Fall Apart: Maritime Disputes and China's Regional

The author thanks Michael Glosny, Michael Horowitz, and Michael Swaine for helpful comments and suggestions.

1. Samuel S. Kim, "China and the World: In Search of a Peace and Development Line," in *China and the World*, ed. Samuel S. Kim (Boulder, Colo.: Westview, 1989), 148.

2. M. Taylor Fravel, "Regime Insecurity and International Cooperation: Explaining China's Compromises in Territorial Disputes," *International Security* 30, no. 2 (Fall 2005): 46–83.

3. This is the story of China's ties with India. See M. Taylor Fravel, "China Views India's Rise: Deepening Cooperation, Managing Differences," in *Strategic Asia 2011–12: Asia Responds to Its Rising Powers—China and India*, ed. Ashley J. Tellis, Travis Tanner, and Jessica Keough (Seattle, Wash.: National Bureau of Asian Research, 2011), 65–98.

4. "USPACOM Facts," http://www.pacom.mil/about-uspacom/facts.shtml. Pacific Command accounts for approximately 20 percent of U.S. armed forces.

5. Peng Guangqian and Yao Youzhi, eds., *Zhanlue xue* [The science of military strategy] (Beijing: Junshi kexue chubanshe, 2001).

6. Michael D. Swaine and Ashley J. Tellis, *Interpreting China's Grand Strategy: Past, Present, and Future* (Santa Monica, Calif.: RAND, 2000).

7. Zhang Baijia, "Cong 'yi bian dao' dao 'quan fang wei': dui 50 nianlai zhongguo waijiao geju yanjin de sikao" [From "lean to one side" to "omnidirection": Reflections on the evolution of China's foreign policy structure over the past 50 years], *Zhonggong dangshi yanjiu*, no. 1 (2000): 21–28.

8. M. Taylor Fravel, *Strong Borders, Secure Nation: Cooperation and Conflict in China's Territorial Disputes* (Princeton, N.J.: Princeton University Press, 2008).

9. Michael A. Glosny, "Heading Toward a Win-Win Future? Recent Developments in China's Policy Toward Southeast Asia," *Asian Security* 2, no. 1 (2006): 24–57.

10. Leszek Buszynski, "ASEAN, the Declaration on Conduct, and the South China Sea," *Contemporary Southeast Asia* 25, no. 3 (December 2003): 343–62.

11. Glosny, "Heading Toward a Win-Win Future?"

12. Ibid.

13. Evan S. Medeiros, *China's International Behavior: Activism, Opportunism, and Diversification* (Santa Monica, Calif.: RAND, 2009).

14. Joshua Kurlantzick, *Charm Offensive: How China's Soft Power Is Transforming the World* (New Haven, Conn.: Yale University Press, 2007).

15. Robert Jervis, "Cooperation Under the Security Dilemma," *World Politics* 30, no. 2 (January 1978): 167–214.

16. For a recent review of China's growing capabilities, see Michael D. Swaine, et al., *China's Military and the U.S.-Japan Alliance in 2030: A Strategic Net Assessment* (Washington, D.C.: Carnegie Endowment for International Peace, 2013).

17. On the security dilemma in territorial disputes, see Thomas J. Christensen, "The Contemporary Security Dilemma: Deterring a Taiwan Conflict," *Washington Quarterly* 25, no. 4 (Autumn 2002): 7–21; M. Taylor Fravel, *Strong Borders, Secure Nation: Cooperation and Conflict in China's Territorial Disputes* (Princeton, N.J.: Princeton University Press, 2008).

18. Kenneth N. Waltz, *Theory of International Politics* (New York: McGraw-Hill, 1979).

19. M. Taylor Fravel, "China's Strategy in the South China Sea," *Contemporary Southeast Asia* 33, no. 3 (December 2011): 292–319.

20. Vietnam occupies twenty-seven of the land features in the Spratlys, more than all the other claimants combined. The Philippines occupies eight features, China seven, Malaysia five, and Taiwan one. Taiwan was the first claimant to occupy a contested feature, when Nationalist troops in 1956 landed on Taiping (Itu Aba) Island, the largest of the islands. See M. Taylor Fravel, "Maritime Security in the South China Sea and Competition over Maritime Rights," in *Cooperation from Strength: The United States, China and the South China Sea*, ed. Patrick M. Cronin (Washington, D.C.: Center for New American Security, 2012), 34–35.

21. Fravel, "Maritime Security in the South China Sea" and "China's Strategy in the South China Sea."

22. Zhiguo Gao and Bing Bing Jia, "The Nine-Dash Line in the South China Sea: History, Status, and Implications," *American Journal of International Law* 107, no. 1 (January 2013): 98–124.

23. Under the UN Convention on the Law of the Sea, a state can only exercise rights to the continental shelf if the CLCS certifies the claim.

24. UN Rules of Procedure of the Commission on the Limits of the Continental Shelf (New York: United Nations, 2008), 22.

25. A list of all submissions and objections is available on the commission's Web site, http://www.un.org/Depts/los/clcs_new/commission_submissions.htm.

26. See http://www.un.org/Depts/los/clcs_new/submissions_files/mysvnm33_09/chn_2009re_mys_vnm_e.pdf.

27. Fravel, "China's Strategy in the South China Sea," 306.

28. M. Taylor Fravel, "The South China Sea Oil Card," *The Diplomat*, June 27, 2012.

29. The vessels from the China Marine Surveillance have been incorporated into the newly established China Coast Guard, which is under the jurisdiction of the State Oceanic Administration.

30. Quoted in Geoff Dyer, "Beijing's Elevated Aspirations," *Financial Times*, November 10, 2010. For Yang's official statement, see "Foreign Minister Yang Jiechi Refutes Fallacies on the South China Sea Issue," Ministry of Foreign Affairs, China, July 26, 2010.

31. "ASEAN Talks Fail Over China Dispute," AFP, July 13, 2012; Ian Storey, "China Pushes on the South China Sea, ASEAN Unity Collapses," *China Brief* 12, no. 15 (August 3, 2012)

32. Greg Torode, "China 'Dictatorial' In Scarborough Shoal Disputes, Says Albert Del Rosario," *South China Morning Post*, November 30, 2012.

33. Social Weather Stations, "Second Quarter 2012 Social Weather Survey," August 13, 2012, http://www.sws.org.ph/pr20120813.htm.

34. Singapore Ministry of Foreign Affairs, press release, "MFA Spokesman's Comments in Responses to Media Queries on the Visit of Chinese Maritime Surveillance Vessel Haixun 31 to Singapore," June 20, 2011, http://www.mfa.gov.sg/content/mfa/media_centre/press_room/pr/2011/201106/press_20110620.html.

35. For Indonesia's letter to China, see http://www.un.org/Depts/los/clcs_new/submissions_files/mysvnm33_09/idn_2010re_mys_vnm_e.pdf.

36. William Jordan, Lewis M. Stern, and Walter Lohman, *U.S.-Vietnam Defense Relations: Investing in Strategic Alignment* (Washington, D.C.: Heritage Foundation, 2012).

37. "Manila Declaration on U.S.-Philippine Alliance," November 16, 2011, http://translations.state.gov/st/english/texttrans/2011/11/20111116141458su0.2878338.html.

38. "Joint Statement of the United States-Philippines Ministerial Dialogue," April 30, 2012, http://www.state.gov/r/pa/prs/ps/2012/04/188977.htm.

39. "Indian Navy to Hold Rescue Drill in Da Nang," VietNamNet Bridge, June 5, 2013, http://english.vietnamnet.vn/fms/government/75969/indian-navy-to-hold-rescue-drill-in-da-nang.html.

40. From the SIPRI Military Expenditure Database, http://milexdata.sipri.org.

41. SIPRI Arms Transfers Database, http://www.sipri.org/research/armaments/transfers/databases/armstransfers.

42. PRC Ministry of Foreign Affairs, "China and Japan Reach Principled Consensus on the East China Sea Issue," June 18, 2008, http://www.fmprc.gov.cn/eng/xwfw/s2510/t448632.htm.

43. "Chinese Premier Wen urges Japan to Release Jailed Captain," *Xinhua*, September 23, 2010.

44. Recent research by Iain Johnston suggests that China did not halt rare earth shipments during this period. See Alastair Iain Johnston, "How New and Assertive Is China's New Assertiveness?" *International Security* 37, no. 4 (Spring 2013): 23–24. Nevertheless, many observers, including Japanese government officials, believe China did take such action.

45. The survey in 2010 was taken in October, after the fishing captain incident. See http://www8.cao.go.jp/survey/h25/h25-gaiko/zh/z10.html.

46. "Joint Press Availability with Japanese Foreign Minister Seiji Maehara," Press Availability, U.S. Department of State, October 27, 2010, http://www.state.gov/secretary/20092013clinton/rm/2010/10/150110.htm

47. Data on Chinese patrols around the Senkakus as reported by the Japanese Coast Guard. See http://www.kaiho.mlit.go.jp/senkaku/index.html.

48. Louisa Lim, "Second Day of Anti-Japan Protests Rock China," NPR, September 16, 2012.

49. PRC Ministry of Foreign Affairs, "Remarks by Assistant Foreign Minister Le Yucheng at Symposium Marking the 40th Anniversary of the Normalization of Relations Between China and Japan," September 28, 2012, http://www.fmprc.gov.cn/eng/topics/diaodao/t975066.htm.

50. Keith Bradsher, "In China, Sales Fall as Political Uproar Hurts Japanese Carmakers," *New York Times*, October 10, 2012.

51. See http://www8.cao.go.jp/survey/h25/h25-gaiko/zh/z10.html.

52. Ibid.

53. "Talks Start with U.S. on New Defense Plan," Kyodo News, January 18, 2013.

54. Julian Barnes, "U.S., Japan Update Plans to Defend Islands," *Wall Street Journal*, March 21, 2013.

55. Ministry of Defense (India), "First Bilateral Maritime Exercise between India and Japan 'Jimex 12' to Commence on 09 Jun 12," June 8, 2012, http://pib.nic.in/newsite/erelease.aspx?relid=84780.

56. Ministry of Foreign Affairs of Japan, "Second Japan-Philippines Dialogue on Maritime and Oceanic Affairs," February 27, 2013, http://www.mofa.go.jp/announce/announce/2013/2/0222_01.html.

57. "Japan Vows to Help Philippines Amid China Sea Row," AFP, June 27, 2013.

58. "Japan, Vietnam to Hold Maritime Security Talks in May," Kyodo News, April 15, 2013.

59. Alexander Martin, "Japan Steps Up Defense Spending as China Tensions Simmer," *Wall Street Journal*, December 24, 2013.

60. Toko Sekiguchi, "Japan to Protect Islands with Drones and Amphibious Units," *Wall Street Journal*, December 17, 2013.

61. Ben Blanchard, "China Detains Vietnamese Fishermen in Disputed Water," Reuters, March 22, 2012.

62. This paragraph draws on M. Taylor Fravel, "All Quiet in the South China Sea: Why China is Playing Nice (For Now)," *Foreign Affairs*, March 22, 2012.

63. "ASEAN, China to Meet on Maritime Code of Conduct," AFP, April 11, 2013.

64. Daniel Ten Kate, "China Agrees to Asean Sea Talks Amid Philippines Warning," Bloomberg, July 1, 2013.

65. "China, ASEAN 'Make Progress' on Code of Conduct in S. China Sea: Official," Kyodo News, September 15, 2013.

66. Pu Zhendong and Zhang Yunbi, "China, Vietnam Set up Naval Hotline," *China Daily*, June 7, 2013.

67. "China, Vietnam Agree to Maintain Maritime Dialogues," *Xinhua*, June 21, 2013.

68. "China, Vietnam Launch Consultations on Sea-Related Joint Development," *Xinhua*, January 9, 2014.

69. M. Taylor Fravel, "Xi Jinping's Overlooked Revelation on China's Maritime Disputes," *The Diplomat*, August 15, 2013.

70. "Xi Jinping zai zhoubian waijiao gongzuohui shang fabiao zhongyao jianghua" [Xi Jinping's important speech at the peripheral diplomatic work meeting], *Renmin Ribao*, October 25, 2013.

71. The new fishing rules generated some concern because of the repeated earlier rules requiring foreign ships to receive approval to fish in waters under Hainan's administration. See M. Taylor Fravel, "Hainan's New Fishing Rules: A Preliminary Analysis," *The Diplomat*, January 10, 2014.

72. "2014, Guoji anquan xingshi shida kandian" [The 10 main aspects of international security in 2014], *Renmin Ribao*, December 9, 2014.

73. Richard Katz, "Why Chinese-Japanese Economic Relations Are Improving Delinking Trade From Politics," *Foreign Affairs*, December 30, 2013.

74. Cui Tiankai and Pang Hanzhao, "China-US Relations in China's Overall Diplomacy in the New Era: On China and US Working Together to Build a New-Type Relationship Between Major Countries," Ministry of Foreign Affairs (China), July 20, 2012. Cui Tiankai is now China's ambassador to the United States.

75. Edward N. Luttwak, *The Rise of China vs. the Logic of Strategy* (Cambridge, Mass.: Belknap Press of Harvard University Press, 2012).

76. Fravel, "China's Strategy in the South China Sea."

77. Ibid.

78. On this dynamic in China's territorial disputes, see Fravel, *Strong Borders, Secure Nation*.

Chapter 12. China's Challenges: Volatility in China–U.S. Relations

The author is grateful for the comments and discussion of this paper by the panel members and participants at the conference session on April 26, 2013.

1. Robert Sutter and Chin-Hao Huang, "China's Growing Resolve in the South China Sea," *Comparative Connections* 15, no. 1 (May 2013).

2. Robert Sutter and Chin-Hao Huang, "Beijing Shifts to the Positive, Plays Down Disputes," *Comparative Connections* 15, no. 3 (January 2014).

3. Don Keyser "President Obama's Re-election: Outlook for U.S. China Relations in the Second Term," November 7, 2012, China Policy Institute, Nottingham University.

4. Robert Sutter, *U.S.-Chinese Relations: Perilous Past, Pragmatic Present*, 2nd ed. (Lanham, Md.: Rowman & Littlefield 2013), chap. 7.

5. Bonnie Glaser and Brittany Billingsley, "US-China Relations: Strains Increase Amid Leadership Transitions," *Comparative Connections* 14, no. 3 (January 2013).

6. Kenneth Lieberthal and Wang Jisi, *Addressing U.S.-China Strategic Distrust*, John J. Thornton China Center Monograph Series, no. 4 (Washington, D.C.: Brookings Institution, March 2012).

7. David Shambaugh, "The Rocky Road Ahead in U.S.-China Relations," *China-U.S. Focus*, October 23, 2012.

8. Daljit Singh, "US-China Dialogue Process: Prospects and Implications," *East Asia Forum*, November 2, 2012.

9. Richard Bush, *Uncharted Strait* (Washington, D.C.: Brookings Institution, 2013), 213–50.

10. Bonnie Glaser and Brittany Billingsley, "U.S.-China Relations: Xi Visit Steadies Ties; Dissident Creates Tension," *Comparative Connections* 14, no. 1 (May 2012): 29.

11. National Security Adviser Thomas Donilon's speech and the officials' media briefing on President Obama's Asia policy were released November 15, 2012, at http://www.whitehouse.gov/the-press-office.

12. Consultations in Washington, DC, involving groups of visiting Chinese specialists assessing U.S.-China relations after the U.S. elections and groups of concerned American specialists, November 8, 15, 16, 2012.

13. Robert Sutter and Chin-Hao Huang, "China Muscles Opponents on South China Sea," *Comparative Connections* 14, no. 2 (September 2012); "China Gains and Advances in South China Sea," *Comparative Connections* 14, no. 3 (January 2013); James Przystup, "Japan-China Relations: 40th Anniversary: Fuggetaboutit!" *Comparative Connections* 14, no. 3 (January 2013).

14. These three paragraphs are adapted from Sutter, *U.S.-Chinese Relations*, chap. 4.

15. Harry Harding, *A Fragile Relationship* (Washington, D.C.: Brookings Institution, 1992), 215–324. This and the next five paragraphs are adapted from Sutter, *U.S.-Chinese Relations*, chap. 5.

16. David M. Lampton, *Same Bed, Different Dreams* (Berkeley: University of California Press, 2001), 55–63.

17. Sutter, *U.S.-Chinese Relations*, chap. 6.

18. Jeffrey Bader, *Obama and China's Rise* (Washington, D.C.: Brookings Institution, 2011); Martin Indyk, Kenneth Lieberthal, and Michael O'Hanlon, *Bending History: Barack Obama's Foreign Policy* (Washington, D.C.: Brookings Institution, 2012), 24–69; Sutter, *U.S.-Chinese Relations*, chap. 6.

19. Bonnie Glaser and Brittany Billingsley, "Friction and Cooperation Co-exist Uneasily," *Comparative Connections* 13, no. 2 (September 2011): 27–40; Minxin Pei, "China's Bumpy Ride Ahead," *The Diplomat*, February 16, 2011; Robert Sutter, *Positive Equilibrium in US-China Relations: Durable or Not?* (Baltimore: University of Maryland School of Law, 2010).

20. Bader, *Obama and China's Rise*, 69–129; Greg Sheridan, "China Actions Meant as Test, Hillary Clinton Says," *The Australian*, November 9, 2010.

21. Wang Jisi, "China's Search for a Grand Strategy," *Foreign Affairs* 90, no. 2 (March/April 2011): 68–79; Dai Bingguo, "Stick to the Path of Peaceful Development," *China Daily*, December 13, 2010, 9–10.

22. Robert Putnam, "Diplomacy and Domestic Politics: The Logic of Two Level Games," *International Organization* 42 (Summer 1988): 427–60.

23. Linda Jacobson and Dean Knox, *New Foreign Policy Actors in China*, SIPRI Policy Paper 26 (September 2010); "Brushwood and Gall" and "Less Biding and Hiding," *The Economist* (special report on China's place in the world) (December 2, 2010); David Shambaugh, "Coping with a Conflicted China," *Washington Quarterly* 34, no. 1 (Winter 2011): 7–27.

24. Sutter and Huang, "China Muscles Opponents on South China Sea" ; "China Gains and Advances in South China Sea"; "China's Growing Resolve in the South China Sea"; Przystup, "Japan-China Relations: 40th Anniversary: Fuggetaboutit!"; James Przystup, "Japan-China Relations: Treading Troubled Waters," *Comparative Connections* 15, no. 1 (May 2013).

25. Przystup, "Japan-China Relations: 40th Anniversary: Fuggetaboutit!"

26. Sutter and Huang, "China Gains and Advances in South China Sea," 72.

27. Robert Sutter and Chin-Hao Huang, "China's Toughness on the South China Sea—Year II," *Comparative Connections* 15, no. 2 (September 2013); "Beijing Shifts to the Positive, Plays Down Disputes," *Comparative Connections* 15, no. 3 (January 2014). This and the next two paragraphs are adapted from Sutter, *U.S.-Chinese Relations*, chap. 7.

28. See discussion of the many Chinese fishing and oil exploration disputes in recent years with neighbors in the East China Sea and the South China Sea covered in the tri-annual reviews of China-Japan relations and China-Southeast Asia relations in the e-journal *Comparative Connections* www.csis.org/pacfor

29. Yufan Hao, "Domestic Chinese Influences on U.S.-China Relations," in *Tangled Titans*, ed. David Shambaugh (Lanham, Md.: Rowman & Littlefield, 2013), 125–50.

30. Suisheng Zhao, "Hu Jintao's Foreign Policy Legacy," *e-International Relations*, December 8, 2012, http://www.e-ir.info/2012/12/08/hu-jintaos-foreign-policy-legacy.

31. See the review of the findings of Harry Harding, Samuel Kim, and Denny Roy on these matters in Robert Sutter, *The Foreign Relations of the PRC* (Lanham, Md.: Rowman & Littlefield, 2013), 10–14.

32. Sutter, *Foreign Relations of the PRC*, 18–22.

33. Robert Ross, "The Problem with the Pivot," *Foreign Affairs* 91, no. 6 (November-December 2012): 70–82.

34. Shawn Brimley and Ely Ratner, "Smart Shift," *Foreign Affairs* 92, no. 1 (January–February 2013): 177–81.

CONTRIBUTORS

Yong Cai teaches sociology at the University of North Carolina at Chapel Hill. Cai is a social demographer whose research focuses on population in China, including changes in fertility decision making in the Chinese family and the relative impact of government birth control policy and people's voluntary choice in the context of drastic social change in producing China's low fertility rate. His articles have appeared in *Demography, Population and Development Review, Asian Population Studies,* and other scholarly journals, and his research has been featured and quoted in the magazine *Science* and in Western and Chinese media.

Jacques deLisle is Stephen A. Cozen Professor of Law, professor of political science, and deputy director of the Center for the Study of Contemporary China at the University of Pennsylvania, and director of the Asia Program at the Foreign Policy Research Institute. His scholarship addresses legal and legal-institutional reform in China, relationships among legal, economic, and political change in China, law's roles in addressing crises in China, and China's engagement with the international legal order. He is co-editor of *China under Hu Jintao* (with T. J. Cheng and Deborah Brown) and *Political Changes in Taiwan under Ma Ying-jeou* (with Jean-Pierre Cabestan). His work has appeared in *Orbis, American Journal of Comparative Law,* and other journals of international affairs and law, and edited volumes.

Jane Duckett is Professor and Edward Caird Chair of Politics at the University of Glasgow. She is also director of the Scottish Centre for China Research. Her recent research focuses on the politics of social policymaking and implementation in China. She is author of *The Entrepreneurial State in China, The Open Economy and Its Enemies* (with Bill Miller) and *The Chinese*

State's Retreat from Health: Policy, Politics and Retrenchment and co-editor of *China's Changing Welfare Mix: Local Perspectives* (with Beatriz Carillo). Her work has appeared in *China Quarterly*, *Modern China* and other scholarly journals and edited volumes.

Andrew S. Erickson is associate professor in the Strategic Research Department at the United States Naval War College, member of the China Maritime Studies Institute, and associate in Research at the Fairbank Center for Chinese Studies at Harvard University. His research focuses on Asia-Pacific defense and other international relations issues and his scholarship has been published in *China Quarterly*, *Asian Security*, *Asia Policy*, *Journal of Strategic Studies*, *Orbis*, and other journals. He is coeditor of the series Studies in Chinese Maritime Development, contributor to the *Wall Street Journal's* China Real Time Report, and recipient of the National Bureau of Asian Research's Ellis Joffe Prize for PLA Studies.

M. Taylor Fravel is associate professor of political science at the Massachusetts Institute of Technology and member of the Security Studies Program at MIT. His research focuses on international security, China, and East Asia. He is the author of *Strong Borders, Secure Nation: Cooperation and Conflict in China's Territorial Disputes* and the forthcoming *Active Defense: Explaining the Evolution of China's Military*, and co-editor of *Rethinking China's Rise: A Reader*. His scholarship has appeared in *International Security*, *Foreign Affairs*, *Security Studies*, *International Studies Review*, *China Quarterly*, *Washington Quarterly*, *Journal of Strategic Studies*, and other journals.

Avery Goldstein is David M. Knott Professor of Global Politics and International Relations, director of Center for the Study of Contemporary China, and associate director of the Christopher H. Browne Center for International Politics at the University of Pennsylvania. Goldstein's research focuses on international relations, security studies, and Chinese politics. His books include *Rising to the Challenge: China's Grand Strategy and International Security* and *The Nexus of Economics, Security, and International Relations in East Asia* (co-edited with Edward D. Mansfield). His articles have appeared in *International Security*, *Foreign Affairs*, *International Organization*, *Journal of Strategic Studies*, *China Quarterly*, *Asian Survey*, *Comparative Politics*, *Orbis*, *Security Studies*, and other journals.

Yasheng Huang is International Program Professor in Chinese Economy and Business and professor of global economics and management at the Sloan School of Management, Massachusetts Institute of Technology. He previously held faculty positions at the University of Michigan and the Harvard Business School, and served as a consultant to the World Bank. Huang's recent research focuses on human capital formation in China and India, entrepreneurship, and foreign direct investment. He is the author of *Inflation and Investment Controls in China, FDI in China, Selling China,* and *Capitalism with Chinese Characteristics.* His research has been profiled and his contributions have appeared in the *Wall Street Journal, The Economist,* and other leading media and academic journals.

Zai Liang is professor of sociology at the University at Albany, State University of New York. He is also director of the Urban China Research Network. Liang's recent research focuses on how migrant children fare in China's rural to urban migration and urbanization processes (including access to education, health services, and health outcomes) and on international migration from China to the United States. He is co-editor of *The Emergence of a New Urban China: Insiders' Perspectives* and editor of *Demography* (in Chinese). His work has appeared in the *American Journal of Sociology, Population Studies, International Migration Review,* and other journals.

Benjamin L. Liebman is Robert L. Lieff Professor of Law and director of the Center for Chinese Legal Studies at Columbia Law School. His current research focuses on Chinese tort law, Chinese criminal procedure, the impact of popular opinion and populism on the Chinese legal system, and the evolution of China's courts and legal profession. His work has appeared in *Berkeley Journal of International Law, Columbia Law Review,* and *China Quarterly,* and in *Chinese Justice: Civil Dispute Resolution in Post-Reform China* (Mary Gallagher and Margaret Woo, eds.), and *Changing Media, Changing China* (Susan Shirk, ed.).

Melanie Manion is Vilas-Jordan Distinguished Achievement Professor of Political Science and Public Affairs at the University of Wisconsin–Madison. Her work has focused on Chinese bureaucratic politics, grassroots electoral democratization in China, the political economy of good governance, and corruption in the PRC and Hong Kong. Her current research focuses on

Chinese local people's congresses. Her books include *Corruption by Design,* *Retirement of Revolutionaries in China,* and *Contemporary Chinese Politics:* *New Sources, Methods, and Field Strategies,* and her articles have appeared in *American Political Science Review, Comparative Political Studies, Journal of Law, Economics, and Organization,* and *China Quarterly.*

Barry Naughton is professor of Chinese economy and Sokwanlok Chair of Chinese International Affairs at the University of California at San Diego. He specializes in issues relating to industry, trade, finance, and China's transition to a market economy. He recently edited and introduced a collection entitled *Wu Jinglian: Voice of Reform in China.* His books include *Growing Out of the Plan: Chinese Economic Reform, 1978–1993* (winner of the Ohira Memorial Prize) and *The Chinese Economy: Transitions and Growth.* His work has appeared in *China Quarterly, Journal of Contemporary China, China Leadership Monitor,* and various other economics journals and edited volumes.

Daniela Stockmann is associate professor of political science at Leiden University in the Netherlands. Her current scholarship focuses on Chinese media, political behavior, the domestic roots of Chinese foreign policy, and the use of digital research methods in China and other authoritarian contexts. Her recent book is entitled *Media Commercialization and Authoritarian Rule in China.* Her other publications include articles in *Comparative Political Studies, Political Communication, China Quarterly,* the *Chinese Journal of Communication,* and edited volumes.

Robert Sutter is professor of practice of international affairs, Elliott School of George Washington University, and previously was visiting professor of Asian Studies at the School of Foreign Service, Georgetown University. In more than thirty years of government service, Sutter worked for the Congressional Research Service, the Central Intelligence Agency, the Department of State, and the Senate Foreign Relations Committee. He is the author of many books and articles on U.S.-China relations, China's foreign relations, and U.S. policy toward Asia. His recent books include *Foreign Relations of the PRC: The Legacies and Constraints of China's International Politics since 1949, U.S.-Chinese Relations: Perilous Past, Pragmatic Present,* and *Chinese Foreign Relations: Power and Policy Since the Cold War.*

Guohui Wang is a lecturer at Yantai University, China. He received his Ph.D. in political science at the University of Glasgow. Wang is author of *Tamed Village Democracy: Elections, Governance and Clientelism in a Contemporary Chinese Village*, a study based on his doctoral research. He has written in English and Chinese on public policy, local governance, and public administration in China.

INDEX

ACKNOWLEDGMENTS

The chapters in this book are based on papers initially presented at the first Annual Conference of the Center for the Study of Contemporary China at the University of Pennsylvania. We are grateful to a distinguished set of discussants at the conference whose comments and suggestions provided valuable guidance as the authors prepared their chapters. These individuals include Deborah Davis, Emily Hannum, Michael Horowitz, Bert Keidel, Marshall Meyer, Carl Minzner, Michael Swaine, Yuhua Wang, and Guobin Yang. We thank all of the conference participants for their helpful comments during lively discussions at our sessions, and thank the anonymous reviewer whose comments on our original manuscript helped improve the chapters. We are also very grateful to Bill Finan at the University of Pennsylvania Press who facilitated the preparation of this volume.

Our conference would not have been possible without the financial support of the Center for the Study of Contemporary China provided by the University of Pennsylvania's provost as well as Penn's School of Arts and Sciences, Law School, Annenberg School for Communications, and Wharton School. Penn's Law School provided the venue for our conference sessions. We thank Amy Liu and Manxian Zhang for their assistance in running the conference. We are especially grateful to Dr. Yuanyuan Zeng, the associate director of the Center for the Study of Contemporary China, whose distinctive combination of substantive expertise and administrative skills made it possible for us to convene a successful conference during our center's first year of operation.